COMPUTER ARCHITECTURE AND ORGANIZATION

To My Father

Deryck East

1921–1989

For the opportunities you helped me find
and never found yourself

COMPUTER ARCHITECTURE AND ORGANIZATION

IAN EAST

University of Buckingham

PITMAN PUBLISHING
128 Long Acre, London WC2E 9AN

A Division of Longman Group UK Limited

© I. East 1990

First published in Great Britain 1990

British Library Cataloguing in Publication Data
East, Ian
    Computer architecture and organization.
    I. Title
    004

    ISBN 0-273-03038-8

OCCAM is a trademark of the INMOS Group of Companies

Printed and bound in Great Britain by
Biddles Ltd, Guildford and King's Lynn

Contents

Preface

I From software to hardware   1

1 Computation   3
1.1 Systems   3
1.1.1 Definition and characterization   3
1.1.2 Classes of system   6
1.2 Automata   7
1.2.1 Switches   7
1.2.2 Finite automata   11
1.2.3 Turing Machines   13
1.2.4 Cellular automata   16
1.3 Processes   18
1.3.1 Nature   18
1.3.2 Concurrency   21
1.3.3 Communication   23

2 Software engineering   29
2.1 Projects   29
2.1.1 Engineering design process   29
2.1.2 Organization   31
2.1.3 Languages   32
2.2 Modular systems design   32
2.2.1 Tasks   32
2.2.2 Processes   36
2.2.3 Objects   38
2.3 Structured programming   41
2.3.1 Primitives   41
2.3.2 Constructs   43

	2.3.3	Partitions	47
2.4		Standard programming languages	48
	2.4.1	Modula 2	48
	2.4.2	Occam	50

3 Machine language — **55**

3.1		Nature	55
	3.1.1	Translation from programming language	55
	3.1.2	Structure	56
	3.1.3	Interpretation	57
	3.1.4	Instructions	59
	3.1.5	Operands	62
3.2		Simple architectures	66
	3.2.1	Sequential processing	66
	3.2.2	Parallel processing	68
	3.2.3	Modular software	72
3.3		Instruction set complexity	74
	3.3.1	Reduced instruction set computer (RISC)	74
	3.3.2	Complex instruction set computer (CISC)	77
	3.3.3	Comparison of RISC and CISC	78

II   From switches to processors — **81**

4 Data representation and notation — **83**

4.1		Notation	83
	4.1.1	Pure binary	83
	4.1.2	Hexadecimal	85
	4.1.3	Octal	86
4.2		Primitive data types	87
	4.2.1	Integer	87
	4.2.2	Character	92
	4.2.3	Real	93
4.3		Structured data types	99
	4.3.1	Sequence association	99
	4.3.2	Pointer association	101

5 Element level — **105**

5.1		Combinational systems	105
	5.1.1	Specification	105
	5.1.2	Physical implementation	108
	5.1.3	Physical properties	115
5.2		Sequential systems	120

	5.2.1	Physical nature	120
	5.2.2	Specification	124
	5.2.3	Physical implementation	129
	5.2.4	Physical properties	143

6 Component level   **149**

6.1	Combinational system design		149
	6.1.1	Boolean algebra	149
	6.1.2	Karnaugh maps	152
	6.1.3	Quine-McCluskey	157
6.2	Sequential system design		159
	6.2.1	Moore machines	159
	6.2.2	Mealy machines	162
	6.2.3	Summary	166
6.3	Components		167
	6.3.1	Logic units	167
	6.3.2	Arithmetic logic units	173
	6.3.3	Registers	178

7 Control units   **193**

7.1	Function of the control unit		193
	7.1.1	Processor organization	193
	7.1.2	Machine language interpretation	197
	7.1.3	Fetch/execute process	200
7.2	Implementation		204
	7.2.1	Introduction	204
	7.2.2	Minimum state method	206
	7.2.3	Shift register method	208
	7.2.4	Counter method	212

III   From components to systems   **221**

8 Processor organization   **223**

8.1	Requirements		223
	8.1.1	General requirements	223
	8.1.2	Throughput	224
	8.1.3	Real-time systems	225
8.2	Accumulator machine		226
	8.2.1	Programming constructs	226
	8.2.2	Data referencing	226
	8.2.3	Booting	228
	8.2.4	Summary	229

8.3	Stack machine		229
	8.3.1	Software partitions	229
	8.3.2	Data referencing	230
	8.3.3	Expression evaluation	233
	8.3.4	Alternation	233
	8.3.5	Summary	234
8.4	Register window + instruction cache machine		236
	8.4.1	Exploitation of locality	236
	8.4.2	Software partitions	237
	8.4.3	Data referencing	238
	8.4.4	Parallel instruction execution	241
	8.4.5	Summary	242
8.5	Queue + channel machine		245
	8.5.1	Process scheduling	245
	8.5.2	Message passing	246
	8.5.3	Alternation	246
	8.5.4	Summary	247

9 System organization — **255**

9.1	Internal communication		255
	9.1.1	System bus	255
	9.1.2	Bus arbitration	257
	9.1.3	Synchronous bus transactions	259
	9.1.4	Asynchronous bus transactions	262
9.2	Memory organization		268
	9.2.1	Physical memory organization	268
	9.2.2	Virtual memory organization	284
9.3	External communication (I/O)		290
	9.3.1	Event driven memory mapped I/O	290
	9.3.2	External communication (I/O) processors	302

10 Survey of contemporary processor architecture — **311**

10.1	Introduction		311
10.2	Motorola 68000		312
	10.2.1	Architecture	312
	10.2.2	Organization	323
	10.2.3	Programming	326
10.3	National Semiconductor 32000		330
	10.3.1	Architecture	330
	10.3.2	Organization	342
	10.3.3	Programming	349
10.4	Inmos Transputer		353
	10.4.1	Architecture	353

10.4.2 Organization 369

10.4.3 Programming 373

Appendix 387

A ASCII codes 387

B Solutions to exercises 389

Bibliography 437

Index 443

Preface

Motivation and philosophy

One does not undertake the task of composing a new textbook lightly. This one has taken more than a year to produce. Furthermore, it does not make the author rich. (It pays better working in a bar!) So why bother?

Having moved to a *computer science* department from an applied physics environment, I was somewhat shocked at just how little students had been expected to learn, or even care, about the physical nature and engineering of the machines themselves. When I arrived at the University of Buckingham, courses in computer architecture were new to the computer science curriculum in most UK universities. On searching for a text suitable for students, who perceived their machines from a purely software perspective, I found two serious problems. First, almost all were written primarily for students of electrical engineering and so devoted too much space to engineering topics and presumed too great a knowledge of electrical theory. Second, all too often they were devoted to one or other "favourite" machine and lacked breadth. It also proved impossible to locate one which comprehensively covered new innovative ideas, such as...

- *Reduced instruction set*

- *Register windowing*

- *Modular software support*

- *Concurrent software support*

In particular I felt that the architecture of the *Transputer* could not be ignored because of the degree of its innovation and the fact that it renders parallel computing accessible and *affordable*, even to the individual.

As a result of the absence of a suitable text I felt myself duty bound to attempt the production of one. At the highest level my intention was to produce, *not* a "bible" on the subject, but a *course text*, containing sufficient material to provide a solid introduction but not so much as to overwhelm. It is intended as support for self-contained introductory courses in computer architecture, computer organization and digital systems. A detailed table of contents and substantial index should facilitate random "dipping in". Occasionally material is duplicated between sections to reduce the amount of cross-referencing necessary. An *italic* font is used for emphasis. A *slanted* one is used to indicate an important term upon its first use (within the current chapter or section) and also to highlight itemized lists.

It seems worthwhile to mention some points of philosophy underlying the book. The current computer science curriculum is a mix of science, technology and engineering, although this seems to be changing as the field matures. (New degree programmes in *computer systems engineering*, as distinct from *computer science*, are becoming commonplace.) I have attempted to emphasize the ideas fundamental to technology and engineering. These include *top-down design* and an *analyse/design/implement/verify* sequential structure to the design process. It seemed to me important to divorce *digital systems* from the *implementation technology* to be employed. I believe that a digital computer should be understood independent of whether it is constructed with electrical, optical, mechanical or even pneumatic switches. As a result space has been devoted to explaining the *switch level* of organization. In summary, the following levels are considered...

- *Switch*

- *Element (Gate, flip-flop)*

- *Component (Register, ALU, counter, shift-register etc.)*

- *Processor*

The distinction between *mainframe*, *mini* and *micro* computers has been considered irrelevant to an introductory course or text. *VLSI* technology is in any case blurring the boundaries. I have intentionally omitted any treatment of highly complex designs in order to concentrate on fundamental ideas and their exploitation. More can be learned from simpler examples. The Transputer and *Berkeley RISC* have shown how simplification can defeat increased complexity. *Scientists simplify, engineers complicate!*

The *programming model* assumed as a default is that of the *procedure* since procedural languages are currently most commonly taught first to students of computer science. Buckingham has opted for *Modula-2*. In addition the *process + message passing* model is used when discussing concurrency support.

"Architecture" is taken to mean those features of the machine which a programmer needs to know, such as *programmer's architecture*, instruction set and addressing modes. "Organization" is taken to mean all features which give rise to the characteristic behaviour and performance of the machine *and/or* the way in which its components are connected together. The distinction between the two definitions is not adhered to with absolute rigidity.

The new *ANSI/IEEE* standard logic symbols are not employed since it is felt that the traditional ones are easier to learn, make simple systems more clear and are still in widespread use. The new symbols are clearly intended to simplify the representation of *integrated* devices, particularly for use in *computer-aided design*. To introduce both would only serve to confuse.

Lastly, only the final chapter depends on any particular design. This is not a book devoted to any favourite machine. The three which are discussed have been chosen purely for reasons of illustration.

To summarize, this book differs from others on the same subject as follows...

- *Better support for students of computer science*

- *No dependence upon any particular machine*

- *High digital systems content*

- *Up-to-date coverage of new issues including...*

  - *Modular software support*
  - *Concurrency support*

- *Up-to-date coverage of new features including...*

  - *Reduced instruction set*
  - *Register windowing*
  - *Synchronous channels (hard & soft)*

Content and course correspondence

The book is divided into three parts...

Part I: From software to hardware is intended to introduce the software-oriented student to the fundamental ideas of physical computation. It begins with a chapter devoted to defining new terminology and describing fundamental concepts such as that of *time-discrete system*, *process* and *protocol*. Chapter 2 offers a summary of the basic ideas of software engineering and introduces some of the ideas fundamental to the engineering design process. Chapter 3 outlines the implementation of the building blocks of a structured program at the *primitive* (or *atomic*) level and includes a contrast of the *RISC* versus *CISC* design philosophies in the context of their efficiency at implementing statements in a high level procedural programming language.

Part II: From switches to processors covers more than the required ground needed in *digital systems*. It includes treatment of design techniques for both combinational and sequential systems. Also finding a home here are Chapter 4, which discusses data representation and notation, and Chapter 7, which discusses the nature and design of both hardwired and microcoded processor *control units*.

Part III: From components to systems seeks to show how components may be *organized* to form central and communication processors and memory units. Chapter 8 covers processor architecture and organization, discussing *accumulator, stack* and *register file* designs. Discussion of the use of register files extends to include *register windowing* and its effect on the procedure call overhead. It also discusses a *"queue + channel"* machine, designed to support the scheduling of concurrent processes and the *synchronous* communication of messages between them. Chapter 9 deals with both internal and external communication and memory organization. Finally, Chapter 10 gives an overview of the architecture of three contemporary processors, the *Motorola 68000, National Semiconductor 32000* and the *Inmos Transputer*. A particularly thorough discussion of the *Transputer* is given because of the extent and importance of its innovation and because a *student accessible* treatment does not yet appear to be available elsewhere.

More than *two hundred* diagrams serve to illustrate ideas in the text. Every picture is worth a thousand words...and took as long to produce! Also more than forty exercises are given , *together with complete solutions*. These are intended as supplementary material for the student, *not* to save the course tutor effort! (I have never understood the point of including exercises without solutions in a textbook.) References used are nearly all to currently available textbooks. Those made to journal papers are restricted to "landmark" expositions.

The course at Buckingham is supplemented with *assembly language* programming experience. Apart from two lectures on assembly language translation and programming tools, the course follows the book except for somewhat reduced coverage of digital systems design and early delivery of material from Chapter 10 on the machine to be programmed, (currently the *NS32000*).

Material on assembly language programming and tools is deliberately omitted for two reasons. First, it requires a particular machine which should be chosen partly on the basis of practical experience and available equipment. Neither of these factors should influence the content of a textbook. Secondly, an alternative possibility is that a full course on compilers might include material and practical experience of code generation and its relationship to architecture design. Teaching assembly language programming is arguably not the best way to introduce students to machine implementation of constructs and procedure invocation, etc.. It totally bypasses the problem of *automatic* generation of code and its implications for architecture design.

Knowledge of a fully structured procedural programming language is the only prerequisite. The level of mathematical skill and knowledge required varies throughout the book. Introductions are included to *propositional logic, Boolean algebra* and *computer arithmetic* which are adequate for their use within the book. Knowledge of *data structures, modular software engineering, parallel processing* and *Occam* would be beneficial but not essential.

The *IEEE Computer Society Model Program in Computer Science and Engineering*,

[IEEE CS 83], calls for the following related core curriculum subject areas to be supported by lecture courses. The degree of overlap with the topics chosen for this text is shown below...

Subject area	Name	Modules	Overlap
6	*Logic design*	1–5	Full
7	*Digital systems design*	1, 2	Partial
		3–5	Full
8	*Computer architecture*	1	Partial
		2–4	Full
		5	Little

The approach taken in this text differs from the recommendations. Many more additional topics are treated than are left out. Overlap at the *module* level may not mean exact correspondence to topics within. Treatment of alternatives, of equivalent merit, within a module is considered sufficient. For example in *Subject area eight/module three:* "*Computer architecture survey*" a different collection of machines will be found to that in Chapter 8.

It was never the intention to match the book to part of *any* preconceived curriculum. Course syllabus should be a matter for the course tutor. I hope very much that the text proves useful to others who share the experience of that responsibility.

Acknowledgements and author's comments

I would like to thank Keith Dimond of University of Kent Electronics Laboratory, for help and advice in reviewing the whole book, Steven Maudsley of Inmos, for comments and advice on the Transputer overview in Chapter 10, Roger Hill of Pitman, for his cheerfulness, encouragement and toleration of many broken deadlines and Nicola for tolerating being a "book widow" for more than a year.

I also wish to thank the staff, students and institution of the University of Buckingham, without whom and which the book might never have been written.

Lastly, and most of all, I wish to thank a mother and father who always knew that education begins at home at the age of zero. My father was responsible for inspiring me with his love for all things technical. Even being subjected to the delivery of science at school could not quell that!

...Do nothing save for love!

Part I

From software to hardware

1

Chapter 1

Computation

1.1 Systems

1.1.1 Definition and characterization

Discrete digital system

A *system* is simply any entity which generates *output* from *input*. A system may have any given number of input and output *ports*. The name "port" is derived from the analogy with shipping. However, unlike shipping, a system port may only be used for either input or output, never both. We may make use of the mathematical concept of a *function* to describe how each possible *input value* causes a particular *output value*. The statement of *system function* then serves to define a particular system. An alternative means of characterizing the behaviour of a system, the *system process*, is described below and is the preferred means used throughout this text.

By *time-discrete system* (Figure 1.1) is meant one whose output changes only at regular, discrete intervals of time. The intervals may be thought of as ending with each tick of a *system clock*. Regardless of any change to the input, no change of output will take place *until* the clock ticks. The input is only *sampled* upon the tick of the system clock. Any system which does not wait for the tick of a clock is called a *continuous system*.

Analogue systems represent a varying *abstract* quantity (e.g. temperature) by varying a *physical* quantity which serves as its analogue. If such a system is implemented using electrical technology the physical analogue may be a current or voltage[1]. In contrast, *digital systems* use an *internal representation* of abstract quantities by first assigning it a *cardinal integer value* and then representing *each digit* separately. Binary representation has a distinct advantage which greatly simplifies implementation. The machine need only physically represent *two* digit values, 0 and 1.

---

[1]Electric *analogue computers* were once common and still find application today.

Figure 1.1: A time-discrete system

Digital systems are thus not able to internally represent *any* value an abstract quantity may take. Before encoding it must be *quantized*. Imagine that you have the task of sorting ball bearings into ten bins, coarsely labelled for bearing size. The obvious procedure is to first measure their size and then place them into the appropriate bin. Someone else will now quickly be able to tell the size of each ball bearing *with sufficient precision* for their purpose. *Quantization* means the selection of the nearest allowed value and is thus exactly like binning.

The *computer* is a special type of *time-discrete digital system*. It is *programmable*.

State

State is a concept fundamental to physics. It is the *instantaneous configuration* of a system. The simplest example is that of a tetrahedron resting on a table. There are four *states* corresponding to the four sides it may rest on. It is possible to label each side with a *symbol* and use it to remind yourself about one of four things. In other words it constitutes a four-state *memory*. *Memories are labelled physical states.*

One kind of symbol you could use, to label the tetrahedron, would be the numeric digits $\{0,1,2,3\}$. It is then possible to use it as a 1-digit memory! We are now able to *store* a multi-digit, base 4, number by employing one tetrahedron for each digit. The group used to store a single value is called a *register*. The *statespace* is the range of values possible and is determined by the number of ways in which the states of the tetrahedra may be combined. N of them allows 4^N values, $0 \rightarrow (4^N - 1)$. If we wish to store many values we simply use many words.

State, or memory, is not necessarily used to store numbers. Symbols, or symbol combinations, may represent *characters* or *graphic objects*. Alternatively they may represent objects in the real world. The *combined* state may then be used to represent *relations* between objects.

Process

A *process* describes the *behaviour pattern* of an object. It consists of a *sequence of events* which is conditionally dependent on both its initial state and communication with its environment, which may be modelled as a number of other processes. Processes are said to *start, run* and then *terminate*.

Each possesses *private state*, which is *inaccessible to any other*, and a number of *channels* by which to communicate externally. The complete set of symbols which may be stored must include those which may be input or output.

The named *description* of a process is called a *procedure*. The fundamental indivisible atomic, or primitive, events of which any process is capable may be categorized...

- *Assignment*

- *Input*

- *Output*

Describing a process is one way of characterizing a system. The *system process* must then possess a channel corresponding to each system port. Any system which runs a process may be called a *processor*.

Processes may be iteratively reduced into *subordinate processes*. For example, an assembly line producing cars may be described as a process with several input channels (one for each component) and one output channel (of cars). This single process may be broken down into lower level processes making sub-assemblies such as engine, gearbox and suspension. These can be further broken down until individual actions of robots (or human workers) are reached. Consider the subordinate process of gearbox assembly. Input channels must be available for receiving gears of each required type. One output channel will transmit finished gearboxes.

Designing a *process network* to implement a complex system such as a car factory is very far from easy. The problem is that of *scheduling* processes onto processors (robots or workers) in such a way as to maximize efficiency at all levels. The solution must ensure the *synchronization* of all necessary communication. In other words, for instance, the gearbox assembly process must have at least one gear of each type available *as it is required*. Further discussion is outside the scope of this book.

Protocol

A *stream* is a sequence of symbols. It may or may not be infinitely long. If finite then it is terminated by a special value, *End Of Transmission (EOT)*. The length of the *stream* is not known *a priori* to either the receiver or transmitter. Upon any given clock tick only the *current* symbol in the stream is accessible to either. Returning to the manufacturing analogy, it may be necessary to represent a worker transmitting a *stream* of identical components to another who requires them to assemble something. This stream may initially be defined as infinite. Later it may be necessary to allow for the possibility that the supply of components is exhausted. The message sent to inform the worker that this has occurred constitutes an *EOT*.

A *channel*, just as in nature, is the means for a stream to flow. Just as a processor is the physical entity which runs a process, a stream is said to *flow* along a channel. In the manufacturing example above, a channel may be a conveyor belt or an "Autonomous Guided Vehicle" (A.G.V.) which allows objects to flow from one process to another.

Unlike a stream, a *string* is characterized by prior knowledge of the length of a *message*. The length must be *finite* and is transmitted first so that the receiver is made aware of the number of symbols which follow. To continue the manufacturing analogy, because the assembly worker (receiver process) has some means to check if any components have been lost or stolen, it is said to be more *secure* if they are sent a batch at a time with the quantity transmitted first. This is then an example of the use and benefit of *string protocol*.

Stream and string are both examples of communication *protocol*. *A protocol is an agreed set of rules by which communication may take place*. Once both transmitting and receiving processes agree a protocol, communication may proceed without difficulty. In the example above of a string, the recipient need know in advance *only* the protocol, i.e. that first to arrive is a quantity followed by that number of components. The origin of the term lies in inter-government diplomacy. Before one head of state may visit another certain events must take place. The *sequence and nature* of these events are agreed before *any* communication occurs. Typically, various officials, of increasing rank, *pass messages* to each other until heads of state themselves talk.

The simplest form of protocol is the *signal* where *no* message is passed. Attention is merely attracted. A common use for the *signal*, by both human and machine, is to cause a process to *alternate* between subordinate processes. An example of this is a person engaged in playing two chess games simultaneously. The process of playing one may be *interrupted* by a signal from the other. Alternation between many processes requires one channel of *signal protocol* for each.

1.1.2   Classes of system

Causal systems

Physics tells us that output can never be simultaneous with, or precede, the input which causes it. This is called the *law of causality*. It is one of the most fundamental laws of physics. All real, natural and artificial systems obey it. There is no explanation of it. The universe is simply made that way.

For a computer, causality means that every output value takes some interval of time to derive from the input stream on which it depends. The interval must always be shorter than that between clock ticks at the level of the primitive action.

Linear systems

There are several specific classes of system which are of interest. Knowledge of them helps in analysing problems. One we shall mention now is that of systems which exhibit *linearity*. In a linear system one can add together several inputs and get an output which is simply the *sum* of those which would have resulted from each separate input. Very few natural systems are linear. However there is a growing range of applications which are benefiting from the simplicity, and thus low cost, of *linear processors*[2].

Deterministic systems

A *deterministic system* is one whose output is *predictable with certainty* given prior knowledge of some or all preceding input. All conventional computers are deterministic systems.

An example of a deterministic system is a processor running a process which adds integers on two input channels placing the result on a single output channel. Here one need only know the input symbols on the current clock tick to predict (determine) the result output on the next one.

Another system, whose process is the computation of the *accumulated* sum of all integers input on a single stream, requires prior knowledge of *all* symbols input since process start.

Stochastic systems

A *stochastic system* is one where it is only possible to determine the *probability distribution* of the set of possible symbols at the output. In other words the output at each clock tick is a *random variable*.

Although it is the more general system, the *stochastic computer* is rare and very much just the subject of research within the field of *artificial intelligence* at the time of writing this book[3].

1.2 Automata

1.2.1 Switches

Normally-open switches

A switch is the simplest system which exhibits *state*. Of the many types of switch, the one we shall consider is the *normally-open switch* (Figure 1.2). Imagine a light switch which is sprung so that the light is immediately extinguished on removal of your finger.

---

[2] Often referred to as *signal processors*.

[3] It is interesting to note that *natural* systems are predominantly *non-linear* and *stochastic* whereas *artificial* systems are predominantly *linear* and *deterministic*.

It only closes, allowing electrons to flow, in response to pressure from your finger, thus turning on the light.

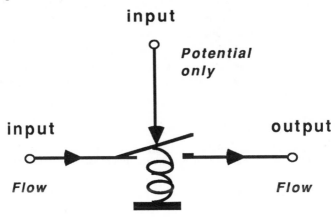

Figure 1.2: Normally-open switch

Now for just a little physics. *Some energy must be expended in closing a normally-open switch.* Our simple model has one output and *two* inputs. Are both inputs the same?

Anything that flows has *kinetic energy*. Something which may potentially flow is said to have *potential energy*. In other words, some energy is available which may be converted into kinetic energy.

We have already met one fundamental law of physics in the law of causality. Here we have a second one. The *first law of thermodynamics* requires the *conservation of energy*. It therefore tells us that flow can only occur if some potential energy is available. A stream of water flows down a hill because the water has *gravitational* potential energy available.

To understand our normally-open switch we observe that potential energy must be available at *both* inputs. In this sense both inputs are the same. They differ in that flow may occur through one and not the other. Different kinds of potential energy may characterize each input. For example, a light switch uses *electrical* potential energy (voltage) on its flow input and *mechanical* potential energy (finger pressure) on its other input.

Another example of a normally-open switch would in fact allow us to construct an entire (albeit rather slow) computer. A *pressure-operated valve* is designed to switch air pressure. It may be referred to as a *pneumatic switch*. The interesting property of this switch is that *the output of one may operate others*. The number of others which may be operated defines the *fan-out* of the switch.

By now it should come as little surprise that the fundamental building block of all *electronic* systems, the *transistor*, is in fact no more than a switch. It is very important to understand that a computer can be built using *any* technology capable of implementing a normally-open switch[4]. There is nothing special to computation about electronics. Nor is it true that there exists only *artificial* computers. Biological evolution may be regarded as a form of computation.

Computers are often rather noisy. Most of the noise comes from a cooling system which is usually just a fan. There is a fundamental reason for this... *switches consume*[5] *energy*. Yet another fundamental law of physics, the *second law of thermodynamics*, tells us that no machine may do work without producing *heat*. This heat is being produced continuously. If nothing is done to remove it the system will overheat. Computers get hotter the faster they run!

There are a lot of switches in a computer. Hence it is very important for the technology chosen to offer a switch which requires as little energy to operate as possible. Designs usually involve a trade-off between *power consumption*[6] and speed.

Switch operation is the most fundamental event in computation. Therefore the operation speed of the switch will limit the speed of the computer. Biological switches (e.g. the neurons in our brains) switch rather slowly. They take $\sim 10^{-3}s$. It appears that the best an electronic switch can do is $\sim 10^{-9}s$. Optical switches, recently developed in the UK, promise switching in $\sim 10^{-12}s$. The reader should have noticed the contrast between the switching speed of the neuron and that of the transistor. The capabilities of the human brain compare somewhat favourably with those of current computers. *It is obvious that we are doing something wrong!*

Memory

"State" is really just another term for *memory*. The number of states of a system is equal to the number of things it can remember. States *are* memories. We may label them how we like, e.g. by writing symbols on the sides of our tetrahedra.

Figure 1.3 shows how normally-open switches may be connected to realize a *binary memory* or *latch*. Flow *resistance* is necessary to ensure that not all potential supplied is lost when either switch closes. The existence of potential is marked "1" and the lack of it by "0". In addition, the medium (e.g. air, electrons or water) is able to flow away through any terminal labelled "0", which may thus be regarded as a *sink*.

Careful study of Figure 1.3 will reveal that there are only two *stable states* in which the latch can exist. It is impossible for *both* switches to be simultaneously either closed or open. The closure of one reduces the potential above it sufficiently to prevent the other from closing. Either point between resistance and the switch flow input may be state-labelled and used as an output. It is unimportant which.

---

[4] Computers using only *optical* switches are now being built.
[5] Energy is not actually *consumed* but is *converted* from one form to another, in this case work into heat.
[6] *Power = energy × time.*

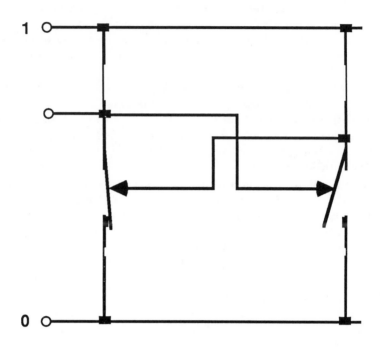

Figure 1.3: Binary memory (latch) constructed from normally-open switches

It may also be used as an input. The application of "0" or "1" will *write* that *datum* into the latch. The output state shown is "0" since the left switch is closed, removing any potential present. Applying a potential will cause the right hand switch to close and thus the left hand one to subsequently open, changing the latch output state. Removing the applied potential does not affect the latch state which now remains "1". In other words, *it remembers it!*

The reader should verify that the latch will similarly remember the application (input) of "0".

Logic gates

Logic gates are devices which implement systems with *binary* input and output values. The presence or absence of a potential, at either input or output, is used to infer the *truth* or otherwise of a *proposition*. A full treatment of the functions they may implement and how they are used in the construction of computers is left for Part II of this book. It is however appropriate now to illustrate how our simple normally-open switches may be used to construct logic gates. Figure 1.4 shows how *AND, OR* and *NOT* gates may be

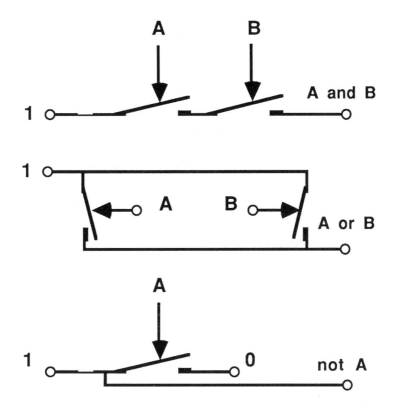

Figure 1.4: Logic gates implemented using normally-open switches

made.

Output is "1" from *AND* only if A *and* B are "1". Output is "1" from *OR* only if A *or* B is "1". *NOT* merely inverts a single input.

In fact logic gates merely define standard ways in which switches may be connected together. Their usefulness is that they allow *formal* (mathematically precise) design of *logic systems* simply by *combination*, i.e. by connecting them together as building blocks. Part II shows how.

1.2.2 Finite automata

An *automaton* is any entity which possesses state and is able to change that state in response to input from its environment. It is a discrete system whose *next* state depends both on input *and* its current state. Figure 1.5 illustrates the idea from both *functional* and *procedural* points of view.

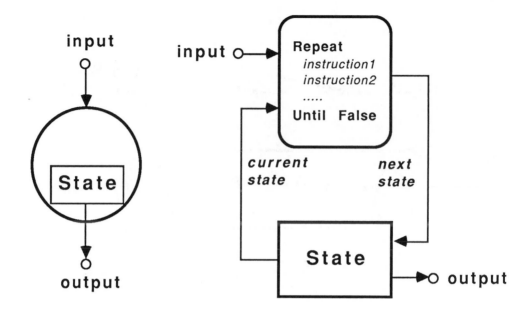

Figure 1.5: Automaton

Imagine you are monitoring an instrument which is equipped with three lights, each of which may be only green or red. It is your job to interpret the meaning of the pattern of lights according to a small *instruction set*. Let us say that the instrument is designed to detect military aircraft and identify them as either friend or foe. A certain pattern is interpreted as "aircraft detected". Subsequently, some patterns mean "friend", some mean "foe" and the rest mean "failure to identify". These are the *states*, you are the (4-state) automaton and the light patterns form a *symbol alphabet*.

Automata are fundamental building blocks of computers. They may be found implemented in both software and hardware. The automaton process may be described as a series of series of *IF... THEN...* statements inside a *REPEAT... UNTIL... FALSE* loop (infinite loop). These form the instruction set of the automaton. Each one is thus composed of...

- *Condition part (state & input)*

- *Action part*

...where the condition is in two parts, state and input symbol. The action is simply the updating of state. To summarize, a procedural description of the behaviour of an automaton is...

```
REPEAT
    IF <symbol> AND <state> THEN <action>
    IF <symbol> AND <state> THEN <action>
    ...
UNTIL FALSE
```

The automaton may have output only in the sense that the *state* may be visible externally. Typically, output forms the input to another automaton. In our analogy the second might be a 2-state automaton enabling a missile to be fired at a "foe". A *formal definition* of an automaton must consist of the following...

- *Set of symbols*

- *Set of states*

- *Set of instructions*

The set of states allowed forms the statespace, the set of symbols the alphabet. It is programmed simply by specification of the instruction set. *No ordering of instructions is needed.*

Finite automata[7] are simply automata with a finite number of states and may alternatively be described by a *state transition graph* which defines how the system proceeds from one state to the next, given both state and input symbol. Part II describes their design.

1.2.3 Turing Machines

Origin and purpose

A *Turing Machine* is built on the concept of an *automaton*. It gains its name from Alan Turing who invented it as a means of investigating the class of *computable functions* [Turing 36].

Turing Machines are *not* used as the basis for the design of real computers. Their most important use is in determining those functions which are not computable. *If a Turing Machine cannot evaluate a given function then neither can any other computer!*

Structure

The Turing Machine is composed of three subsystems. One of these is a *processor*, which is much like an automaton except that it can also output a symbol *distinct* from its state. Symbols are input from, and output to, a *linear memory* composed of a sequence of memory "cells". The processor is also able to move one position in either direction along memory.

---

[7] In the field of hardware design automata are usually referred to as *state machines*. The two terms mean the same.

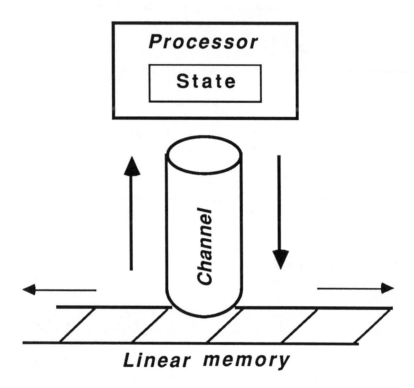

Figure 1.6: Turing Machine

The linear memory forms a second subsystem which contains symbols drawn from an *alphabet*. One of the symbols is special and usually termed *blank*. Each memory cell is capable of storing a single symbol. The operation of the machine is *cyclic*. A single cell is *read*, then one of *just three* actions is carried out.

The third subsystem is a *channel* which allows the processor to *read* or *write* a memory cell. Note that moving along the linear memory may equally well be performed by...

- *Moving the processor*
  (as if it slid back and forth along the memory)

- *Moving the communication channel*
  (as if it were a pipe, through which symbols pass)

- *Moving the memory*
  (as if its symbols were on a tape)

A Turing Machine may be summarized as...

- Processor *with internal memory for instruction execution*

- Linear memory *composed of a sequence of memory cells*

- Channel *allowing processor to read and write memory*

It may help to imagine the processor as a "rubber stamp" stamping new symbols onto a tape (linear memory) which depend on the current one it sees and an internal memory (Figure 1.6).

Programming

As with automata, instructions are solely of the *if...then* kind. The condition part of the instruction is simply made up of the state and the symbol which has been read. The action part has three possibilities only...

Instruction type	Action
modify <sym>	Modify symbol at current position to *sym*
move <dir>	Move in direction *dir*
halt	Halt computation

The input to a Turing Machine is the contents of the memory at the start. The output is the memory contents when it halts. If it fails to halt then the function is not computable. The program is the (unordered) set of instructions.

A particular Turing Machine is defined by specifying the following...

- **Q** : *Finite set of states*

- **Σ** : *Finite set of* symbols *including* blank *which is not allowed as an input*

- **I** : *Finite set of* instructions

- **q** : *Initial state*

- **$F \subseteq \Sigma$** : *Finite set of final states*

Computability

One model of computation is that of a *process* which evaluates a *function*. Not all functions are computable. There is no known way of distinguishing the incomputable from the computable. Each problem must be investigated in its own right. The Turing Machine is a useful model for such investigation because of the *Church thesis* [Church 36] which may be paraphrased thus...

> Church thesis: *Every effectively computable function may be computed using a Turing Machine.*

The term "effectively" implies that it must be possible to write a program for a computer to achieve the evaluation of the function. In other words it must be possible to describe the process of evaluation. For a good introduction to the subject of computability see [Rayward-Smith 86].

1.2.4   Cellular automata

Origin

Here the reader may be introduced to part of the legacy of another great person who helped create a science of computation... *J. von Neumann.* von Neumann wished to compare living entities with artificial systems. The element of life is the living cell. *Cellular automata* were his invention to promote understanding of *self-replicating* systems [von Neumann 66].

Interest

Just as the study of *finite automata* promotes understanding of *sequential* computation, the study of *cellular automata* promotes that of *parallel* computation. It is an area of research which is progressing rapidly, at the time of writing, and promises machines which might earn the adjective "intelligent".

Structure

An *automata network* is any *graph* of finite automata which evolves by means of discrete interactions which are both *mutual* and *local*. A graph G is defined as a set of *sites* $s_i \in S$ together with a *neighbourhood system* $F = \{F_c | s_i \in F_j \Rightarrow s_j \in F_i\}$. Hence $G = \{S, F\}$.

Programming

There is no *global* program for a cellular automata network. Cells share a common *local* program which describes how to interact with their *neighbours* to update their (purely local) state. It may define either a *deterministic* or a *stochastic* process.

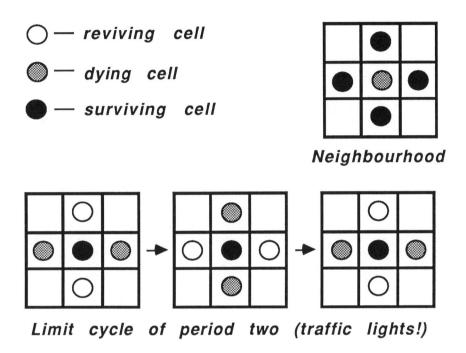

Figure 1.7: Game of Life

Perhaps the most frequently investigated deterministic process is that of the game of *Life* (Figure 1.7) [Conway 82]. Here the graph is a set of sites (cells) arranged as a two-dimensional array with a simple neighbourhood (e.g. the four cells surrounding any given specimen). Each cell is a simple two-state automaton, the states being labelled "alive" or "dead". There are just two state-updating actions for the cell, *birth* and *death*. Values input are simply the neighbour states. Local state is assigned according to some simple rules and output to its neighbours. These rules are (typically)...

- *A cell is born if and only if it has exactly three living neighbours*

- *A cell dies unless it has exactly two or three living neighbours*

If the state of the entire graph is displayed as an *image* (two dimensional array of brightness, or colour, values) behaviour cycles emerge as patterns which move or repeat themselves. Those cycles which infinitely repeat are known as *limit cycles*.

1.3   Processes

1.3.1   Nature

Events

The atomic (indivisible) element which characterizes a process is the *event*. The *observed* behaviour of any process is considered to be a *discrete sequence of events*. Each event is idealized to be instantaneous. It is the accomplishment of an *action* in response to a single *command* of the process *specification*.

The *alphabet* of a process is the set of all events of which it is capable. For instance, the alphabet of a Turing Machine is simply {All defined `modify` events, `move` forward, `move` backward, `halt`}.

In order to be useful, a process must possess one special event in its alphabet... `succeed` Passage of this event means successful *termination*. The equivalent for the Turing Machine is `halt`.

Example process

Recall that a process is the *behaviour pattern* of an object. This consists of a *sequence of events* which is conditionally dependent on both its initial state and communication with its environment. A process *starts*, *runs* and then *terminates*.

For an example of a process, consider an *economy* (Figure 1.8). We here adopt an extremely naïve model. A number of *supplier/manufacturer/consumer* chains run concurrently without communicating with each other. Each supplier inputs raw materials and then outputs goods (perhaps refined raw materials or components) to a manufacturer from whom it also inputs money. A manufacturer simply inputs from its supplier and outputs goods to its customer, from whom it also inputs money. Part of the definition of this process, not rendered explicit in the diagram, is that it cannot output money until it is first input. The customer inputs goods, for which it pays, and then outputs waste. Another omission from the diagram is any hint of how the process or any of its subordinates *terminate*.

The *alphabet* of the process includes communication events between pairs of subordinates which cause update of its internal state. Input and output events for subordinates must be *synchronized* to form a communication transaction internal to the parent process. The effect is then to *update the state* of the parent.

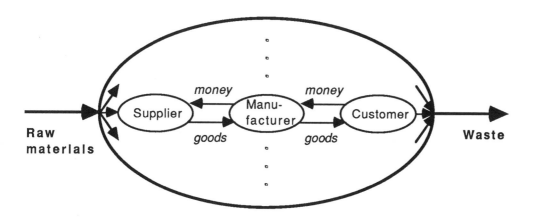

Figure 1.8: Naïve process model of an economy

Traces

The actual sequence of events *observed* is called a *trace* and will end with a special **succeed** event if the process terminates.

An example of a process is the behaviour *pattern* of a vending machine which outputs different kinds of chocolate bar depending on the coin input. Its internal *state* is the number of each kind of chocolate bar. The process (behaviour pattern) may be described as a *procedure* such as on the left below...

```
REPEAT                                  input 5p
    CASE input OF                       output small bar
        5p:  output small bar          input 10p
        10p: output big bar            output big bar
    UNTIL FALSE                         input 10p
                                        output big bar
                                        . . .
```

An example trace start for the process is shown on the right above. It is just one possibility of many.

STOP and SKIP

Some special processes may be defined which are useful to the designer who must *specify* and *verify* a process. **STOP** starts but never terminates. Its presence indicates a *fault* in the design. It is possible to reveal the presence of a STOP using *transformations* of the specification. Any process which has a subordinate STOP will itself never terminate.

SKIP simply *succeeds* and thus terminates immediately. It is most useful in the development of a process specification. Substitution of SKIP for a section of code allows the remainder to be tested independently.

Recursion

Processes may sometimes possess a *recursive definition*. This means that they may be *defined in terms of themselves*. A very simple example of such a definition is that of a *clock* whose alphabet is simply composed of a single *tick* event, and never terminates. This would be formally described by...

$$Clock = tick \rightarrow Clock$$

The initial event must always be specified and is called a *guard*. The idea is that the process is a *solution of the equation*. Equations may be manipulated rather like algebra. *Mutual recursion* is the name given to a definition specified as the solution of a set of *simultaneous equations*.

Primitive processes

Primitive processes are the simplest things we need consider. In the process model there are just three primitive processes (in addition to *STOP* and *SKIP*)...

- *Assignment*

- *Input*

- *Output*

Assignment refers to the assignment of *purely local state*. In the process model of software there can be no global variables and no references to non-local variables whatsoever. All resources (e.g. a database) must either be *distributed* or belong solely to a single process.

Just as assignment is of a variable to an expression, *output* is of an expression and the corresponding *input* is of its value into a variable. The correspondence of assignment to input and output is no coincidence and shows that all computation may be regarded as communication, as we shall see.

Construct processes

Constructs may be employed to specify a process in terms of subordinates. The possibilities are as follows...

- *Sequence*

- *Parallel*

- *Selection*

- *Iteration*

The three possible means of process selection are by...

- *Guard event*

- *Condition*

- *Expression value*

Qualification may be required to determine the process selected by *guard* since it is possible that more than one choice may exist at the instant of selection. Thus the program must specify *prioritization*. In the absence of prioritization the process selection will be *nondeterminate*.

Iteration is terminated by a condition in the usual way.

1.3.2   Concurrency

Synchronization

Any pair of processes *running* in the same window of time are said to be *concurrent* (Figure 1.11). Of interest are those processes which *interact* by communication.

Consider the economy example above. The manufacturer process is unable to send money to its supplier until it has first received money from its customer. As a result the supplier must *wait idle* until the manufacturer is ready and the transaction may proceed. This is what is meant by *synchronization*. Communication is delayed until both parties are ready.

Of course, the constraint of payment before supply may result in the supplier delaying the sending of goods until payment has been received. In other words, the supplier will not be ready for that transaction until after the other has occurred.

Deadlock

One of the most insidious problems which can occur with the specification of concurrent systems is that of *deadlock*. The classic example of this is the *dining philosophers* problem (Figure 1.9).

A number of philosophers (say three) share a common dining room. Each has his own seat and fork and is right handed. They eat nothing but spaghetti which requires *two* forks with which to serve a helping. Being either stupid or utterly selfish, they are incapable of assisting each other and so must each make use of the fork of another or

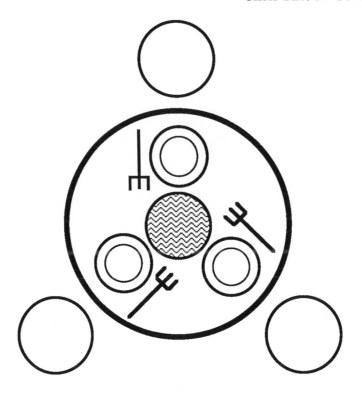

Figure 1.9: Dining philosophers problem

starve to death if all dine together. The problem is that they cannot all serve themselves at the same time[8]. If they do not talk to each other and reach agreement how can they avoid *starvation?*

Each philosopher dining may be described as a process defined by the following procedure...

1. *Input fork from left-hand neighbour (input fork)*

2. *Pick up own fork and eat (update state)*

3. *Give fork to neighbour (output fork)*

4. *Leave (succeed)*

---

[8] A similar situation has been used to illustrate the difference between *heaven* and *hell*. The same physical scenario is present in both. *In hell they starve, in heaven they eat!*

The philosophers come and go as they please and the dining system will work *except when they start together!* If they all start simultaneously, no-one will be able to commandeer their own fork. They will all **STOP** and never **succeed**. This situation is an example of *deadlock*.

One solution is to create a new process whose task it is simply never to allow a full table at any one time. This is an example of a *monitor* process which permits secure access to a *shared resource*. Although it prevents the philosophers from deadlocking (starving), it enforces a degree of *sequentiality* which is obviously not maximally efficient.

1.3.3 Communication

Successive processes

Communication is *fundamental* to computation. Computation may be regarded as purely assignment and communication *at all levels*, from hardware upwards.

In the purely procedural model of computation, and hence pure procedural programming languages, communication is rarely formalized. No concurrency is allowed since usually only a single processor is assumed available. Communication is reduced to that between processes which run in sequence, i.e. *successive processes*. The *only* way in which they may communicate is by means of a *shared variable* called a *buffer*. Figure 1.10 shows the relationship between successive processes and the variable they share which belongs to their mutual *parent process*.

The situation is like that in a market when a vendor is waiting for an expected customer who is to purchase his last item of stock. If the vendor *knows* the customer cannot arrive until he has already sold the rest of his stock, it is obviously *secure* and *efficient* for him to leave the purchase in an agreed location for the customer to collect. This is only secure if the agreed location is *not known to anyone else*. Leaving the purchase is equivalent to *assigning a value* to a buffer at the previously declared (agreed) location. The location and the *data type* form the *protocol* for the transaction (communication event).

This form of communication is said to be *asynchronous* because sending and receiving take place at different times. Rather than characterize processes as *successive* or *concurrent* it is sufficient, and arguably more meaningful, to simply relate them by whether their communication is asynchronous or synchronous. *Communication between successive processes is asynchronous and uses a shared variable called a buffer.*

Concurrent processes

Communication between *concurrent* processes is a different problem. Figure 1.11 illustrates communication between concurrent processes within their *time window of overlap*. The input and output events of receiver and sender processes respectively are *synchronized* to form a single event of their mutual parent. *Communication between concurrent processes is synchronous and uses a channel.*

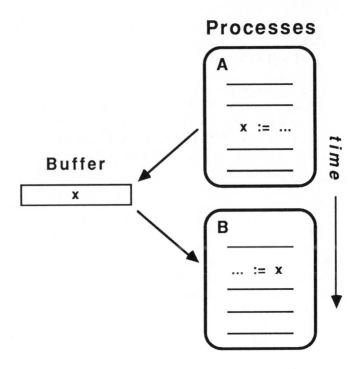

Figure 1.10: Communication between successive processes

Communication, whether synchronous or asynchronous, may be categorized by the number of senders and receivers as follows...

- *One-to-one*

- *One-to-many (broadcast)*

- *Many-to-one (multiplex)*

It is enough to consider the simplest case of *one-to-one communication* where only two processes are involved. Once this can be achieved, so can *one-to-many* and *many-to-one* communication. The same criteria of security and efficiency apply but another difficulty arises in synchronization. One or other process may not be ready. For example our market vendor may be waiting to sell without a customer wanting to buy. The result is that he is *idle* which indicates *inefficiency*. The solution is for him to busy himself with something else and *suspend* the process of selling. In other words, each processor must be capable of *scheduling* multiple processes *in order to be efficient*.

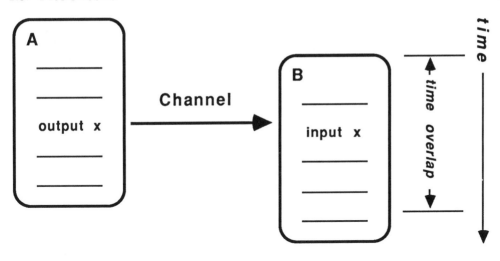

Figure 1.11: Communication between parallel processes

Synchronous communication requires something which corresponds to the part played by the buffer in asynchronous communication. The mechanism required is called a *channel* and must also be agreed (declared) by both parties prior to any transaction. In our market analogy the channel used for a transaction is the method of payment. The vendor may not accept credit cards in which case... *no transaction!* The particular channel employed and the types of value passed form the channel *protocol.*

Input of a value is into a variable. Clearly, it will be hard work computing any given function if all that is possible is to relocate values, although the Turing Machine demonstrates that such is possible. The *output* primitive must be capable of sending the value of some *function of state*. The arguments of this function are therefore local variables. To summarize, a processor must be capable of. . .

- Assignment *of state to a function of state*

- Input *of a value to state*

- Output *of a function of state*

Further reading

Computers may be modelled as a network of processors running processes which communicate with each other and an environment which may be modelled *in the same way*. The process model of computation may be applied to the lowest level of computation even unto the level of the *normally-open switch*.

The model very briefly introduced here originates with [Hoare 78]. A full and fascinating account is given in [Hoare 85], which the reader is strongly recommended to read.

Exercises

Question one

i *Protocols* may be *layered* one above the other. For example *natural language* employs rules collectively called a *syntax* to determine the valid structure of symbols called *words* in each *sentence*. Part of this protocol is the rule that a sentence is a *stream* with EOT ".". Below that protocol lies another, part of which takes the form of a *dictionary* defining the valid structure of symbols called *characters* in each word.

If both writer and reader of this book are regarded as processes, what is the protocol used in their communication?

ii Detail any other kinds of protocol you can think of, which are used for channels of communication in the everyday world.

Question two

i Summarize the instruction set of the (human) automaton discussed in Section 1.2.2.

ii Suggest an implementation of this automaton in *Modula-2* or other structured procedural programming language.

Question three

Show how *normally-open switches* may be used to implement a *NAND* logic gate, which has output "1" unless both inputs are "1". *Use only two switches.*

Question four

i Describe an example, of your own, of a process where *some* of the subordinate processes run *concurrently*. Having done that, now describe an example where *all* the subordinate processes run *successively*.

ii A process is composed of four subordinate processes, *A, B, C, D*. The following communication paths must exist...

- *A → B (asynchronous)*
- *B → D (synchronous)*
- *C → D (asynchronous)*
- *C → A (synchronous)*

Two processors are available, which do not share memory but which possess physical (hardware) communication channels (one input and one output channel each). How must the processes be assigned to processors?

iii   Is there any possibility of deadlock?

Chapter 2

Software engineering

2.1 Projects

2.1.1 Engineering design process

The following universal *design process* is employed in all fields of engineering...

1. *Analyse*

2. *Design*

3. *Implement*

4. *Verify*

Systems analysis should result in a *requirements specification*. The designer then uses this in order to produce a *design specification*. A solution is then implemented, sufficiently *self-documenting* for any other engineer to understand. Figure 2.1 shows a flow diagram for the design process, which terminates only when the implementation has been verified against the requirements.

Failure to specify a requirement properly *prior* to designing a solution is clearly stupid. It is amazing to find how often such failure occurs. Specification means first breaking up the requirement into smaller, more manageable, blocks and identifying the interfaces between them. Systems analysis is most vitally concerned with specifying *interfaces*, particularly the *human/machine interface*.

Systems design requires a means of specifying how the requirement may be met. It proceeds by one or other means of *reduction* of the requirements into manageable *modules* which may in turn be broken down by...

- *Procedure*

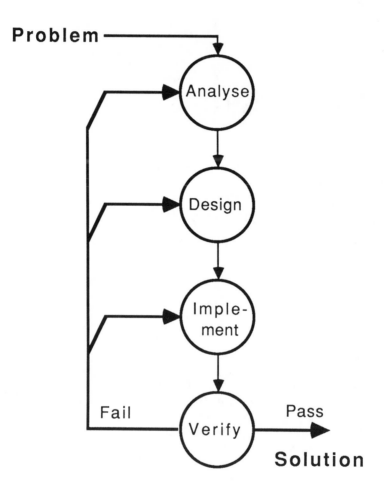

Figure 2.1: How to solve a problem

- *Process*

- *Object*

- *Relation*

- *Function*

In any one design, all modules must be of the same kind to make interfaces between them possible.

Some means of dividing the implementation into corresponding *software partitions* must be available which permits *separate development* and *separate verification*.

Verification is usually the greater problem. One can rarely be certain that an implementation is totally correct. The best that is often possible is to do some tests to verify that the requirements specification is met with the largest possible set of inputs. *Exhaustive verification* means testing the system output for *every* legal input and is usually prohibitively expensive. It is often possible to classify input. If so, a *test set* of inputs may be selected with members from each class. *Formal verification* implies the use of *mathematical transformations* to establish analytically that the *algorithm* used will give correct output for any valid input.

2.1.2 Organization

A project itself may be thought of as a process whose output is the implementation of systems which meet requirements input. This time however the process is carried out by people. The implementation for a particular requirement is known as an *application*.

Projects make use of the design process described above. Each sub-process is usually carried out by a separate team. The reader should think of a line leading from requirement to verified solution and a sequence of sub-processes along it. At the design stage the requirement meets prior knowledge and a very poorly understood process known as human thought produces a solution.

The processes of *analysis, design, implementation* and *verification*, when applied to computer systems, are collectively known as *software engineering*. A readable text on software engineering is [Sommerville 85].

Few systems are simple to engineer, most are complex. Projects are usually constrained to a tight time scale because of the need for a product to reach the market before its competition. As a result it is essential to *distribute effort* across a team.

Three problems arise here. . .

- Distribution: *How may the project be broken down between team members?*

- Interface: *How may team members work together effectively?*

- Co-ordination: *How may the project now be managed?*

The problem may be summarized as *how to get a ten man-year job done in a single year!*

There is no single clear answer to any of these questions. They are still the subject of much research. The ideas in *modular software engineering* go some way towards a solution.

2.1.3 Languages

Requirements

The concept of *language* is central to both *computer science and software engineering.* There is need for a language to communicate each of the following things. . .

- *Requirements specification*

- *Design specification*

- *Implementation (programmer readable)*

- *Implementation (machine readable)*

The language used to specify requirements is usually the local *natural language* (e.g. English). Design and implementation languages should be *compatible* since the programmer must *translate* the design specification into an implementation.

A *semantic gap* is said to separate the two implementation languages of the programmer and machine and is of a width which depends on the *design philosophy* of the machine and is crossed via translation. The *machine language* is in terms of capabilities of the machine itself which will reflect both its design philosophy and the *model of computation* chosen.

2.2 Modular systems design

2.2.1 Tasks

Top-down task diagram

We commence by thinking of the requirement to be met as a *task* to be performed. Now we repeatedly subdivide it into a number of others which are simpler, or easier, to perform. Each task is considered done if all its offspring have been completed. Reduction proceeds until we reach a point at which a single engineer can easily specify software to perform each task at *any* level.

Figure 2.2 illustrates a top-down task diagram for the task of writing a textbook such as this.

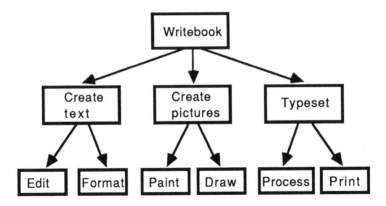

Figure 2.2: Top-down task decomposition diagram for the composition of this book

Balanced loading

The principle of *balanced loading* may be roughly stated as follows...

All tasks, regardless of level, should require roughly equal effort to perform.

It does not help at all if we decompose a task without making its offspring significantly easier to perform. Ideally all tasks at all levels should be of *equal* difficulty to minimize the overall effort required and maximize its distribution.

These ideas can be usefully illustrated by the analysis of *management structure*. Figure 2.3(lower) represents the better structure. It may not necessarily be very good in practice. It is easy to imagine that one middle manager may have less to do than colleagues at the same level. The result would be an *imbalance* of load between them. There is no easy way to assess relative task loading. An initial design may have to be revised after it has been tested. Although it may appear easy, obtaining a decomposition of a task, which is balanced in *both* dimensions, is far from it. It requires skill on the part of the designer which takes experience to gain.

Population growth

Following *balanced loading*, a second principle of top-down task decomposition may be stated...

Each partition of a task should be into between two and five offspring.

The size of the "box" population should not grow too fast or too slow. Between two and five children per parent is recommended.

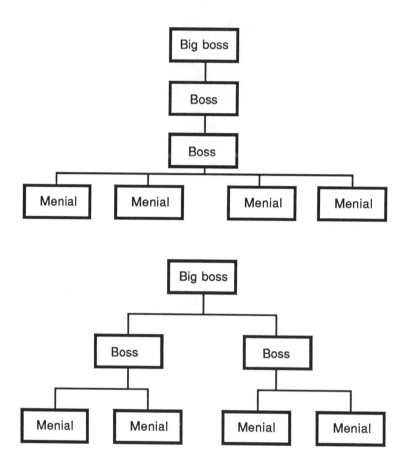

Figure 2.3: Two alternative management structures

No single analysis should consider more than a few levels. A sensible number is three. Each *terminal* (lowest level) task should subsequently be the subject of a further analysis if necessary.

To continue with the management analogy, compare the two alternative structures in Figure 2.3. It is hard to imagine how balanced loading could ever be achieved with the upper structure. Still worse is that extra, unnecessary, *interaction* must occur. The path of command is twice as long as in the lower structure.

Interaction

Once a satisfactory top-down diagram is obtained, the interface between each task and its parent must be rendered clear within the specification of both. A third principle is necessary...

No interaction should occur except between parent and child.

The precise description of the interaction between parent and offspring tasks is called the *interface*.

The ideas detailed here are based on those of *Edward Yourdon*. For a full account of top-down design see [Yourdon & Constantine 78].

Modules

The top-down diagram is progressively developed until each task may be delegated to a single engineer (or team of engineers) who may be expected to produce a *verified* system prior to a declared *deadline*. The software to perform each task delegated in this way is called a *module*. Each module will eventually exist in the following guises...

- *Definition module*

- *Implementation source module*

- *Implementation object module*

The *definition module* defines the module interface, whilst the *implementation source module* contains the software itself in humanly readable form using a *programming language*. The *implementation object module* contains the same but in machine readable form using a *machine language*.

To summarize, in order to render a large requirement manageable we break it down into tasks until a point is reached where individuals (or small teams) are able to implement software to perform each one. The system design is then a number of definition modules, corresponding to each task, which each specify the interface to both parent and offspring. It must be emphasized that *all* tasks at *all* levels are represented by modules. The first definition module to be written is the topmost.

Top-down decomposition is applicable with all programming models. However, tasks are most easily related to procedures (which perform them). In the *procedural model* the communication of...

- *Procedures*

- *Variables*

- *Constants*

- *Data types*

...is undertaken. A parent is said to *import* any of these from its offspring. An offspring is said to *export* them to its parent.

The reader must be wary of confusion here. Modules are purely descriptive. They offer a hierarchical method of describing the required system for human benefit only. For the sake of *performance* (i.e. fast execution) the machine should be as unhindered as possible by inter-module boundaries. It is not possible to have modular software without *some* performance diminution so modularity may need to be traded-off against performance.

In order to reduce development cost it is vital that software be *reused* whenever possible. *Library modules* of previously written software should be built up and used later. To summarize...

- *Low development cost requires software reusability*

- *Reusability requires software modularity*

- *Modularity may require some trade-off against performance*

The benefits of modules are twofold. Firstly, modules make the development of large systems *manageable*. Secondly, *reusable* software drastically reduces development cost. Modules should be thought of as hardware "chips". They prevent "reinvention of the wheel" and unnecessary duplication of effort. They form a *software resource* which need only be developed once and then used in conjunction with any (correctly interfaced) higher level modules. The interface, as detailed in the definition module, should be all that it is necessary to know in order to use a library module. It should *not* be necessary to even have available the corresponding implementation source module.

2.2.2   Processes

Data flow graph

A *data flow graph* is a graph where processes form nodes and channels (or buffers) form edges, through which "flow" data. It is a directed graph and may or may not be fully

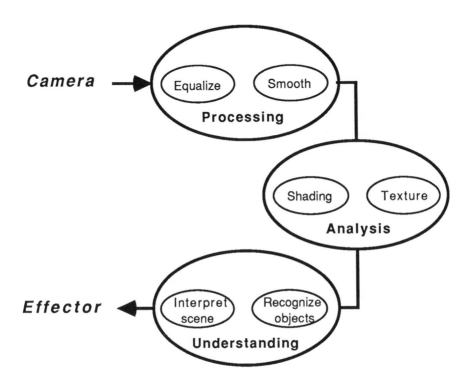

Figure 2.4: Data flow diagram for a vision system

connected. A *data flow diagram* is a pictorial representation of the data flow graph. Figure 2.4 shows an example.

No information is contained in the data flow graph about *when* the processes run, i.e. which must run concurrently and which must run successively. This information must be drawn separately out of the requirement specification.

The analysis of data flow renders clear the *communication* inherent in the requirement. Now we are able to identify precisely what we require for a *process interface specification*. It is simply a formal or informal specification of the *protocol* of both incoming and outgoing data.

Partitions

There is one other benefit gained from data flow analysis. A means of *process oriented design* is afforded which conforms to the notion of *stepwise refinement*. Each node on the data flow graph may be reduced to a new subgraph. This continues until processes are reached which may be implemented without further reduction. In other words the system is partitioned into a network of processes. Each process may then be separately developed, maintained, verified and reused as a software module.

2.2.3   Objects

Nature

The reader is expected to be familiar with the *procedural programming model* where software specifies system behaviour in terms of *procedures* which act upon *data structures* which may be either static or dynamic. The *object oriented programming model* unifies data and procedure with the concept of an *object*. The idea is rather like an extension of that of a *record* by allowing *procedure* fields which alone may act upon the associated data fields. These are termed *methods* and are invoked only by sending the object an appropriate *message*. State is said to be *encapsulated* with methods and can only be updated by the arrival of a message. For instance, a graphics system may require the ability to draw a circle. A *circle object* is defined which responds to the message "draw" by invoking a suitable method to update the screen (state). *Polymorphism* is the name given to the ability of different objects to respond differently to the *same* message. A *line object* may also respond to "draw" with a completely different result.

Objects in the real world may be represented by rendering an *abstract data type* which represents not just its state but also the *operations* which may be performed on it. A system is represented as a network of communicating objects very similar to one composed of processes. The only truly significant difference is that objects possess a property known as *inheritance*. It is possible to declare the...

- *State*

- *Methods*

- *Messages*

...of an entire *class* of objects. When an object is required it is declared to be an *instance* of a given class and *inherits* its state, methods and messages. This is not all, for it is then possible to modify the instance to possess further properties. Even whole new classes may be declared as modifications of existing ones. This property promotes the reusability of software to an unprecedented degree. A number of classes turn out to be very common natural classes and hence are usually provided within an object-oriented programming system. It is possible to implement a very wide range of applications very efficiently using these as a starting point. A few of them are discussed below.

In short the most important characteristics of the object model are...

- *Encapsulation*

- *Message passing*

- *Polymorphism*

- *Inheritance*

See [Thomas 89] for a more thorough and very readable introduction. The archetype object-oriented language is *Smalltalk* [Goldberg & Robson 83]. The use of objects in system design is thoroughly treated in [Meyer 88].

The implementation of objects using a procedural language is limited since message passing and inheritance are not explicitly supported. However [Stubbs & Webre 87] is an excellent introduction to the implementation of abstract data types given such limitations.

Lists

A *list* is a *dynamic* abstract data structure, i.e. it may change in size while the process to which it belongs is running. List elements may be physically either *sequence associated* or *pointer associated* depending on implementation.

Arguably the list is the simplest object of all. The minimum set of messages it should recognize is...

- *Insert*

- *Remove*

Both are followed by a *key* which identifies the element affected. Typically other messages would allow an element to be inspected without removal and check to see if a given key is present.

A list is referred to as a *generic* type of data structure. In other words it defines a *class* of object. Lists are linear and thus are ordered. Each element has precisely one *successor* and one *predecessor* except those at each end. Extra messages may be defined which exploit the structure best for a given application.

Stack

At the purely data level a *stack* is identical to a list. It is also a linear, ordered structure. It is its message protocol that differs (see Figure 2.5).

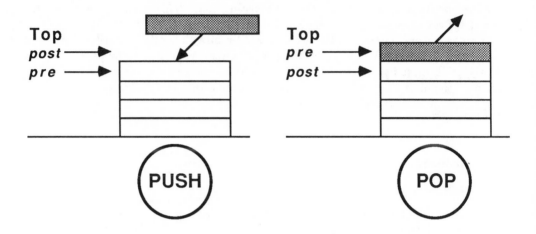

Figure 2.5: Internal operations of a stack object

The minimum set of stack messages is...

- *Push*

- *Pop*

Push is followed by an element which is to be placed on top of the stack. *Pop* causes a responding message containing the element which has been removed from there. Great care should be taken in defining the pop protocol that the response be defined should the stack be *empty*. Similarly the push protocol must also be carefully defined since, in practice, no machine has infinite memory and so any stack can become *full*.

Stack protocol is referred to as *last in first out (LIFO)*, or *first in last out (FILO)*, since the last element in is the first out and the first in is the last out.

Stacks are particularly important in computer organization and will be returned to later in this book. Their chief use is in *expression evaluation*.

Queue

The last object class to be introduced has the following minimum message set...

- *Enqueue*

• *Serve*

... and is also linear and ordered like a list.

Enqueue is followed by the element to be placed at the back of the queue. *Serve* causes a responding message containing the element found at the front. Care must be taken to ensure that the protocol covers the possibility of the queue being either full or empty. Figure 2.6 depicts the operation of the methods on receipt of each message.

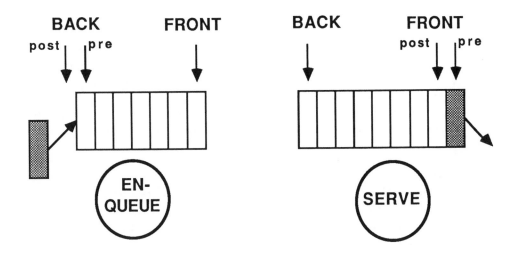

Figure 2.6: Internal operations of a queue object

The queue protocol is referred to as *first in first out (FIFO)* since the first element in is always the first out.

Like the stack, the queue is of great importance in computer organization and is used for *buffering* data in *asynchronous communication*.

An extension is the *priority queue* object where elements are enqueued internally according to an associated priority. Hence when an item arrives of priority higher than that of the back element, it is placed further up as appropriate.

2.3 Structured programming

2.3.1 Primitives

Assignment

Variables are distinct, named items within the memory subsystem of a computer. The name of a variable is a symbol which denotes its *location*. A variable is said to have a value which must be chosen from a set known as its *range*. Two variables with ranges which differ in *size* or *content* are said to be of different *data type*.

Variables of a process constitute its *state*. Values of variables may change while the process to which they belong runs.

Constants are symbols which denote a value which remains unchanged while the process to which they belong runs. Their type must be chosen from those of the variables belonging to the same process. Each is then said to be *compatible* with variables of that type.

Binary operators are *primitive functions* which take two *arguments* and evaluate a result. A simple example is the **add** operator, which when applied to the arguments {3,4} evaluates to 7. The set of operators supplied in a programming language will depend on the applications for which it is designed. For instance, a language used to develop mathematical applications must have, at very least, a full set of algebraic operators. One used to develop graphics or image processing applications will need (at least) a full set of logical operators.

Expressions are combinations of operators, variables and constants which are *evaluated* by first evaluating each operator in turn. The arguments of each binary operator are considered to be expressions. A variable or constant is just a *primitive* expression.

The order in which expressions must be evaluated will be dictated by the *syntax* (rules) of the language. It is common to use parenthesis to allow the programmer to indicate any particular meaning. In order to reduce ambiguity the language usually defines an *operator precedence* which defines the order in which operators are evaluated. Responsibility for removing all ambiguity usually rests with the programmer.

Assignment means the assignment of a value to a variable. In procedural programming an assignment statement *commands* the assignment to occur at a specific point in the procedure. The variable to which the value is assigned appears on the left hand side of a symbol denoting assignment. On the right hand side is an expression, e.g. ...

```
answer := 42
```

In a purely *sequential* programming language assignment is the *only* available primitive.

Input

See Chapter 1 for a discussion of the process model of computation.

An *input* command causes the assignment of a value input (over a channel) to a variable. In the *Occam* programming language (see 2.4.2) the variable name appears on the right hand side, the channel name on the left and a symbol denoting input lies in between, e.g. ...

<code>c.keyboard ? key.pressed</code>

Hence this means... "input a value over channel 'c.keyboard' into variable 'key.pressed'".

Output

Point-to-point communication is the most fundamental within any network. It is that between just two nodes and in one direction only. It constitutes a *single* event for the network but one event *each* for sender and receiver (output and input). Out of this, many-to-one (multiplexing) and one-to-many (demultiplexing or broadcast) communication can be achieved.

An *output* command causes the output of the value of an *expression* onto a channel. Consequently the channel name and expression must be stated. In Occam the expression appears on the right hand side, the channel name on the left and a symbol denoting output lies in between, e.g. ...

<code>c.screen ! 6*7</code>

Hence this means "output the value of '6 * 7' onto channel 'c.screen'"

2.3.2 Constructs

Sequence

The *SEQ* construct is used to *directly* define an event sequence. Each statement is a command causing one or more events to occur (see Figure 2.7).

Each statement may be a primitive or a procedure name and may be regarded as a process which must terminate before the next starts.

Parallel

The *PAR* construct is the means by which the programmer specifies which processes are to run concurrently. It must itself be considered a *sequential process* whose event order will depend upon communication between the component processes.

The events of a process defined by a parallel construct are the assignments belonging to each component process and each communication (i.e. input + output) between them, (see Figure 2.8).

Once again, each statement within the construct is either a primitive or a procedure name.

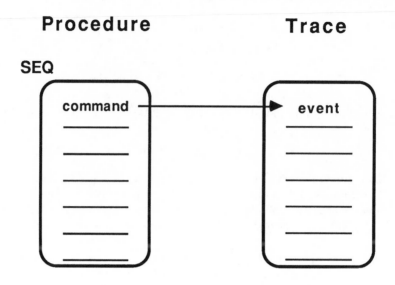

Figure 2.7: Sequence construct

Iteration

A *WHILE* construct specifies the iteration of a process while a condition (expression of Boolean type) remains true. The body will *never* run if the condition is false initially. Strictly speaking, only one iteration construct is necessary to program any process. WHILE would do nicely!

A *REPEAT* construct specifies the iteration of a process until a condition becomes true. The body will *always* run once regardless of whether the *condition* is true when it starts (unlike WHILE).

A *FOR* construct specifies iteration of a process a number of times equal to the value of an expression. If this has value zero initially then the body will never run.

Selection

Selection means choosing one process from a number of stated possibilities. The choice is made immediately before the one chosen is to start. There are three ways in which the choice may be made...

- *Expression value (CASE)*

- *Condition (IF)*

- *Guard (ALT)*

Procedure   Trace

PAR

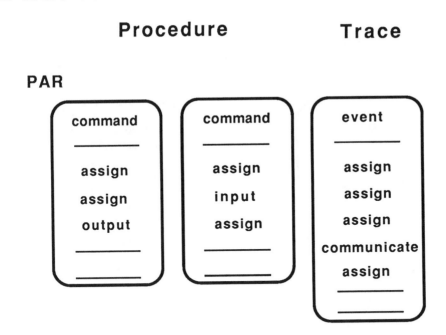

Figure 2.8: Parallel construct

Selection by *either* expression or condition is sufficient in a programming language to program any process. Selection by guard is used to define *efficient* behaviour given multiple input channels. The *guards* used are the input events on each channel. Hence each associated process is the one which uses that channel. The process which has input and thus *can* run is selected and allowed to do so.

It is quite possible to program input from multiple channels without selection by channel input guard. It is not however possible to do it *efficiently*. Input could be taken from each channel alternately. In any real system this would result in serious underuse of the processor, which would spend most of its time idle, *waiting* for input.

For instance a *word processor* used by a *single* typist spends most of its time waiting for the next key to be pressed since it operates much faster than any typist. One which is shared by a number of typists, and which is able to activate the process appropriate to whichever keyboard on which a key is pressed, will make much more efficient use of the processor, which itself then becomes a guarded shared resource.

CASE selects between a number of processes by the value of an *expression*. The expression is thus restricted to ordinal types. There is no ambiguity since the expression can only possess a single value. It may be thought of as a *multiway switch* between the

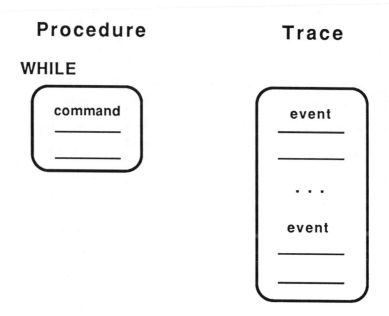

Figure 2.9: While construct

various processes specified.

IF... THEN... ELSE selects between two processes by the success of a *condition*. It may be regarded as a subset of case, since a condition is just a Boolean expression, and selects between just two processes. As with CASE, no ambiguity is possible since the condition may only take a single value at a time. It may be thought of as a *two-way switch*.

Occam, however, extends the construct to have an arbitrary number of conditions. On entry, a process is selected by the success of its associated condition. Ambiguity thus arises, should more than one succeed, which is overcome by *prioritization* of entries by their listed order.

ALT selects between a number of processes, each guarded by an input primitive. The process selected is the one for which the corresponding input is ready. Obviously this construct is only needed in a language which supports *synchronous communication* between concurrent processes. If more than one input is ready, the selection is *nondeterminate*. A condition may be appended to a guard to effectively allow inhibiting of the input.

2.3.3 Partitions

Modules

Modules are simply a means of partitioning software for human benefit. They do not reflect any partition relevant to execution. The whole point of a module is that an individual (or team) may take responsibility for its *separate development* and *separate test*. They have the added advantages of *reusability* between applications (like hardware chips) and *maintainability*. To facilitate reusability, there should ideally be no difficulty in *interfacing* modules when they are designed, implemented or run.

Modules of a procedural language contain the following...

- *Interface (exports and imports to parent and child modules respectively)*

- *Data type definitions*

- *Data declarations*

- *Procedure definitions*

Each of these should have their own, clearly delineated, section in the *source module*, see Figure 2.10.

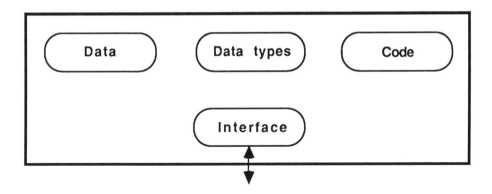

Figure 2.10: Module content

Procedures

Procedures offer a means of further partitioning software. Once again they exist to ease development, maintenance and modification. They do not enhance performance but if anything reduce it. Like modules they are to some extent reusable. They should be thought of as implementing a single *task*. Neither the task nor the procedure should be bigger than a single human can understand easily at one time. A guideline recommended by the author is that the procedure source should all fit on the screen of a terminal at once. All *statements* of a program should be thought of as belonging to one or other procedure.

Procedure parameters are variables on whose value the precise action of the procedure depends. *Value parameters* are variables whose current *value* is passed to the procedure. These variables thus remain unaltered after procedure execution. *Reference parameters* are variables whose *location* is passed, allowing the procedure to alter their value.

The *scope* of a variable is the software partition in which it is visible. Variables declared within a procedure are called *local variables* hence their scope is that procedure only. The same goes for constants. Parameters are said to have local scope only. Local scope usually includes any procedures declared locally, although this is not true of Occam.

Recursive definition of a procedure is possible. This may be understood from the following...

> *Something is said to possess a recursive definition if it may be defined in terms of itself.*

Recursion must terminate and hence must be subject to selection. A commonly quoted example is the definition of the factorial function of a number...

```
factorial(x) =
  IF x>0 THEN
    factorial := x * factorial(x-1)
  ELSE
    factorial := 1
  END
```

...where recursion terminates when x is zero.

2.4   Standard programming languages

2.4.1   Modula 2

Primitives

There is only *assignment* in Modula 2. There is no support for concurrent or parallel processing at the *primitive* level. *Expression evaluation* is well supported with operators to support mathematical, graphics and text processing applications.

Constructs

All the purely sequential constructs discussed above are available. A sequence is defined as any set of statements separated by ";". There is no support at the construct level either for concurrency or parallel processing. (No PAR or ALT.)

In addition to WHILE, REPEAT and FOR constructs Modula 2 has another iteration construct... *LOOP*. Multiple exits are possible using a command *EXIT* which may be *conditionally* selected. Use of the LOOP construct is *not* recommended for the inexperienced programmer!

Partitions

Software partitions are the strength of Modula 2! Procedures and modules are fully supported. Functions are not quite the same as in other languages. They occur in Modula 2 in the guise of *function procedures* which are able to take *reference* as well as value parameters *(caution!)* and unfortunately are unable to return *structured* data objects. The effect of this can be simulated by using a reference parameter (although it will lead to less readable source code) or by returning a pointer to the structured data.

The *procedure data type* is provided *allowing procedures to be passed as parameters.* This is a powerful feature which should be used with great care.

Modula 2 was the first language to provide modules as an *explicit, readable* part of the language. It is possible to clearly delineate between all four sections listed above.

Concurrency

It is at this level that support is found for concurrent processing though *not* for parallel processing. A special module, guaranteed always available, called "System" exports two procedures and one data type which facilitate extra processes called *coroutines* to run *quasi-concurrently* with a procedure defined in the usual way. These are...

- NewProcess: *A procedure which creates, but does not start, a new process. It must be passed a parameter of procedure type which defines the new process and returns a variable of process type*

- Transfer: *A procedure which transfers control between two processes specified by their descriptors which are passed as value parameters*

- Process: *A data type used for process descriptors*

Procedures are provided, exported from module "Processes", to support inter-process communication. The technique used is based on the use of *shared resources* which are protected by *semaphores*, see [Deitel 84] or [Lister 84]. (*Channels* are not provided.)

Considerable expertise and care is required of the programmer to ensure...

- *Secure communication*

- *Mutual exclusion (of processes from shared resources)*

- *Synchronization*

It is certainly for experts only. Unfortunately, even experts make mistakes which in this area can be disastrous.

Support for concurrent processing in a programming language should be provided at the *primitive* level. The same facilities should also (transparently) support parallel processing and be simple to use. This is only possible if the idea of shared resources is abandoned and each process has its own private memory. Computer architects must provide support for both concurrent processing (scheduling, soft channels) and parallel processing (hard channels).

Applicability

Modula 2 is especially recommended for *large* projects. It renders large projects *manageable* because of the availability of modules for design, specification and implementation. The high degree of the source readability eases its maintenance. Development costs may be cut by exploitation of module reusability.

The range of operators available make it appropriate to mathematical, textual and graphics applications. Not discussed above are facilities for *systems level programming* which are reasonable.

As a vehicle for applications requiring concurrent processing it is usable (with great care) by experts only. It is not equipped for parallel processing at all.

Further reading

The purpose of this brief summary is to set the background for subsequent discussion of hardware architectural support of modular, procedural programming. It is not the intent to be thorough.

The discussion should be enough for a student who has successfully traversed a course in procedural programming using *any* fully block-structured language (e.g. Pascal).

[Knepley & Platt 85] is recommended as a readable tutorial, accessible to any student, with a fair amount of example code. [Wirth 85] is the official summary given by the author of the language, *Niklaus Wirth*, and is recommended as a tutorial and reference text for those experienced in at least one other programming language. Modula 2 is now well established. Many good texts are thus available.

2.4.2   Occam

Primitives

Probably the most important and novel feature of Occam is that it supports concurrency at the *primitive* level. There are three main primitives. . .

- *Assignment*

- *Input*

- *Output*

Communication is *synchronized* via a mailbox form of *rendezvous*. The first process to arrive at the rendezvous leaves its identity and *suspends* itself. The second completes the communication and causes the first to *resume*. Note that *either* process may be the one suspended. One cannot determine which prior to their running.

A second novel feature of Occam is that *everything* is a process. Recall (from Chapter 1) that a process is a sequence of events which *starts, runs* then *terminates*. In addition to the three above, two extra primitives are defined...

- STOP *which starts but never terminates*

- SKIP *which starts and immediately terminates*

All five are fully fledged processes in their own right but, from the point of view of the programmer, are *indivisible*.

Data types available unfortunately differ between variable and channel. For instance, variable length *strings* and *records* are supported as *channel protocols* but not as the data types of variables.

Constructs

Occam succeeds beautifully in being at once both *simple* and extremely *expressive* in its facilities to construct sequential processes. Construction of a sequence of subordinate processes, i.e. where the event ordering is explicitly stated, is made possible using a *SEQ* construct. *Iteration* is provided via a *WHILE* construct, conditionally terminated in the usual way.

Construction of a single sequential process from a number of concurrent ones is enabled with the *PAR* construct. *All specified processes start together*. The PAR itself terminates only when *all* the subordinate processes have terminated. If just one of them STOPs so does the PAR. It is essential to understand that, although its subordinate processes run concurrently, the PAR itself forms a single process which is *sequential* like any other.

All three forms of selection (mentioned earlier) are available. *CASE* selects a process from a list by expression value. *IF* selects from a list by the truth of an associated condition. *Care is required here!* Should no condition evaluate true the process STOPs. A wise programmer thus adds the condition *TRUE* and an associated SKIP process to the list. There exists a second problem with IF. Given more than one condition succeeding in the list specified, *which process is run?* In Occam it is the one following the *first* successful condition. Nothing is gained by nesting IF constructs in Occam. All conditions may simply be entered in the list of a single construct. This has the effect of improving readability.

Selection by *channel* is supported by the *ALT* (ALTernative) construct. A list of input guards is specified each with an associated process. The process associated with the first ready guard is the one which runs. If no guard is able to terminate the ALT is suspended until one can.

Each guard may be supplemented with a condition to selectively exclude inputs from consideration. A guard may be an input from a *timer* process, which outputs time. The *AFTER* qualifier may be used to prevent the guard from succeeding until after a stated time thus effectively allowing a "timeout" process to be triggered if no other input arrives.

Replication

Replication of SEQ, IF, PAR and ALT construct level processes is supported. If the design calls for a number of *procedurally identical* processes, which differ only in elements chosen from arrays of either channels (PAR, ALT) or variables (SEQ, IF), extremely concise elegant programs may be written. Replication renders Occam very expressive.

Partitions

We have already met one of the weaknesses of Occam in its limited set of data types for variables. A second weakness is arguably in its support of partitions to benefit software design. There are no *modules* which can encapsulate packages of procedures for reuse between applications. The effect can, of course, be achieved by shuffling text between files using an appropriate editor. Occam does however go part way towards the concept of a module. *Individual* procedures may be *separately compiled* and then linked into any number of applications.

Procedures in Occam are well supported as *named processes* which take reference parameters by default. Value parameters are also supported. If invoked as a subordinate of a SEQ, a procedure must be passed *variables* with which to communicate with its neighbours. If that of a PAR it needs the appropriate *channels*.

Functions also form part of Occam. Only value parameters are allowed. All parameters *must* be variables and not channels. Hence functions which communicate together must communicate via variable sharing and hence must run successively. Neither may they contain any *nondeterminacy* in the form of ALT or PAR constructs.

Neither procedures nor functions may be recursively defined. This constitutes a third weakness in that it places a limit on its expressivity, especially for mathematical applications.

Applicability

Concurrent functions or procedures cannot share variables and thus cannot inflict *side effects* upon each other. A newcomer to Occam might well start off with the notion of it as "Pascal with no shared variables". The idea of doing away with the sharing of any state between processes is central and responsible for Occam being able to offer simple yet unrestricted access to the power of parallel processing.

Event processing is the essence of creating systems which effect *real time control* over automation (e.g. production lines, robots, washing machines, watches, kettles etc). Such systems are known as *embedded systems* and now account for the greatest and fastest growing number of computers. Languages such as Ada and Occam were originally designed for real time control and embedded systems.

Problems in the real world almost always possess a high degree of concurrency. It is the exception which is purely composed of successive processes. Occam is the simplest programming language with which to adequately describe such problems. It is much simpler to describe a problem composed of concurrent, communicating sequential processes with a language which is equipped for it than to *mentally* transform it into a purely sequential form. Unfortunately the majority of practising software engineers are firmly rooted in thinking sequentially and thus often find Occam difficult and natural concurrency obscure.

The *simplicity* of Occam, together with its *expressive power* over the behaviour of both natural and machine systems, give it an accessible range of applications limited only perhaps by their scale due to its limited modularity.

Further reading

We can only afford a brief summary of Occam here, enough to serve subsequent discussion of hardware architectures which support the process model of computation. [Burns 88] is an excellent tutorial which includes a comparison with *Ada*. [Pountain & May 87] offers an alternative introduction. [Inmos 88#1] is the official language definition and manual which also contains many useful examples. It is absolutely indispensable.

Exercises

Question one

i Define *in your own words* the meaning of the following terms and how they may be used in the engineering of software...

- *Module*

- *Top-down task diagram*

- *Data flow diagram*

Question two

i Explain the evolution of a software *project* in terms of the various phases of its life.

ii Identify the phase at which the following must be specified...

- *Definition modules*

- *Pseudocode*

Question three

i What are *library modules* and why are they commercially important to software engineering?

ii In what form would you expect to use library modules?

Question four

If neither *procedures* nor *modules* should affect the machine execution of a program, *why should a machine language support them?*

Chapter 3

Machine language

3.1 Nature

3.1.1 Translation from programming language

Machine language is used for the description of the system process which may be presented to the *raw machine*. On the other hand, a *programming language* is used for a description of the same thing but presented in a manner understandable to a human. The programming language should also render the *software modularity* clear to a human. In other words the boundaries and interfaces of procedures and modules should be *opaque* in the programming language but *transparent* in the machine language.

The language understood by different machines varies greatly. *Portability* of programs between computers is achieved via use of common *programming* languages. The machine language program is *not* portable, except between machines of identical design.

The problem of informing a machine of the procedure you wish it to follow is much like that of informing a person, who speaks another language, how to perform a task. The language of the speaker (programmer) must be *translated* into that of the listener (machine). If the translation is carried out word by word, as it is spoken, it is referred to as *interpretation*. If it takes place after everything has been said it is referred to as *compilation*. Figure 3.1 illustrates the problem.

The difference between the programming and machine language is called the *semantic gap*. It is possible to argue that hardware architecture should evolve so as to *narrow* this gap. This begs the question of the *choice* of programming language. Since it is now comparatively cheap to develop a new processor, a number of new designs are appearing which are optimized to close the semantic gap for a variety of programming languages.

An alternative view is that the semantic gap is an inevitable consequence of the conflict between the machine requirements (for performance) and those of humans (for maintainability and ease of development). In this case the machine language design may take more account of the requirements of the compiler *code generator*, which must

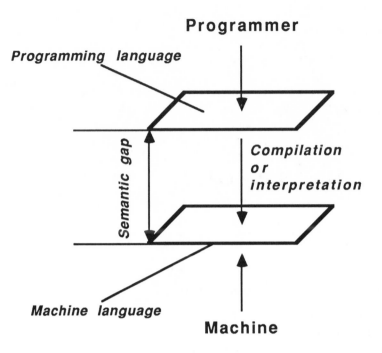

Figure 3.1: Translation of natural language to machine language

generate machine language "code" *automatically*. It must then be made easy to make choices logically where alternatives exist.

3.1.2 Structure

A machine language program takes the form of a stream of independent *instructions*. They are conventionally encoded as binary numbers and are *executed* sequentially in the order in which they are found. Each is made up of two parts...

- *Operation*

- *Operands (0,1,2 or 3)*

When the instruction is executed, the operation, whose encoding is known as an *opcode*, is performed upon the operand(s).

Behaviour of *some* instructions must be *conditional* or conditional behaviour of the process as a whole would not be possible. Some memory of the outcome of the execution of previous instructions is always provided and is referred to as the *processor state*. For example, a single *latch* will recall whether the result of the previous operation (e.g. a subtraction) was zero or not. Hence, for example, two numbers may be compared and subsequent action rendered dependent upon whether or not they share a common value. All processor state is stored collectively in the *processor state register (PSR)*.

Machine code for the running process is stored in a large *linear memory* (Figure 3.2) which may be referenced *randomly* as an *array*. The array index is called an *address* and each memory cell a *location*. Array bounds are simply zero and its size (minus one). The address of the next instruction to execute is stored in another register, wide enough to accomodate any address, called the *program counter (PC)* (Figure 3.3). Sequencing is obtained automatically by incrementing the program counter after each instruction is executed.

Conditional instructions may be used to modify the *control flow* by conditionally updating the program counter. All selection and iteration constructs may be implemented using a single instruction, the *conditional branch*, which adds its single operand to the program counter if the condition succeeds but otherwise does nothing.

Almost all modern computers make use of the idea that the machine code should reside in the same memory device as data. Obviously care must be taken that the two occupy *distinct* areas of memory. However *shared memory* simplifies the architecture and, hence lowers the cost, of the whole computer. Computers using this principle are often referred to as *von Neumann machines*, after the person credited with the innovation. Those which employ separate memories for code and data are referred to as *Harvard machines*.

3.1.3 Interpretation

It is the function of the *processor control unit* to interpret machine language. In other words it *translates* each instruction, one at a time, into a sequence of physical *micro-operations*. There may be two *parallel* components to a micro-operation...

- *Register transfer*

- *Control of functional unit*

As an example, consider a two-operand instruction **add r0,r1** which adds together the contents of two registers (**r0** and **r1**) and places the result in the second (**r1**). This will be translated into the following micro-operation sequence...

$$
\begin{array}{rrcl}
(1) & alu.in.0 & \leftarrow & r0 \\
(2) & alu.in.1 & \leftarrow & r1, alu(add) \\
(3) & r1 & \leftarrow & alu.out
\end{array}
$$

$alu.in.0, alu.in.1, alu.out$ denote the two inputs and one output of an *arithmetic logic unit (ALU)*, which is a device capable of evaluating a number of arithmetic functions.

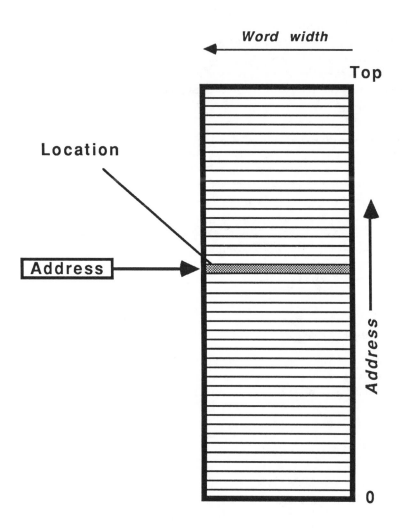

Figure 3.2: Linear memory

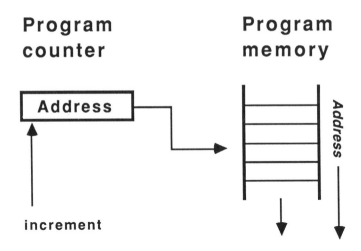

Figure 3.3: Program counter sequencing of instruction execution

The means used to express a micro-operation sequence is called a *register transfer language (RTL)*. "A ← B" denotes the transfer of the contents of register B into register A. Two items separated by a comma are understood to take place in parallel. The second item will always be the control of a functional unit if only a single transfer may take place at a time. This is indicated as a function bearing the name of the unit, whose argument is the "switch" to be set. Thus *alu(add)* means switch the ALU to "add". There is no universally accepted standard RTL. The one used throughout this text is somewhat different to that found elsewhere. It has been designed to render clear each individual transfer rather than to be concise.

3.1.4 Instructions

Assignment and expression evaluation

The first group of instructions is that which implements assignment of an expression value to a variable. Actual assignment is achieved with the **store** instruction which typically takes two operands, the value and the variable, usually referred to as *source* and *destination*.

Expressions are evaluated by iteratively evaluating sub-expressions, usually from right to left or according to level of parenthesis. The term "expression" simply means a description of a function in terms of variables, constants and primitive functions called *operators*.

So far, two *special registers* have been mentioned, the program counter and the processor state register. In addition to these, a number of *general purpose registers (GPRs)*

will be provided which are used to hold the value of both an expression and its sub-expressions as they are evaluated. Since *local variables* are implemented as memory locations, there must be two kinds of *data transfer*...

- *Register to memory (*`store`*)*

- *Memory to register (*`load`*)*

A `store` performs an assignment. A `load` of each required variable prepares the *register file* for expression evaluation.

Instructions which implement functions at the *binary operator* level are essential for expression evaluation. It may be shown that *any* computable function may be computed using just a few *binary logical operators*. In fact the set {`and or not`} is sufficient.

In reality any operator requires a sequence of operations (and hence some time) to be evaluated. For example, the function *plus(a,b)* will usually require transfering the values of *a* and *b* to the input of a *physical* adding device and then transfering the result to *plus*. In addition the adder must be *activated* at the right moment. It must run some process to generate a sum. We postpone these problems until Part II. It is vital to understand that the machine language represents the operation of the hardware at its *highest* physical level, not its lowest. Operator instructions may give the effect of "instant" evaluation when executed, but in fact many distinct *register transfer* operations may be required[1].

Control flow

The use of a *conditional branch* instruction to modify the contents of the program counter depending on processor state is discussed above. We now turn to how it may be used to implement selection and iteration constructs.

Shown below are code segments for the machine language implementation of both *WHILE* and *IF... THEN... ELSE* constructs. In order to avoid binary notation, *mnemonics* are used for all instructions.

```
; start                        cb <else>
cb <exit>                      ...
...                            br <exit>
br <start>                     ; else
; exit                         ...
                               ; exit
```

The meaning of the mnemonics used is as follows...

- `cb` ≡ *Branch if condition fails*

---

[1] It is possible to devise a *functional architecture* where the need for assignment is eliminated. In this case the result of each operator is used as an argument to a function. The value of the function is used as an argument to another, and so on until the *system function* is evaluated.

- `br` ≡ *Branch always*

`<exit>` denotes the offset to the next instruction in memory. `<else>` denotes the offset to the code to be executed should the condition fail. Note how much more convenient it is to have an instruction which branches only if the condition *fails*. Of course the actual condition needed may be the negated version of the one available.

The conditional branch may be regarded as the *programming atom*, or *primitive*, from which all constructs are made. Together with a sufficient set of logical operators and {`load store`}, anything may be computed. Additional instructions are required to support the partitioning of software for the sole benefit of the software engineer. They add nothing to the capacity to compute and if anything reduce performance. *Arithmetic operators* are always included since they are almost universally required. However, it is quite possible, though laborious, to compute them using just logical and shift operators.

Linkage

In order to ease the engineering of software, it is necessary to provide support for procedure invocation. Procedure code, at the level of the machine, is referred to as a *subroutine*. Invocation requires the following...

- *Branching to subroutine*

- *Returning from subroutine*

- *Passing parameters*

The first is directly implemented with another branch instruction which we shall give the mnemonic `bsr`. It is beyond the scope of this chapter to discuss support for *nested* procedure invocation. The method adopted here is simply to save the incremented program counter value in a register as the *return address*. As well as doing this, `bsr` adds its operand to the program counter register in order to enter the subroutine.

Returning from subroutine is achieved by the `ret` instruction which simply copies the return address back into the program counter and must be the last in the subroutine. The *thread of control* is shown in Figure 3.4.

Parameters may be passed by placing them in general purpose registers prior to `bsr`.

Application support

The fourth group of instructions is that which support a given set of applications. For example, graphical applications require *block move* operations.

Although not strictly essential, such a group is necessary if the design is to be competitive as a *product*. Many manufacturers now offer a range of *co-processors* which extend the instruction set or enhance the performance of a given subset for a specified applications group.

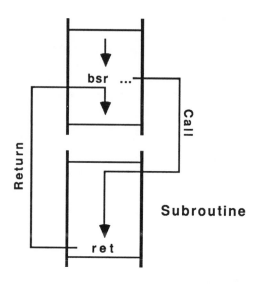

Figure 3.4: Thread of control through subroutine

3.1.5   Operands

Number of operands

The number of operands depends on a design decision and on the instruction itself. It is possible for a design to require *zero* operands. This assumes that the *computer organization* is such that the operand(s) have a predetermined source (e.g. on top of a stack) and the result a predictable destination. At the other extreme *three* operands may be required for each operator (two arguments and one result).

There is disagreement among computer architects as to which is the better number. Fewer operands generally means shorter code but can mean more micro-operations per instruction.

Storage class

The *arguments* to the instruction describe where to find the operands. Memory devices are usually grouped into *storage classes*. The concept of storage class represents the *programmer's* view of where the operand resides. A hardware engineer usually only perceives devices.

For example, the only complete computer we have so far met, the Turing Machine, has just two storage classes, processor state and the linear memory. We have met only two storage classes for a real modern computer, the register file and linear "main" memory.

It is also necessary to distinguish between two *areas* of memory, *program memory* and *workspace*. Constant data is often located within the program memory. The area of memory reserved for *local variables* is referred to as workspace. Each local variable is said to be *bound* to an *offset* from the value of yet another register, the *workspace pointer*. To summarize, the minimum set of storage classes usually found is...

- *Program memory*

- *Register*

- *Workspace*

The actual set found depends strongly upon its architecture design but the above is typical.

Due to constraints imposed by the ability of current technology to meet *all* the requirements of typical applications, real computers have two, three or more distinct memory devices. At least some of these will be available as distinct operand storage classes. Others will require special software to communicate with external processors which *can* gain direct access.

Access class

The *access class* of an operand is the manner in which it is referenced. It describes what happens to it and whether it is updated. There follows a summary...

- *Read (R)*

- *Write (W)*

- *Read-Modify-Write (RMW)*

Read access implies that the operand value remains unaltered by the reference and simply has its value used, for example as an operand of an operator. A two-operand addition instruction may be defined to overwrite the second operand with the result. The first operand is of access class *read* and the second *read-modify-write*. An example of *write access* is the destination of a **store**.

The access class of each operand must be specified in the definition of each instruction since it depends almost totally on the nature of the operation performed.

Addressing modes

Each instruction encodes an *operation*. Operations act on *operands*. Also encoded within the instruction is *how to find the operands*. For instance, if just one operand is required and it resides in memory then a further *instruction field* must communicate this fact and an *instruction extension* must indicate its address. An instruction is therefore a *record* with the following fields...

- *Opcode*

- *Addressing mode(s)*

- *Address(es)*

The *addressing mode* defines the storage class of the operand. When the operand is in memory it is called *absolute* or *direct* addressing. Absolute addressing has become progressively less common since the whole machine code program will need editing if the data area is moved. *Relative addressing*, where data is referenced via offsets from a workspace pointer, removes this difficulty. Only the pointer need be changed. Similarly code (or data) in program memory may be addressed relative to the program counter. Everything may be accessed via an offset from one or other register, be it data, a subroutine or construct code segment. *Position independent code* is said to result from such an architecture.

Immediate mode indicates to the processor that constant data follows in an instruction extension instead of an offset or an address. It may be thought of as a special case of program counter relative addressing. However, the data should be regarded as *contained within* the instruction.

Some addressing modes do not require qualification with an address. For example *register addressing* may be encoded as a distinct mode for each register. Hence no further qualification is required.

There follows a summary of common addressing modes...

- *Immediate*

- *Register*

- *Workspace relative*

- *Program counter relative*

- *Absolute (direct)*

Addressing mode modifiers

Addressing modes may be used to reference either *scalar* data or the *base* of a *vector*. Vector elements may be *sequence associated* or *pointer associated*. An addressing mode may be modified to locate an operand by either of the following...

- *Indexing*

- *Indirection*

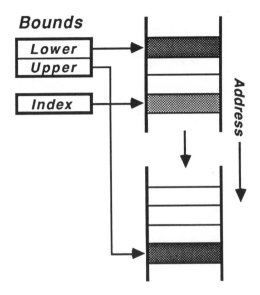

Figure 3.5: Indexing as an address modifier

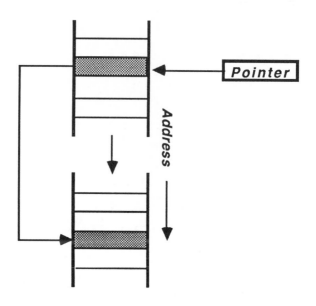

Figure 3.6: Indirection as an address modifier

Figure 3.5 illustrates indexing and Figure 3.6 indirection.

Indexing allows referencing of an element within an array. An index must be specified which must be checked *first* to see if it lies within *array bounds*. The array shown has only one dimension. Multi-dimensional arrays require one index per dimension specified, which are then used to calculate the element address. (Memory has just one dimension so some *mapping* is necessary.)

Indirect addressing means, instead of specifying the operand address, specifying the address of the address. Indirection is like crossing a pond via stepping stones. Each stone represents one level of indirection.

3.2   Simple architectures

3.2.1   Sequential processing

Programmer's architecture refers to just that set of registers which a machine level programmer needs to know about. *Architecture* more generally refers to *everything* such a programmer needs to know, including the available instruction set, addressing modes etc..

Figure 3.7 shows the programmer's architecture for purely sequential processing. As may be seen, very little is needed. The size of the general purpose register file shown

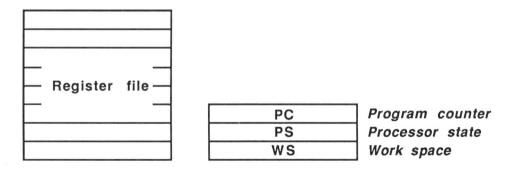

Figure 3.7: Programmer's architecture for purely sequential processing

is arbitrary although it is generally agreed that about eight registers are sufficient for expression evaluation. They may still be used for parameter passing if subroutines are not called while an expression is being evaluated.

The following addressing modes should suffice and permit position independent code. . .

- *Immediate*

- *Register*

- *Workspace relative*
  (Optional index modifier)

The following instruction set represents the minimum absolutely necessary to support structured programming with a single level of procedure invocation. . .

Assignment	Operators	Control flow	Linkage
load	and	cb	bsr
store	or	br	ret
	not		
	shl		
	shr		

Assignment and operators may be two-operand instructions where the second is always the destination. Those for control flow and linkage take a single offset operand except **ret** which takes none. **shl** and **shr** are *shift left* and *shift right* operators where the first operand is the number of bits (see Chapter 4) to shift.

It is quite possible to make do with even fewer instructions without loss of generality. For instance {**and or not**} may be replaced with **nand**. A computer with just a *single* instruction has also been reported! Such machines, however, are most probably not a delight to generate code for.

3.2.2 Parallel processing

Global processor scheduling

Imagine a manager for a construction company who is to build a house with a given number of workers. Each worker can take on any task so long as it is unambiguously described. Obviously *there are a lot more tasks than there are workers.* Procedures describing how to perform each task already exist. It remains for the manager to *schedule* processes between workers in such a way as to promote *efficiency.* Figure 3.8 depicts the problem of scheduling processes onto processors.

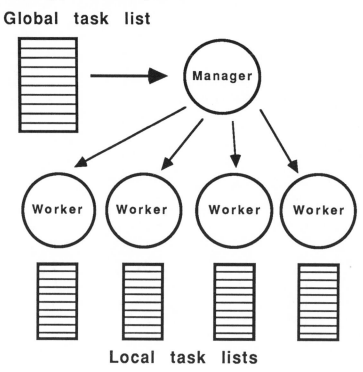

Figure 3.8: Global scheduling of processes to processors

Also previously defined is which tasks may proceed concurrently. Some tasks will be specified as necessarily proceeding in a given sequence. The manner in which tasks relate (communicate) with each other must be specified. An example of a procedure which cannot commence until another has finished is the erection of the roof. Clearly this should not begin until all four walls are built.

The manager of a computer is termed an *operating system* and is distinct from the running application. One of the operating system activities is *process management*. Let us assume that this is the only activity of the operating system and hence forward simply refer to it as the *process manager*. It is the job of the process manager to schedule processes to processors (workers) in such a way as to...

- *Balance load between workers*

- *Minimize worker idleness*

- *Guarantee absence of deadlock*

See Chapter 1 for a discussion of these and related problems.

Local processor scheduling

Each worker will have a number of tasks to perform. Hence he now has the problem of *scheduling himself*. There are some facilities which a processor (or worker) needs to make this possible, and some which just make it easier. (A building site-worker might make do with a pencil and a scrap of paper but a processor needs a bit more.)

Each processor must maintain a *ready queue* holding the identities of all processes which are *ready*. The ready queue might form the basis of a *round robin* schedule such that, when its turn comes, each process is executed until...

- *It terminates*

- *Waits for communication*

- *It has been executing for more than* a timeslice

A *timeslice* on a computer is typically about a millisecond. Round robin scheduling is fairer to shorter lived processes than most alternatives.

It is obviously inefficient to maintain a queue in a computer by moving all the remaining members when one leaves. Instead a sequence associated structure is kept with two pointers. *Queue front* points to the head of the queue (the next member to leave) and *queue back* points to its tail (Figure 3.9).

Two new instructions are required to support a process ready queue. **endp** terminates a process and causes the next in the queue to be *despatched* to the processor. **startp** places a newly ready process at the back of the queue. These can both be made very simple if the queue entry is just a pointer to the value required in the *program counter* for that process to run or continue.

The change of process on a processor requires a *context switch*. The context is simply the processor state and process state. When a process terminates there is obviously no

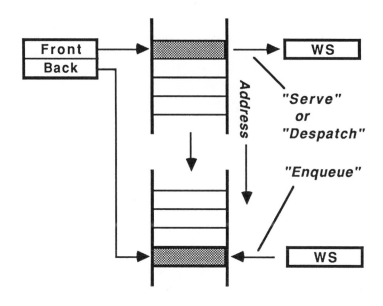

Figure 3.9: Local process scheduling

need to save context. If it is just *suspending*, to *resume* later, context must be saved and later restored. Context switching is reduced almost to zero by two simple expedients. First, maintain *all* process state in workspace except when evaluating expressions. Second, forbid suspension while expression evaluation is in progress. As a result no process state is in registers when suspension occurs *except* program counter and workspace pointer. The program counter may be saved at a reserved offset within workspace and the workspace pointer used as *process identifier*. A context switch is thus very fast because it only involves saving and loading just two registers, *WS* and *PC*.

The implementation of PAR and ALT constructs is beyond the scope of this chapter and must wait for Part III which also considers the architecture support for concurrency in considerably greater depth and detail.

Communication

Where only one processor is involved there must be a mechanism establishing *synchronization*. The problem is exactly like meeting up with a friend during the day when only the location of the *rendezvous* has been established. Suppose that you arrive to find your friend is not yet there, i.e. you have arrived first. Obviously you must *suspend* the process which involves the meeting. In order not to suspend all your processes you sensibly decide to leave a note giving your location for the rest of the day. Having arrived, your friend is able to find you and the suspended process is free to resume.

There is no need for the system to maintain a list of suspended processes since each may be *rescheduled* by the *second process* to arrive at the rendezvous, who knows their identity.

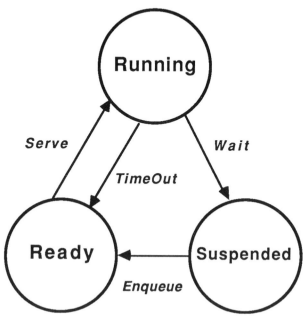

Figure 3.10: Process states and state transitions

To summarize, a process may be...

- *Running*

- *Ready*

- *Suspended*

Figure 3.10 shows the relationship between the process states.

The minimum additional instructions needed to support synchronous inter-process communication may be given the mnemonics **in** and **out**. They operate in a highly symmetric manner. A previously declared *memory location* suffices for a channel rendezvous and is initialized with a value denoting "empty". If either instruction finds the rendezvous empty, it deposits its process identifier and suspends. The second to arrive detects that the rendezvous is *not* empty, completes the communication (in either direction) and reschedules the first process by simply enqueing its identifier.

The rendezvous mechanism is considered in greater detail in Part III.

Summary of concurrency support

The minimum programmer's architecture to support concurrent sequential processes on a single processor is shown in Figure 3.11.

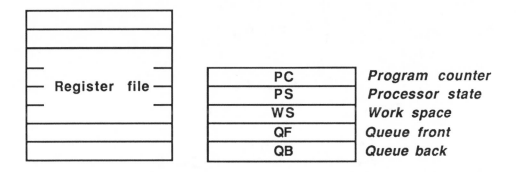

Figure 3.11: Programmer's architecture to support concurrent sequential processes

The minimum additional instructions needed to support both process scheduling and synchronous inter-process communication is {`startp endp in out`}.

3.2.3   Modular software

Refer to Chapter 2 for a full account of the use of modules in software engineering.

There is a *performance overhead* with invocation of a procedure in another module due to the extra level of *indirection* required. Remember that modules serve the purposes of development, maintenance and cost, *not* the application performance. As such they may be thought of as the software equivalent of hardware *chips*.

A *module descriptor* is required to support linkage with other modules and is made up from the following pointers...

- *Program base*

- *Static base*

- *Link table*

An extra processor register is shown provided in Figure 3.12 to house a pointer to (address of) the descriptor of the current module.

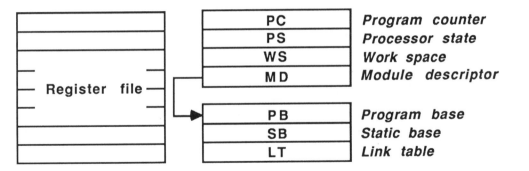

Figure 3.12: Programmer's architecture for module support

Program base is the address of the base of module code, which consists of the *concatenated* code for all its constituent procedures. A given procedure is thus referenced via an offset from this pointer.

Static base is the address of the base of workspace reserved for the module *as a whole*. Variables therein have *scope* which is *global* to all module procedures. Referencing *global variables* can cause highly undesirable *side effects* and should be kept to an absolute minimum or (preferrably) altogether eliminated.

Link table is the address of the base of a table of absolute addresses and *procedure descriptors* allowing procedures in the current module to reference variables and procedures, respectively, in others. A procedure descriptor consists of its parent module descriptor together with its offset from program base.

A special instruction is required to invoke an external procedure and an extra addressing mode to reference external variables.

3.3   Instruction set complexity

3.3.1   Reduced instruction set computer (RISC)

Decsription

RISC philosophy calls for little more than the minimum necessary set of instructions which enables all possible programs to be compiled. Correct selection of instructions is therefore critical and has been helped by inspection of usage by existing compiler generators. Instructions themselves are kept *simple* and are of common, small size. To summarize the principal features of a *RISC* design...

- *Small instruction set optimized for*

  - *Programming language*
  - *Compiler code generation*

- *Common, small instruction size*

- *Fast instruction execution*

- *Single addressing mode*

- *Load/store register file expression evaluation*

All of these features interact in such a way as to coexist *harmoniously*. The small instruction set promotes rapid *decoding* and execution. Decoding requires less hardware which instead may be devoted to a large register file. Hence the register file may be large enough to be used for local variables as well as expression evaluation.

Just because the instruction set is small does *not* mean that it cannot effectively reduce the semantic gap. Much progress may be made by *simultaneous* consideration of language, compiler and architecture. An effective match may be maintained between the architecture and compiler code generation strategies. The arrival of RISC in fact champions at least two causes...

- *Improved compiler/architecture interface*

- *Reduction of processor complexity*

A more complete description of the features and principles of RISC design must wait for Part III.

Reducing processor complexity has two motivations. It improves reliability and reduces the development time and so gets a new processor to market more quickly. The author has first hand experience of more traditional devices arriving *years* late and still with serious flaws. Indeed this had become the rule rather than the exception. How much trust can one put in a device when notice of a serious defect is announced long after it was brought to market. *Lives* now frequently depend on computer reliability. RISC design has already been demonstrated as an answer to this problem. A relatively small company in the UK has recently developed its own RISC . The *Acorn ARM* arrived on time and for four years (at time of writing) has proved free from "bugs". It also delivers a *cost/performance ratio* which is an embarrassment to its non-RISC competitors.

We now turn to the underlying reason why a smaller instruction set is able to deliver an enhanced performance...

Exploitation of locality

It is *not* the case that a RISC delivers improved performance because more, faster instructions simply reduce the total execution time from that required by fewer, slower ones. It is the *choice* of instructions to implement that counts. Because RISC designers set out to have fewer, they had to think more carefully about which are *really* needed and which are not essential.

Temporal locality is an extremely important concept for processing. It is the property of software to reference the same set of stored items in memory within a given time window (Figure 3.13).

The process model of execution encourages this by only allowing references to *local* variables and procedure parameters. Structured programming also strongly enhances the effect since a loop body will reference the same variables on each iteration.

The RISC philosophy is to reap the maximum possible benefit from temporal locality. The idea is that, on process start (or procedure entry), all local variables are *loaded* into registers where they may be accessed much more rapidly. Afterwards they are *stored* in memory. This is called a *load/store memory access* scheme. If, in addition, parameters are passed in registers then *spatial locality* is introduced. References will all be to the same *spatial* window. The idea may be extended by keeping all the local variables of the currently executing *group* of processes in an enlarged register file.

The load/store scheme plus the drive for simplicity require that only one or two addressing modes are provided. However these are defined in a flexible manner so that cunning use of registers may be used to create *synthesized addressing modes*.

The most important consequence of load/store access, and its associated single addressing mode, is that *memory references are minimized*. This is responsible for a large proportion of the performance improvement seen. A secondary consequence is that the compiler code generation is simplified. Another mechanism, called *register windowing*, almost eliminates the (conventionally high) performance overhead of procedure invocation. Discussion of this is left for Part III.

History

The RISC story began with an *IBM* project around 1975 called the *801*, [Radin 83]. This was never sold commercially. However the results were used in the *IBM RT* which is now

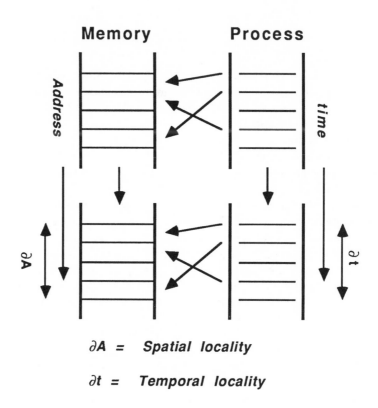

Figure 3.13: Temporal and spatial locality

available. The term RISC, together with many of the fundamental ideas, surfaced in the Berkeley designs called *RISC I* and *RISC II*, [Patterson & Ditzel 80].

An account of the Berkeley projects, and a fascinating comparison of several recent academic and commercial RISC systems, may be found in [Tabak 87]. Also very highly recommended is [Colwell et al. 85] which seeks to define a RISC, separates and assesses the various associated ideas and gives a thorough contrast with *CISC*s.

3.3.2 Complex instruction set computer (CISC)

Description

In *CISC* design no attempt is made to minimize the size of the instruction set. As well as there being a larger set, the instructions themselves are more complex. Many different formats are possible and a plethora of addressing modes are provided. For example the DEC VAX architecture supplies addressing modes which *auto-increment* or *auto-decrement* an array index after, or before, carrying out an operation.

The result is a complex processor executing instructions rather more slowly than its RISC counterpart. However, some of the instructions and addressing modes achieve much more, *when* they are required. Given both application and compiler which make use of the powerful features, a superior performance *may* be demonstrated by a CISC.

The chief characteristics of a CISC are...

- *Large instruction set to suit broad range of* applications

- *Variable size instructions (some very large)*

- *Many addressing modes (some highly complex)*

Motivations for complexity

The motivations towards complexity are largely due to attempts to continue the upgrading of existing, successful products. They may be summarized...

- *Speed up specified application operations via hardware implementation*

- *Reduce semantic gap via hardware implementation of programming language statements*

- *Maintain upwards compatibility in product line*

- *Reduce size of machine code software because of high memory cost*

Here, the focus of attention for performance increase is the *application*. The high cost and low speed of reference of memory which prevailed for many years persuaded designers to turn their attention to reducing code size and the number of memory references by "migrating" subroutines to hardware implementation. Programming language and the compiler/architecture interface were rarely considered. New instructions could not *replace* old ones because of the need for upwards compatibility. (Old code had to still run on new machines.) Some new instructions actually operated *more slowly* than the series of old ones they were supposed to replace, though this was not generally the case. Many of the new instructions were highly specialized, thus rarely used. As complexity increased, so design and development time *rapidly* increased, as did the incidence of design error.

Closure of the semantic gap

It is possible to implement some procedural constructs in machine language more directly on a CISC. An example is the `case` instruction of the *NS32000* CISC (see Chapter 10). The termination of an iterative *FOR* loop usually consists of several distinct instructions. The NS32000 provides for this combination in a single instruction, `acb` (add, compare & branch), which adds a signed value to the loop index, compares it to zero and then conditionally branches.

Referencing elements in structured data objects is also made much simpler in CISC machine language by the addition of extra addressing modes. Even elements within *sequence-associated* structures, themselves inside pointer-associated ones, may be referenced directly.

Applications support

Applications specific machine language extensions or (performance) enhancements are usually readily available. For example, graphics applications frequently require moving, or applying a common logical operator to, a *block* of memory at a time. A special addressing mode may be supplied to cope with this. Similar provision is often found nowadays for string processing and for mathematical *(floating-point)* operators.

3.3.3 Comparison of RISC and CISC

Closure of the semantic gap and applications support look very good in the catalogue and have proved popular. However, once the CISC machine language is implemented, an application may not run faster than it would on a RISC. The reasons are twofold. Firstly, the powerful instructions take time to translate into a sequence of primitive operations. Secondly, all that CISC complexity could have been exchanged for a larger register file, to gain greater benefit from locality, *or even for another separate processor*. The latter would reap benefit if parallelism exists at the problem level and hence at the algorithmic level.

To summarize, the advantages of RISC are improvements in...

- *Performance for structured software via exploitation of temporal locality*

- *Reliability and freedom from design errors*

- *Design and development path*

- *Compiler/architecture interface*

Those factors which a CISC maintains in its favour are...

- *Code length*

- *Application specific performance*

- *Upwards compatibility with older machines*

It must be emphasized that RISC machines demonstrate *several* innovations. Each must be considered separately. Research is still under way to discover which truly offer the greatest rewards. The reader is strongly encouraged to read [Colwell et al. 85] for an up-to-date account of these matters.

Although there is great controversy over the RISC vs CISC issue, several new machines are now available visibly benefiting from RISC architecture. These include the *Acorn Archimedes, SUN 4* and *IBM RT*.

The only arguable disadvantages to a RISC are that the size of object module is increased and that programming at machine level is slightly more work. It is not *harder* work since the machine language is simpler. Neither of these is of great importance to someone whose primary concern is performance and who programs in a high level language (as most do).

Apart from an uncompetitive performance, CISC has a more serious disadvantage. The design and development paths are long and risky[2]. By the time some have reached the market they are almost out of date. The cost of development is high and rapidly rising. The greater complexity also impacts reliability.

By contrast the development of RISC designs is short and cheap. For example the *Acorn ARM* processor was developed on a very short time scale and the very first chip made was reported to function perfectly. It was designed on an Acorn *home micro* using their own software. The cost and reliability of the chip set make it very competitive.

Designing optimized code generators for a RISC is generally easier than for a CISC. Part of the motivation behind the RISC concept is that existing compilers were not making sufficient use of complex instructions.

---

[2]No pun intended!

Exercises

Question one

i When a book is *translated* from one natural language to another, is it *interpretation* or *compilation*?

ii Explain what is meant by *semantic gap.* In your own words, summarize the arguments for and against designing a computer architecture to reduce it.

Question two

The instruction...

        add r0,0400

means...

> *Add the contents of register zero, in the register file, to the memory location whose address is 0400 and put the result back in register zero.*

State the *storage class, access class* and *addressing mode* of each of the two operands.

Question three

A rather basic *processor* has only the following instructions...

- nand Bitwise logic operator *which operates on its one and only register and an operand in memory. Its result is placed automatically in the register.*

- shift Shift operator *which shifts the contents of the register left by one bit.*

- load ...*direct addressed operand from memory to register.*

- store ...*operand in register to direct addressed memory location.*

- branch ...*on the condition that the process state is set, the number of words forward or back specified by the immediate addressed operand.*

It also has only a one bit *processor state* which is *cleared* if the result of a nand is zero and *set* otherwise. Both memory locations and the register are four bits wide.

Write a program which computes the *AND* of two variables stored in memory whose addresses may be referenced symbolically as x and y. Ensure that a *zero* result clears the processor state and sets it otherwise.

Part II

From switches to processors

Chapter 4

Data representation and notation

4.1 Notation

4.1.1 Pure binary

Binary words

A number is written as a sequence of digits which are collectively referred to as a *word*. Symbols, called *numerals*, must be decided upon to represent each distinct digit value from zero to a maximum which is one less than the *base*. The *arabic* system, using base ten, is the one with which we are all familiar. Digits increase in significance from right to left, representing increasing powers of the base.

Pure binary notation uses *base two*. The arabic symbols "0" and "1" denote binary digit *(bit)* values. The quantity of bits required to represent a number is given by $\log_2$ of its value rounded upwards to the nearest integer. For example...

- *7 requires 3 bits ($2^3 = 8$)*

- *60 requires 6 bits ($2^6 = 64$)*

- *129 requires 8 bits ($2^8 = 256$)*

Each time a single extra bit becomes available, the range of values which may be represented *doubles* since the quantity of available states doubles. A *value* is just the *label* of a *state*.

Physical representation

Pure binary notation is special to current computer technology because it *directly* corresponds to the physical data representation inside any contemporary computer. The reason for this is that it is comparatively easy to *store* and *communicate* binary digits in a reliable manner. A *1-bit memory cell* may be made using any physical process which yields just *two stable states*. Such a process is referred to as *bistable*[1].

Each variable stored within the machine requires a number of *memory cells* grouped together into a *register* of width equal to that of the word. Registers are usually all of a common width within a computer. They may not be large enough to accomodate some values required. Unfortunately the computer cannot suddenly materialize more wires and memory cells. It starts off life with a fixed *word width*, for each number stored or communicated within it, and that remains constant until its life is over. Each digital computer may be partially characterized by word width which varies from machine to machine.

Negative and fractional values

A minus sign may be employed with pure binary for negative number notation in exactly the same way as with decimal notation. Similarly, fractions may be written using a *binary point*, used in just the same way as a decimal point. Digits after a binary point denote *negative* powers of two with significance increasing from right to left as usual (e.g. $0.1111 = 2^{-1} + 2^{-2} + 2^{-3} + 2^{-4} = 0.9375_{10}$). However, neither minus sign nor binary point have obvious physical representations. To represent a *positive* integer value we simply *enumerate* states. Negative values pose a problem.

You are reminded that only the set of positive integers have any physical meaning. All "numbers" less than unity are *abstractions*. It is not surprising that their *direct* representation with wires and switches is impossible. After all, *have you ever eaten a negative number of apples?*

As we shall see later, pure binary is always useful for enumerating physical states but in order to represent negative or fractional values it is necessary to establish a *standardized* state labelling scheme.

Word partitions

It has become customary to divide up word width into standard "chunks" called *bytes* and *nibbles* where...

$$nibble = 4 \ bits, \quad byte = 8 \ bits$$

---

[1] It should be pointed out that it is quite possible (though less easy) to render machines which physically represent values using bases other than two. A memory cell would have to be devised with a number of stable states equal to the new base. Communication elements (wires) would face similar requirements. An electrical solution might use a number of voltage ranges to distinguish states.

Not surprisingly perhaps, a byte is equivalent to two nibbles!

Each location in a memory map (see Figure 4.1) shares the common word width of the machine, which is nowadays usually an integral number of bytes.

The problem for humans using binary notation is that numbers take a lot of writing. For example, the number which is written 65,535 in decimal notation becomes 1111111111111111 in binary! It is somewhat relieved by using a point (not to be confused with the binary point) to break up the word into *fields* (e.g. 1111.1111.1111.1111) but life can still get extremely tedious.

4.1.2 Hexadecimal

Notation/representation correspondence

If writing numbers in pure binary notation is too tedious, why then do we not use decimal? Given, say, a 4-bit binary word, every state has a corresponding 2-digit decimal value. Sadly, not every 2-digit decimal value has a corresponding 4-bit binary state. The redundant values mean that we would have to take great care when using decimal notation. It is simply too inconvenient.

Consider a 4-bit word carefully. It has 16 (2^4) states. Wouldn't it be nice if we had a notation where each *digit* had 16 states. We could then use a single digit to denote the value represented by the word. *Every possible digit value would correspond to just one state and vice versa.* What we require then is a *base sixteen*, or *hexadecimal*, notation, often abbreviated to just *"hex"*.

Digit symbols

The symbols used for hexadecimal digits are partly arabic numerals and partly alphabetic characters...

$$\begin{array}{rcl} \textit{Zero to nine} & \rightarrow & 0\dots 9 \\ \textit{Ten to fifteen} & \rightarrow & A\dots F \end{array}$$

Just in case you are confused, remember that the concept of *number* is simply a consequence of that of *counting*. A new digit is required to the left of the old when the count reaches a chosen value which is called the *base*. The separate historical origins of writing and counting explain why we write text from left to right but numbers from right to left.

Multi-nibble word notation

The real beauty of hexadecimal notation is that we can now conveniently interchange between a concise notation of *value* and the *state* which represents it. The mapping works in either direction as long as the word breaks up into an integral number of nibbles. In other words hexadecimal is ideally suited to notation of the values represented in 8-bit, 16-bit, 32-bit etc. registers...

$$8\text{-}bit \quad \rightarrow \quad 00_{16} \dots FF_{16}$$
$$16\text{-}bit \quad \rightarrow \quad 0000_{16} \dots FFFF_{16}$$
$$32\text{-}bit \quad \rightarrow \quad 0000.0000_{16} \dots FFFF.FFFF_{16}$$

Leading zeros are included to infer the word width. Note how a point may be used to aid clarity by breaking up a value into fields of four hex digits, which each correspond to 4×4 bits.

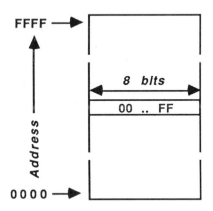

Figure 4.1: 16-bit address word/8-bit data word memory map

Figure 4.1 depicts a (currently) not uncommon memory map where the *data* word width is one byte and the *address* word width is four bytes. (One byte requires two hex digits.)

It should be clear from this how awkward life would be if decimal notation were used for either address or data. One would have to think carefully whether a particular value actually corresponded to a real address (or real data).

4.1.3   Octal

Some machines use a word width which is divisible by *three* instead of four. Each three bits can physically take 8 (2^3) states. Hence it is sensible to employ a notation of *base 8* and divide the word up into 3-bit fields, the value of each one denoted by a single *octal* digit. Once again there will be a one-to-one correspondence between notation and state. For example...

$$9\text{-}bit \quad \rightarrow \quad 000_8 \dots 777_8$$
$$18\text{-}bit \quad \rightarrow \quad 000.000_8 \dots 777.777_8$$
$$27\text{-}bit \quad \rightarrow \quad 000.000.000_8 \dots 777.777.777_8$$

As before leading zeros are included to infer word length. This time points are used to separate fields of 3×3 bits.

Obviously bases other than eight or sixteen are possible. However, small bases are not very useful and those given by powers of two larger than four require too many symbols per digit.

Figure 4.2 illustrates the alternative notations and their correspondence to groups within the word. It also serves as an example of translation between them via pure binary.

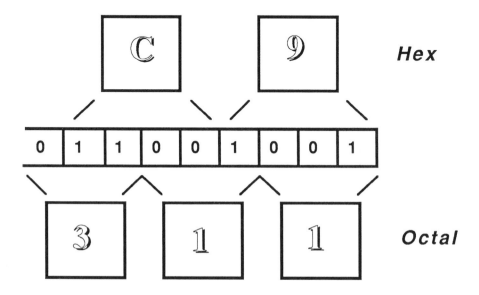

Figure 4.2: Alternative notations for a pure binary number

Lastly, it is true to say that hex has now become more useful than octal. This is because of the success of 8-bit machines which have subsequently evolved into 16-bit, 32-bit and even 64-bit versions.

4.2 Primitive data types

4.2.1 Integer

Sign-magnitude

We now turn to the means of representing *integers* including *negative* as well as positive values.

To summarize, data is represented physically as distinct states of registers, each made up of a collection of bistables. Each possible register *state* is interpreted as a distinct *value*.

Any interpretation of register states other than pure binary constitutes what is called a *virtual data type*, by which we mean the particular translation required of (pure binary) state into value. The translation is most easily understood as via the *labelling of states*.

With integers the problem boils down to one of deciding how to divide states between positive and negative *labels*. The simplest and perhaps most obvious is to reason in the following way...

> There are only two states needed to represent sign so let's use one bit within the word specifically to represent it. Make it the leftmost bit since the sign is usually written leftmost. All states with this bit set are labelled negative. The state of all bits to the right of the sign bit are simply labelled with their pure binary value.

Figure 4.3 shows a pure binary and a sign/magnitude labelling of states. There are two serious drawbacks and one advantage to this simple scheme.

As pointed out earlier, the very concept of "number" is drawn from that of *counting*. Similarly that of addition implies counting forwards or *incrementing* a number. On the "clock" representation of states depicted, counting corresponds to a hand moving clockwise. The *modulus* of the register is simply its pure binary range. For the register depicted this is simply 16 (2^4). A pure binary addition whose result is greater than the modulus is said to be correct *modulo 16*. Unfortunately an addition which crosses the boundary between sign values gives the *wrong* answer using the sign/magnitude labelling.

The second drawback is that there are *two representations of zero*. It is clearly inefficient and confusing to use two states for a single value.

Sign/magnitude representation of signed integers has one redeeming feature. It is extremely easy to *negate* a number. All that is necessary is to invert the leftmost bit. To summarize...

- *Modulo signed addition gives wrong results (Disadvantage)*

- *Two states for zero (Disadvantage)*

- *Negation is easy (Advantage)*

There is a better way to achieve an integer labelling.

Twos-complement

The "clock" diagram for the *twos-complement* state labelling scheme is depicted in Figure 4.4.

So how is this labelling arrived at? All that we do is...

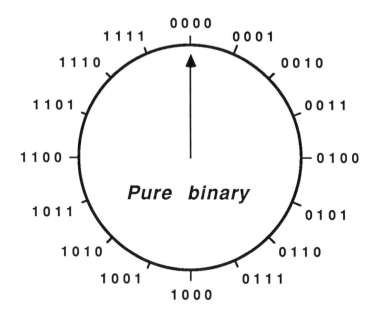

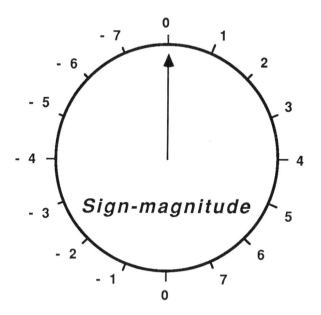

Figure 4.3: Pure binary and sign/magnitude state labelling represented as a clock face

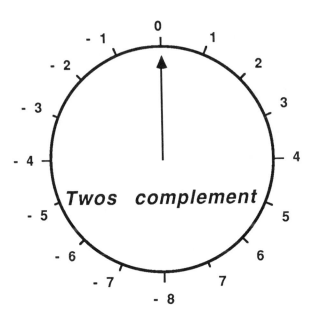

Figure 4.4: Twos-complement state labelling represented as a clock face

1. Subtract the value we wish to represent from the modulus (16)

2. Increment the register (move hand clockwise) from zero that number of times

There is a single *major* advantage and one disadvantage with this scheme. First the disadvantage. *Negation is hard!* One way is to make use of the definition of twos-complement...

The twos-complement representation (state) of a value α, given a word width N (modulus $M = 2^N$), is...

$$\alpha^{(2)} = M - \alpha$$

The procedure for labelling the clock diagram is consistent with this.

The negation operation derived directly from the definition unfortunately turns out to be very hard to achieve automatically. It is also dependent upon the word width (or modulus). A much better way (for human and machine) is to employ the following procedure...

1. *Ones-complement*

2. *Increment*

Ones-complement is usually referred to as just "complement" and may be achieved simply by *bitwise negation*. In contrast with twos-complement, the complement operation is *independent of word width*. It is formally defined...

> The ones complement representation (state) of a value α, given a word width N (modulus $M = 2^N$), is...

$$\alpha^{(1)} = (M - 1) - \alpha$$

Taking the definitions of twos-complement and ones-complement we may eliminate M...

$$\alpha^{(2)} = \alpha^{(1)} + 1$$

...which yields our new algorithm for twos-complement negation and shows that it is *independent of word width*. Unlike the earlier method, we may apply it without concerning ourselves with the word width of the operand.

Now for the *overwhelming* advantage of twos-complement representation of integers which has resulted in its universal acceptence and use. *Addition works across sign boundaries!* Every state has a single unique labelling. Note that the twos-complement range of a register of modulus M is $-\frac{M}{2} \ldots +(\frac{M}{2} - 1)$. That of the register depicted is $-8 \ldots +7$. Addition of twos-complement signed values will give the correct result as along as they, and the result, are *within range*.

You are strongly urged to try some simple sums yourself using the clock diagram for twos-complement. (Recall that addition simply means counting forward by rotating the hand clockwise and subtraction means counting backwards by rotating the hand anticlockwise.)

To summarize the pros and cons of twos-complement signed integer representation...

- *Two phase negation required (Disadvantage)*

- *Addition works across sign boundaries (Advantage)*

It is the scheme adopted almost universally for representing signed integers.

Overflow and underflow

Obviously, in any signed arithmetic computation it is vital to have the computer cope correctly with a result which is outside the range of valid representation. In other words the *processor state register* must include a memory of whether the range boundary has been crossed in either direction.

Our clock is a form of computer capable of arithmetic computation. The computation process is the rotation of the hand in the direction corresponding to addition or subtraction as desired. *Overflow* is said to have occured if the hand passes the range boundary in the *clockwise* direction, *underflow* if it does so in the *anticlockwise* direction. With a little imagination one might devise a mechanical contrivance to set some sort of bistable which would record either event and thus form the processor state required.

Neither overflow nor underflow can occur if the arguments are of different sign and are in range themselves. This observation leads to a simple rule for detecting over/underflow. . .

> *Overflow or underflow may be deemed to have occured in an arithmetic computation only if the arguments share identical sign which differs from the result.*

Recall that the *most significant bit (MSB)* of a twos-complement representation is alone sufficient to indicate sign.

4.2.2   Character

Printing characters

All that is necessary to represent printing characters is to decide a *standard* labelling of states. The equivalent pure binary state label is referred to as the *code* for the corresponding character.

It is desirable that some subsets are *arranged in order* to ease text processing algorithm design. For example, a program which swaps character case will benefit from the codes for 'a. . . z' and 'A. . . Z' being in order. Alphabetical ordering also facilitates the sorting of character *strings*.

Codes will also be needed for other printing characters such as *space*, punctuation and numeric (decimal) characters.

Appendix A contains a table of the *American Standard Code for Information Interchange*, more commonly known as *ASCII*, which is now the almost universal code used for representation of both printing and *control* characters.

A useful summary is. . .

$$
\begin{aligned}
\text{`a'} \ldots \text{`z'} &\rightarrow 61_{16} \ldots 7A_{16} \\
\text{`A'} \ldots \text{`Z'} &\rightarrow 41_{16} \ldots 5A_{16} \\
\text{`0'} \ldots \text{`9'} &\rightarrow 30_{16} \ldots 39_{16} \\
\text{Space} &\rightarrow 20_{16}
\end{aligned}
$$

Control characters

Control codes are included for controlling text-oriented devices, such as. . .

- *Display screens*

- *Keyboards*

- *Printers*

In addition they also permit grouping of text according to...

- *Line*

- *File*

To summarize the most frequently used (by a long chalk)...

$$
\begin{array}{lcll}
LF & = & 0A_{16} & \text{\textit{Causes a display device cursor to move one line down}} \\
CR & = & 0D_{16} & \text{\textit{Causes a display device cursor to move to the start of line}} \\
DEL & = & 7F_{16} & \text{\textit{Deletes previous character}} \\
EOT & = & 04_{16} & \text{\textit{End Of Transmission}}
\end{array}
$$

Unfortunately the standard does not stipulate *precisely* what codes are used to *delimit* text lines and files. As far as lines are concerned, either or both LF and CR may be used. The situation is worse for file delimitation. The operating system or compiler designer has a free hand here. As a result *they all do it differently!*

The *UNIX* operating system uses LF alone as a line delimiter and *nothing at all* as a file delimiter[2].

4.2.3 Real

Fixed-point representation

There are three things we should care (and thus *think*) about when deciding the numeric data type for a variable...

Dynamic range *is the difference between the largest and smallest values the variable might possibly assume as the process runs and may be denoted by* ΔV.

Resolution *determines the difference between a desired, true value and the nearest one that can be represented and may be measured as the difference in value represented by neighbouring states, denoted by* δV.

Precision *is the ratio of the difference between the value represented by a state and that by its neighbour to the value itself and may be denoted by* $\frac{\delta V}{V}$.

---

[2]The process which is reading it is sent a *signal* instead. However a process (for instance a user at a keyboard) writing out a file signals its end using ASCII EOT.

Precision is the proportional uncertainty inherent in a value. Resolution determines how close a representable value can get to the truth. All *fixed-point* representations exhibit constant resolution, but variable precision, over their range. *Floating-point* representations exhibit rather the reverse.

Twos-complement integers form an example of a fixed-point type. The location of the binary point is *implicit* and lies *to the right of the rightmost bit*.

It is a simple matter to represent fractional quantities (less than unity) using a fixed point. We simply change our assumption about the location of the point to one where it lies *to the left of the leftmost bit*. Addition still works correctly as before. *Only our interpretation of states has changed!* An *implicit scale factor* has simply been introduced which we will only need to make use of when we display our results (via graphics or text). Its value is simply given by M^{-1} (where M is the modulus of the word width in use).

We must take note of some important observations about use of fixed-point representation of the *real* data type as compared to that of the *integer* data type...

- *There is no loss of resolution*

- *There is no gain in dynamic range*

- *There is no loss in the number of distinct values represented*

The range has merely been translated by an amount equal to the implicit scale factor. Because of the implicit scale factor the programmer must scale abstract level quantities (e.g. distances, angles etc.) before representing them at the virtual level as fixed-point reals. This is an inconvenience to the programmer but *not to the user*, who cares more about the performance and the cost of the system than any tough time the poor programmer had tailoring it!

Floating-point representation

In floating-point representation a word is partitioned into two fields, as shown in Figure 4.5. A *mantissa* is represented (labelled) as a fixed-point value with the point assumed *to the right of the leftmost bit*. This means that the mantissa represents numbers between zero and two. Secondly, an *exponent* is represented as an integer value (point to the right of the rightmost bit).

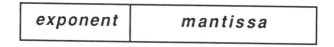

Figure 4.5: Floating-point representations as mantissa + exponent

The exponent may be thought of as an *explicit scale factor* in contrast to the implicit one associated with any fixed-point representation.

Floating-point representation sacrifices resolution for dynamic range! In other words if you want *resolution* it is a much better to use a fixed-point representation. If you want *dynamic range*, beyond that available in the local word width, and roughly *constant precision* it is better to use a floating-point representation.

The decision of which to choose should be settled by careful consideration of the *abstract* quantity to be represented. Supposing we have a 10-bit word available to represent the output of an *encoder* which measures the angle of rotation, say, of a robotic wrist. It is thus required that the *uncertainty* of orientation be *constant* over the full 360^0 range, which may be represented with a precision of one part in 1024 using fixed-point, pure binary encoding.

Now consider a different abstract quantity, say, temperature from zero up to thousands of degrees Kelvin. A tenth of a degree near the bottom of the scale has the same significance as a hundred near the top. It is *precision* required here, not resolution. Scientists also often wish to represent quantities with a vast *dynamic range*. For instance, the *mass* of objects can vary from 10^{-27}g for an electron up to 10^{33}g for a star!

Fixed-point data may be processed more quickly and with simpler, cheaper hardware. It is surprising how often they suffice and how often floating-point is used unnecessarily. *Think* before you choose.

Floating-point degeneracy

A little thought will reveal a problem with the floating-point type. *There are many representations for most values!*

Consider a 4-bit mantissa with a 4-bit exponent. Shifting the mantissa right one bit is exactly equivalent to dividing by two. Incrementing the exponent by one is exactly equivalent to multiplying by two. If we do both the value represented will remain utterly unchanged. For example...

$$1100 : 0011 \;=\; 1.5 \times 2^3 \;\;=\;\; 12$$
$$0110 : 0100 \;=\; 0.75 \times 2^4 \;=\; 12$$
$$0011 : 0101 \;=\; 0.375 \times 2^5 = 12$$

The existence of more than one state per value is called *degeneracy*. The ambiguity so caused is unacceptable. It is removed by enforcing a rule which states that *the leftmost bit in the mantissa must always be set*. Thus the mantissa always represents values between *one* and *two*. Representations obeying this rule are said to be of *normalized form*. All operators on floating-point variables *must* normalize their result.

Because it is always set, there is no point in including the MSB. Hence it is simply omitted. It is referred to as the *hidden bit*. The normalized floating-point representation of 12 is thus $1000 : 0011 = 1.5 \times 2^3 = 12$.

When set, the MSB of the mantissa now contributes 0.5 and we have an *extra* bit of precision available. *Neat trick eh!*

Signing

Unfortunately twos-complement signing of the mantissa results in *slow normalization*. Hence we resort to the sign-magnitude approach and include a sign bit.

Signing of the exponent uses neither twos-complement nor sign-magnitude representation. The reason for this is that it is highly desirable to compare two floating-point values *as if they were sign-magnitude integers*. Sign-magnitude encoding of the exponent is therefore not a possibility since it introduces a second sign-bit. Twos-complement is not on since the pure binary interpretations are not ordered by value (e.g. the representation of 1 appears less than that of -1).

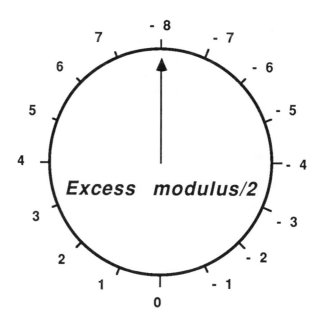

Figure 4.6: Excess $M/2$ state labelling represented as a clock face

The exponent may be signed using *excess $M/2$ representation*, where M is the modulus of the exponent field. A value is arrived at simply by subtracting $M/2$ from the pure binary interpretation. Two floating-point values using excess $M/2$ exponent representation may be compared by simply comparing the pure binary interpretations of each entire word. The clock diagram for the state labelling of a 4-bit register is given in Figure 4.6.

IEEE 754 standard for floating-point representation

The *IEEE 754 single precision standard* is as described above except that the exponent is represented using *excess* $(M/2 - 1)$ representation and a 32-bit word width is called for. The range of valid exponents is thus -126...+127. The extreme states are used to indicate exceptional conditions such as...

Meaning	Exponent	Mantissa	Sign
Not-a-Number (NaN)	FF_{16}	$\neq 0$	0 /1
$+\infty$	FF_{16}	0	0
$-\infty$	FF_{16}	0	1
$+0$	0	0	0
-0	0	0	1

NaN may be used used to signal invalid operations such as divide by zero. Another special state, not included in the table above, is used to indicate a result too small to be encoded in the usual way. Instead it is encoded via a *denormalized* mantissa, whose validity is indicated by a *zero exponent*.

There is also a 64-bit double precision standard (see Figure 4.7).

It should be noted that not all computers adhere to the standard. For instance there are some very common machines to be found which use *excess M/2* exponent representation.

Floating-point operations

There are three phases in the algorithm for addition or subtraction...

1. *Align both variables (render equal their exponents)*

2. *Add or subtract the mantissas*

3. *Normalize the result*

Similarly there are three phases in the algorithm for multiplication or division...

1. *Add or subtract exponents*

2. *Multiply or divide mantissas*

3. *Normalize result*

In each middle phase the mantissas are processed exactly as if they represented pure binary values. The position of the point remains fixed and in no way affects the operation.

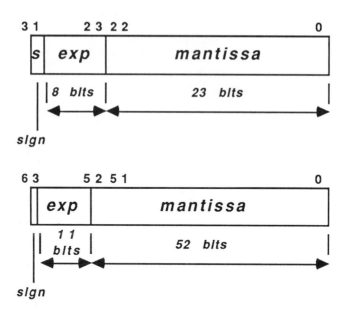

Figure 4.7: Floating-point representations as mantissa + exponent

Summary

The following observations are noted about floating-point representation of the *real* data type...

- *Dynamic range increased by 2^{M_e}, where M_e is the modulus of the exponent (Advantage)*

- *Precision is roughly constant across range (Advantage)*

- *Virtual representation of very large or very small abstract quantities without scaling (Advantage)*

- *Higher cost or reduced performance (Disadvantage)*

- *Resolution is reduced and varies across range (Disadvantage)*

It must be emphasized that the direct representation of very large or very small quantities without scaling is advantageous to the programmer but *not* to the user, who cares more about cost and performance *which will be lost!* Choosing floating-point real typing is justified if the abstract quantity calls for high dynamic range and roughly constant precision.

4.3 Structured data types

4.3.1 Sequence association

Arrays

Given a linear memory organization, the *sequence-associated* data structure known as an *array* needs very little work to implement. In fact a memory map is itself an array, whose index is the current address.

All that is needed to represent an array is to specify its start and its end (Figure 4.8). The start and end are known as the *array bounds*. The only other thing required is a variable elsewhere in memory to act as an index. To summarize, an array representation consists of...

- *Upper bound (Constant)*

- *Lower bound (Constant)*

- *Index (Variable)*

The bounds form a simple example of data structure *descriptor*. The linear organization of memory takes care of finding neighbour elements. (All structures are *graphs* of one kind or another.)

What we mean by an array is a sequence of elements of *common type*. No hardware can guarantee that. It is up to the programmer to write well behaved software.

Records

Records are represented in much the same manner as arrays. Actual representations vary with compiler implementation but bounds remain at least part of the descriptor and an index is still required. A record differs from an array in that differing types of variable are allowed to appear within it.

Each entry in a record is referred to as a *field* (e.g. a floating-point representation may be thought of as a record consisting of three fields...sign, mantissa and exponent).

Security

Two forms of *security* should be provided...

- *Type checking*

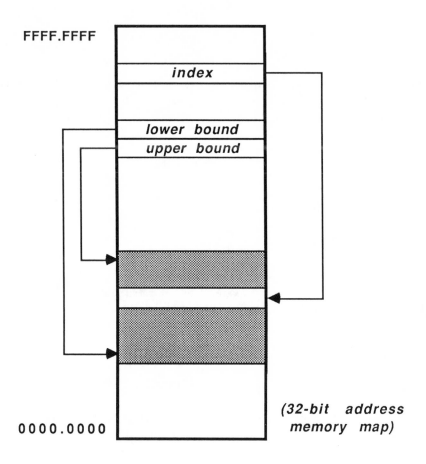

Figure 4.8: Sequence-associated data structure in memory map

- *Bounds checking*

It must be possible to verify, on a reference, the *type* of structure in order to check the validity of an assignment or communication. Secondly, it must also be possible to verify, on a reference, that an element lies inside its parent structure. This is called *bounds checking*.

The structure descriptor should include enough information to allow the compiler (or programmer) to render code secure.

Note that arrays and records are *static data structures*. Once declared they can change neither in element type nor in size. Hence abstract structures built out of them may only maintain the illusion of being dynamic within strict size limits.

4.3.2 Pointer association

Pointer type

A *pointer* is just the address of an item of data (either elementary or structured). It is the counterpart of an index but within a *pointer-associated data structure*. It references an individual element (Figure 4.9).

Abstract data structures may be constructed using records, one or more fields of which contain a pointer. They present an alternative to the use of array indices and permit truly *dynamic* structures to be built and referenced.

Security

Exactly the same criteria for security of access apply as to sequential structures. However both *bounds checking* and *type checking* are much more difficult *when using a linear spatial memory map*.

Programmer declared type labels *tagged* to pointers are used in most conventional languages to facilitate type checking. But since these are static they can only delineate the element type of which the structure is composed. They do not delineate the type of the whole dynamic structure.

Dynamic type tagging of pointers fulfils part of our security requirement but provides no means of checking whether a variable (perhaps structured itself) is to be found within another.

The action of assigning (moving) a pointer structure is very difficult to render secure and impossible to render efficient given a linear spatial memory map.

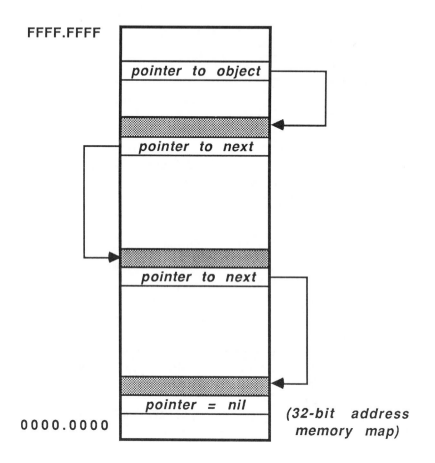

Figure 4.9: Pointer-associated data structure in memory map

Exercises

Question one

i   What is the smallest register word length such that a given number each of octal and hex digits may denote a valid *state* for every *value*?

ii   Write down the octal and hex notations for each of the following numbers...

- 011001010100001100100001

- 000111110101100011010001

iii   Write down the pure binary notations for the following numbers...

- $8000.002C_{16}$

- $076.543.210_8$

Question two

i   Prove that the arithmetic negation of a twos-complement value is equivalent to the ones-complement incremented by one.

ii   Give the interpretation in decimal notation of the following pure binary states assuming first sign-magnitude, then excess-M/2 and finally twos-complement interpretation...

- FF_{16}

- $C9_{16}$

Comment on your answer.

iii   Add the above two numbers together, assuming twos-complement encoding, showing that the answer is consistent regardless of whether hex, pure binary or decimal notation is used. Comment on your answer.

Question three

i   ASCII was designed at a time when terminals were just *teletypes*, which simply printed everything they were sent on paper and transmitted everything typed immediately. In what ways is it inadequate for present day terminals and how is it extended to remedy the situation?

ii ASCII is very convenient for transmitting *textual* data. What is the problem with transmitting raw binary data (e.g. a machine executable file) ? Suggest a solution *which makes use of ASCII*.

Question four

i What is meant by *degeneracy* of a number coding system? Give two examples of degenerate number coding systems.

ii Give, in hex notation, *normalized single precision IEEE floating-point* representations for the following...

- -1.375

- -0.375

- -0.34375

Question five

i Summarize the circumstances when it is sensible to make use of floating-point, rather than fixed-point, number representation, and those when it is not.

ii Perform the floating-point addition of 1.375 and 2.75 showing details of each phase of the operation. (Assume IEEE standard single precision representation.)

Chapter 5

Element level

5.1 Combinational systems

5.1.1 Specification

Propositional logic

Propositions are *assertions* which are either true or false. Assertion is typically denoted in natural language by verbs, most often the verb "to be". In a *formal language* (i.e. a mathematical one) it is denoted by "=". No *action* is implied.

Examples are...

- P = "The cat is fat"

- Q = "Fred is a cat"

- R = "Cats are lazy"

- S = "Fred is lazy"

Propositions do not allow one to express assertions about whole classes of object or about exceptions within classes. Such assertions are called *predicates*.

Connectives are the means of joining propositions together. Because they are *associative* it is sufficient that they are *binary*. Because there are four possible ways of combining two binary objects there are sixteen (2^4) connectives (see Table 5.1). In addition to the binary connectives a single *unary* one is defined called *logical negation* (Table 5.2).

Formulæ are formed by joining propositions together with connectives. For instance...

$$F_1 = P \wedge Q \quad \text{The cat is fat} \quad AND \quad \text{Fred is a cat}$$
$$F_2 = R \wedge Q \quad \text{Cats are lazy} \quad AND \quad \text{Fred is a cat}$$
$$F_3 = F_2 \Rightarrow S \quad \text{Cats are lazy} \quad AND \quad \text{Fred is a cat} \quad IMPLIES \quad \text{Fred is lazy}$$

A	B		↓			∧			⇔	⊕			|	⇒		∨	
F	F	F	T	F	F	F	T	T	T	F	F	F	T	T	T	F	T
F	T	F	F	T	F	F	T	F	F	T	T	F	T	T	F	T	T
T	F	F	F	F	T	F	F	T	F	T	F	T	T	F	T	T	T
T	T	F	F	F	F	T	F	F	T	F	T	T	F	T	T	T	T

Table 5.1: Truth table for all sixteen binary logical connectives

A	¬A
T	F
F	T

Table 5.2: Unary logical connective: Negation

Formulæ themselves are propositions and thus are either true or false. Consider especially that F_3 may be either true or false.

Classification of formulæ is possible into one or other of the following categories...

- Tautologies *are always true (e.g. The cat is fat* OR *the cat is thin)*

- Contradictions *are always false (e.g. The cat is fat* AND *the cat is thin)*

- Consistencies *may be either true or false (e.g. Fred is a cat* AND *the cat is fat)*

A number of theorems exist which allow propositional formulæ to be *reduced* or proved logically equivalent. It is sometimes possible to reduce one to either a tautology or contradiction and hence *prove* or *deny* it. Such manipulation is a rudimentary form of *reasoning*. The author recommends [Dowsing et al. 86] as a concise and readable introduction to the subject, set in the context of computer science in general and computer architecture in particular.

Truth functions may be specified via a *truth table*. Truth tables may be used to define a truth function of any number of propositions. The possible combinations of proposition truth values are tabulated on the left hand side. A single column on the right hand side defines the value of the function for each combination (see Table 5.3).

The logical connectives described earlier are thus *primitive* truth functions. *Sufficiency sets* of connectives are those from which *every* truth function can be generated. An example is $\{\land, \lor, \neg\}$. This idea is of enormous importance to computer architecture. *Any machine capable of computing* $\land$, $\lor$ *and* $\neg$ *is capable of computing any truth function.*

Interestingly, there are two connectives which *alone* form sufficiency sets. These are ↓ and |. Although this is interesting, the formula expressing the function will (usually) contain *more terms* than it would using $\land$, $\lor$ and $\neg$. ↓ and | are thus, in a sense, less efficient.

A	B	C	Q
F	F	F	F
F	F	T	T
F	T	F	T
F	T	T	T
T	F	F	T
T	F	T	T
T	T	F	T
T	T	T	T

Table 5.3: Example of a truth function: $Q = A \vee B \vee C$

To summarize, three sets of binary logical connectives, sufficient to compute any function of any number of propositions, are...

- *AND, OR, NOT ($\wedge, \vee$ and $\neg$)*

- *NAND ($|$)*

- *NOR ($\downarrow$)*

Boolean algebra

Boolean variables are variables with range $\{1,0\}$. It is hoped that the reader has already met and used them as a *data type* of a programming language. *Boolean algebra* is designed to appear much like ordinary algebra in order to make it easy to write and manipulate truth functions. *Boolean operators* are primitive functions, out of which expressions may be constructed, and comprise the single sufficiency set...

- *AND (represented by ".")*

- *OR (represented by "+")*

- *NOT (represented by (e.g.) "$\bar{A}$")*

The concepts of *operator* and *connective* are *not* identical. A connective is simply a means of *associating* propositions into a formula. Its meaning is purely symbolic. An operator, meanwhile, is a primitive function, i.e. it has a *value*. Since no function may be physically evaluated without execution of some process, *action* is implied. To summarize, an operator yields a value, a connective expresses the form of association between propositions. Operators imply a *time axis*, i.e. a "before" and "after".

The reason for choosing symbols in common with those of ordinary algebra for AND and OR is that they obey the laws of *distribution* and *association* in exactly the same way as addition and multiplication respectively.

Boolean expressions are equivalent to propositional *formulæ*. They are formed by combining operators and variables, exactly as for ordinary algebra, and evaluate to {1,0} as do Boolean variables which may be regarded as primitive expressions. Boolean functions, like Boolean variables, evaluate to the range {1,0} only. They may be specified by...

- *Boolean expression*

- *Truth table*

The truth table is a *unique* specification, i.e. there is only one per function. There are, however, often many expressions for each function. For this reason it is best to initially specify a requirement as a truth table and then proceed to a Boolean expression.

Boolean functions are important to computer architecture because they offer a means of *specifying* the behaviour of systems in a manner which allows a *modular* approach to design. Algebraic laws may be employed to *transform* expressions. Table 5.4 shows a summary of the laws of Boolean algebra.

5.1.2   Physical implementation

Logic gates

If we are going to manufacture a real, physical system which implements a Boolean function, we should first query the *minimum set* of physical primitive systems needed.

We know from a theorem of *propositional logic* that any truth function may be formulated using the set of operators {AND, OR, NOT}. This operator set must therefore be implemented physically. Each device is known as a *logic gate* (or just *gate*). Figure 5.1 depicts the standard symbols for {AND, OR, NOT}.

As an alternative to implementing the {AND, OR, NOT} set, either {NAND} or {NOR} alone may be implemented. Figure 5.2 depicts the standard symbols used for these logic gate devices. Note that Boolean algebra does not extend to either of these operators[1].

Implementing a truth function by use of *combining* logical operators is known as *combinational logic*. It was pointed out earlier that a propositional logic formula, to express a given function, which uses either NAND (|) or NOR (↓) alone will usually contain more terms than if it were to use AND, OR, NOT alone. It was also pointed out that, *in a sense*, it would thus be less efficient. However, physical truth is the province of the engineer and *not* the mathematician. Manufacturing three things the same is much *cheaper* than three things different. The reader is recommended to open a catalogue of electronic logic devices and compare the cost of NAND or NOR gates to those of AND, OR and NOT. Using NAND or NOR to implement a combinational logic system usually turns out to be more efficient in the sense of *minimizing production cost*, which is of course the most important sense of all.

---

[1] It is obviously easy to define Boolean functions which implement them.

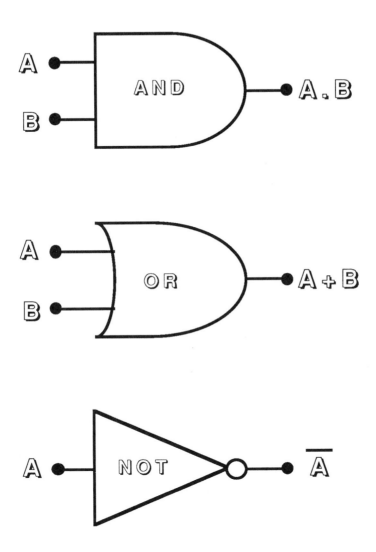

Figure 5.1: Logic gates implementing the {AND, OR, NOT} sufficiency set of operators

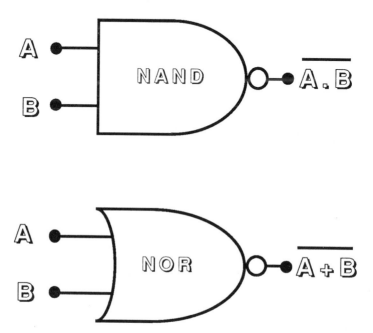

Figure 5.2: Logic gates implementing the {NAND} or {NOR} sufficiency set of operators

Commutation	$A + B$	$=$	$B + A$
	$A.B$	$=$	$B.A$
Distribution	$A.(B + C)$	$=$	$A.B + A.C$
	$A + (B.C)$	$=$	$(A + B).(A + C)$
Association	$A + B + C$	$=$	$(A + B) + C = A + (B + C)$
	$A.B.C$	$=$	$(A.B).C = A.(B.C)$
Complementation	$A.\bar{A}$	$=$	0
	$A + \bar{A}$	$=$	1
Zero	$A.0$	$=$	0
	$A + 1$	$=$	1
Identity	$A.1$	$=$	A
	$A + 0$	$=$	A
Idempotence	$A + A$	$=$	A
	$A.A$	$=$	A
Absorption	$A + A.B$	$=$	A
	$A.(A + B)$	$=$	A
	$A + \bar{A}.B$	$=$	$A + B$
DeMorgan's laws	$\overline{A + B + C}$	$=$	$\bar{A}.\bar{B}.\bar{C}$
	$\overline{A.B.C}$	$=$	$\bar{A} + \bar{B} + \bar{C}$

Table 5.4: Laws of Boolean algebra

The last combinational logic gate to mention does *not* constitute a sufficiency set. The *exclusive-or* operator is so useful that it is to be found implemented as a logic gate (Figure 5.3).

It is useful because...

- *It inverts (complements) a bit*

- *It is equivalent to binary (modulo 2) addition*

Once again Boolean algebra does not include this operator[2]. However, with care it is possible to extend it to do so. The $\oplus$ symbol is used to denote the XOR operator. It is *commutative...*

---

[2]But as with NAND or NOR we may define a Boolean function.

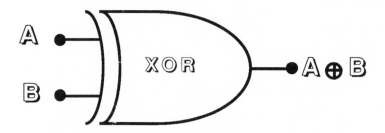

Figure 5.3: Logic gate implementing the XOR operator

$$A \oplus B = B \oplus A$$

and *associative*...

$$(A \oplus B) \oplus C = A \oplus (B \oplus C)$$

XOR from AND, OR & NOT

From the truth table of XOR (Table 5.5) we note that the operator value is 1 (true) when...

$$\bar{A}.B = 1$$
$$A.\bar{B} = 1$$

A	B	Q
0	0	0
0	1	1
1	0	1
1	1	0

Table 5.5: Truth table of XOR function

These two are called *minterms*. Any Boolean function may be written as either...

- *Standard sum of products (minterms)*
- *Standard product of sums (maxterms)*

Minterms are easily deducible from a truth table, simply by writing down the pattern (as if spoken in English) which produces each 1 of function value. The value of the function is 1 if the first minterm is 1 OR the second OR the third... and so on.

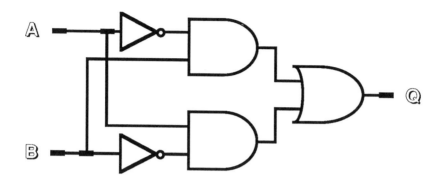

Figure 5.4: Exclusive-or function implemented using AND,OR and NOT gates

Thus the *combinational logic* implementation of XOR, using just AND, OR and NOT, is just...

$$F_{xor} = \bar{A}.B + A.\bar{B}$$

This is shown pictorially in Figure 5.4.

AND/OR structures

Because every truth function may be realized as either the *standard product of sums* or the *standard sum of products* it is not uncommon to find structures of the form depicted in Figure 5.5. They are called *two-level structures*. The first level produces the minterms or maxterms, the second yields the function itself.

Recall *DeMorgan's laws*...

$$\overline{A + B + C} = \bar{A}.\bar{B}.\bar{C}$$

$$\overline{A.B.C} = \bar{A} + \bar{B} + \bar{C}$$

Recall also that economy demands use of a single type of gate, either NAND or NOR. Application of DeMorgan's laws results in a very useful *design transform*. We may, it turns out, simply replace every gate in a standard product of sums design by NOR, or every gate in a standard sum of products by a NAND, *without affecting its function*. The equivalent networks for those in Figure 5.5 are shown in Figure 5.6.

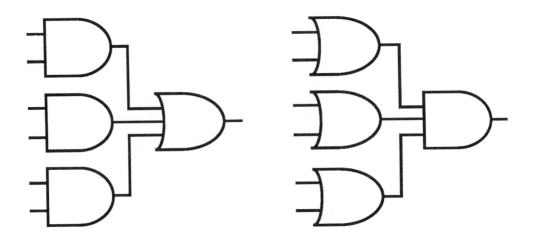

Figure 5.5: Two-level AND/OR gate structures

There is one further advantage in using NAND/NOR gates. Typically some of the inputs to the first level gates will require *inversion*. It is a simple matter to achieve inversion of a single signal with either a NAND or a NOR gate[3].

Bitwise logical operations

Most computations deal with numbers and symbols which require *word widths* greater than one. The memory of a computer is arranged accordingly. There are, however, still many occasions when this is inefficient, inconvenient or downright impossible. For example, ...

1. *Packed Boolean variables (e.g. Processor Status Register)*

2. *Packed ASCII character codes*

3. *Packed short integer variables*

As a result it is necessary to work out how to access individual bits and groups of bits within a word. In order to achieve access within word boundaries we introduce *bitwise logical operators* which operate on each bit of a word *independently* but in parallel. The technique used is known as *bit masking*. We will consider three kinds of access...*Set*, *Clear* and *Invert*.

First let's deal with *Set*. The initial step requires the creation of a *mask*. This is a constant binary word with a 1 in each position which requires setting and a 0 in every

---

[3] A minor exercise for the reader.

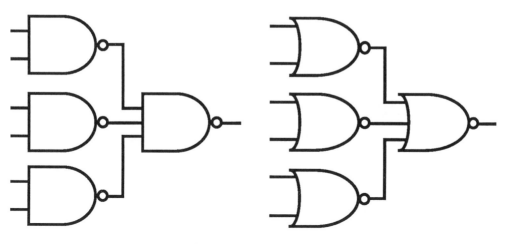

Figure 5.6: Two-level NAND/NOR gate structures

other. For example 1111.0000_2 would be used as a mask to set the *most significant nibble (MSN)* of a 1-byte word. This is shown below (left) along with how to clear and invert it.

```
      1010.1010              1010.1010              1010.1010
   or 1111.0000          and 0000.1111          xor 1111.0000

   =  1111.1010           =   0000.1010           =   0101.1010
```

Note that the mask needed with XOR for *Invert* is the same as is used with OR for *Set* but its inverse is required with AND for *Clear*.

5.1.3 Physical properties

Nature and operation

Logic gates are simply *configurations* of *normally-open switches*, (Figure 1.2). Figure 1.4 shows how switches form logic gates. A discussion of the nature and operation of the normally-open switch may be found in Chapter 1.

Logic polarity

Boolean states ($\{0,1\}$) must be represented in some way by physical states in order for the computer to possess memory. In addition to those physical states, some kind of potential energy must be employed to communicate state, which implies that we must

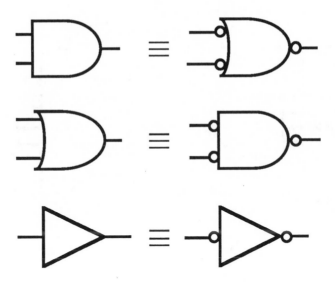

Figure 5.7: Negative logic symbols

decide on two *standard* potentials, one for *logic 1* and one for *logic 0*. One must be
sufficiently greater than the other to ensure rapid *flow*.

- Positive logic *simply means the use of the* high *potential for logic 1*

- Negative logic *simply means the use of the* low *potential for logic 1*

It is very easy to become confused about the meaning of design schematics using
negative logic[4]. Remember that *design* and *implementation* are *separate* issues. Design
may take place without the need to know the logic polarity of the implementation.

Sometimes *part* of a design needs to be shown as negative logic. The logic symbols
used to indicate this are shown in Figure 5.7. The "bubble" simply indicates *inversion*
and has been seen before on the "nose" of NAND and NOR gates.

Negative logic gates are shown with their equivalents in positive logic. Each equivalence is simply a *symbolic* statement of each of *DeMorgan's laws. This is the easy way
to remember them!*

Propagation delay

It is hoped that the reader is familiar with the concept of *function* as a *mapping* from a
domain set to a *range* set. If we are to construct *physical* systems which realize functions
(e.g. logical operators) we must prove that we understand what that concept means.

---

[4] *Positive* logic is the norm and should be assumed unless stated otherwise.

There are two interpretations of a function. The first is that of *association*. Any input symbol, belonging to an *input alphabet*, is *associated* with an output symbol, belonging to an *output alphabet*. For example, imagine a system where the input alphabet is the hearts suit of cards and the output alphabet is clubs. A function may be devised which simply selects the output card which directly corresponds to (associates with) that input.

The second interpretation is that of a *process* whose output is the value of the function. For example, both input and output alphabets might be the set of integers and the function value might be the sum of all inputs up to the current instant. An *algorithm* must be derived to define a process which may then be physically implemented.

The association interpretation is rather restrictive, but for *fast* implementation of simple *primitive* operators may offer a useful approach.

The purpose of the above preamble is to make it clear that, since a *process* must always be employed to physically evaluate a function, *time must elapse between specification of the arguments and its evaluation!* This elapsed time is called the *propagation delay*.

Race condition

Logic gates are typically combined into *gate networks* in order to implement Boolean functions. Because of the gate propagation delay a danger exists that can bring about unwanted *non-determinacy* in the system behaviour.

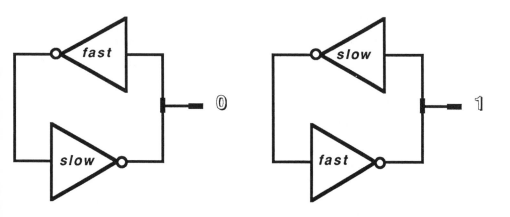

Figure 5.8: Race condition in a cyclic combinational logic network

Figure 5.8 illustrates the two different outputs which can result from the same input. It is *history* that decides the output! Although we might make use of this property later for implementing *memory*, it is totally unwanted when implementing a truth function (independent of time or history).

A simple precaution at the design phase will eliminate *race conditions* from deciding output. The following rule must be obeyed...

No gate network may include a cycle.

Races may result in *unstable* states as well as stable ones, as we shall see later.

Power consumption and dissipation

Communication between interacting devices is made possible by the flow of some medium from *high to low* potential energy. Flow requires converting some potential to kinetic energy (to do *work*). Power[5] is thus consumed. The simplest analogue is water flowing downhill where *gravitational* potential energy is converted into the (kinetic) energy of motion. Potential energy is required by our "something" to *push closed a switch* and help operate the logic gate. Before sufficient energy can be mustered, enough of the medium must have arrived. This is known as *charging*.

The most relevant example is that of the electrical technology used to implement contemporary computers. The electrical switch employed is called a *transistor*, the medium which flows is *electric charge* and the channel through which it flows is simply a wire. "Charging" thus refers to the build up of charge in a *capacitance* at the switching input of a transistor.

The *charging time* is totally dependent on the operating potential of the switch and is responsible for the majority of the propagation delay of any gate.

The *first law of thermodynamics* may be (very coarsely) stated...

The total amount of potential and kinetic energy in a system is constant.

...and is popularly known as the law of *conservation of energy*. The *second law of thermodynamics* basically says that *all machines warm up as they operate* and may be (very coarsely) stated...

The complete conversion of potential energy into kinetic energy is not possible without some proportion being dissipated as heat.

The first law implies that we cannot build a logic gate, a computer or any other device without a *power supply*. Gates *consume energy* each time an internal switch operates. The second law of thermodynamics states that we cannot build a logic gate, a computer or any other machine which does not *warm up* when it operates.

Race oscillation

Race oscillation is related to the race condition discussed earlier. It was mentioned that, in addition to obtaining more than one possible output state, it was possible to obtain *unstable* output states. Figure 5.9 shows how this may arise.

---

[5] For those who failed their physics... *power* is energy "consumed" per unit time.

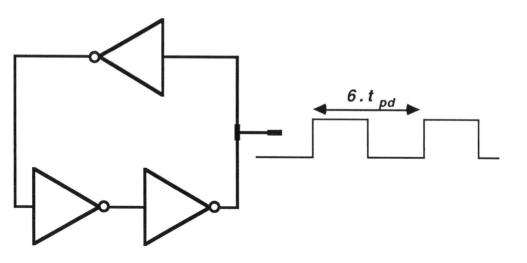

Figure 5.9: Combinational logic system which results in race oscillation

Let's suppose we begin with an input state at $\bar{S}$ which brings about an output state of 1 after one gate propagation delay, t_{pd}. The $\bar{S}$ input is then immediately disconnected. The output is fed back to the input, forming a cycle in the network, via any gate which will generate an extra delay. This *feedback* signal causes the output state to be reset to 0. The cycle of events repeats itself indefinitely. It is an example of a *recursive* process called *oscillation*.

The *frequency* of oscillation is the number of complete cycles per second. A little thought shows that, for the network shown, this is given by...

$$F_{osc} = (6.t_{pd})^{-1}$$

Fan-out

As discussed above, gates are fabricated from normally-open switches which require a certain potential to close. The input must be charged for a period of time until this potential is reached and the switch closes. The *charging time* is thus dependent on two factors...

- *Flow rate*

- *Operation potential*

The rate of flow out of a gate is dependent on the available energy from the power supply to the gate. Some constriction or *resistance* to flow is essential since gates must share the available energy.

The flow rate into the gate depends on that *out* of the previous one. The *fan-out* is the number of gates which may be connected to the output of a single gate and still work reliably. The flow available at the output of a single gate is fixed and determined by its effective *output resistance*. Connecting more than one gate input to it implies dividing up this flow. As a result, a longer charging time is required for each successor gate and their propagation delay is thus increased. Fan-out and propagation delay must therefore be *traded-off* against one another.

5.2 Sequential systems

5.2.1 Physical nature

Synchronization

Processes are entities which possess *state* and which *communicate* with other objects. They are characterized by a *set of events* of which they are capable.

All this may seem a little formal and mysterious. *Not so!* You are surrounded by such processes. For instance, a clock or watch (digital or analogue) is such a beast. It has state which is simply some means of storing the time. This is likely to be the orientation of cog wheels if it is analogue and a digital memory if it is digital. It also communicates with other processes, such as yourself, by means of some sort of display. Note that this is a *one way* communication, from the clock to you. There is likely also to be some means for you to communicate *to* it, e.g. in order to adjust it. Its reception of the new time and your transmission of it are events which belong to the clock and you respectively. The two combined form a *single event* of an abstract object of which both the clock and you are part (e.g. your *world*).

All events fall into three classes...

- *Assignment of state*

- *Input*

- *Output*

Communicating sequential processes (CSP) were discussed in Part I. They form a universal model, *equally applicable to hardware and software!* A process is *any sequence of events* and forms a powerful paradigm for analysis of objects which are observed to change with time, or which are required to change with time. Computers obviously fall into the latter category.

As was stated right at the start of this book, a computer is a *programmable system*. A program may be thought of as a list of commands (which may or may not be ordered). A computer is capable of causing a process to occur following a *single* command. Sometimes that process infinitely repeats a block of events. Such a process may often be defined *recursively*. The simplest example is that of a clock which increments then displays the time (notionally) forever. We formally write this as...

$$Clock = increment \rightarrow display \rightarrow Clock$$

Right at the heart of a computer there is a device which causes a single pre-defined process to occur as a result of each command (or *instruction*) from an *alphabet* (or *instruction set*). It is called a *control unit*. It is discussed in detail in Chapter 7.

This section forms the first step towards an understanding of it, without which it is impossible to truly understand a computer. The reader is warned to remember the above definition of a *process* and to always return to it when confused. Any process, except those composed of single events, may be broken down into smaller processes which may run *concurrently* or *successively*. In this part of the book we shall discover how to assemble more and larger *hardware processes* until we are able to construct a complete computer. From that point on, larger processes are constructed in *software*.

Two (or more) processes are said to run *synchronously* if some of their events occur simultaneously (i.e. at the same instant of time). It is impossible for processes to synchronize without *communication*. The necessary communication may not be direct. Indeed it is inefficient to synchronize a large number of processes directly. A much better way is to have all of them share a common *clock*.

The world may be thought of as a (very) large collection of processes which are synchronized to a single common clock (or *time base*). It is the job of a *standards institute* to define this clock to a high degree of precision. To most of us the clock on the wall suffices.

Synchronous communication is...

- Simple *because it requires only a signal (e.g. from a common clock)*

- Efficient *because it requires no extra state to implement*

- Secure *because the sender "knows" the message has been received*

Synchronous communication is thus generally well suited to (low level) hardware processes. The one severe disadvantage is that either the receiver or sender process must wait *idle* for the other to be ready.

Processes are said to be *asynchronous* if they share *no* events which occur simultaneously. No signals are received from a common clock. With *asynchronous communication* the sender cannot know *if or when* a message has been received. Extra memory (state) is required to form the *buffer* where the message awaits the receiver process. When it is known in advance that the sender...

- *Will always be ready in advance of the receiver*

- *Is able to usefully perform other processes*

...asynchronous (buffered) communication may improve performance. The cost however is extra memory for the buffer.

Memory

Memory is equivalent to the concept of a *stable physical state*. Any physical system with only a *single* stable state will eventually attain that state if left to itself. If disturbed, then left alone, it will return to that state. Such a system is referred to as a *monostable*. The simplest example is that of a ball-bearing in a smoothly curved well. We shall simplify things further by considering the two-dimensional equivalent shown in Figure 5.10. The state of the ball is its position (*height* will do). The state at the bottom of the well is stable because the ball cannot reduce its potential energy. *We can deduce nothing of its history upon inspection!*

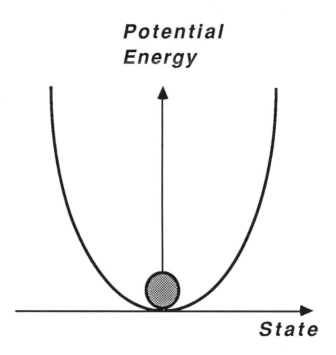

Figure 5.10: System with a single stable state

Figure 5.11 shows a different physical system with *two stable states*. Such a system is referred to as a *bistable*. This time we can deduce something of the ball's history. Assuming there has been no random disturbance (i.e. *noise*), such as a minor earthquake etc., we can safely deduce that somebody put it in whichever hollow it sits. *Bistables have useful memory!* All that remains is to label the states (e.g. 0 and 1) and we have a *1-bit* memory.

Writing such a memory requires *injecting potential energy* to push the ball up the

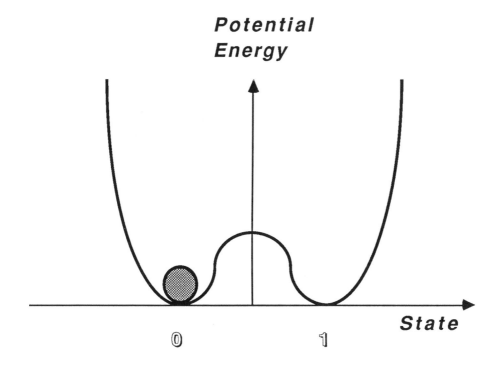

Figure 5.11: System with two stable states

slope. If insufficient potential is available the ball will remain in the first state. Hence there is a *threshold potential* which may cause a state change.

Hysteresis is the formal term given to the reluctance of a system to change its state. Whatever the physical process required to change state, we require it to be *reversible* in as symmetric a manner as possible. It must also need significantly more energy than is available locally in the form of noise but no more than necessary to ensure reliability. Figure 5.12 shows the *hysteresis diagram* which relates input (in the form of applied force) to state for the system shown in Figure 5.11. The total energy required to effect a change of state is given by integration (area under the graph).

Systems (such as the one discussed) which exhibit hysteresis form useful memories because they remain in one or other stable state *when the disturbing force disappears!* This property is called *non-volatility*.

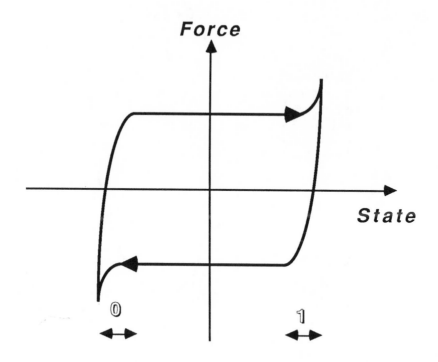

Figure 5.12: Hysteresis in a bistable system

5.2.2   Specification

Temporal logic

A theory is needed on which to base usable methods of specifying systems which *change with time*. *Temporal logic* is at present an active field of research which promises many applications within computer science, such as...

- *Knowledge-based temporal reasoning*

- *Formal verification of software*

- *Formal specification of software*

- *Formal specification of hardware*

It is the last application that is of interest here.

You live in exciting times for computer science. The development of temporal logic for formal process specification is going on around you. Because the dust has not yet settled it is not possible to present a full description of how it may be employed. However, methods will doubtless be built on what is so far understood of this subject. The author therefore feels a *brief* summary of the fundamental concepts to be of value. Further reading is recommended (at the time of writing) of [Turner 84] and [Bentham 83]. Direct application to the specification and verification of hardware systems is presented in [Halpern et al. 83] and [Moszkowski 83].

Propositional logic was sufficient for specifying systems which implement *truth functions*. In this theory something was asserted true or false *for all time!* It is necessary to extend this theory in order to make assertions which are understood to be true at some time and false at another. Three things are needed in order to define time, in a logical sense, and relate it to propositional logic...

- *Set of discrete instants*

- *Successor operator*

- *Timed truth function*

The *successor operator* operates on two instants and evaluates true if the first precedes the second. The *timed truth function* of an instant and a proposition evaluates true if the proposition is true at that instant. This function effectively maps the truth of the proposition for all time.

Temporal operators are *unary* operators which establish the truth of a proposition with respect to time. Intuitively these operators must fall into the following categories...

- Future: *The proposition will be true at some instant in the future*

- Past: *The proposition was true at some instant in the past*

Assertions that something will *always* be true in the future and/or the past may be constructed via negation. For example, $\overline{Future(\overline{Rain})}$ might be used to state *"From now on, it will rain forever."*. It may be interpreted[6] literally as *"It is not true that, at some future time, it will not rain."*. The *timed truth function* decides the truth or otherwise of the assertion. In reality, in this case, it would take forever to evaluate. This clearly places some sort of constraint on the range of applications of temporal logic. It would seem well suited to the formal specification of system behaviour.

One problem which exists for system specification is that of how to specify *precisely when* an event, within the system process, is to occur. It is possible either to specify that an event coincides with an instant or that it occurs within the interval between the instant and its predecessor. What is needed is a set of temporal operators which suits

---

[6]Note how, in English, we often have to resort to phrases, such as *"from now on"*, to convey simple propositions.

the needs of the process model computation. This means that it should be tailored to specify and reason about *sequences* of events. Such a set is composed of three unary and two binary operators as follows. . .

Operator	Notation	Meaning
Next P	$\bigcirc P$	*P is true at the next instant*
Always P	$\square P$	*P is true at all future instants*
Eventually P	$\diamond P$	*P is true at some future instant*
P_1 Until P_2	$P_1 \cup P_2$	*P_1 is true until P_2 becomes true*
P_1 Then P_2	$P_1 \supset P_2$	*P_1, if true, is followed by P_2*

Temporal formulæ are propositions constructed from. . .

- *Temporal operators ($\bigcirc, \square, \diamond, \cup, \supset$)*

- *Boolean connectives ($\vee, \wedge, \neg$)*

- *Set of atomic propositions*

These atomic propositions correspond with communication and state assignment primitives appropriate to the system.

Specification of a system means construction of formulae which describe its behaviour as a process, i.e. the sequence of events that we wish to witness. In terms of physical systems these events fall into two categories. . .

- *A given state being observed (e.g. a logic 0 in a flip-flop)*

- *Transmission or reception of a logic signal*

Properties of temporal logic allow the abstraction of requirements and thus the proper separation of *specification* from *design*. It is possible to merely consider what is *wanted*, without consideration of the constraints of what is available for implementation.

One great advantage of such an approach is that *theorems* of temporal and propositional logic may be applied to the specification to verify that it is *consistent*, i.e. that no pair of requirements *conflict*. This is a form of *temporal reasoning*.

A second formidable advantage is that the same reasoning may be applied to *transform* the specification into a design given. . .

- *Set of available primitives*

- *Set of constraining parameters (such as cost, complexity etc.)*

The ideas discussed here are inadequate for such ventures. For instance *predicate logic* is used, to achieve the *expressivity* required, rather than simple propositional logic. The (brave) reader is referred to [Halpern et al. 83] and [Moszkowski 83].

State transition graphs

State machines are systems whose *state* evolves according to values input. State evolution may be represented by a graph whose nodes represent state and whose edges represent *state transitions*.

The sole type of event considered is the *observation* of state. Each subsequent state is the consequence of both input and previous state. In other words inputs are considered to have occured *prior* to the current state but *after* the previous one. Only the value delivered is of interest[7].

Output is derived in two *alternative* ways giving rise to two alternative kinds of *state machine...*

- Moore machine: *Output is derived from state alone*

- Mealy machine: *Output is derived from state and input*

Although the Mealy machine is the more general formulation, the Moore machine is just as general *in application* but may require more state (memory). Figure 5.13 depicts a schematic of both.

Moore machine				Mealy machine				
State	Output	Next state		State	Output		Next state	
		$x = 0$	$x = 1$		$x = 0$	$x = 1$	$x = 0$	$x = 1$
A	0	A	B	A	0	0	A	B
B	0	C	B	B	0	0	C	B
C	0	D	B	C	0	0	D	B
D	0	A	E	D	0	1	A	B
E	1	C	B					

Table 5.6: State transition tables for Moore and Mealy state machines

One way to document a state transition graph is to make up a *state transition table*. This looks slightly different for Moore and Mealy machines. Table 5.6 documents the same *specification* for both a Moore and a Mealy state machine. Note that nothing has been said about how either machine may be *designed*. That must wait for the material in the next chapter.

---

[7] This is rather like picking up the mail on coming home in the evening. Who cares when the postman came! One only cares about what the mail actually is.

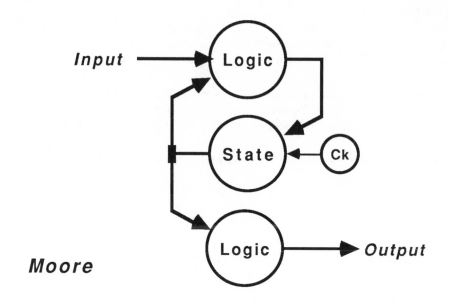

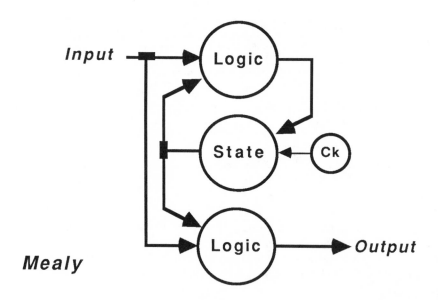

Figure 5.13: Moore and Mealy state machines

5.2.3 Physical implementation

Requirements

In order to implement simple processes as real physical (i.e. hardware) systems we may use the model of one or other type of *state machine*.

Synchronous communication will be used for the sake of simplicity (using nothing more complicated than a wire, given electrical technology).

This reduces our problems to those of implementing...

- *1-bit memory*

- *Clock*

A *1-bit memory* is a bistable whose state may be written and read *synchronously* with a *clock*, which is an *unstable* system, oscillating between two states, outputting *ticks* to all components of the system.

From these two primitives it is possible to build systems implementing simple *communicating sequential processes*. Systems constructed in this way are referred to as *sequential logic*.

Clock

Figure 5.9 offered a possible solution for a clock. (A thing to be avoided in combinational logic is the key in sequential logic.) This system has two states, neither of which is stable. The rate at which it oscillates between them is totally dependent on t_{pd}, the propagation delay of the gates employed. Here lies a problem.

In combinational logic it is highly desirable to minimize t_{pd} since it largely determines how fast a truth function may be computed. *We cannot predict or control the interval between ticks.*

Let's backtrack to physics once more to remind ourselves of what is really happening. A medium *flows* from the output of one gate to the input of the other. Enough must arrive in the storage "bucket" at the input for there to be enough *potential energy* available to push a switch closed and operate the gate[8].

We can gain control of this flow by employing our own "bucket", *much bigger than the one inside the second gate*, and our own flow constriction , *narrower than the output of the first*. For those familiar with electrical terminology we place a *resistance* in series and a *capacitance* in parallel. The time taken to charge the capacitance through the resistance will now virtually completely determine the state switching time and thus the frequency at which it ticks[9]. Such a clock is depicted in Figure 5.14.

---

[8] Like water flowing downhill into the lake behind a dam until a sufficient weight of water is available to break it down.

[9] A tick being one or other, but not both, state changes. The remaining state change might be thought of as a "tock". (Imagine it's audible!)

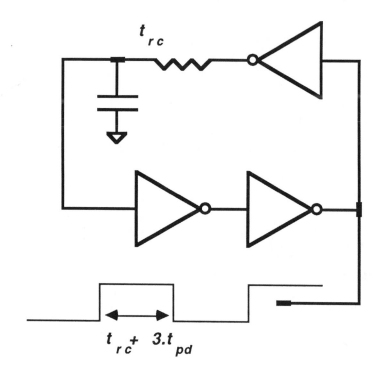

Figure 5.14: Clock whose frequency is determinable

The physics of oscillation dictates that *energy must be stored*. Any means of storing energy may be used to make a clock. A very important requirement for our clock is that it does not vary in frequency. *Quartz crystals* are currently used as the energy storage for clocks within computers. They allow the construction of oscillators with suitable range and stability of frequency. It may be that other devices will have to be found with typical charging times more suited to future computers.

1-bit memory

It is very important to realize that *any* bistable system may be used to implement a 1-bit memory. Such a system may be made from normally-open switches, as shown in Figure 1.3. Figure 5.15 shows the same bistable in gate form.

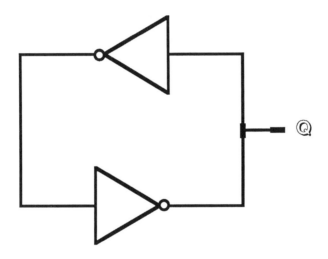

Figure 5.15: 1-bit memory constructed from NOT gates (invertors)

The state adopted when energy is supplied will depend on which gate (switch) wins the *race*. However, the system may be *disturbed* into one or other state by some external process as we shall see.

In order to consider the function of 1-bit memory cells we shall consider various types. Because we know all about gates now, we shall use them to implement memory. Figure 5.16 (upper) shows a bistable gate configuration which should be compared with Figure 5.8. The two inputs are *Reset* and *Set*. Their function should be plain from the state transition table below...

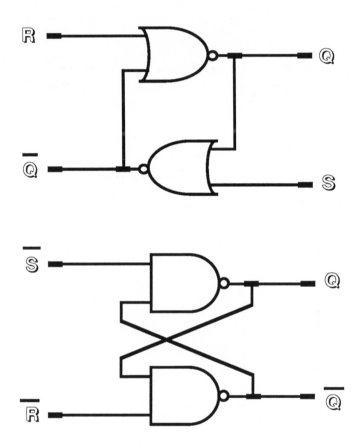

Figure 5.16: RS latch fabricated from both NOR and NAND gates

Present state	Next state			
	$RS = 00$	$RS = 01$	$RS = 10$	$RS = 11$
0	0	1	0	?
1	1	1	0	?

It is equally common to use NAND gates to implement a latch, in which case the inputs are *negative logic* and thus labelled $\bar{R}$ and $\bar{S}$. Figure 5.16 (lower) depicts such a latch and shows how it is usually drawn, with inputs and outputs on opposite sides.

The system behaviour with $RS = 00$ is exactly the same as that depicted in Figure 5.8. When power is first applied the output is determined solely by whichever is the faster gate (regardless of by how little). Subsequently it is determined by the *previous state*, i.e. its memory. The behaviour with $RS = 11$ is rather boring and not usable. Depending on gate type used the output is 0 or 1 on *both* outputs. As a result it is usual to treat this input configuration as *illegal* and take care to ensure that it can never occur. The remaining two possible input configurations are used to *write* data into the latch. As long as $RS = 00$, previously written data will be "remembered".

The disadvantages of an *RS latch* are twofold...

- *Both inputs must be considered when writing the memory*

- *There is no means of synchronization*

The primitive systems discussed in the remainder of this chapter are all built around the RS latch since it is the simplest possible bistable system which may be *written* as well as read. We will show how the idea may be extended to enable synchronous communication with other primitive systems, and simple programming of function.

A modification to the RS latch which frequently proves very useful (e.g. in system initialization) is the provision of extra inputs for...

- *Set (Force Q=1)*

- *Clear (Force state Q=0)*

- *Enable (Allow response to R and S)*

Figure 5.17 shows how this may be achieved.

The *D latch* (Figure 5.18) overcomes the disadvantages, inherent in the RS latch, to some extent. It has the following state transition table...

Present state	Next state	
	$D = 0$	$D = 1$
X (Don't care!)	0	1

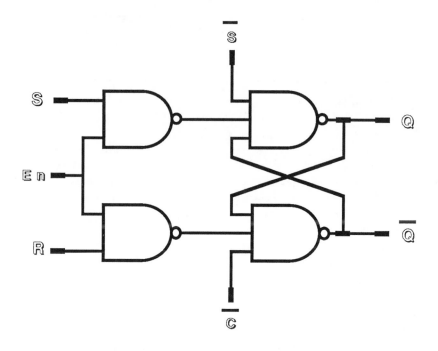

Figure 5.17: RS latch with added set, clear and enable inputs

The input gating allows a clock to switch it on and off so that the system will ignore data except when it is *enabled*. When enabled, output will follow input with only the propagation delay, which we assume to be small compared to the clock period. This property is referred to as *transparency* and has an effect on communication which is sometimes useful and sometimes highly undesirable. A second device connected to the output of a transparent one will receive its input effectively simultaneous with the first. A latch is a transparent memory cell which implies that it *cannot be both read and written simultaneously*. To summarize...

> *Latches cannot engage in secure synchronous (clocked) communication since they possess only a single memory which is simultaneously visible to both input and output ports.*

In order to construct a system, whose internal communication is synchronous, it is necessary for the components to possess the ability to both *input* and *output* simultaneously, i.e. upon a single instant. A latch cannot do this because *it has only a single memory* which cannot simultaneously be read and written.

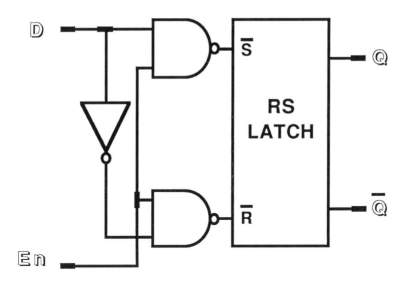

Figure 5.18: D latch (transparent) memory)

This is a general problem whose solution is known as *double buffering* (Figure 5.19). Two identical memories (buffers) are provided which we denote by A and B. The operation of the double buffer may be described using RTL[10] as follows...

$$(1) \quad A \leftarrow input, \quad output \leftarrow B$$
$$(2) \quad B \leftarrow A$$

It is this *swapping* which gives the *flip-flop* its name!

One problem is obvious. Extra synchronization is required for the buffer swap event. Think of this as the need for the clock to *"tock"* as well as *"tick"*. Because our clock is a 2-state machine, and thus has no choice but to tock after it ticks a solution is already to hand. The enable connections of the latches may be used to...

- *Isolate the two latches from each other*

- *Synchronize the buffer swap*

The two halves of a *clock-cycle* are known as *phases*. We can use two D latches to construct a *D flip-flop* as shown in Figure 5.20. Note that the state transition table is exactly the same as for the D latch. The differences are that input and output are now *synchronized* to a clock and that the new device may be simultaneously read and written.

---

[10] See Chapter 3.

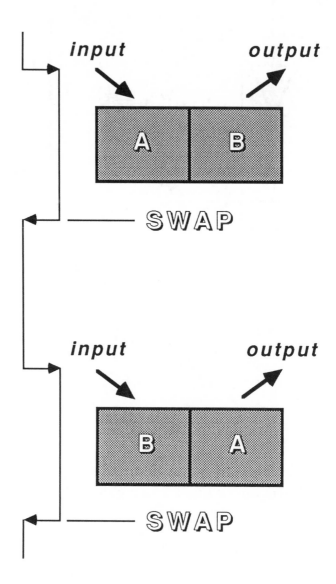

Figure 5.19: Double buffering

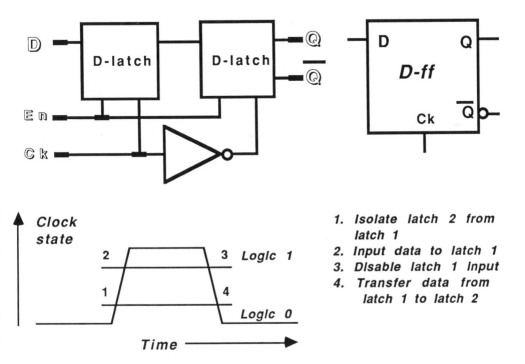

Figure 5.20: D flip-flop showing double buffer operation

The second problem is that some way of *disabling* the memory is required so that the memory may be *commanded* to input *or* do nothing. The solution to this one is simply to duplicate the *enable* connections of both latches and join one from each together.

Values are said to be *clocked* in and out on each clock tick. Synchronous communication with other components of a system is therefore possible. The system may be *programmed* to a small extent. It may be regarded as a very simple *processor* whose *process* is determined by the state in which the *enable* connection is found. *It is this device which we employ as the 1-bit memory which is fundamental to computer structure!*

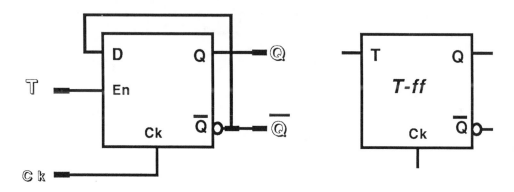

Figure 5.21: T flip-flop fabricated from D flip-flop

The result of programming the D flip-flop, with the output inverted and fed back to the input (Figure 5.21), is called the *T flip-flop*. It turns out to be very useful indeed. This time, if $T = 1$, the output will be *inverted* or *toggled*. If $T = 0$ it will remain in its previous state. The state transition table is as follows...

Present state	Next state	
	$T = 0$	$T = 1$
0	0	1
1	1	0

A more complicated processor may be constructed whose process may be programmed more fully. The *JK flip-flop* is shown in Figure 5.22. It has state transition table...

Present state	Next state			
	$JK = 00$	$JK = 01$	$JK = 10$	$JK = 11$
0	0	0	1	1
1	1	0	1	0

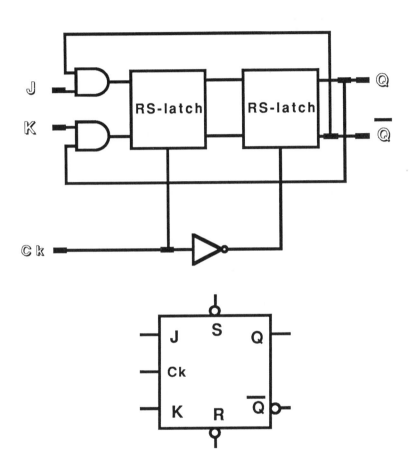

Figure 5.22: JK flip-flop

Feedback is once again employed to determine the state. Its effect is perhaps best understood as preventing the RS latch from being both *set* and *reset* simultaneously. RS latches may be used with added set and clear inputs which may be used *asynchronously*, to implement *JK flip-flops*. Table 5.7 shows the functions which may be programmed.

Operation	Control	Effect
Input	$J = 1, K = 0$	*Synchronous*
Not Input	$J = 0, K = 0$	*Synchronous*
Toggle	$J = 1, K = 1$	*Synchronous*
Set	$\bar{S} = 0, \bar{R} = 1$	*Asynchronous*
Reset	$\bar{S} = 1, \bar{R} = 0$	*Asynchronous*

Table 5.7: Programmable functions of a JK flip-flop

$\bar{R}, \bar{S}$ are called *direct inputs* and act *asynchronously*, i.e. their effect is immediate regardless of the clock. They allow the state of the flip-flop to be ensured at a time prior to the start of a process.

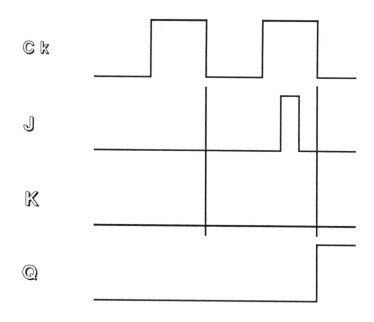

Figure 5.23: The ones-catching problem

One major problem arises with the JK flip-flop. It is known as the *ones-catching* problem (Figure 5.23). An input *transient state* is recorded by an enabled JK flip-flop. D flip-flops do not suffer from this problem. A transient $D = 1$ causes a transient *Set* input to the RS latch (inside the D latch) which is quickly followed by a *Reset* input.

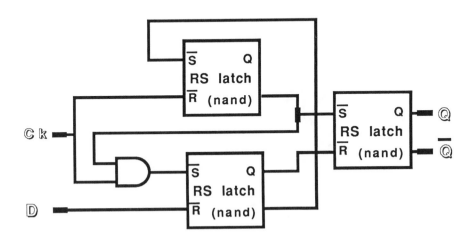

Figure 5.24: Edge-triggered D flip-flop

We would very much like input states to be inspected only at *discrete* points in time so that systems may be *noise immune* and so that synchronous communication may be rendered secure. An *edge-triggered* design for the D flip-flop is shown in Figure 5.24. The explanation of its operation is left as an exercise.

Figure 5.25 shows an edge-triggered JK flip-flop design. No input which fails to persist over a *state transition* is recorded by the flip-flop. An explanation of its operation is also left as an exercise. We shall see later how this device may form a useful programmable processor within a computer.

Lastly, an edge-triggered T flip-flop may be implemented simply by substituting an edge-triggered D flip-flop in Figure 5.21.

Summary

Flip-flops are *clocked*, latches are only *enabled*. This is an easy way to remember the difference. Flip-flops usually have an *enable* connection too, so that they may avoid communication on any given clock tick. They offer *synchronous communication* through use of a shared clock.

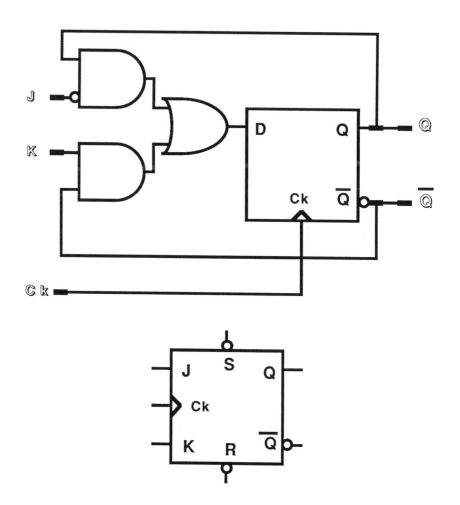

Figure 5.25: Edge-triggered JK flip-flop

Latches are *transparent*, flip-flops are not. *Edge-triggered* devices are totally blind to any state at the input connection(s) *which does not persist over a clock tick* and are preferred for their *noise immunity*.

"D" is for *Data*, "T" is for *Toggle!* "D" is also for *Delay* since data at the input of a D flip-flop cannot be input to a second one until the following clock tick. A delay is therefore afforded in passing data along a string of flip-flops of one clock period per device.

The JK flip-flop allows a number of different processes to be programmed, some with asynchronous and some with synchronous effect. It may be thought of as the most primitive possible programmable processor.

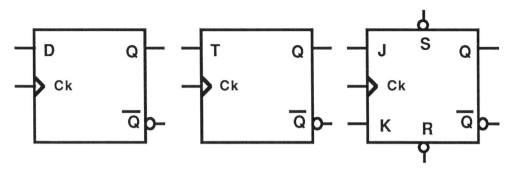

Figure 5.26: Elementary building blocks of sequential logic

Figure 5.26 summarizes the elementary building blocks of *sequential logic*. All these flip-flops have been discussed using logic gates for implementation. The reader must realize that they represent *any* physical bistable system.

5.2.4 Physical properties

Time intervals

Nothing in reality can ever happen truly instantaneously. No gate can change state simultaneously. Enough potential must be accumulated at each switch within it to cause it to operate. For this reason the input to any flip-flop must be correct at least t_{setup} prior to the clock tick, typically measured from half way between clock states. The value of t_{setup} will be specified by the manufacturer.

t_{hold}, once again to be specified by the manufacturer, is the time for which input values must remain valid *after* a clock tick. Sometimes the value of t_{hold} is actually *negative*, meaning that the value input may actually *fail to persist to the tick!*

The value output will become valid t_{pd} after the clock tick. The value of t_{pd} is likely to differ according to which of the two possible state changes occurs. The manufacturer must specify its (or their) value(s).

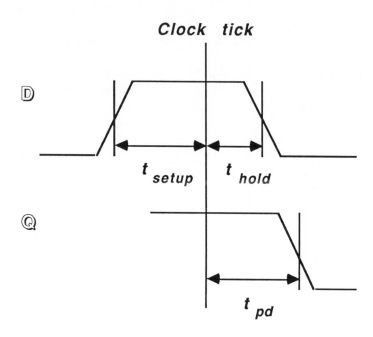

Figure 5.27: Setup, hold and propagation delay time intervals of a flip-flop

Timing considerations of memory devices may be summarized...

- *Setup time*

- *Hold time*

- *Propagation delay*

...and are shown in Figure 5.27.

Power considerations

The same comments apply to flip-flops as did to logic gates, under this heading. *Thermodynamics* tells us that it is impossible to change the state of something without converting potential energy into kinetic or some other form of energy, i.e. to do *work*. It also tells us that it is also impossible to do work without *heat dissipation*. *Flip-flops thus both consume energy and get hot when they operate.*

The same comments about *fan-out* apply to flip-flops as were made with regard to logic gates. The output of each is only able to drive a limited number of inputs to other devices, depending on both its own output flow resistance and the input potential required to operate the others *in the time available*. *Fan-out and speed of operation must be traded-off by the designer.*

Depending on the physical bistable employed a flip-flop *may* require energy to maintain one (or both) of its operating states. If the actual state itself of the bistable is not to be used to drive the output, then it is possible for the device to *retain its state when the power supply is removed*. Such a memory is referred to as *non-volatile*. A non-volatile bistable memory has a *potential function* like that shown in Figure 5.11 and must exhibit *hysteresis* . A volatile memory has no hysteresis and must be maintained in its upper state by some other source of energy (such as a stretched spring). *Energy is always required to change the state of any bistable, but not necessarily to maintain it.*

Power considerations of memory devices may be summarized. . .

- *Consumption*

- *Dissipation*

- *Fan-out*

- *Volatility*

Exercises

Question one

Use Boolean algebra to prove that...

1. *A two-level NAND gate structure may be used to implement* a standard sum of products

2. *A two-level NOR gate structure may be used to implement* a standard product of sums

(Use the examples shown in Figures 5.5 and 5.6 reduced to just four inputs in each case).

Question two

i Show how a *bitwise logical operator* might be used to *negate* an integer stored in memory using *sign-magnitude* representation.

ii Describe how the same operator is used in the negation of a value represented in twos-complement form.

Question three

Show how both NAND and NOR gates may be used to implement the Boolean functions...

- *NOT*
- *OR*
- *AND*

Question four

i Using Boolean algebra, derive implementations of the following function using only...

- *NAND*
- *NOR*

$$Q_{aoi} = \overline{A.B + C.D}$$

ii Devices which implement this truth function are available commercially and are referred to as *and-or-invert* gates. Prove that, alone, they are sufficient to implement any truth function.

Question five

i Expand the NAND implementation of the *RS latch*, shown in Figure 5.16, into a network of *normally-open switches*.

ii Discuss the requirements specification that an engineer would need in order to implement a practical device.

Question six

Explain, in detail, the operation of the system shown in Figure 5.28.

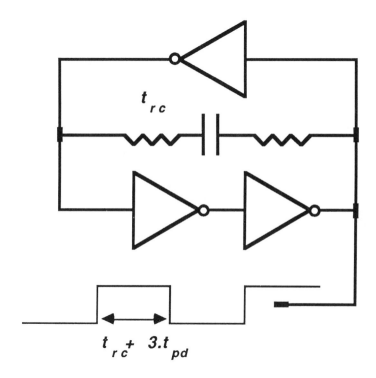

Figure 5.28: An alternative clock system

Question seven

i Explain the difference between a *latch* and a *flip-flop*. What are the limitations of latches when used as 1-bit memories?

ii   Explain, in detail, the operation of the *edge-triggered D flip-flop* of Figure 5.24.

Chapter 6

Component level

6.1 Combinational system design

6.1.1 Boolean algebra

Specification

The behaviour of a purely combinational system must be determined by the specification of a *function*. If the system input and output *channels* are of *binary digital* form then we may regard each as a set of Boolean variables. Each output may thus be specified as a Boolean function of the input variables. It is simplest to generalize by specifying each output as a function of *all* input variables.

A	B	C	Q_1	Q_2	Q_3	Q_4
0	0	0	1	0	0	0
0	0	1	1	1	1	0
0	1	0	1	1	1	1
0	1	1	1	0	1	0
1	0	0	0	0	1	0
1	0	1	0	1	1	1
1	1	0	0	1	1	1
1	1	1	0	0	0	1

Table 6.1: Truth table for three input, and three output, variables

The easiest way to derive the function is to specify the *truth table*. On the left-hand side are written all permutations of the values of input variables. Given n input variables there will thus be 2^n rows. Columns correspond to the variables themselves. On the right-hand side are written the desired values for each output variable. Table 6.1

shows an example. Note that Q_1 is in fact only a function of A and is quite independent of B and C[1]. Q_2 is only a function of B and C and is independent of A[2]. Only Q_3 and Q_4 need be expressed as functions of all three input variables.

You should now pause for thought about the precise *meaning* of a truth table such as the one shown. Writing a "1" in a right-hand column indicates that the function value will be 1 *if* the input variables take the values found in the same row on the left-hand side. For example, $\{A, B, C\} = \{0, 0, 1\}$ is the first condition in the table upon which $Q_3 = 1$. The output variable is asserted given the truth of *any one* of the conditions. Hence the function may be defined by the Boolean expression formed from the *OR* of all of them.

The expression so formed is called the *standard sum of products*. Each product is called a *minterm*. Thus the specification of the Boolean function called Q_3 may be deduced from the truth table to be...

$$Q_3 = \bar{A}.\bar{B}.C + \bar{A}.B.\bar{C} + \bar{A}.B.C + A.\bar{B}.\bar{C} + A.\bar{B}.C + A.B.\bar{C}$$

Note that this is not the *simplest* expression of the function. Like arithmetic algebra, it is possible to *reduce* the number of terms and hence the number of gates needed to implement the system.

It is quite possible to draw up a table which represents the function as a *standard product of sums*. For some reason this does not appeal to intuition. Our minds seem to prefer to AND together variables and OR together terms.

Both the standard sum of products and the standard product of sums form equally valid expressions of the function. *DeMorgan's laws* may be used to interchange between the two.

Reduction

We now come to the first of three methods which may be employed to arrive at a useful design of a combinational logic system to meet a specification given by either...

- *Truth table*

- *Boolean function(s)*

Recursive absorption is the technique employed to reduce an expression. The aim is to reduce the number of primitive operations required to implement the specified function. This is obviously important in order to reduce both cost and complexity. Reducing complexity helps to improve reliability.

The following are perhaps the most useful transformations in reducing a standard sum of products...

---

[1] $Q_1 = \bar{A}$.
[2] $Q_2 = B \oplus C$.

$$
\begin{aligned}
A &= A + A \\
A.B + A.\bar{B} &= A \\
A + A.B &= A \\
A + \bar{A}.B &= A + B
\end{aligned}
$$

Examples

The reduction of Q_3 proceeds as follows. First we note down *all pairs of terms which differ in just one variable*. Numbering terms from left to right, these are...

- $\{1,5\}$

- $\{1,3\}$

- $\{2,6\}$

- $\{4,6\}$

Those terms which appear more than once in this list are *duplicated*, by using the *law of idempotence* $(X = X + X)$, until one copy exists for each pairing. Pairs are then combined to reduce the expression.

$$
\begin{aligned}
Q_3 &= \bar{A}.\bar{B}.C + \bar{A}.B.\bar{C} + \bar{A}.B.C + A.\bar{B}.\bar{C} + A.\bar{B}.C + A.B.\bar{C} \\
&= \bar{A}.\bar{B}.C + \bar{A}.\bar{B}.C + \bar{A}.B.\bar{C} + \bar{A}.B.C + A.\bar{B}.\bar{C} + A.\bar{B}.C + A.B.\bar{C} + A.B.\bar{C} \\
&= \bar{B}.C + B.\bar{C} + \bar{A}.C + A.\bar{C}
\end{aligned}
$$

In fact, some further simplification may be obtained by remembering that...

$$
X \oplus Y = \bar{X}.Y + X.\bar{Y}
$$

...yielding...

$$
\begin{aligned}
Q_3 &= (B \oplus C) + (A \oplus C) \\
&= A \oplus B \oplus C
\end{aligned}
$$

The disadvantages of this method of simplification are that it is not very easy to spot the term pairs (especially given many input variables) and that it is prone to error.

6.1.2   Karnaugh maps

Derivation

An alternative to presenting and manipulating information in *textual* form is to use a *graphical* one. Where information is broken into a number of classes, such as the values $\{0, 1\}$ of an output variable, a graphical form is usually much more effective.

The graphical alternative to a truth table or Boolean function is the *Karnaugh map*. A box is drawn for each state of the input variables and has a "1", "0" or "X" inscribed within it, depending on what is required of the output variable. "X" denotes that we *don't care!* In other words, each box represents a *possible minterm*. Each "1" inscribed represents an *actual minterm*, present in the expression.

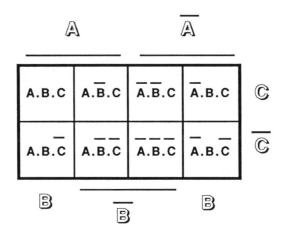

Figure 6.1: Karnaugh map for three variables

The *K-map* graph in fact wraps around from top to botom and from right to left. In reality it has a *toroidal* topology, like that of a doughnut. It must, however, be drawn in the fashion shown in Figure 6.1. A separate K-map must be drawn for each output variable. Figure 6.1 shows an example of a Karnaugh map for three input variables and thus has eight (2^3) boxes.

It is simple to derive a K-map from a truth table specification by transferring each 1 (minterm) into its appropriate box. The K-map makes the process of reduction much easier[3] because it renders as *neighbours* minterms differing in one variable only.

---

[3] ...for a human! This method is not suitable for automation.

Reduction

Each minterm is said to be an *implicant* of a function Q because it *implies* $Q = 1$. A *prime implicant* of Q is one such that the result of deleting a single *literal*[4] is *not* an implicant.

The minimal implementation of Q is the smallest sum of prime implicants which guarantees the specified function correct for all possible input configurations. Deducing prime implicants requires the reduction of terms which are *logically adjacent*, i.e. those which differ in just one variable. Groups of implicants of size 2^i are formed. The largest groups which it is possible to form are the prime implicants.

The procedure begins with isolated minterms. Groups are iteratively enlarged subject to the following rules. . .

1. *Group area must be 2^i where i is integer*

2. *Groups must be as large as possible*

3. *Groups must be as few as possible*

4. *Groups may overlap* only *if it enlarges at least one of them*

Sometimes this process yields a *unique* solution, sometimes it does not.

Examples

Figure 6.2 depicts the K-maps for Q_3 and Q_4 as specified in Table 6.1. In the case of Q_3, no group with more than two minterms is possible. The solutions depicted may be presented as Boolean expressions. . .

$$Q_3 \;=\; \bar{A}.C + A.\bar{B}. + B.\bar{C}$$
$$Q_3 \;=\; A.\bar{C} + \bar{B}.C + \bar{A}.B$$

Which of the two possible solutions *is* optimal (if any) will depend on practical circumstances[5].

Just one solution is possible for Q_4. . .

$$Q_4 = A.C + B.\bar{C}$$

---

[4] Variable or negated variable.
[5] e.g. existing availability of spare gates or sub-expressions.

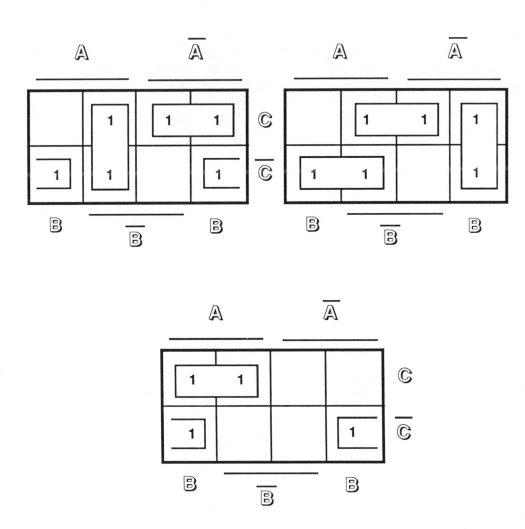

Figure 6.2: K-maps for Q_3 (upper) and Q_4 (lower)

Hazards

One potentially serious problem emerges from the physical nature of switches and hence logic gates. The finite *gate propagation delay*, together with the unsynchronized nature of communication between gates, gives rise to the possibility of momentarily *invalid* output.

Such *hazards* occur when a *single* variable appearing in a *pair* of prime implicants changes value. One becomes 0 as the other becomes 1. In any real physical system it is possible that, for a brief period, both will be 0.

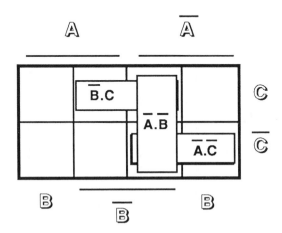

Figure 6.3: Karnaugh map elimination of a hazard

On a K-map potential hazards may be identified as *vertical or horizontal transitions* between prime implicant groups. The solution is to add a *redundant term* overlapping *both* groups as shown in Figure 6.3. This ensures that a valid implicant is asserted while the input variable makes its transition.

In practice hazards are just as likely to be caused by the (approximately) simultaneous change of *two* input variables which manifests itself as a *diagonal* transition between two prime implicant groups on the K-map. The solution is the same as before, to provide an extra overlapping implicant. However, this time it is only possible to do so if the extra minterms thus included are each "X" ("don't care").

Limitations

K-maps for more than three variables are possible. The form for four variables is shown in Figure 6.4. They become cumbersome for more than four or five variables. It becomes difficult to recognize logical adjacency by eye. They are, however, quick and easy for four variables or less. The method is not suitable for automation.

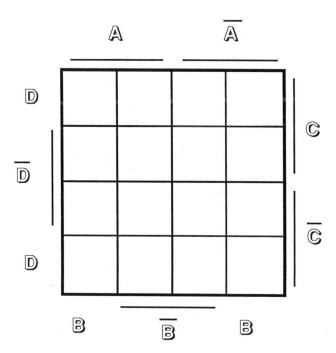

Figure 6.4: Karnaugh map for four variables

6.1.3 Quine-McCluskey

Reduction

This method is generally applicable to problems with large as well as small numbers of input variables. It is also suited to automation due to its *tabular*, rather than graphical, approach.

Minterms			Prime implicants		
A	B	C	A	B	C
1	1	0	1	★	0
1	0	1	★	1	0
0	1	1	1	0	★
1	0	0	★	0	1
0	1	0	0	1	★
0	0	1	0	★	1

Table 6.2: Quine-McCluskey reduction of Q_3

There are two phases, one of reduction to a complete set of prime implicants and a second to eliminate those which are unnecessary. The reduction phase begins by tabulation of minterms *according to the number of 1s*. Terms differing by just one variable are thus located nearby rendering them quick to find.

Minterms			Prime implicants		
A	B	C	A	B	C
1	1	1	1	★	1
1	1	0	1	1	★
1	0	1	★	1	0
0	1	0			

Table 6.3: Quine-McCluskey reduction of Q_4

A second table is derived, of prime implicants, where an asterisk replaces the literal which differs. Arrows may be added for each to indicate its "sponsors". Further reduction is often possible in the same way. It requires an asterisk in the same location in each of a pair of terms *and* just one literal differing between them. If such is possible a new table of further reduced terms is created. Several iterations of further reduction may be required. *QM reduction* is shown for Q_3 and Q_4 in Tables 6.2 and 6.3 respectively. A large number of reduced terms are deduced which are prime implicants but whose sum is definitely not minimal. You should verify for yourself that further reduction is impossible in the examples shown.

Minimization

Once the process of reduction has proceeded as far as possible, a minimal set of prime implicants must be selected. Not all prime implicants are necessary, in the sum, in order to assert all minterms required by the specification. A minimal set may be selected with comparative ease using a table of prime implicants (row) against minterms (column). A selection is made which is no larger than is necessary to provide a complete set of minterms. One method is to follow up a random initial selection avoiding those which duplicate a tick in a column already dealt with.

Prime implicants	Minterms			
	111	110	101	010
• 1 ⋆ 1	•		•	
• ⋆10		•		•
11⋆	•	•		

Table 6.4: Quine-McCluskey elimination of redundant terms for Q_4

The table and selection for Q_4 is shown first (Table 6.4) because it is simpler. A unique solution is possible as can be deduced through the use of a K-map.

Prime implicants	Minterms					
	110	101	011	100	010	001
• 1 ⋆ 0	•			•		
• ⋆10	•				•	
• 10⋆		•		•		
• ⋆01		•				•
• 01⋆			•		•	
• 0 ⋆ 1			•			•

Table 6.5: Quine-McCluskey elimination of redundant terms for Q_3

The table and selection for Q_3 (Figure 6.5) demonstrates the derivation of both solutions determined previously by K-map. One follows an initial selection of the topmost prime implicant, the other the bottom one. Each solution is arrived at quickly using the method mentioned above.

6.2 Sequential system design

6.2.1 Moore machines

State assignment

We begin this section with a brief recapitulation of the nature of a *Moore state machine*. Figure 5.13 shows that the internal state of the machine is updated by a functional mapping from a value input upon each tick of a clock. Values output are similarly derived and synchronously communicated.

The property which distinguishes the Moore machine from the Mealy machine is that output is strictly a function of state alone. It is decoupled from the input by the internal state. The consequences of this are primarily...

- *Moore machines generally require more state than Mealy machines*

- *They thus often tend to require more complicated excitation logic which is also slightly harder to design*

- *They are easier to understand intuitively since each input/output event directly corresponds to a unique state*

State machines are used within computers to cause some predetermined process to run upon receipt of a single simple instruction. The next and final chapter in this part of the book will demonstrate how they are used to execute a *stored program*, i.e. a sequence of instructions.

The example used below, to illustrate a logical approach to designing both Moore and Mealy state machines, turns this idea around. Instead of causing a sequence of events following a signal, we shall investigate how to cause a signal following receipt of a given sequence. In other words, the machine has to *recognize a pattern*. It illustrates some very important ideas which have wide technological application.

Any state machine may be designed using the logical approach employed here. The first thing to do is to *assign state*. This entails deciding just what events you wish to occur and in what order. Once that is decided, each state is given a label to provide a brief notation. It is sensible to include in the *state assignment table* a brief description of the event corresponding to each state. The number of states will dictate the number of flip-flops required.

Table 6.6 shows the state assignment table for the Moore state machine which is to detect (recognize) the bit string 1001. Since there are five states three flip-flops will be needed[6]. The binary representations of each state are completely arbitrary. It is easiest to simply fill that part of the table with a binary count, thus assuring that each state is unique. Here, each state is just a memory of events that have already occurred. In this instance they provide memory of various partial detections of the bit string sought.

---

[6]Recall that the number of flip-flops i must be such that $2^i \geq n$ where n is the number of states.

Label	State			Description
a	0	0	0	Nothing acquired
b	0	0	1	Leading 1 acquired
c	0	1	0	10 acquired
d	0	1	1	100 acquired
e	1	0	0	Sequence detected

Table 6.6: State assignment table for Moore sequence detector

State transition graph

The second step in the design process is to specify the *behaviour* of the machine. It is easier to do this graphically via a *state transition diagram*. This is a pictorial representation of the *state transition graph* in which states form the *nodes* and transitions form the *edges*. Figure 6.5 illustrates the state transition graph for the sequence detector. From the diagram it is easy to build up the *state transition table*.

State	Output	Next state	
		$x = 0$	$x = 1$
a	0	a	b
b	0	c	b
c	0	d	b
d	0	a	e
e	1	c	b

Table 6.7: State transition table for Moore sequence detector

Table 6.7 is a formal specification of the Moore version of the sequence detector. Unlike the output, the next state *does* depend on the current input. Hence there is a separate column for each possible value. On the diagram this is represented by two separate edges leaving each node, one for each input value.

State and output excitations

All that remains to be done now is to design the combinational logic which determines both output from current state and next state from current state and input.

By referencing back to the state assignment table it is possible to derive truth tables for the output, and for the input of each flip-flop, from the state transition table. Tables 6.8 and 6.9 are truth tables defining the required logic.

Because there are few variables input to the logic it is sensible to exploit the ease and speed of K-maps. The two needed to complete the design are shown in Figure 6.6.

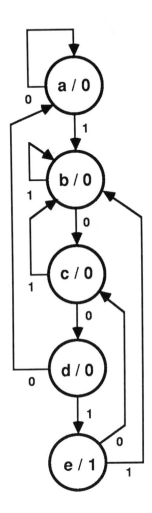

Figure 6.5: State transition graph for Moore sequence detector

Q_2	Q_1	Q_0	Y
0	0	0	0
0	0	1	0
0	1	0	0
0	1	1	0
1	0	0	1

Table 6.8: Truth table for output of Moore sequence detector

X	Q_2	Q_1	Q_0	D_2	D_1	D_0
0	0	0	0	0	0	0
0	0	0	1	0	1	0
0	0	1	0	0	1	1
0	0	1	1	0	0	0
0	1	0	0	0	1	0
1	0	0	0	0	0	1
1	0	0	1	0	1	1
1	0	1	0	0	0	1
1	0	1	1	1	0	0
1	1	0	0	0	0	1

Table 6.9: Truth table for flip-flop excitations for Moore sequence detector

Finally the reduced Boolean algebra specification for the combinational logic for a Moore state machine which detects the sequence 1001 is as follows...

$$
\begin{aligned}
D_2 &= X.\bar{Q}_2.Q_1.Q_0 \\
D_1 &= \bar{Q}_2.\bar{Q}_1.Q_0 + \bar{X}.Q_2.\bar{Q}_1.\bar{Q}_0 + \bar{X}.\bar{Q}_2.Q_1.\bar{Q}_0 \\
D_0 &= \bar{X}.Q_1.\bar{Q}_0 + \bar{X}.Q_2.\bar{Q}_1 + X.\bar{Q}_2.\bar{Q}_1.\bar{Q}_0 \\
Y &= Q_2
\end{aligned}
$$

6.2.2 Mealy machines

State assignment table

That which seems to add complication, namely the extra dependence of output upon input as well as state, very often simplifies design. The cost is that the Mealy machine (Figure 5.13) is a little less easy to intuitively understand.

The significant difference is that a distinct state representing the event of detection of the entire bit string is no longer necessary. We can rely on the state representing the

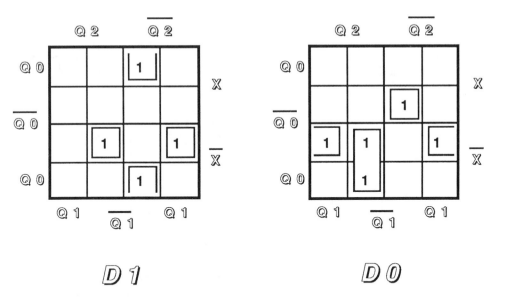

Figure 6.6: K-maps for Moore machine to detect the sequence 1001

detection of the first three bits. Once in this state the output can be configured so as to become asserted should the next value input be a 1. Thus the machine can detect the whole string with one less state. Table 6.10 shows the Mealy machine requirements.

In this instance, one less state allows the removal of one flip-flop. Although this may not seem a significant economy it represents a 20% reduction. Of greater importance is the simplification of the combinational logic design required. Removing a single flip-flop *halves* the size of the truth table and each K-map.

Label	State		Description
a	0	0	Nothing acquired
b	0	1	1 acquired
c	1	0	10 acquired
d	1	1	100 acquired

Table 6.10: State assignment table for Mealy sequence detector

State transition graph

The state transition graph is altered somewhat from that of the Moore machine as can be seen from the state transition diagram (Figure 6.7).

Output can no longer be associated with present state alone and thus cannot be depicted within a node as before. Because it is now associated with input, as well as present state, output must be depicted on *edges*.

State	Output		Next state	
	$x = 0$	$x = 1$	$x = 0$	$x = 1$
a	0	0	a	b
b	0	0	a	b
c	0	0	a	b
d	0	1	a	b

Table 6.11: State transition table for Mealy sequence detector

The state transition table (Table 6.11) appears a little more complicated, with the addition of an extra column specifying the precise dependency of output on input.

State and output excitations

A single truth table may now specify the combinational logic required since both flip-flop excitation and output are now functions of state *and* input (Table 6.12). Note that the two K-maps required are visibly simpler than before (Figure 6.8).

X	Q_1	Q_0	D_1	D_0	Y
0	0	0	0	0	0
0	0	1	1	0	0
0	1	0	1	1	0
0	1	1	0	0	0
1	0	0	0	1	0
1	0	1	0	1	0
1	1	0	0	1	0
1	1	1	0	1	1

Table 6.12: Truth table for output and flip-flop excitations of Mealy sequence detector

As expected the combinational logic required is also simplified...

$$D_1 = \bar{X}.\bar{Q}_1.Q_0$$

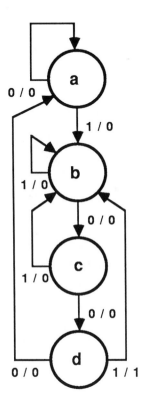

Figure 6.7: State transition graph for Mealy sequence detector

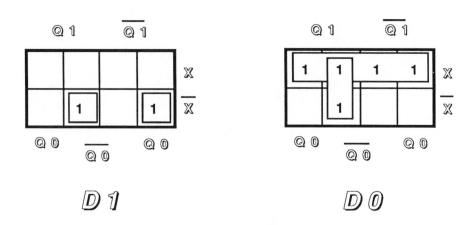

Figure 6.8: K-maps for Mealy machine to detect the sequence 1001

$$D_0 = X + Q_1.\bar{Q}_0$$
$$Y = X.Q_1.Q_0$$

6.2.3   Summary

There follows a brief summary of the process of designing a state machine. It applies equally to either Moore or Mealy types.

1. State assignment table: *Decide the events which are to occur and arbitrarily assign them binary states. Their number will dictate how many flip-flops are required.*

2. State transition diagram: *Decide, and specify pictorially, how you wish the system to behave.*

3. State transition table: *Tabulate the relationship of present state to next state and output.*

4. Truth tables for output & flip-flop excitation: *These are derived directly from state assignment table and state transition table.*

6.3 Components

6.3.1 Logic units

Introduction

Before we are in a position to discuss typical components of a contemporary computer architecture we must first discuss commonly used sub-components. Sometimes these form part of a component[7], sometimes they are found in the *"glue"* which joins components together. Only then will we approach the components themselves which may be divided into two categories...

- Registers *which hold and sometimes synchronously operate on data words*

- Logic units *which asynchronously operate on the contents of registers*

Several different types of register are discussed, some of which are capable of carrying out *operations* on data words and thus are of great assistance in implementing machine instructions.

Binary decoder

The first sub-component of interest is a system which *decodes* a binary value. By "decoding" is meant the assertion of a unique signal for each possible value input. Hence a 2-bit decoder has an input consisting of two signals, one for each bit of a binary word, and four separate outputs, one for each input value. Figure 6.9 shows a schematic diagram and Table 6.13 the truth table of a 2-bit decoder.

D_1	D_0	Q_3	Q_2	Q_1	Q_0
0	0				1
0	1			1	
1	0		1		
1	1	1			

Table 6.13: Truth table for a 2-bit binary decoder

Perhaps the most important use of decoders is in *bus communication*, which is treated fully later on in this book. For now it is enough to know that data signals for each bit in a data word are connected in common to, and thus *shared* by, a number of separate systems. They are collectively referred to as the *data bus*.

Each system on the bus has a unique *bus address*. The one which is to receive the data on any given communication event is dictated by the current address. Typically

---

[7]...such as the use of *multiplexers* in a *bidirectional shift register*.

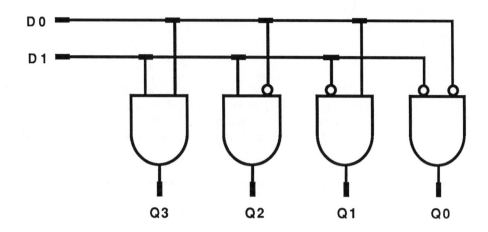

Figure 6.9: 2-bit binary decoder

the address will be *binary encoded* for efficiency. For example, if there are 256 systems, an address may be binary encoded using 8 ($\log_2 256$) signals instead of 256. A binary decoder is used to drive the *enable* inputs of each system from the address word. The decoder shown would be sufficient to select one of four systems from a 2-bit address.

The only alternative to employing an encoded address is to use a separate signal for each system. This will often prove prohibitive because of the number of connections required. The extra cost of the decoder required is often insignificant when compared to the cost of the alternative interconnections. However, the decoder takes time to operate which may degrade the performance of a system unacceptably. This represents a typical *cost vs. performance* design decision.

Binary encoder

It is sometimes necessary to *binary encode* the selection of one signal from a collection of them. The device shown in Figure 6.10 effectively does the reverse of a decoder. The diagram has been kept simple by showing only two bits. It should be fairly obvious how to extend the system. One OR gate is required for each output bit. Its truth table is shown in Table 6.14.

Each input bit which requires an output bit set is connected to the appropriate OR gate. For example, the gate for the LSB must have inputs connected to every alternate input bit so that the output LSB is set for all odd-valued inputs.

There exists two major problems with the simple system shown...

- Invalid output: *Should more than one input signal be active, output will be invalid*

D_3	D_2	D_1	D_0	Q_1	Q_0
			1	0	0
		1		0	1
	1			1	0
1				1	1

Table 6.14: Truth table for 2-bit binary encoder

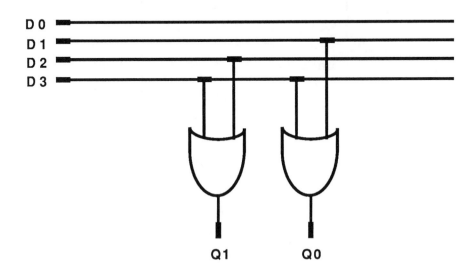

Figure 6.10: 2-bit binary encoder

- Ambiguity: *Identical output is achieved for both the least significant input signal active and no input signal active*

A simple solution would be to XOR all pairs of input lines to derive a *valid output signal*[8]. An alternative is to *prioritize inputs* and design the system so that the output is the consequence of the *highest priority* input. Such a system is referred to as a *priority encoder* and proves to be much more useful[9] than the simple system shown in Figure 6.10. The design of such a system is left as an exercise in combinational logic design.

---

[8] This may be achieved in parallel by 2^n XOR and one OR gates (fast but expensive) or in *ripple-through* fashion by $n - 1$ XOR gates (slow but cheap).

[9] e.g. to encode an *interrupt vector* in a *vectored interrupt system* (see Chapter 9).

Read-Only-Memory (ROM)

Read-Only-Memory is a contradiction in terms, or at least a description of something which would be totally useless. In truth the system described here is *Write-Once-Only-Memory* but the author does not seriously intend to challenge convention. Unfortunately, computer engineering is full of misleading (and sometimes downright wrong) terms.

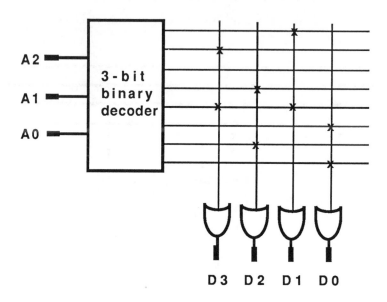

Figure 6.11: Read-Only-Memory (ROM) with 3-bit address and 4-bit data

A *ROM* may be thought of as a linear memory system which receives an address as its input and produces as output the data word "contained" in the "register" at that address. The width of address and data words form parameters of the system.

It may also be thought of as a *decoder/encoder system*. *Binary code* is used at the input. The code at the output is decided by the complete "memory contents". ROM is in fact implemented in this fashion, as shown in Figure 6.11.

As stated above, in order to be used as a memory, the system must be written at least once. ROM is written (once only) by *fusing links* between the inputs of the output gates and the output of the *address decoder*. EPROM[10] is a widely used *erasable and reprogrammable* ROM which allows multiple attempts to get the contents right!

Perhaps the most important use of ROM is as *non-volatile memory* for *bootstrapping* computers, i.e. giving them a program to run when they are first switched on. We will see

---

[10] Erasable Programmable ROM.

in the next chapter that ROM is also sometimes used in the implementation of *processor control units.*

Multiplexer (MUX)

The purpose of a *multiplexer* is to switch between channels. It is simply a *multi-way switch.* An example of a *MUX* is the channel selector on a television. The *source* of information for the channel to the system which builds images on the screen is switched between the many available TV broadcast channels. Its truth table is shown in Table 6.15 and schematic diagram in Figure 6.12.

S_1	S_0	Q
0	0	D_0
0	1	D_1
1	0	D_2
1	1	D_3

Table 6.15: Truth table for multiplexer (MUX) with four inputs

Another common use of a MUX is to share a single available channel between multiple sources. For example, there might be only a single telephone cable between two countries. Multiple telephone connections are possible over the single cable if a MUX is connected at the source and its inverse, a *DEMUX*, at the *sink.* The sources are rapidly switched in and out such that *packets* of each conversation are transmitted in sequence. The *DEMUX* must know this sequence in order to *route* each packet to the correct receiver. This is known as *time-multiplexing.* The users are unaware that only one *physical channel* exists. They are said to be exploiting *virtual channels.*

MUXs are used in computers for selecting one of a number of binary signals[11] or for sharing limited numbers of physical channels.

Demultiplexer (DEMUX)

A *DEMUX* performs the inverse function of the MUX. A single input value is routed to an output channel selected by the two *select* control inputs. Figure 6.13 shows the combinational logic required. Its truth table is shown in Table 6.16.

It was described above how a decoder might enable (switch on) a system selected from a number of others by an address. If all the systems are connected to a common data bus, only the one enabled will read or write a data word. This assumes *parallel* transmission of all data word bits.

Given serial transmission of a word, only *state transitions* infer any meaning. A DE-MUX may be used to route data to the currently addressed system simply by connecting

---

[11] ... as in the *bidirectional shift register.*

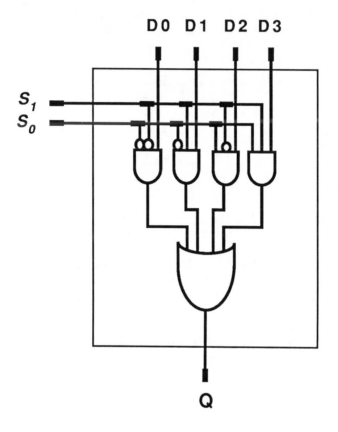

Figure 6.12: Multiplexer (MUX) with four inputs

D	S_1	S_0	Q_3	Q_2	Q_1	Q_0
d	0	0				d
d	0	1			d	
d	1	0		d		
d	1	1	d			

Table 6.16: Truth table for demultiplexer (DEMUX) with four outputs

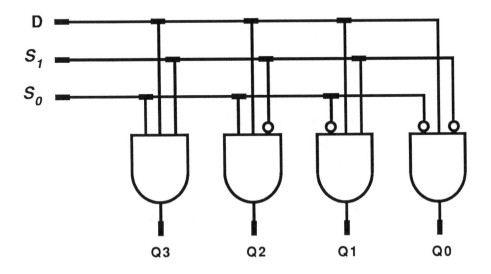

Figure 6.13: Demultiplexer (DEMUX) with four outputs

the address bits to its select control inputs. Refer back to the telephone example of time-multiplexing given above. Assuming the signal is digitally encoded, make an estimate of how rapidly the MUX and DEMUX must switch to form a useful speech communication system[12].

6.3.2 Arithmetic logic units

Half-adder

The truth table for 1-bit binary addition is shown in Table 6.17.

---

[12] For "hi-fi" sound quality approximately $50,000$ 12-bit samples of a microphone output must be transmitted per second.

A	B	S	C
0	0	0	0
0	1	1	0
1	0	1	0
1	1	0	1

Table 6.17: Truth table for half-adder

It is easily seen that 1-bit binary addition is equivalent to a XOR operation and that the carry may be generated by an AND. The system which performs a 1-bit binary addition with carry output is called a *half-adder* and is depicted in Figure 6.14.

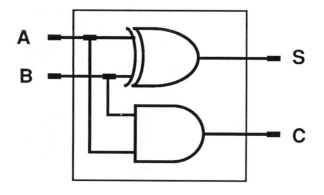

Figure 6.14: Half-adder

A half-adder cannot be used in the addition of multiple-bit words because it cannot add in a carry from the next less significant bit.

Full-adder

The *full-adder* adds one bit from each of two data words *and* an incoming carry. It is easily made from two half-adders. As is readily seen from the truth table below, the outgoing carry is the OR of the carry outputs from both half-adders. Figure 6.15 shows the complete combinational logic system of a full-adder. Its truth table is shown in Table 6.18.

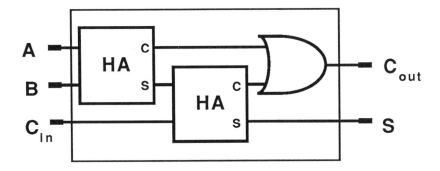

Figure 6.15: Full-adder

A_i	B_i	C_{i-1}	S_i	C_i
0	0	0	0	0
0	0	1	1	0
0	1	0	1	0
0	1	1	0	1
1	0	0	1	0
1	0	1	0	1
1	1	0	0	1
1	1	1	1	1

Table 6.18: Truth table for full-adder

Ripple-through arithmetic logic unit

Now it is time to confront the problem of how to combine full-adders in order to achieve arithmetic operations on data words.

Addition is simple. One full-adder is used for each bit of the result word. Each outgoing carry output is connected to the incoming carry input of the next most significant bit. The carry input of the LSB adder is connected to logic zero and the carry output of the MSB adder provides a signal to any interested system that a carry from the result word has occurred.

To *twos-complement negate* a word we need to *complement* and then *increment* it. Complementing is easy, we only need to XOR each bit with logic one. To increment we might use the adder described above, with the second word zero, and set the LSB carry input.

If we combine these ideas it is possible to design an *arithmetic logic unit (ALU)*, such as that shown in Figure 6.16, which can add or subtract *according to function control*

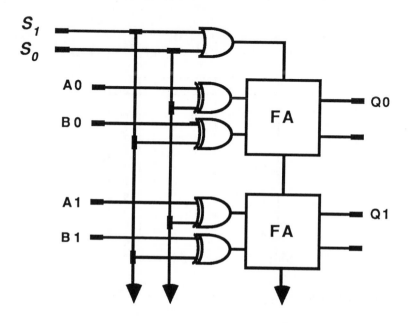

Figure 6.16: Ripple-through arithmetic unit

inputs. It is relatively easy to expand this system to get logic functions too. The one shown performs an operation according to its control inputs as shown in Table 6.19.

Select	Operation
00	$A + B$
01	$B - A$
10	$A - B$
11	*Not allowed!*

Table 6.19: Ripple ALU operations

There is but one serious disadvantage with this system. The result output will not be valid until the carry has rippled through from LSB to MSB. The time taken for this to finish would limit the speed of arithmetic computation. For this reason, although it is quite instructive, the ripple-through arithmetic unit is rarely used nowadays. There is a better way.

Look-ahead-carry (LAC) adder

When both data words are presented at the input of an adder all the necessary information is present to immediately compute both sum and carry. A *LAC* adder seeks to compute sum and carry independently and in a *bit-parallel* fashion.

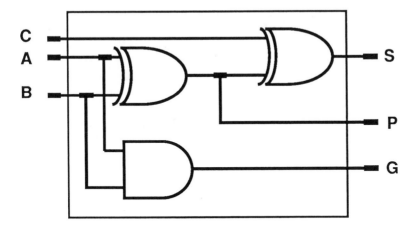

Figure 6.17: Look-Ahead-Carry (LAC) sum generator

If we study the logic required to generate both sum and carry for each bit of the result word we find a general specification possible. . .

$$S_i = A_i \oplus B_i \oplus C_{i-1}$$
$$C_i = A_i.B_i + C_{i-1}.(A_i \oplus B_i)$$

Note that the specification of C_i is *recursive*. If we wish to compute C_i without first waiting for C_{i-1} to be computed we must obviously expand the specifying expression. The terms which may be evaluated in *bit-parallel* fashion are called *generate* and *propagate* and are denoted by G_i and P_i respectively. They may be specified via. . .

$$G_i = A_i.B_i$$
$$P_i = A_i \oplus B_i$$

Sum and carry are thus generated via. . .

$$S_i = P_i.C_{i-1}$$
$$C_i = G_i + P_i.C_{i-1}$$

Figure 6.17 shows the logic for the system which replaces the full-adder, in the arithmetic unit, for generating the sum. A separate system to generate carry must also be included for each bit of the result word. Figure 6.18 shows the schematic for the logic required. The products may be generated merely by adding an extra input to the AND gate for each term. A complete 4-bit *LAC adder* is shown in Figure 6.19.

LAC adders, as shown, may be connected together so that the carry output of each is connected to the subsequent carry input. The final carry output relies on its predecessors carry values *rippling through*. It is however possible to design a multiple-bit LAC adder which allows for larger scale carry generation. In addition to the sum outputs *group generate* and *group propagate* outputs are generated, formed from the G_i and P_i. These are then used as inputs to a carry generator as before to generate, bit-parallel, the carry inputs to each adder and the final carry output. The deduction of these combinational functions is left as an exercise.

6.3.3   Registers

Data register

A *register* is simply a collection of flip-flops wide enough to contain one complete word of data. Registers are *read* onto, and *written* from, a data bus, which is of width equal to that of the registers themselves. Some means must be provided to enable the connection of any one particular register to the bus and to ensure that it either reads or writes the bus *but not both simultaneously*.

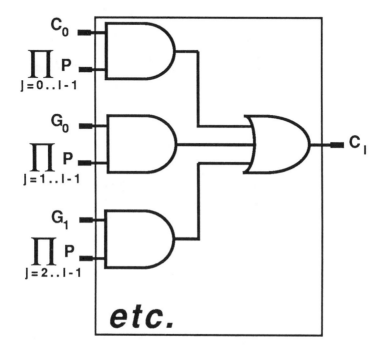

Figure 6.18: Look-Ahead-Carry (LAC) carry generator

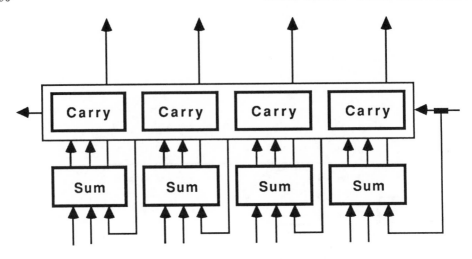

Figure 6.19: 4-bit LAC adder

The gates connected between the flip-flop outputs and the bus may be regarded merely as switches. Their connection to the bus is said to form a *tristate* channel because *three* different events may occur upon each clock tick...

- *Logic 1 passed*

- *Logic 0 passed*

- *Nothing passed (Flip-flop completely disconnected from bus)*

The need for *tristate buffering* is clear. Without it the outputs of a register may be connected via the bus to the outputs of another, leaving the state of the bus (and hence the inputs of any third register enabled for reading) undecided. Figure 6.20 shows the two least significant flip-flops of a *data register* and their *direct* input, and *tristate* output, connection to the data bus.

The data register is one of the most common components of contemporary computers. Its function, on any clock tick, may be defined by *previously* setting or clearing the following control inputs...

- *R/W (Read/Write)*

- *En (Enable)*

R/W means "read not write" when set and therefore "write not read" when clear. It is standard practice to refer to control signals by their function *when asserted*. *En* serves to decide whether a read or write operation is to be allowed or not. Remember that,

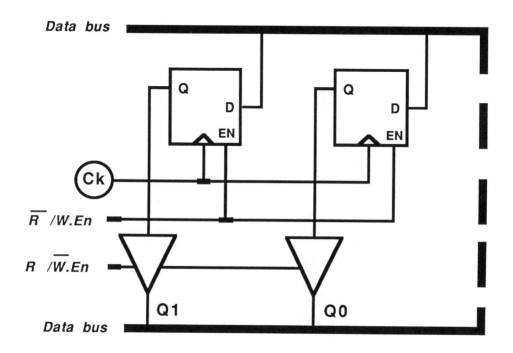

Figure 6.20: Data register

unlike the data inputs, control inputs are *asynchronous*. They must be set up *prior* to
the clock tick when the operation is required.

Bi-directional shift register

We now progress to consider registers which are capable of *operating* on the data they
contain.

The *bidirectional shift register* is capable of *shifting* its data right or left by one bit
each clock tick. Each flip-flop input is connected via a MUX to one or other of the
following. . .

- *The output of itself*

- *The output of the next flip-flop to the right*

- *The appropriate bit of the data bus*

- *The output of the next flip-flop to the left*

. . . according to the value of the MUX select inputs, which form the control inputs
to the register. As well as shifting data right or left, the bidirectional shift register can
read and write the data bus. A schematic diagram is shown in Figure 6.21.

Flip-flops at each end of the register are able to read from an external source, which
may then be shifted further through the word. The external source may be a data source
external to the computer in the form of a *serial channel*. If the two ends are connected
together the shift operation is then known as *register rotation*.

Select	Operation
00	Retain state and read
01	Shift right
10	Write
11	Shift left

Table 6.20: Bidirectional shift register operations

The control inputs to the bidirectional shift register are two MUX select bits. . .

- S_0

- S_1

. . . whose effect is summarized in Table 6.20.

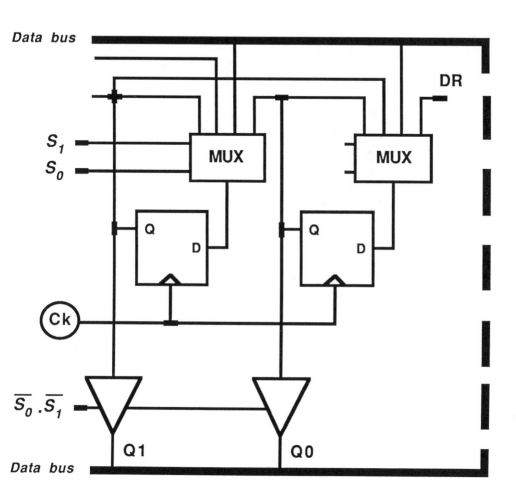

Figure 6.21: Bidirectional shift register

Up/down counter

Now consider the design of a register which is capable of *counting* up or down in binary.
As we shall see in the next chapter, such a register is very useful indeed in the design of
a processor.

A counter is a state machine since it has state which varies in a controlled manner.
We shall consider a Moore machine design. Real counters have *finite state* and hence can
only count from 0 up to M-1, where M is the modulus of the register (2^N for a register
of width N). In order not to obscure an example with unnecessary detail, we shall follow
the design of a *modulo-8 counter*[13].

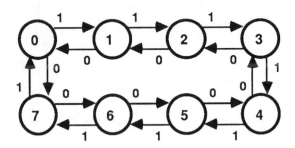

Figure 6.22: State transition graph for modulo-8 up/down counter

There is no need for a state assignment table since we know there are eight states and
will choose to label them by decimal enumeration. Figure 6.22 shows the state transition
diagram for a Moore state machine with a single input, U, which decides the direction
of count. Notice that the state returns to 0 after reaching 7. From this we deduce the
state transition table, Table 6.21. Having chosen to use T flip-flops, a truth table may
be deduced for the flip-flop inputs (Table 6.22).

It is quite sufficient to employ K-maps in the design of the *count logic* since only four
input variables need be considered. Figure 6.23 gives them for the excitation logic for the
two most significant bit flip-flops. It is obvious from the truth table that $T_0 = 1$[14]. From
this observation and the K-maps we conclude that the combinational logic required for
a modulo-8 up/down counter may be specified via. . .

$$
\begin{aligned}
T_2 &= \bar{U}.\bar{Q}_1.\bar{Q}_0 + U.Q_1.Q_0 \\
T_1 &= \bar{U}.\bar{Q}_0 + U.Q_0 \\
T_0 &= 1
\end{aligned}
$$

---

[13] This is another useful example of the design of a *state machine.*
[14] The LSB always toggles as the count alternates between odd and even.

State			Next state					
			$U = 0$			$U = 1$		
Q_2	Q_1	Q_0	Q_2	Q_1	Q_0	Q_2	Q_1	Q_0
0	0	0	1	1	1	0	0	1
0	0	1	0	0	0	0	1	0
0	1	0	0	0	1	0	1	1
0	1	1	0	1	0	1	0	0
1	0	0	0	1	1	1	0	1
1	0	1	1	0	0	1	1	0
1	1	0	1	0	1	1	1	1
1	1	1	1	1	0	0	0	0

Table 6.21: State transition table for Moore modulo-8 up/down counter

If you are wide awake you just might have noticed something very useful. It is possible to rewrite the expression for T_2 as...

$$
\begin{aligned}
T_2 &= (\bar{U}.\bar{Q}_0 + U.Q_0).(\bar{U}.\bar{Q}_1 + U.Q_1) \\
&= T_1.(\bar{U}.\bar{Q}_1 + U.Q_1)
\end{aligned}
$$

... which suggests a *recursive* derivation of T_i, which is not surprising given a little thought.

When counting up, a bit only toggles when all less significant bits are *set*. When counting down, a bit only toggles when all less significant bits are *clear*, i.e....

$$
\begin{aligned}
T_i^{up} &= \prod_{0 \le j < i} Q_j \\
&= T_{i-1}.Q_{i-1}
\end{aligned}
$$

$$
\begin{aligned}
T_i^{down} &= \prod_{0 \le j < i} \bar{Q}_j \\
&= T_{i-1}.\bar{Q}_{i-1}
\end{aligned}
$$

It is simple to combine these to yield the combinational logic specified above for the up/down counter shown in Figure 6.24. The count logic may be specified *via* recursion as...

$$
\begin{aligned}
T_{i \ge 1} &= T_{i-1}.(\bar{U}.\bar{Q}_1 + U.Q_1) \\
T_0 &= 1
\end{aligned}
$$

U	Q_2	Q_1	Q_0	T_2	T_1	T_0
0	0	0	0	1	1	1
0	0	0	1	0	0	1
0	0	1	0	0	1	1
0	0	1	1	0	0	1
0	1	0	0	1	1	1
0	1	0	1	0	0	1
0	1	1	0	0	1	1
0	1	1	1	0	0	1
1	0	0	0	0	0	1
1	0	0	1	0	1	1
1	0	1	0	0	0	1
1	0	1	1	1	1	1
1	1	0	0	0	0	1
1	1	0	1	0	1	1
1	1	1	0	0	0	1
1	1	1	1	1	1	1

Table 6.22: T flip-flop excitations for modulo-8 up/down counter

One further useful observation may be made. Should $T_0 = 0$ counting would *cease* since all subsequent T inputs are effectively combined via *conjunction* (AND) with T_0. Hence we may utilize T_0 as an *enable* input. When it is asserted the counter counts up or down according to the value of U, otherwise it simply maintains its state.

Lastly, it must be said that JK flip-flops could have been used with J and K inputs connected together (at least when counting). Toggle flip-flops simply make the design of counters easier and more natural[15].

Counters are extremely important to the construction of computers and related systems. They represent a means of *generating states* which is relatively easy to understand intuitively. They have very many uses outside the world of computers as well.

To summarize, the control inputs to the up/down counter are...

- U

- *En*

- *Clr*

U determines the direction of count (1 $\Rightarrow$ up). *En* enables counting when set and disables it when clear. *Clr* clears the whole register to zero.

---

[15] An isolated T flip-flop is itself a *modulo-2* counter!

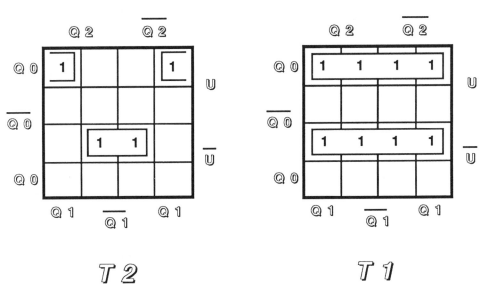

Figure 6.23: K-maps for modulo-8 up/down counter

Active register

The final register considered here (Figure 6.25) forms a very powerful system at the cost of a fairly high degree of complexity. It combines an *up/down counter* with a *data register* to yield a register which could relieve much of the processing burden from an arithmetic unit. Use of several of them would allow exploitation of *word parallelism* by allowing several words to be processed simultaneously.

It is possible to extend the register to include *shift* and *rotate* operations as well through the addition of a MUX for each bit. This might be of assistance in implementing a multiply instruction.

The control inputs for the active register are summarized below *(only one control input is allowed asserted upon any single clock tick!)*...

- *Increment*
- *Decrement*
- *Read*

- *Write*
- *Zero*
- *Complement*

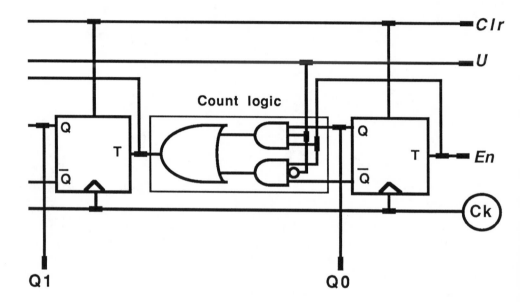

Figure 6.24: Up/down counter register

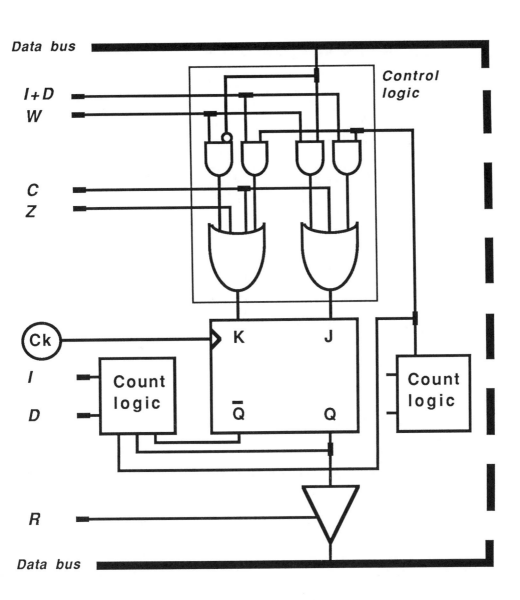

Figure 6.25: Active register with several control inputs

Exercises

Question one

Derive a *combinational logic* design for the two truth functions specified in Table 6.23 using each of. . .

1. *Boolean algebra recursive absorption*

2. *Karnaugh map simplification*

3. *Quine-McCluskey minimization*

A	B	C	Q_1	Q_2
0	0	0	0	0
0	0	1	0	1
0	1	0	0	0
0	1	1	1	1
1	0	0	0	0
1	0	1	1	0
1	1	0	1	1
1	1	1	1	1

Table 6.23: Truth tables for question one

Question two

i   Prove using truth tables, and then Boolean algebra, that two half-adders and an OR gate may be used to implement a *full-adder*.

ii   Using Boolean algebra, derive the combinational logic for a 4-bit adder with *look-ahead carry* generation.

iii   Show how two 4-bit adders with look-ahead carry may be combined to yield an eight bit adder with *full* look-ahead carry (i.e. no ripple through between adders).

Question three

A *linear memory map* is a *one dimensional* array of *data registers* whose index is known as an *address*. The address appears as a binary word on a channel known as an *address bus*. The data, read or written, appears on a channel known as a *data bus*.

Using a memory map of only eight words as an example, show how a *binary decoder* may be used to derive the *enable* input of each data register from the address.

Question four

i *Binary coded decimal (BCD)* representation often proves useful because of the human preference for decimal representation. Show, using examples, how you think such a code is implemented.

ii Design a one (decimal) digit BCD up-counter.

Question five

Design a *4-input priority encoder*. Output consists of two binary digits plus a *valid output* signal.

Chapter 7

Control units

7.1 Function of the control unit

7.1.1 Processor organization

Internal communication

In Chapter 3 the organization of a processor was presented from the *programmer* or *compiler* perspective. This consisted of a number of *special registers*, which were reserved for a specific purpose, and a file of *general purpose registers*, used for the manipulation of data. Now we are to be concerned with processor organization from the machine perspective.

There are a number of ways in which a processor may be organized for efficient computation. The subject will be treated in detail later in the book. In order to discuss the function of the *processor control unit* it is necessary to consider some fundamental ideas of the subject.

A processor may be pictured as a collection of registers, all of which communicate together via an *internal data bus*[1] and share a common *word width*. Each register is connected to the bus for...

- *Read*

- *Write*

...operations.

Connecting registers onto the bus is very much like *plumbing*. The *read* and *write* register control inputs act to turn on or off valves as shown in Figure 7.1.

The control inputs of all processor registers collectively form part of the *internal control bus* of the processor. It is this which allows the implementation of a protocol for

---

[1] If the technology is electrical, each data bus bit-channel may simply be a conductor.

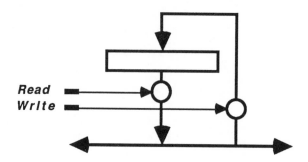

Figure 7.1: Plumbing in of a processor register

the communication between registers. To transmit a value from one register to another the read input of the sender and the write input of the receiver must be asserted, as shown in Figure 7.2. Note that communication may be...

- *One-to-one (Point-to-point)*

- *One-to-many (Broadcast)*

The control bus is usually omitted from diagrams since it adds clutter and conveys little information. One must simply remember that *all* registers have control inputs.

The problem for the graphic artist is unfortunately shared by the design engineer. Current technology is essentially restricted to *two dimensions*. A third dimension is necessary in order to connect registers to both data and control bus[2]. Use of a third dimension is currently expensive and hence must somehow be minimized. One way to picture a processor is as three planes (Figure 7.3). The middle one contains the registers, the others the control and data buses. Connections are made, from buses to registers, from the appropriate outer plane to the inner one. It is the function of the control unit to cause the correct internal control bus signals to be asserted through each clock cycle.

The fact that executing any given machine instruction requires a *sequence* of events is almost wholly the result of all communication internal to the processor sharing a *single* communication channel in the form of the internal data bus. Full connectivity, where every register is connected to every other, would allow execution of any instruction within a single clock cycle.

Logic units

In addition to registers the processor also contains combinational logic components such as the *arithmetic logic unit (ALU)*. These systems possess *asynchronous* inputs and

---

[2] If the system is electrical short circuits would otherwise result.

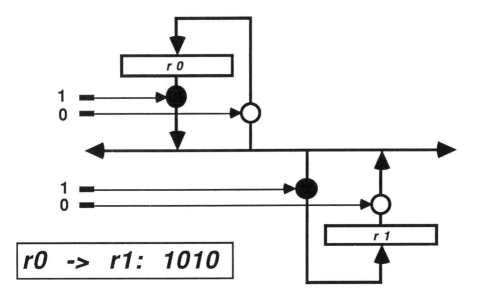

Figure 7.2: Register to register bus communication

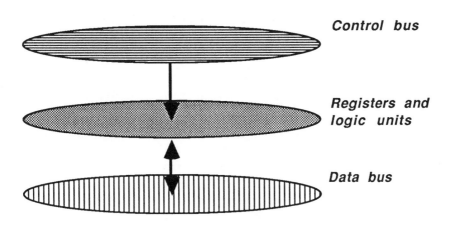

Figure 7.3: Bus plane register connection

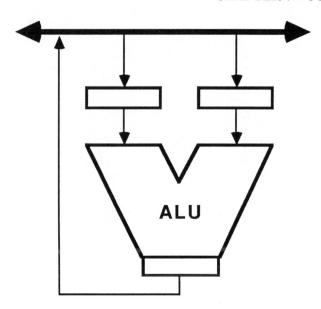

Figure 7.4: Connection of a combinational logic component to internal data bus

outputs whose values must be communicable to any chosen register. There is clearly a problem here. The solution is simply to connect data registers on the internal bus such that register outputs are permanently connected to logic unit inputs and register inputs permanently connected to logic unit outputs as shown in Figure 7.4. The control inputs to combinational logic components make up the rest of the internal control bus.

External communication

In the strict sense, any system which may be characterized by a *process* may be referred to as a *processor*. Within a computer the term is usually taken to mean any device which executes a program. The program in machine language may be thought of as a process description or *procedure*.

No processor will be *useful* unless it can communicate with *external processors* (for example the user). Hence every useful processor must contain at least one component capable of external communication. It is quite possible to imagine a processor with a sufficient quantity of registers to hold both...

- *Program*

- *Data*

Unfortunately, there are serious practical problems with this approach. Firstly, the width of the control bus grows in direct proportion to the size of memory and quickly becomes unmanageable. Secondly, it is by no means obvious how data may be *bound* to their location or how instructions might be conveniently sequenced. Contemporary computers separate memory and (programmable) processor. A single memory is used for *both* program and data.

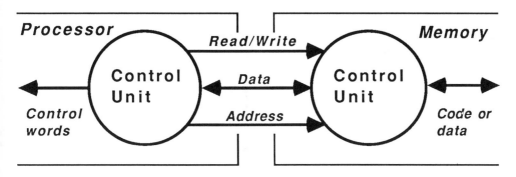

Figure 7.5: Processor to memory communication channels

It is advantageous to consider the activities of both processor and memory each as a process when considering *processor to memory communication* (Figure 7.5). The *bandwidth* of a channel is a measure of the frequency of communication transactions it can support. The bandwidth of the processor to memory communication channel largely limits performance in any computer.

The processor to memory channel is typically made up of data, address and control buses. The protocol includes synchronization (with respect to a clock) and a means of establishing the direction of communication[3]. The combinational logic component which implements this protocol is usually called the *bus control unit (BCU)*.

7.1.2 Machine language interpretation

Microcode

We have established above that the control unit is responsible for generating the correct sequencing of the control signals which make up the control bus.

In a *programmable* processor, the correct sequencing is determined by the program. The program is itself a sequence of instructions. The control unit must cause the correct sequence of *control words* to be output onto the control bus to execute each instruction.

---

[3] A detailed description of the operation of external bus communication may be found in Part III.

Because they are sequenced just like instructions, they may be thought of as *micro-instructions* and any sequence of them as *microcode*. The sequence of events they bring about may be termed a *microprocess*. Each event is termed a *micro-operation*.

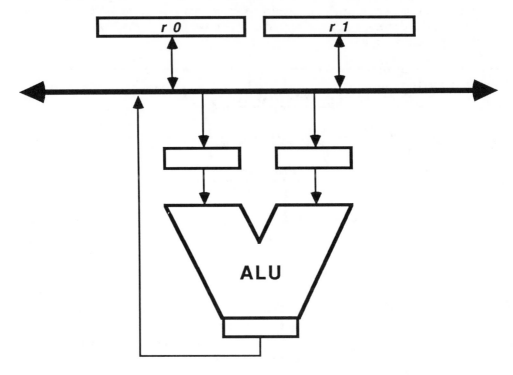

Figure 7.6: Simple example of processor architecture

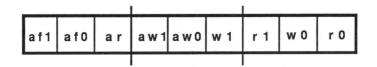

Figure 7.7: Possible micro-instruction format

A micro-instruction, at its simplest, is just a control word placed on the internal control bus which causes a micro-operation to be performed. The *micro-instruction format* is then just the arrangement of control signals within the control word. For example, an architecture which has just...

- *Two data registers with read/write control inputs r1, w1, r0, w0*

- *Arithmetic unit with control inputs af1, af0...*

- *... and register control inputs aw1, aw0, ar*

...as shown in Figure 7.6, might have a *micro-instruction format* as shown in Figure 7.7.

The correct *microprocess* for a given instruction must be determined. A signal is required to *trigger* the correct one for each instruction. These signals are generated as the result of *instruction decoding*.

Instruction format

An *instruction format* comprises a number of distinct fields, each containing a binary code as follows...

- *Opcode*

- *Addressing modes*

"Opcode" is an abbreviation of "operation code" and encodes the operation to be performed. Although all operations required may have a code, not all codes may correspond to operations. There must be one addressing mode field for each operand which describes how the control unit may fetch it. Some addressing modes imply an *instruction extension* such as an memory address, offset from special register or even the operand itself.

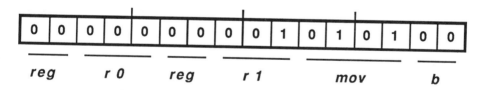

Figure 7.8: Instruction format for a NS32000 register move

As an example, the format of a register move instruction for the *National Semiconductor 32000* processor, is shown in Figure 7.8. From right to left we have the following fields...

- *2-bit operand size (byte)*

- *4-bit opcode (move)*

- *5-bit destination addressing mode (register)*

- *5-bit source addressing mode (register)*

The addressing mode field may be further broken down. The most significant two bits being zero indicates register mode, and the remaining bits binary encode *which* register.

State generation

We have now established that the control unit must *decode* instructions and generate a sequence of *micro-instructions*, or *control words*, for each one in order to bring about the appropriate *microprocess*. We now turn to how the necessary *state generation* may be achieved.

Each micro-instruction corresponds to a state of the internal control bus. Some of these states may be repeated as the microprocess runs, so fewer states than events may suffice. Nor is it necessary to generate a control word directly. In each case it will be found that the majority of the signals will not be asserted (i.e. are 0) which suggests that to do so would be inefficient. The designer need only enumerate the *distinct* states required and design a state machine to cause these to occur in the sequence required. Control words are then *decoded* from each state. Other approaches are possible as we shall see in the next section.

State decoding

Each control bus state must be decoded from the flip-flop states of the state machine. This is rendered fairly easy usually, despite the fact that the control word is often very wide and few states are required per instruction, because most signals in the control word are typically not asserted. The general form of a control unit is thus that shown in Figure 7.9.

7.1.3 Fetch/execute process

Microprocesses

The operation of any computer may be described as the execution of the following procedure...

```
REPEAT
    fetch instruction
    execute instruction
UNTIL FALSE
```

The loop forms the *fetch/execute process*, iteratively (or recursively) defined in terms of the loop body which is traditionally known as the *fetch/execute cycle*, which may be expanded into four microprocesses...

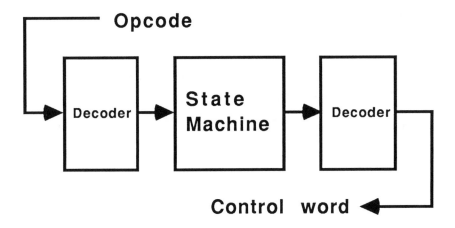

Figure 7.9: General form of a control unit

```
REPEAT
  fetch instruction
  fetch operands
  execute instruction
  IF interrupt.signalled THEN interrupt
UNTIL FALSE
```

Fetch instruction

Any microprocess may be reduced to a number of events, expressed using a *register transfer language (RTL)*. We shall continue to use the RTL introduced in Chapter 3. *Instruction fetch* reduces to...

$$
\begin{array}{lllll}
(1) & EAR & \leftarrow & PC \\
(2) & DIR & \leftarrow & Mem, & BCU(read) \\
(3) & IR & \leftarrow & DIR, & PC(increment)
\end{array}
$$

This assumes a processor organization with the following functional unit and registers, of which only the PC would be of concern to the machine language programmer,...

$$
\begin{array}{rcl}
BCU & \equiv & Bus\ control\ unit \\
PC & \equiv & Program\ counter \\
EAR & \equiv & Effective\ address\ register\ of\ BCU \\
DIR & \equiv & Data\ in\ register\ of\ BCU \\
IR & \equiv & Instruction\ register
\end{array}
$$

The first micro-operation copies the contents of the PC into the EAR. Subsequently, upon a *read* command, the BCU copies the contents of the memory location, whose address is in the EAR, into the DIR. It is assumed here that both BCU and memory operate fast enough that the instruction at the address in the EAR arrives in the DIR on the the next clock tick so that the final operation can then go ahead and copy it into the IR, ready for execution. At the same time, the PC is incremented to point to the next instruction to be fetched.

Note the parallelism by *division of function* made possible by the fact that the PC can increment itself without the need to be transferred to an *arithmetic logic unit (ALU)*. Only three clock-cycles are therefore needed.

Fetch operand

Operands may be classified according to their location, i.e. they belong to one or other *storage class*. Typical storage classes are...

- *Program memory*
- *Register*
- *Workspace*

It is useful to distinguish the *basic instruction* from *instruction extensions*. The basic instruction is fetched first and contains the *opcode* and *addressing modes* for all operands.

When each addressing mode in the instruction is decoded it may signal the start of a subsequent microprocess which fetches the corresponding operand from memory. For example, given *immediate addressing*, where the operand resides in *program memory*, the following microprocess will run...

$$(1) \quad EAR \quad \leftarrow \quad PC$$
$$(2) \quad DIR \quad \leftarrow \quad Mem, \quad BCU(read), \quad PC(increment)$$

The microprocess required to load a *direct addressed* workspace operand is slightly different...

$$(1) \quad EAR \quad \leftarrow \quad PC$$
$$(2) \quad DIR \quad \leftarrow \quad Mem, \quad BCU(read), \quad PC(increment)$$
$$(3) \quad EAR \quad \leftarrow \quad DIR$$
$$(4) \quad DIR \quad \leftarrow \quad Mem, \quad BCU(read)$$

The first two steps load the address, which is assumed to be an instruction extension, following the basic instruction in program memory. *Indirect addressing* requires repeating steps 3 and 4 once for each level of indirection. After indirection, DIR is in exactly the same state as for direct addressing.

Register addressing is very efficient because operand fetch cycles are not required. The full specification of the operand location may be encoded within the addressing mode field of the basic instruction itself. No (slow) transaction with external memory need take place. The operand may be copied directly to the destination required by the opcode.

Execute instruction

Their will be one unique *execute microprocess* for each opcode. The extent to which this is separate from *operand fetch* microprocesses depends very much on implementation[4].

A very simple example of an execute microprocess is that implementing the register move instruction of Figure 7.8. Only a single micro-operation (register transfer) is required.

$$(1) \quad r1 \quad \leftarrow \quad r0$$

A slightly more interesting example is that of adding the contents of two registers and placing the result in one of them. The microprocess for this operation, given the architecture shown in Figure 7.6, is as follows...

$$
\begin{array}{llll}
(1) & au.i0 & \leftarrow & r0 & & 021_8 \\
(2) & au.i1 & \leftarrow & r1, & ALU\,(add) & 244_8 \\
(3) & r0 & \leftarrow & au.o & & 102_8 \\
\end{array}
$$

Given the micro-instruction format of Figure 7.7, it is microcoded as shown on the right-hand side.

Conditional branch instructions require microprocesses where *selection* of microoperation is required. *Condition signals*, which represent processor state, are used to make the selection. Selection is between either...

- *Control signals asserted*

- *Sequence of micro-operations*

Just the control signals asserted upon inspection of the conditione may differ *or* the subsequent sequence itself.

Interrupt

It is usually necessary for the processor to be capable of switching between a number of distinct processes upon receipt of appropriate signals. Each process generates its own signal demanding attention. These signals are known as *interrupt requests* since they each ask the processor to *interrupt* the process currently running.

---

[4]In some architectures, any addressing mode may be used with (almost) any operation. Such an architecture is referred to as *symmetric*.

The processor itself may be considered as a process receiving *interrupt requests* and whose state changes according to the current running process. Switching between processes is termed *alternation*. A useful analogy is that of a person playing several chess games concurrently. When ready, an opponent signals the "multi-player" who must then switch to that game until some other opponent transmits a similar signal. The "multi-player" must however always finish a move before responding to a new signal.

Processors often manage using a single interrupt request signal allowing only two processes and hence just two programmed procedures. The procedure which is switched in, following receipt of an interrupt request, is called an *interrupt routine* and must have a start address known to the processor. It is usually either a fixed value or contained in an internal special register.

The arrival of an interrupt request is recorded as a bit in the *processor status register* which is interrogated after the execute microprocess, at the start of the *interrupt microprocess*. If set then the following (fixed) microprocess is executed...

$$
\begin{aligned}
&(1) \quad EAR \;\leftarrow\; SP \\
&(2) \quad DOR \;\leftarrow\; PC, \qquad SP(increment) \\
&(3) \quad Mem \;\leftarrow\; DOR, \quad BCU(write) \\
&\qquad\quad PC \;\leftarrow\; INT
\end{aligned}
$$

The following extra processor registers are used...

$$
\begin{aligned}
SP \;&\equiv\; \textit{Stack pointer (see Chapter 1)} \\
DOR \;&\equiv\; \textit{Data out register of BCU} \\
INT \;&\equiv\; \textit{Interrupt routine address register}
\end{aligned}
$$

The contents of the PC are first saved at a known location, usually the top of a stack located by a special register *SP*. Subsequently the contents of another special register *(INT)*, containing the address of the *interrupt routine*, are copied into the PC. Program execution proceeds from there.

7.2 Implementation

7.2.1 Introduction

There are three functional components to a control unit...

- *Opcode decoding*

- *State generation*

- *State decoding*

There are traditionally three ways to implement a control unit according to method of *state generation*...

- *Minimum state*

- *Shift register*

- *Counter*

Each method tends to dictate how *opcode decoding* (to trigger state generation) and *state decoding* (to derive control word) are carried out.

Timing requires careful consideration. The control word must be ready *before* each operation is to take place. Each processor component must have the correct values at its *control inputs* before a clock tick causes it to execute an operation. This is easiest to implement if we distinguish two clocks ("tick" and "tock") which *interleave*. We need use just a single oscillating bistable system as before to generate instead a *two-phase clock* where alternate state changes form each phase (Figure 7.10). The two phases might be termed...

- *Command phase*

- *Operation phase*

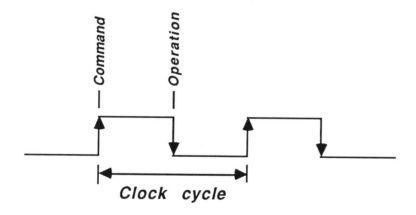

Figure 7.10: Command and operation clock phases

The implementation of control units is a large and complicated subject with many areas which are subject to fashion, preference and current technological capabilities as well as rapidly advancing knowledge and rapidly changing application. This section is thus intended only as a brief introduction. A more thorough coverage may be found in [Hayes 88].

7.2.2   Minimum state method

Sequencing

The first means of state generation to be considered here is the *minimum state* method.
This is the standard method, discussed in the previous chapter for the design of *state
machines*. It may be summarized as follows...

1. *Enumerate and label required states in a state assignment table*

2. *Define behaviour via state transition graph represented first by diagram, then by
   table*

3. *Design combinational logic for outputs and flip-flop excitation*

Where a fixed sequence of states is required, usually only a single input signal is needed
which triggers execution. Once the first state is attained, the *microprocess* continues until
termination. The exception to this occurs when the design calls for an instruction to be
interruptible. A second *(interrupt request)* input will then be required which must cause
execution to be *aborted* and an interrupt microprocess to start.

Here is an example of the design of a control unit to implement the single instruction...

add r0, r1

...which was discussed in the previous section.

First we must decide and label the necessary states in the *state assignment table*
(Table 7.1).

Label	State	Micro-operation		
a	00		*Inactive*	
b	01	$au.i0$	$\leftarrow$	$r0$
c	10	$au.i1$	$\leftarrow$	$r1,$ alu(add)
d	11	$r0$	$\leftarrow$	$au.o$

Table 7.1: State assignment table for add instruction control unit

Next the *state transition table* must be deduced and the output function specified.
Table 7.2 assumes the use of a *Moore machine* and the micro-instruction format given in
the previous section. The 1-bit input signals the start of instruction execution. Subsequent input values are ignored until completion. If the unit is not executing, its output
is forced inactive.

It now remains to deduce how to generate the required output values and excite each
flip-flop. For this we require a truth table (Table 7.3).

Design of the necessary combinational systems may proceed as described in Chapter 6.
Note that C_8, C_3, C_1 are never asserted and hence require no design effort.

Input	Present state	Next state	Micro-instruction
0	a	a	000_8
1	a	b	000_8
X	b	c	021_8
X	c	d	244_8
X	d	a	102_8

Table 7.2: State transitiont table for add instruction control unit

I	Q_1	Q_0	D_1	D_0	Control word ($C_{8\rightarrow0}$)
0	0	0	0	0	000.000.000
1	0	0	0	1	000.000.000
X	0	1	1	0	000.010.001
X	1	0	1	1	010.100.100
X	1	1	0	0	001.000.010

Table 7.3: Truth table for add instruction control unit

Conditional sequencing

Conditional sequencing of states will be required to implement the *conditional branch* instructions required to implement *selection* and *iteration* constructs of a procedural programming language. It is achieved through the use of an additional input to the state machine which possesses the value of the condition. Condition states are stored within the *processor state register (PSR)*, each as a 1-bit field known as a *flag*.

Selection of micro-instruction sequencing is also required according to *opcode*. Hence inputs to the state machine may be of two kinds...

- *Processor state*

- *Opcode*

If the opcode is used directly, any slight change in its definition will require considerable redesign effort. The use of a decoder to generate state machine inputs from the opcode is thus very advantageous. Remember also that adding a single extra input bit *doubles* the size of the state transition and truth tables!

Pros & cons

There follows a brief summary of the advantages and disadvantages of the *minimum state* method of control unit design...

- Hard to design: *Number of combinations of state and input can become excessively large for the whole system*

- Hard to develop/maintain: *Structure has no intuitive interpretation implying difficulty in locating repeated patterns or cycles.*

- Efficienct to implement: *Minimum number of flip-flops used but quite a lot of combinational logic*

7.2.3   Shift register method

Sequencing

An alternative to the above is to adopt the following approach...

1. *Generate one unique timing signal per required event*

2. *Use an OR gate to drive each control bit output, thus allowing more than one signal to cause it to become asserted*

3. *Connect each timing signal to a gate input for each control bit which is then required asserted*

For a reason made clear below, this is commonly called the *shift register, delay element* or *one flip-flop per state* approach. The timing signals are easily achieved by feeding a 1 through a shift register, leading to the structure shown in Figure 7.11.

Conditional sequencing

As mentioned previously, there are two kinds of selection...

- *Selection of control signals asserted on a given control unit state*

- *Selection of a control word sequence (from two, or more, possibilities)*

Selection of control signals asserted, depending on the value of an input, may be achieved through a little combinational logic as shown in Figure 7.12.

This is the form which may select the microcode sequence according to *opcode!* A decoder is used to produce a single signal (O_i) asserted for each valid opcode. These are used together with timing signals (T_j) derived from the shift register, to generate the control word C.

Supposing the control word bit C_5 is required asserted as follows...

- ...for opcode 3 as part of micro-operation 2

- ...for opcode 7 as part of micro-operation 1

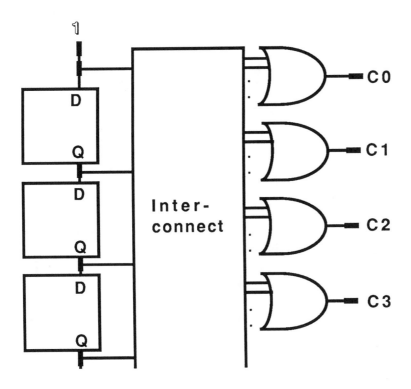

Figure 7.11: The basic structure of a shift register control unit for a single instruction

The derivation of C_5 requires combinational logic to implement the function...

$$C_5 = O_3.T_2 + O_7.T_1$$

The second form of selection upon value of an input, where the choice is between two distinct *sequences*, requires switching between two chains of flip-flops. A simple instance of this is shown in Figure 7.13. Here the assertion of control signal n occurs at one of two *times* depending on the value of condition m.

Obviously completely independent microprocesses might be implemented for each value of m. Each solution would be known as a *timing chain*. This is the kind of selection used to implement conditional branching. The input selecting a chain would be a flag from the processor state register. Rather than implement a separate chain for each flag, a MUX would typically be employed to provide a single selection input to the control unit. The selection inputs of the MUX itself might be provided by an appropriate field of the IR.

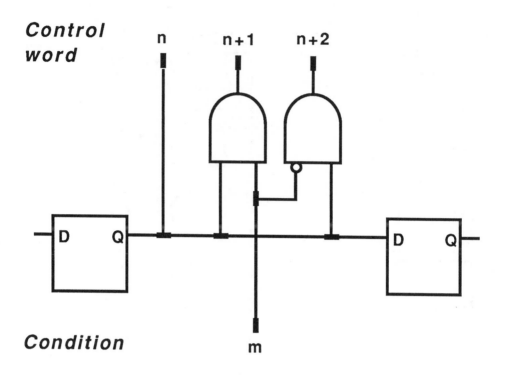

Figure 7.12: Conditional selection of control signal assertion

Integration

The design of a shift register control unit to implement a given processor operation is easy compared to that of a minimum state one. The reason is that a *control flow analysis* may be performed to produce a *flowchart* which has a one-to-one correspondence with the hardware. Figure 7.14 shows a set of symbols which may be employed in the flowchart together with their corresponding hardware implementation. The design is thus *intuitive*, a fact which greatly simplifies development and maintenance. It is the most significant advantage of this method.

Integrating the implementation of a number of distinct processor operations requires...

- *Timing signals* (T_i)

- *Operation signals* (O_i)

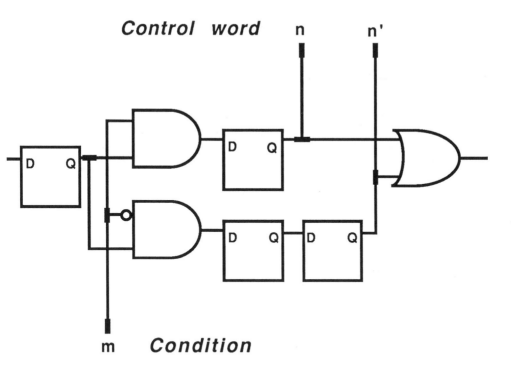

Figure 7.13: Conditional selection of control word sequence

The timing signals are developed from timing chains of flip-flops. Some of them (T_i^s) will be conditional asserted according to the state (s)of a PSR flag. Operation signals are the result of decoding the current opcode. Only one will be asserted at a time, corresponding to the opcode. The combinational logic for driving each control word signal has the general structure shown in Figure 7.15.

Pros & cons

Below is a brief summary of the advantages and disadvantages of the shift register approach to control unit design...

- Easy to design: *Use of standard forms to establish all necessary timing chains*

- Easy to develop: *Intuitive interpretation speeds development and debugging*

- Inefficient to implement: *One flip-flop per event per chain is expensive*

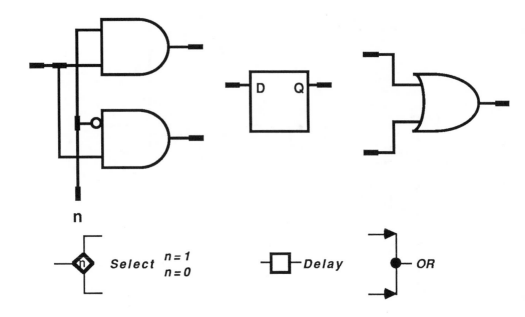

Figure 7.14: Flowchart symbols for shift register control unit design

7.2.4   Counter method

Sequencing

We have so far seen how either a specially designed *state machine* or a *shift register* may be used for generating state within a control unit. It should not be surprising that another standard component, the *counter*, may also be employed. Each time the counter is incremented a new distinct state is arrived at. Two advantages are immediately apparent. Firstly, counters are *standard* components, so there is no need to design a special one for each instruction or each processor. Secondly very much fewer flip-flops are needed for a given number of states ($\log_2 n$ for counter, n for shift register).

There is a further advantage. Control words may be simply stored as values in memory since the state generated by the counter may be treated as an *address*. They are thus rendered easily understood as *micro-instructions*, sequenced exactly as are instructions.

ROM may be used to conduct the decoding from state to control word. Alternatively, the development of such a control unit may be rendered very convenient through the use of a *writable microcode memory* instead.

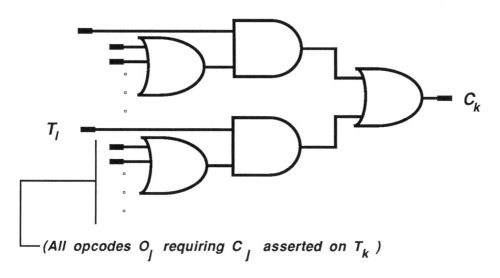

T_l

(All opcodes O_j requiring C_j asserted on T_k)

C_k

Figure 7.15: Combinational logic structure driving each control word structure

Integration

Microprocedures for the interpretation of all instructions may be held within the *microcode ROM*. Execution of the correct one is ensured by loading the counter with the correct start address as the first event in the *execute microprocess*.

Acronym	Name	Function
MMROM	Microcode mapping rom	*Opcode decoding*
CAR	Control address register	*State generation*
MROM	Microcode rom	*State decoding*
AMUX	Address mux	*Multiplex CAR data input*
CMUX	Control mux	*Multiplex CAR control input*

Table 7.4: Components of microprogrammable, counter-based, control unit

The simplicity of this approach may be extended further by employing a *microcode mapping ROM* for opcode decoding. The opcode is used to address a location in the mapping ROM whose contents are used as the start address of a microprocedure in the microcode ROM. Figure 7.16 shows the form of a control unit built in this way. Figure 7.17 shows the relationship between microcode ROM and microcode mapping ROM. The structure of a complete counter-based control unit is shown in Figure 7.18. Two

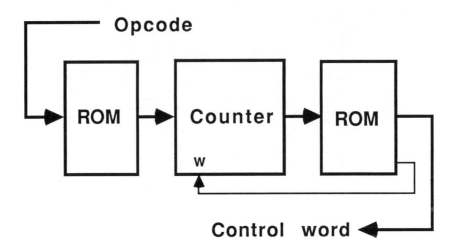

Figure 7.16: Form of a counter-based control unit

MUXs are required to permit both conditional sequencing and microprogrammed selection or iteration (see below). The list of complete components is tabulated in Table 7.4.

Microprogramming

Micro-instruction formats may be designed in two alternative ways. The simplest way to represent a micro-instruction is simply as the *raw* control word. This is called *horizontal format*. A large amount of *parallelism* is made possible in this way, at the microcode level. Many combinations of simultaneous micro-operations might be desired and all are accessible this way.

Unfortunately, control words are typically very wide indeed and, in the majority of micro-instructions, have very few bits set. Hence it is very inefficient to use a horizontal format for storage of microcode. Instead a *vertical format* may be employed, where the control word is composed of one or more fields which are *encoded* in some way to reduce the number of bits required to store them[5]. If, say, an 11-bit control word field is only ever used with twenty-six configurations (bit patterns), then it may be replaced with a 5-bit encoded *micro-instruction* field.

The price of vertical format is *reduced parallelism* at the microcode level and the requirement of an *extra decoder* for each encoded control word field.

---

[5] Note that such encoding is not necessary with the *minimum state* or *shift register* approaches since neither calls for the storage of microcode.

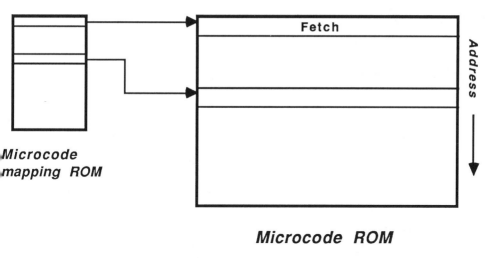

Microcode ROM

Figure 7.17: Relationship between microcode ROM and microcode mapping ROM

Micro-instruction fields include the following. . .

- Control word: *Only field output from control unit and composed of sub-fields of control signals (when decoded if necessary) controlling the operation of each register and combinational logic unit*

- Jump/Enter: *Single bit field which provides the control input for switching the CAR input (AMUX) between a new start address (from microcode mapping ROM) or jump destination (see below)*

- Jump destination: *Field containing a new value for the CAR and used to implement either constructs or microprocedure invocation/return*

- Flag select: *Field used as control input to the CMUX to select a condition signal input or force the CAR to unconditionally increment or load new start address*

Selection and iteration may be achieved via the **jump** micro-instruction. The *Jump/Enter* bit must be set in the micro-instruction executed immediately prior to the first of the microprocedure. A valid *jump destination* field must also be supplied. The last requirement is that the *flag select* field must be be set appropriately to select 1 in order to force the CAR to load a new value from the AMUX.

Termination of each *execute microprocedure* is effected by invoking the *fetch microprocedure*, which will usually be stored at the base of the MROM, i.e. at address zero.

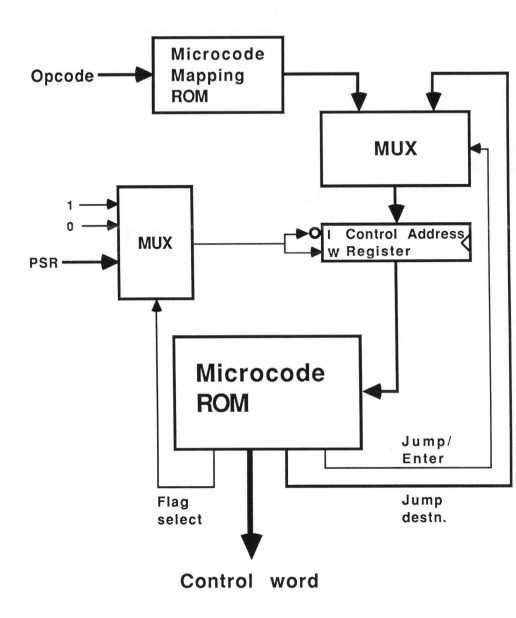

Figure 7.18: Fully microprogrammable counter-based control unit

n turn, zero must then be stored at address zero in the MMROM. Ensuring zero in the opcode field of the IR when the machine is first switched on will cause the first instruction to be fetched[6].

Correct termination therefore requires all execute microprocedures to end with the micro-instruction...

```
jump #0000
```

Microprocedures may be invoked and returned from using the jump mechanism. They may be shared between execute microprocedures and thus reduce the total microcode required in implementing an entire instruction set.

Pros & cons

Below is a brief summary of the advantages and disadvantages of the *counter* approach to control unit design...

- Easy to design: *Standard components (counter, ROM, MUX) are used, all of which have a simple, regular structure*

- Easy to develop: *Microcode may be developed and debugged in similar manner to any normal program*

- Inefficient to implement: *Sparse use of MROM since typically very few bits set in any control word*
  (Improved by use of vertical format at the expense of micro-operation parallelism)

Counter-based microprogrammable control units have found favour with contemporary *CISC* designers on account of the facility they offer in debugging a complex machine (too often *after* it has been brought to market).

---

[6] Typically, all registers are *automatically cleared to zero* when a processor is switched on. This offers a simple way of obtaining predictable behaviour on *power-up*. Hence the system designer must ensure the *power-up boot procedure* begins at address zero in main memory since the program counter will be cleared also.

Exercises

Question one

Suggest a *control word* format for a processor with the following components...

- *Three active registers*

- *Program counter*

- *Processor state register*

- *Arithmetic unit capable of four operations*

The active registers are as described in Chapter 6 except that they have two extr
control inputs, one for *shift left* and one for *shift right*. The *carry* flag in the PSR i
arranged to appear at the end of either register so that, after a shift, it will contain th
value of the previous LSB, if a right shift, or MSB, if a left shift.

Question two

Design a *minimum state control unit* (from a *Moore state machine*) for the processc
described in question one, which negates the contents of a single active register (assumin
twos complement representation).

Question three

i   Pseudocode for a *shift and add* algorithm for multiplication of unsigned integers, whic
requires no dedicated hardware, is as follows...

```
result := 0
WHILE multiplier > 0 DO
  multiplier >> 1
  IF carry = 1 THEN
    result := result + multiplicand
  END
  multiplicand << 1
END
```

...where $\ll$ denotes the *shift left* operator and $\gg$ the *shift right* operator[7]. Carr
being set after a shift right is equivalent to the multiplier ending in 2^{-1} which is take
into account by adding half the new multiplicand (simply the old unshifted version) to th

---

[7]The algorithm relies on the fact that a left shift is equivalent to multiplication by two, and a righ
shift division by two.

result register. Satisfy yourself, using examples, that you understand how the algorithm works.

Suggest an additional step which precurses the algorithm to improve its performance over a large random set of pairs of operands. How might it be further extended to deal with *signed* operands?

ii Assuming the processor architecture described in question one, give the *microprocedure*, expressed in RTL, which implements a multiplication instruction employing the algorithm shown above (without extensions) given that the result, multiplier and multiplicand already occupy the active registers. (Remember to terminate it correctly.)

Question four

i Establish a *horizontal micro-instruction format* for the microprogrammable control unit shown in Figure 7.18 which includes the control word format given as your answer to question one. (Make a reasonable assumption for the width of the MROM address and that of the PSR.)

ii Give the complete microcode, in binary, octal or hex, to implement the *shift and add* multiplication microprocedure described in answer to question three. Take care to exploit all possible *word-level parallelism*.

Question five

Design a *shift register control unit* which implements the algorithm for unsigned integer multiplication given in question three. Make the maximum possible use of parallelism between micro-operations.

Part III

Computer organization

Chapter 8

Processor organization

8.1 Requirements

8.1.1 General requirements

There are no hard and fast rules applying to processor organization. In this chapter, four designs are considered as distinct. Commercially available designs are either *hybrids*, employing a mixture of the ideas presented here, or a *combination* of more than one philosophy allowing the *system designer* freedom of choice over which to exploit. This is illustrated in Chapter 10 with a discussion of three commercially available designs.

Two requirements dominate long term design aims...

Efficient execution requires the minimization of the time taken to translate each element of a software *source* module into *micro-operations*. Virtually all software is now written in a high level language. It is important to understand that the architecture must be optimally designed for the *compiler code generator*. The fact that an alternative architecture may permit more rapid execution of a process, given *machine level* (assembly language) programming, is completely immaterial.

Efficient development requires architectural support for *software partitions* such as *procedures* and *modules*. Software partitions should correspond to *problem partitions* in the most direct fashion possible. *Separate development* of each partition requires *separate compilation* which in turn requires support for code and data referencing across partition boundaries. With the procedural programming model this implies the ability for a procedure in one module to reference variables and procedures within another, ideally *without* the need to recompile or relink more than just the one (referencing) module.

223

8.1.2   Throughput

Instructions

The purpose of a processor is to translate machine language instructions into *micro-operations*. The speed of execution depends on the *average* time taken to translate each instruction. The *instruction throughput*[1] is simply the mean number of instructions executed per unit time.

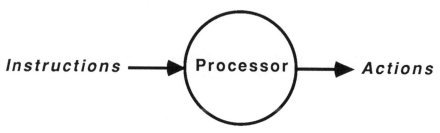

Figure 8.1: Simplest model of processor function

A number of methods are known which improve instruction throughput and they are often the first thing of which a designer or manufacturer will boast. Prominent among them currently is the *instruction cache* and *pipelining* which are both discussed below. Caution is however required since some instruction sets achieve more per instruction than others *at the problem level!*

Data

Like the *Turing Machine*, a contemporary computer employs *separate* processor and memory. The two are connected by some kind of communication channel. Unlike the Turing Machine processor, which can only reference a single location and move to its successor or predecessor, a contemporary processor has *random access* to its memory[2]. It may reference any element in memory, whenever it chooses.

The limit on the instruction throughput of a processor is largely determined by its *data throughput* which is the number of memory references per unit time that the processor to memory communication channel is capable of supporting. This is referred to as its *bandwidth*[3]. The channel is typically a bus, thus an important factor will be the *bus width*, equal to the number of bits transferred per *bus cycle*.

Most contemporary computers employ a *shared memory* for both instructions and

---

[1] ... usually stated in *MIPS*, Millions of Instructions Per Second.

[2] The memory is still linear, like that of the Turing Machine.

[3] In its strict sense the term refers to the difference between the lowest and highest *frequency* of *sinusoidal* analogue signal which may be transmitted over the channel.

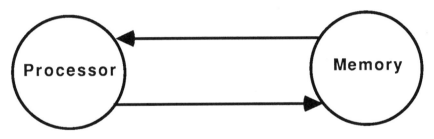

Figure 8.2: Processor to memory communication

data. This philosophy is credited to *J. von Neumann*[4] [von Neumann 46]. Thus the bandwidth of the processor to memory channel is important because, more than any other single factor in contemporary computer design, it determines the limit of both instruction and data throughput. It is thus commonly referred to as the *von Neumann bottleneck*.

8.1.3 Real-time systems

In addition to these universal requirements will be the *applicability* of the design. It is now becoming cost effective to design processors which are optimized to a *specific* application. Arguably the most important growth is in *real-time systems* which are capable of *synchronous* communication with their environment. Such systems require *event-driven software*. An *event* occurring external to the system *immediately* causes appropriate processing to generate the required response. The delay between the event and execution of the first relevant instruction is known as the *latency* and must be minimized. Such a processor must also possess the capability of *alternation* between distinct environment processes. As a result it must itself be capable of scheduling multiple processes[5].

Applications of real-time systems range from aircraft flight control to robotics. The principles are also highly applicable to the *human/computer interface* process of a computer work-station.

---

[4] ...who is also credited with the very idea of the *stored program*. Previously, computers had to be *physically altered* in order to change their program. Those machines which employ *separate* memories for instructions and data are said to possess a *Harvard architecture*.

[5] See discussion in Chapter 1.

8.2 Accumulator machine

8.2.1 Programming constructs

The most basic construct, the sequence, is implemented using a counter called the *program counter (PC)*. It contains the address of the next instruction to be fetched from memory and then executed. It is incremented after each *instruction fetch* micro-operation.

Useful computations require selection and iteration constructs both of which may be implemented by means of *conditional branch* instructions. Branching[6] occurs if a specified *condition flag* is set[7] in the *processor state register (PSR)*. Processor state depends on the results of previously executed instructions. For example, if the result of a preceding addition instruction was zero, a flag (usually denoted by Z) will be set. The *arithmetic logic unit (ALU)* will automatically have caused it to be so.

The *organization* of the accumulator machine is shown in Figure 8.3 and its *programmer's architecture* in Figure 8.4. Note that there is no obvious means to reuse *software partitions* of any kind.

8.2.2 Data referencing

The *accumulator* is so called because it is said to *accumulate* the value of the computed function. Its contents repeatedly form one argument of a function computed by the ALU. The result of each ALU operation is communicated back into the accumulator. For example, summation of an array of integers may be performed as a sequence of binary addition operations each of which takes the result of the last as one operand.

The *X register* gets its name from "eXtension" or "indeX" and is used to contain either. For example multiplication of two integers will require a result register twice as large as required for each operand and will use X as an extension of the accumulator. X also renders *multiple precision* arithmetic more efficient by *reducing the number of memory references* required by acting as a temporary store. It would also be used as the array and loop index in the summation example mentioned above. An instruction to decrement X would be employed in the loop body. The loop would terminate with a conditional branch instruction which interrogates the Z flag in the PSR.

Accumulator machine instructions need take only a *single* operand. Typical addressing modes are...

- Immediate: *Operand embedded within code immediately following instruction*

- Absolute (direct): *Operand to be found in memory location whose absolute address is embedded within code immediately following instruction*

---

[6]The addition of a signed integer to the PC.

[7]...or clear as required.

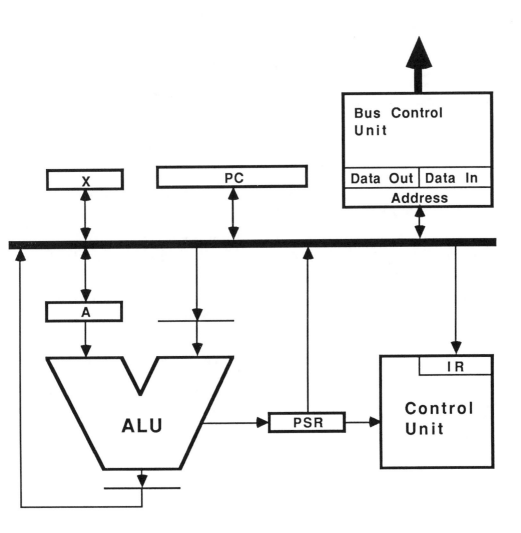

Figure 8.3: Accumulator machine organization

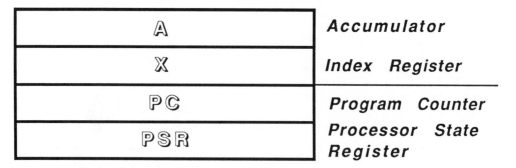

Figure 8.4: Programmer's architecture of accumulator machine

- Indexed: *Operand to be found at effective address given by the sum of an absolute address (array base) and the contents of the X register (array index)*

- Indirect: *Effective address of operand found in memory at specified absolute address (vector), i.e. the address of the address of the operand is specified following the instruction*

- Indirect indexed: *Effective address of operand is a vector to which is added the contents of the X register (i.e. indexing takes place after indirection)*

- Indexed indirect: *Effective address of operand is the vector address to which is added the contents of the X register (i.e. indexing takes place before indirection)*

Immediate mode is used for referencing constants and *absolute mode* for scalar variables. The others support the access of elements within sequence-associated and pointer-associated structured variables.

8.2.3 Booting

By *booting* or *bootstrapping* we mean the correct initiation of the process we wish to run. This first of all requires that all registers possess a suitable state. In particular the PC must point to the first instruction of the *boot code*. Traditionally this is first achieved by *clearing all registers*, which implies that the first instruction to be executed must exist at the memory location whose address is *zero*[8]. Similarly, judicious design can ensure that a satisfactory *boot state* is achieved with all flags in the PSR cleared to zero.

---

[8] At a lower level, clearing the instruction register of a *microcoded* control unit is satisfactory if the *fetch instruction* microprocess lies at the base of *microcode memory*. This will cause the first micro-operation to be to fetch the first instruction of the boot code.

8.2.4 Summary

The *accumulator machine* described here has many similarities with the *von Neumann machine* [von Neumann 46]. It supports programming a complete set of procedural constructs via a *program counter, processor state register* and *conditional branch* instructions.

Indirection and *indexing* support the referencing of both sequence-associated and pointer-associated data. The referencing of constant and scalar variable data are supported via *immediate* and *absolute addressing modes*.

One-address instructions are adequate, the accumulator being used for both one operand and the result of an operator. The other operand must *always* be fetched from memory. Thus the bandwidth of the processor-to-memory communication channel is paramount in determining performance in most applications.

No support is provided whatsoever for *software modularity* at the machine level.

8.3 Stack machine

8.3.1 Software partitions

The *stack machine* directly supports a *stack* data object (see Chapter 2) through the inclusion of a *stack pointer (SP)* register to contain the address of the *top-of-stack (TOS)*. It may be automatically incremented after each **push** and decremented after each **pop** instruction. In addition it should also be possible to reference TOS without actually removing the top item, i.e. without affecting SP.

A *subroutine* is simply a section of code which may be executed repeatedly when a program runs, *avoiding the need for code repetition*. When combined with a mechanism for parameter passing it becomes a *procedure*. With a further mechanism to return a value it implements a *function*[9]. Two special instructions facilitate subroutine invocation and return...

- **bsr <offset>**...*branch to subroutine*

- **rts**...*return from subroutine*

bsr causes the following microprocess to run...

$$
\begin{array}{rrll}
(1) & PC & \leftarrow & (PC + length(bsr)) \\
(2) & EAR & \leftarrow & SP \\
(3) & DOR & \leftarrow & PC, & SP(increment) \\
(4) & PC & \leftarrow & (PC+ <offset>), & BCU(write)
\end{array}
$$

---

[9] The computation of a *function* is by means of a *process*! Take great care to distinguish between the mathematical definition of *function* and its implementation as a *subroutine* which receives parameters and returns a value.

Note that the semantic level of the RTL in use has now been raised by extending it to allow the right-hand side to be specified as an *arithmetic sum*, whose evaluation requires a number of unlisted micro-operations and hence takes more than one clock-cycle. Depending on the total length of the `bsr` instruction, it may actually be quicker to use the *increment* function of the PC than to cycle it through the ALU. Some machines are equipped with a second ALU dedicated to *effective address computation*.

Step 1 adjusts the PC to point to the next instruction of the main routine. Steps 2 and 3 push the PC contents onto the stack $(TOS \leftarrow PC)$. Step 4 adjusts the PC to point to the subroutine start. An immediate operand forms the offset from the current PC value to the subroutine start. `rts` simply pops the address of the instruction following the `bsr` off the stack and back into the program counter $(PC \leftarrow TOS)$...

$$
\begin{array}{rrcl}
(1) & EAR & \leftarrow & SP \\
(2) & DIR & \leftarrow & Mem, \quad BCU(read), \quad SP(decrement) \\
(3) & PC & \leftarrow & DIR
\end{array}
$$

8.3.2   Data referencing

It should be clear from the above that *a stack provides direct support for subroutines*. In order to implement procedures and functions the correct *reference scoping* for the following classes of data must be guaranteed...

- *Global data*

- *Local data*

- *Parameters*

- *Function value*

Note that all data are *dynamic* except global data. The *stack frame* is the mechanism for referencing all dynamic data. The *frame pointer (FP)* register contains the address of the first free location at the bottom of the frame, which contains all *local variables* and whose size must be decided by the compiler by inspecting their number and type. Directly beneath the stack frame is found the *old* frame pointer value and return address followed by parameters and possibly space reserved for a function value return. This structure is created by the compiler generated code in implementing a procedure or function call and is shown in Figure 8.5.

To summarize the compiler generated code for a procedure or function call...

1. *Push space for return value (function only)*

2. *Push parameters*

3. *Branch to subroutine*

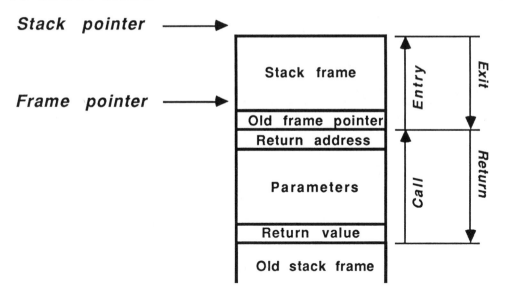

Figure 8.5: Stack format within a procedure or function

... and for procedure/function entry...

1. *Push old frame pointer*

2. *Copy stack pointer to frame pointer*

3. *Increment stack pointer by frame size*

... and for procedure/function exit...

1. *Copy frame pointer to stack pointer*

2. *Pop old frame pointer value to frame pointer register*

3. *Decrement stack pointer by parameter block size*

The function value returned (if any) will now be easily accessible at TOS. There follows a summary of addressing modes available with a stack machine ...

- Immediate: *Operand embedded in code immediately following instruction*

- Register relative: *Operand is at a specified offset from the address held in a register*

- Register indirect: *Vector to the operand is located at the effective address formed by the sum of an offset and the contents of a register*

The registers available for *register relative* addressing are detailed in Table 8.1. The *static base register (SB)* contains a pointer to an area of memory reserved for global access by all procedures of a software module.

Acronym	Register	Application
PC	Program Counter	*Subroutine entry* *Conditional branching in constructs*
SP	Stack Pointer	*Subroutine exit* *Expression evaluation*
FP	Frame Pointer	*Local variable access (+ve offsets)* *Parameter & return access (-ve offsets)*
SB	Static Base register	*Global variable access*

Table 8.1: Stack machine registers and their application

A vector may be maintained as a reference into a structured data object whose elements are thus recovered or inserted by indirection. A little thought about this leads to the realization that a mechanism must be provided to *generate the run-time effective address* of one of the above modes to serve as a pointer to an object. *No indexing is required* since the vector may be adjusted as necessary to point to an element of a static, *sequence associated*, data structure (array or record). The mechanism takes the form of a special instruction which generates the *effective address* specified and places it at TOS. There follows the procedure to reference an element in an array, given a variable representing the array index,...

1. *Generate the array base address at TOS*

2. *Add this to array index, result to TOS*

3. *Reference with SP indirect addressing*

One-address instructions are quite adequate. The stack machine uses TOS like the accumulator machine uses its accumulator. TOS always serves as one operand and the result of a binary operator so it remains only to specify the other operand.

All data referencing is therefore made relative to addresses stored in processor registers. Variables are bound to *offsets*, not absolute addresses! This has the very important consequence that code may run *independent of position* in memory. No absolute addresses need appear in the code at all. It is thus known as *position independent code*.

8.3.3 Expression evaluation

Expressions may be evaluated with very few instructions purely using the stack[10]. In a given assignment, the left-hand side is a variable which is referenced via a special register and an offset to which it is bound. Which register (FP or SB) depends on the scope of the variable as discussed above. The right hand side is the expression which is computed at TOS. Each variable appearing in the expression is pushed onto the stack as it is required. When the computation is complete the value of the expression rests at TOS. The assignment is then completed by a pop to the location of the variable.

Instructions take the form of *operators* which operate on the stack. Typically they pop the top two items as operands and push a result back. This may then be used as an operand to the next instruction and so on until the value of the whole expression is to be found at TOS, e.g. to compute $(9+3) \times (7-4)$...

```
push #7      7
push #4      7,4
sub          3
push #9      9,3
push #3      3,9,3
add          12,3
mul          4
```

"#" denotes immediate addressing mode. The status of the stack is shown on the right hand side.

A great deal of code is (or may be) written with only short expressions to be evaluated. On some machines stacks have been implemented specifically and solely for the purpose of expression evaluation, taking the form of a small number of processor registers. By eliminating the need for memory references a significant performance increase is obtained.

It is quite possible to survive without an index register to reference array elements by using a variable to act as an indirection vector. The vector into the array (base + index) is maintained and use made of indirect mode to recover or set the element value. This does have the unfortunate consequence however of incurring two memory accesses per element reference, one to acquire the vector, a second to acquire the operand.

8.3.4 Alternation

Alternation between environment processes is provided by the mechanism known as the *interrupt*. A hardware channel, which supports a *signal* protocol, is connected to the control unit . When a signal is received, the control unit completes the current instruction, increments the PC, then saves it on the stack[11]. The address of the *interrupt routine* is

[10] If the required computation is expressed purely as a function *it is possible to avoid the need for the notion of assignment altogether! Functional programming* is outside the scope of this book.

[11] The *interrupt microprocess* of a control unit is discussed in Chapter 7.

copied from the INT register into the PC. The activity is very much like that of calling a subroutine. Return from interrupt routine is achieved by a pop of the return address back to the PC.

In this way the processor is able to switch rapidly between two routines, although the means of switching in each direction are not symmetric. The interrupt allows rapid switching from a "main" routine into the interrupt routine but subsequent interrupts are disabled upon entry and execution continues until *programmed* return.

To communicate with *multiple* environment processes, *polling* must be used. On entry into the interrupt routine, all such processes are interrogated (polled) until the one which sent the interrupt signal is found.

8.3.5 Summary

Figure 8.7 shows the organization of the stack machine, Figure 8.6 the *programmer's architecture*.

Stack machines permit software *modularity* by supporting procedures and functions at *machine level*. However, each invocation requires considerable time overhead, reducing performance for the sake of both reducing code size and easing the development and maintenance of source. They are very efficient, with respect to code length, at expression evaluation and require only *one-address* instructions.

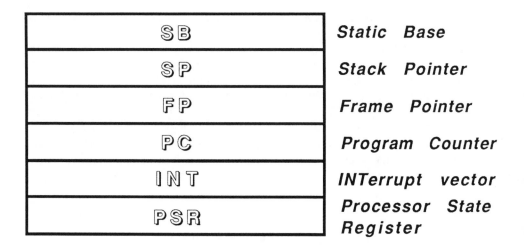

Figure 8.6: Programmer's architecture of stack machine

Stack machines require only a small instruction set composed solely of the operators required together with **push** and **pop**. An additional *"generate address"* instruction is

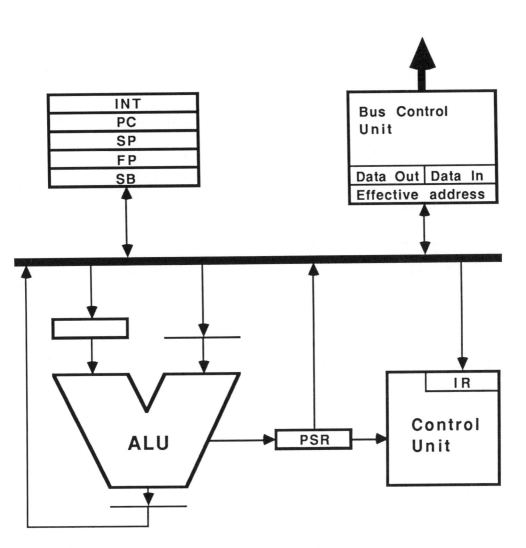

Figure 8.7: Stack machine organization

required to support access within sequence-associated or pointer-associated structured data. They are compact and simple in architecture and machine code. The instructions themselves may be compactly encoded and implemented simply because there are few of them. Their single severe disadvantage is that every data reference is to main memory which is time and power consuming.

A form of *alternation* is possible, via the mechanism of the *interrupt*, which requires further support (e.g. software *polling*).

8.4 Register window + instruction cache machine

8.4.1 Exploitation of locality

Both stack and accumulator machines suffer from the same handicap of the need to access memory for each variable reference. This is particularly severe when evaluating an expression. The inclusion of a file of processor registers, directly controlled by the control unit, may greatly reduce the problem by housing all variables local to a procedure while it runs. Registers may be used to contain any type of data for any purpose and hence are collectively referred to as a *general purpose register file*.

The efficiency derived from a register file is a result of *structured programming*. Research has shown that the use of structured programming results in *temporal locality*, i.e. the processor tends to access the same group of variables within a certain size time window. *Spatial locality* is the tendency to reference variables closely situated within memory. The exploitation of locality is discussed in Chapter 3.

When the procedure is entered all local variables are initialized within the register file. If the *register file* is not large enough, only those most frequently referenced are housed there. In order that the calling procedure does not have its local variables corrupted, the new procedure must, as its very first act, save the register file at a known location. Parameters may be passed and values returned in the register file but great care must be taken. A procedure implementation must pay regard to register usage. As a result conventions exist with some compilers and architectures, for instance the use of *r0* in the "C" language for a function return value.

Register files are usually combined with a stack architecture. The stack now provides two facilities. . .

- *Temporary storage for special registers (e.g. PC, PSR)*

- *Temporary storage for general purpose registers*

Considerable performance improvement may be gained with a register file and stack if the compiler makes *effective* use of the registers. This means *always* using them for expression evaluation, and *as much as possible* for local variables. The need for a compiler to be portable among a wide variety of machines often results in their less than optimal exploitation. Unfortunately, there are also still the memory references required on every procedure call that are due to the architecture *and not the problem*. We now move on to discuss the removal of this inefficiency.

8.4.2 Software partitions

The advantages of a stack machine over an accumulator one are attractive but the penalty can be reduced performance. Each procedure invocation requires parameters, return address and frame pointer to be written to the stack. The two latter items must later also be read on exit and return. All this implies memory access over a bus which can only transmit one item at a time. There is a way to avoid as many references and greatly speed up those remaining.

A large register file is provided within the processor. A *register window* is notionally laid over the register file so that only those visible through the window are accessible. The *window* now takes the place of the stack in implementing local variables, parameters and return value as depicted in Figure 8.8.

Accessing data in processor registers is very much faster than accessing memory locations because each one is accessed directly without the need for *address decoding* and *bus protocol*. The problem with registers is one of interconnection. Bussed memory requires only one extra signal connection each time the number of locations *doubles!* Registers require another signal pair (at least) for each and every one added. For this reason it is costly, *particularly with a 2-d technology*, where overlapping connections are not allowed. A large area of silicon "real estate" is given over to *interconnect* that could just as easily be used for a large bussed memory or even another processor!

A compromise is where the register file is broken up into equal sized windows which overlap to allow parameter passing. Only one window is active at a time whose address is the *current window pointer (CWP)* for which a register is provided. For example, we might have eight windows of twenty-two registers. Each window may overlap its successor or predecessor by six registers. Hence the window advances across sixteen registers on each procedure call. In this example the register file thus consists of...

- *128 physical registers*

- *8 windows each of 22 logical registers*

...and requires a CWP of just three bits[12].

Instructions only ever refer to one of twenty-two registers, hence the control unit need only send control signals for these. No internal bus collision will occur because the *current window pointer* is decoded to allow only one group of registers to respond to the signals. Inspection of Figure 8.9 should render clear the fact that each register need only be connected to just *two* pairs of control signals. Each physical register is visible within only two possible windows. The CWP decoded will provide the select signal to choose which signals each register must obey.

---

[12]This example is based on the *Berkeley RISC I* processor.

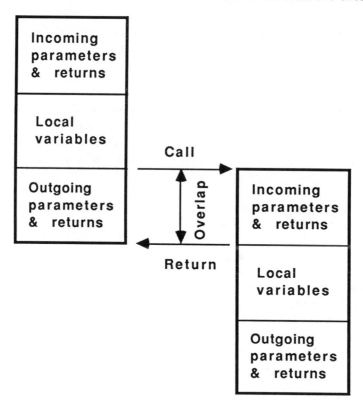

Figure 8.8: Contents of a register window

8.4.3   Data referencing

Global data, although undesirable since it allows side effects to occur, is still perceived by many as essential for an architecture to support. A register window machine deals with this in an elegant fashion. Figure 8.10 shows how it is achieved. A partition at one extreme of the *logical* register file remains permanently bound to the same set of physical registers and holds global variables visible to all procedures. Given ten global registers, the total size of the logical register in our example will be thirty-two.

There need only be a *single* principal addressing mode for a register window machine! Absolute, register relative and indexed register relative access to main memory may be *synthesized* quite simply. The principal mode uses two arguments to an instruction. The first specifies a register in the logical register file. (We assume that the PC may be referenced simply as an extension to the logical register file.) The second argument contains more bits than the first including one which indicates its interpretation, which

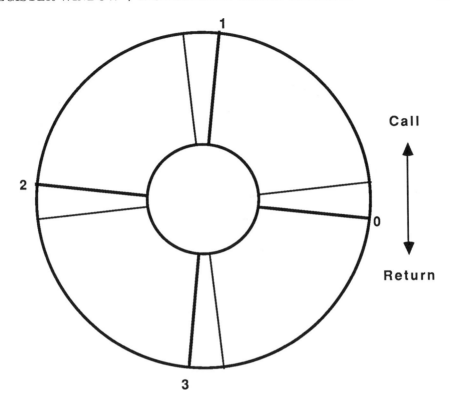

Figure 8.9: Connectivity between register windows

may be either a logical register number (like the first) or an *immediate operand*. The effective address of an operand in memory is thus given by[13] ...

$$EA = (reg) + arg2$$

There follows a summary of possible *synthesized addressing modes*...

- Absolute: reg *is any register containing the value zero,* arg2 *is an immediate operand specifying the required absolute address*

$$EA = imm$$

- Register relative: reg *contains the address of the operand,* arg2 *is either any register containing the value zero or a zero immediate value*

$$EA = (reg)$$

---

[13] "(...)" should be read as *"contents of ...".*

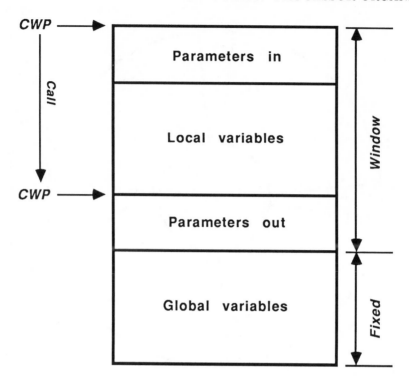

Figure 8.10: Logical register file supporting global, local and parameter variables

- Register relative + index: reg *is once again a vector,* arg2 *is a register containing the required index*

$$EA = (reg) + reg$$

- PC relative: reg *is the logical register number of the PC,* arg2 *is an immediate operand whose value is the required offset*
(Used solely for conditional branching)

$$EA = (PC) + imm$$

Arguments may be used to derive either one or two operands depending on the effect of the operation encoded within the opcode. The single operand effect will be restricted to *load/ store instructions* which transfer any data to be processed within a procedure into *local register variables.* In this way memory references are kept down to the absolute minimum necessary. Logical and arithmetic operators will require two arguments.

8.4.4 Parallel instruction execution

In Chapter 7 the process performed by the processor control unit was described in pseudocode by...

```
REPEAT
    fetch instruction
    execute instruction
UNTIL FALSE
```

There is an assumption here that the two components of the loop body must be executed sequentially when in fact such is not the case. The *sub-processors* which perform each *sub-process* are in fact independent except for a single *asynchronous* channel of comunication...the *instruction register*. In machines where the above is a true description of control unit behaviour, each sub-processor is idle while the other does its job. Borrowing some notation from the *Occam 2* programming language [Inmos 88#1] we can describe the transformation we require thus...

```
SEQ                             PAR
    fetch instruction               fetch instruction
    execute instruction    →        execute instruction
```

Things are not quite this simple however. The processor responsible for the *fetch* process is the *bus control unit (BCU)* which is required to perform other tasks which are subsidiary to the *execute* process. This leads to the possibility remaining that execution might be delayed until a fetch terminates. Also a fetch typically takes less time than an execute which leads to valuable machinery lying idle once again.

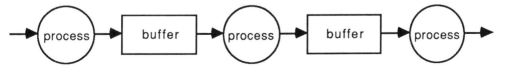

Figure 8.11: An asynchronous pipeline

The answer is to have a queue of instructions called an *instruction cache* which is topped up whenever the bus is not in use for instruction execution. A fresh instruction is always present, waiting at the front of the queue, whenever a new execute process is ready to start *provided the queue is large enough*. The use of a *queue* data object in this fashion is called *buffering* and is vital for efficiency in *asynchronous communication*. The idea of *pipelining* is shown in Figure 8.11 and is precisely that employed on a production line such as is found in a car factory. Parallel execution of fetch and execute is but a simple example.

One other problem remains. The result of the execution of a conditional branch instruction may change the identity of the following instruction depending on processor state. The contents of the entire instruction cache must then be discarded and replaced. However, a good standard of *structured programming* should make this comparatively rare. Of the order of only 1% of instructions are a conditional branch. Also the condition will only fail an average of 50% of occasions, leaving the contents of the instruction cache still valid.

An *interrupt* will also invalidate the contents of the instruction cache. Again interrupt events are comparatively rare.

Further pipeline parallelism may be obtained by breaking down *execute* microprocesses. However, if this is pursued too far the *overhead incurred in buffer transactions* and growth in *control unit complexity* can defeat performance gained.

Parallel operation of different functional units is obviously desirable to avoid machinery lying idle unnecessarily. If a number of instructions present in the instruction cache each require to operate different functional units (e.g. multiplier, ALU) on *independent* operands there is no reason why they should not. Ensuring that the operands concerned are indeed independent is not always easy however.

Multiple identical functional units become useful once an instruction cache is included in the design. Typically this means multiple ALU architectures. A significant increase in instruction throughput may be gained in many applications at the cost of a reasonable increase in control unit complexity.

8.4.5 Summary

The organization of the instruction cache + register window machine is shown in Figure 8.12. Note that *only two* special registers are required, PC and CWP. The most significant performance advantage is that very much less external memory access is required upon...

- *Subroutine invocation*

- *Expression evaluation*

This fact gives rise to an observed performance increase *with very little added complexity* compared to an accumulator or stack machine.

The *programmer's architecture* is shown in Figure 8.13 and is clearly very simple to understand and for which to generate code[14].

There is no technical reason for associating the presence of an *instruction cache* and *register windowing* in processor design. They are quite independent ideas and are brought

---

[14] Remember that the compiler code generator author need not be concerned with how the windowing operates and need only consider the *logical* register file.

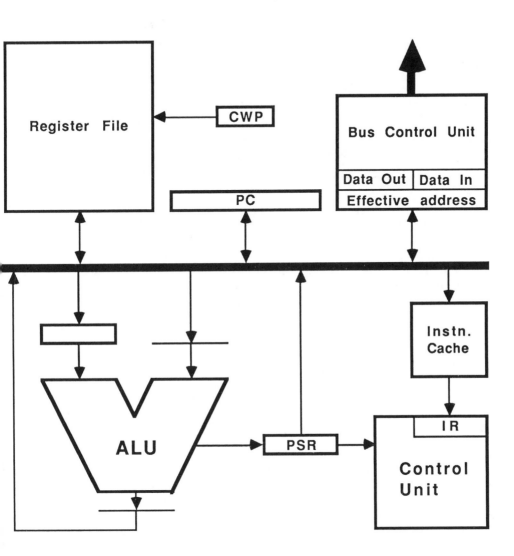

Figure 8.12: Instruction cache + register window machine organization

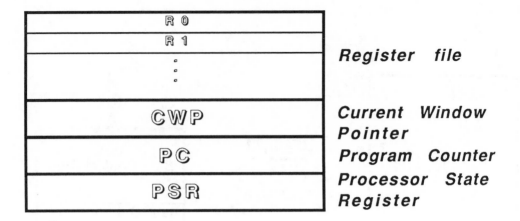

Figure 8.13: Programmer's architecture of cache + window machine

together here merely to reduce the number of designs illustrated. However, they do complement each other very well since...

- *Instruction pipelining seeks to optimize instruction throughput*

- *Register windowing seeks to optimize data throughput*

Pipelining is a concept of extreme importance to the field of *parallel processing*. It is interesting to carry the idea onwards towards its logical conclusion where each instruction has its own processor. Much more promising is the *data-led* approach where *each variable* has its own processor! Further comments would be outside the scope of this text.

Another idea which suggests itself given this design is that of establishing memory as purely for code. The idea of separate memory for data and code predates that of a single memory shared by both. Machines with separate memories for each are referred to as *Harvard architectures*. The compiler would obviously have to attempt to ensure that sufficient *procedure activation depth* exists. Recursion would be risky, but then again it is anyway given a stack machine. The implementation technology would have to permit a sufficiently large register file. This requires reducing the cost of *interconnect* implicit with a 2-d technology.

The origin of many of these ideas is (historically at least) associated with the drive for the *RISC*[15] architecture. A good survey of RISCs is to be found in [Tabak 87].

---

[15] Reduced Instruction Set Computer.

8.5 Queue + channel machine

8.5.1 Process scheduling

Process networks

The design of this machine is to fully support the software model of a *process network* which communicates, internally and externally, by passing messages over *channels*[16]. Processes may be hierarchically reduced until the structure of each process is purely sequential and composed of the following primitives...

- *Assignment*

- *Input*

- *Output*

Only *synchronous communication* is possible between processes, which *suspend* while awaiting *rendezvous*. For any *processor* network to be efficient, *every node must itself be multiprocessing*, otherwise they would be idle while their single running process is suspended.

Scheduling algorithms

The support required for multiprocessing is some kind of *scheduling algorithm*. The two simplest are...

- *First In First Out (FIFO)*

- *Round Robin*

The *FIFO* algorithm simply stores ready processes in a *ready queue*. A process is *served* (or *despatched*) to the processor and then runs till it terminates. *Round Robin* also employs a *ready queue* but each process is timed-out after one *timeslice* if it has not already terminated or suspended. The magnitude of the timeslice depends upon the overhead in *context switching* between processes and may be either fixed or variable. If variable it might be made proportional to the *priority* of the process, though that would not be easy to implement.

Scheduling support

The minimum support necessary for process scheduling is simply a *front pointer* and a *back pointer* for a ready queue. The process is represented in the queue simply by its *workspace pointer (WS)*. When suspended, the PC value is located at a fixed offset

---

[16]The *communicating sequential process* model of a system is described in Chapter 1. Detailed accounts may be found in [Hoare 78], [Hoare 85].

from the start of workspace. Context switching between processes is rendered extremely simple by applying the constraint that *it is postponed until completion of any expression evaluation already under way on time-out*. This means that no registers need be saved except the PC. The contents of WS are simply placed in the ready queue, when timed-out, or at the rendezvous, when suspended (see below).

We shall assume processes to be *static* objects which must all be declared prior to compilation so that the compiler can allocate *workspace* for each process. There is no mechanism to allocate workspace for *dynamic processes* (created at run-time).

8.5.2   Message passing

Channels

Channels which venture to processes running on external processors are referred to as *hard channels*. They clearly require special hardware mechanisms. The mechanism implementing the transmission and reception of data over a hard channel may be built around a *bidirectional shift register* (see Chapter 6). The transmission must be inhibited until the receiving processor is ready. A subsidiary channel of *signal protocol* must be provided, alongside the data channel, to effect this[17]. *Input* and *output* instructions are unaffected by whether the partner process is running on the same or another processor.

Soft channels are those which serve to connect processes which share a processor. They are implemented in a fashion which appears identical with hard channels to the processor at the *instruction* level. Both employ *rendezvous* and differ only in the *rendezvous location* and the mechanism by which data is transferred.

Rendezvous

Rendezvous requires a rendezvous location agreed *a priori* by both processes partaking in the transaction. This may simply be a memory location which is initialized with a value denoting *empty* (Figure 8.14). The first process to arrive at the rendezvous, on finding it empty, leaves behind its identifier (WS value) and suspends itself by simply quitting the processor, causing the despatch of the next ready process from the queue. When the second process arrives it completes the transaction by direct access to the workspace of the first, which it subsequently reschedules (enqueues). Note that it is quite irrelevant whether the sender or receiver arrives first. The second process to arrive will either read or write the workspace of the first, depending on which one it is.

8.5.3   Alternation

Alternation is natural and simple to implement on the queue/channel machine. Concurrent processes may be programmed, each to look after communication with a single

---

[17]The two taken together effect what is known as a *Busy/Ready protocol*.

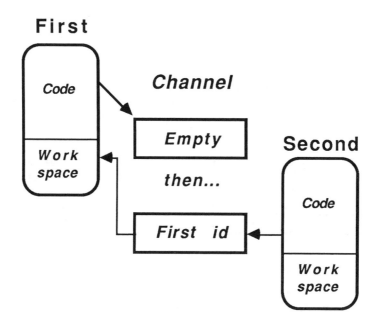

Figure 8.14: Implementation of rendezvous using single memory location

environment process. Any which are not currently communicating will be suspended. Any which are will be scheduled to run or be running.

For very low *latency* in real-time systems, a high priority process may *preempt* the one running in response to a signal on a special hard channel (which supports signals only).

8.5.4   Summary

The design of a processor to support both local multiprocessing and connection within a processor network need not be complicated. All that is needed to support *static non-prioritized processes* is a pair of *queue pointer* registers and the necessary hardware for transmitting and receiving data on each *hard channel*. Processes are represented in a *ready queue* by their *workspace* pointer. Workspace is private to each process and includes a record of the program counter value when the process is not running. Context switching is kept simple and fast by obviating the need to save any registers except PC. This is achieved by denying the possibility to suspend or time-out any process while an expression evaluation is under way. Figure 8.15 shows the organization of the processor and Figure 8.16 the programmer's architecture.

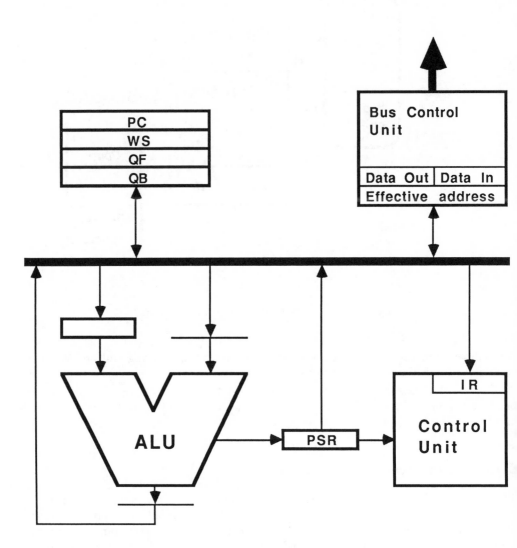

Figure 8.15: Process queue + message channel machine organization

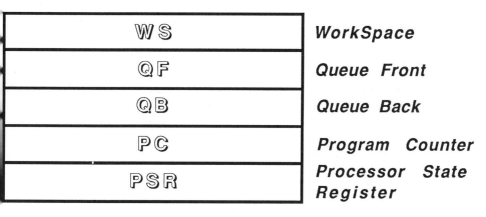

Figure 8.16: Programmer's architecture of queue + channel machine

Prioritized processes may be supported by employing a *round robin* algorithm with timeslice proportional to priority. An alternative, which is much simpler to implement, is to employ a separate ready queue for each distinct priority and allowing any process to pre-empt one of lower priority.

Soft channels and *hard channels* are unified by employing an identical *rendezvous* mechanism. They differ purely in the memory locations used as *rendezvous locations*[18] and data transfer mechanism. Processes awaiting rendezvous are suspended (with little processing overhead) on awaiting communication and rescheduled later by the other process partaking in the transaction. It is irrelevant whether *sender* or *receiver* is first to arrive at rendezvous location.

This design is *ideally* suited to real-time systems because it enables easy implementation of *alternation*. However many such applications would require *prioritization* and *preemption* in process scheduling.

Processes provide a problem-level *abstraction*, software-level *modularity* and machine-level *reusability*.

---

[18]i.e. a memory location is reserved for each hard channel.

Exercises

Question one

i   As described in the text, the implementation of a *function invocation* by a compile
on a pure *stack* machine implies the creation of a suitable stack structure containing...

- *Local variables*

- *Parameters*

- *Return value*

Explain how the compiler initializes...

- *Value parameters*

- *Reference parameters*

ii   Draw a diagram showing the stack structure created to implement an invocation of th
following procedure and function, defined using the *Modula-2* programming language...

```
PROCEDURE HexStringToCard(String : ARRAY OF CHAR;
                          VAR Value : CARDINAL;
                          VAR Error : BOOLEAN)
VAR
  Index : CARDINAL;

BEGIN
  ...
END HexStringToCard


PROCEDURE Random(Seed : CARDINAL;
                 VAR NextSeed : CARDINAL)
                 : REAL;
BEGIN
  ...
END Random
```

Note: A *function* in *Modula-2* is referred to as a *function procedure* and is still de-clared as a procedure, but with the addition of a *return type*. Assume that *CARDINAL* and *REAL* variables are of length four bytes and that *BOOLEAN* and *CHAR* variables are each represented within a single byte. *ARRAY OF CHAR* is called an *open array parameter* whose size is determined on invocation at run-time. The stack pointer points to the *topmost item* and not to the first free byte.

Question two

Many architectures build their stacks *downward* in memory. Use your solution to question one to show in each case how each parameter and each variable would be referenced using only the *frame pointer*.

Note: Use the notation "<offset>(fp)". Also assume that any address is *three* bytes long and that the least significant byte of anything is always found at the lowest address.

Question three

Consider three processors...

- *Zero-address stack machine*

- *One-address accumulator machine*

- *Two-address register file machine*

...with simplified instruction sets, respectively...

- { push pop mul div add sub}

- { load store mul div add sub}

- { load store mul div add sub}

For all three machines assume a *basic instruction* length of one byte and an address length of four bytes. An immediate operand may be encoded within one, two or four bytes as required using twos-complement integer representation.

Stack machine   push and pop alone take a single address locating the operand to be moved. The arithmetic instructions all operate on the topmost two items on the stack, leaving the result on top. Where ordering of operands is important, the top item is equiv-alent to that on the left of a written expression. Assume all variables are located as *byte* offsets from either *frame pointer* or *static base register*. Hence both *move* instructions will be just two bytes long (one byte for an instruction plus one byte for an offset).

Accumulator machine   One operand is always the accumulator, corresponding to that on the left of a written expression. The result is always placed in the accumulator.

Register file machine   The second address identifies both the righthand operand and the destination of the result of an arithmetic operation. In the case of a *move* instruction the first and second address identify *source* and *destination* respectively. Assume sixteen registers allowing up to two to be specified within a single byte, additional to the basic instruction and an address or immediate operand (if required). Note that there is no *register windowing*, so all variables are bound to memory and *not* to registers.

i   The execution time of an instruction is almost completely determined by the number of *bus cycles* required. Why does it take much longer to perform a (*read* or *write*) bus cycle than any other processor operation? Need it always be true?

ii   Assuming a unit of time equal to that taken to perform a bus cycle, enumerate the time taken to execute each instruction of each processor described above.

iii   Summarize the advantages and disadvantages of the *stack machine* in the light of your answers to parts i and ii of this question. How might the worst disadvantage be alleviated.

Question four

i   For each of the processors described in question three compose the code which a *compiler* might produce to implement the following assignment...

$$\text{RootSquared} := (\text{b*b} - \text{4*a*c})/(\text{2.a})$$

...given that the order of operations will obey the following rules...

- *Parenthesized expressions evaluated first (from innnermost out)*

- *Expression evaluated from right to left*

- *Operators evaluated according to precedence order (*, /, +, -)*

ii   Discuss your solution to i and give a *quantitative* comparison between architectures with regard to...

- *Number of instructions required*

- *Execution time*

- *Code length*

Quantify the improvement in the execution time on the *stack machine* yielded by arranging that the topmost three stack items are always to be found in special dedicated processor registers.

Note: You may assume that $a > 0$ and that *single precision* arithmetic is sufficient (i.e. forget about *carry*).

Question five

Enumerate all bus operations required for a *stack machine* to *invoke, enter, exit* and *return* from a function. Assume that three parameters are passed and that all parameters and return value each require just a single bus operation to read or write.

Compare your result with the operations required to achieve the same thing on a *register windowing* machine. What are the limitations of *register windowing*?

Question six

What is the difference between a *procedure* and a *process* and what (if any) are the similarities? Include a brief comparison between *procedure oriented* and *process oriented* software design.

Chapter 9

System organization

9.1 Internal communication

9.1.1 System bus

Bus devices

A top-level functional decomposition of a computer may be made yielding a requirement for the following components. . .

- *Processor*

- *Memory*

- *External communication (Input/Output or I/O)*

A computer system may typically be broken down into a number of components called *devices*, each of which implements, or *cooperates* in implementing, one or other system function. A minimum of one device is required to implement each function[1]. The use of multiple devices cooperating to implement memory and external communication is commonplace and is discussed in this chapter. Systems with multiple processor devices are rapidly becoming more common but suffer complication and are outside the scope of this book.

Devices must be able to communicate with each other. The form of *communication channel* employed is the *bus*[2]. In general a *bus* permits both *one-to-one* and *one-to-many* communication. On the *system bus*, however, communication is restricted to just *one-to-one*. Figure 9.1 shows how devices are connected to the *system bus*.

---

[1] This approach is *reductionist* and may not be the only way to approach constructing a computer. *Artificial neural systems* [Vemuri 88] [Arbib 87] inspired by models of brain function, offer an example of a *holistic* approach .

[2] We have met the *bus* before as a means of communication *inside a processor* (see Chapter 7).

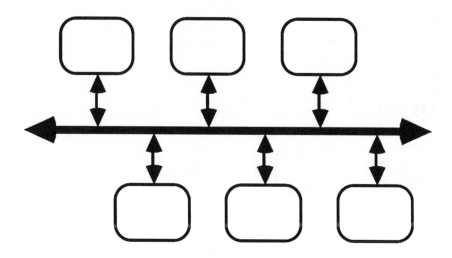

Figure 9.1: Devices communicating over the system bus

It is of the greatest importance to understand that the *system bus* constitutes a *shared resource* of the system. A device must wait its turn in order to use it. Whilst waiting it will be *idle*. The *bandwidth* of a bus is the number of *symbols* (binary words) which may be transmitted across it in unit time. The bandwidth of the single system bus used in contemporary computers determines the limit of their performance [3].

Bus structure

The term *system bus* is used to collectively describe a number of separate channels. In fact it may be divided into the following subsidiary bus channels...

- *Address*

- *Data*

- *Control*

Address bus and *data bus* are each made up of one physical channel for each bit of their respective word lengths. The *control bus* is a collection of channels, usually of *signal* protocol (i.e. single bit), which collectively provide system control. The structure of the system bus is depicted in Figure 9.2.

---

[3] The purchasor of many a processor "upgrade" has been sadly disappointed to find only a marginal increase in performance because of this.

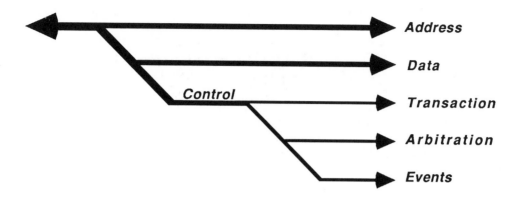

Figure 9.2: Subdivision of system bus into address, data and control buses

Control signals may be broken down into groups implementing *protocols* for the following communication...

- *Arbitration*

- *Synchronous transaction*

- *Asynchronous transaction (Events)*

These form the subject matter of the remainder of this section.

9.1.2   Bus arbitration

Arbitration protocol

While a bus transaction occurs, an *arbiter* decides which device, requesting use of the bus, will become *master* of the next transaction. The *master* controls the bus during the whole of a *bus cycle* deciding the direction of data transfer and the address of the word which is to be read or written.

Arbitration must take into account the special demands of the processor fetching code from memory. As a result most commercial processors combine the tasks of arbitration with that of executing code by implementing both in a single device called a *central processing unit (CPU)*.

The *arbitration protocol* operates cyclically, concurrent with the bus cycle, and is composed of two signals...

- *Bus request*

- *Bus grant*

One physical channel for each signal is connected to each potential master device. A device which requires to become master asserts *bus request* and waits for a signal on *bus grant*, upon receipt of which it disasserts *bus request* and proceeds with a transaction *at the start of the next bus cycle*. Note that *bus request* is a signal which is transmitted continuously whereas *bus grant* is instantaneous. A useful analogy is the distinction between a red *stop* sign, which is displayed continuously while active, and a factory hooter, which simply sounds briefly once. Both may be considered to be of *signal* protocol but care must be taken to distinguish which is intended. In digital systems we talk of a *level*, meaning a continuous signal usually communicated by *maintaining a potential*, or an *edge*, meaning an instantaneous signal usually communicated by *changing a potential*.

Slave devices are typically memory devices, all of which must be located within unique areas of the *memory map*. Masters are usually *I/O processors* which drive devices for such purposes as mass storage, archival or communication with other remote computers.

Device prioritization

How does the arbiter decide which device is to be the next master if there are *multiple* requests pending? As is often the case, the answer to the question lies waiting in the problem as a whole. Here we find another question outstanding... How do we ensure that the more *urgent* tasks are dealt with *sooner*? Both questions are answered if we assign a *priority* to each device and provide a mechanism whereby bus requests are granted accordingly. The simplest such mechanism is that of the *daisy chain* shown in Figure 9.3.

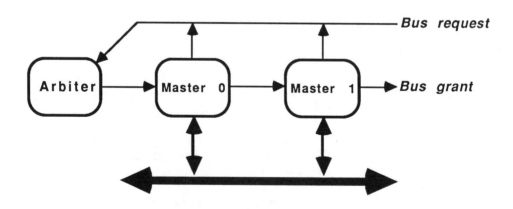

Figure 9.3: Bus arbitration with daisy chain prioritization

9.1.3 Synchronous bus transactions

Bus cycle

A *transaction* is a single communication event between two bus devices. Each transaction is *synchronous*, i.e. each participating device must complete a transaction before proceeding. Asynchronous communication may also be achieved as we shall see later in this section. On each transaction a single device becomes master and communicates a message to or from just one slave. One transaction occurs on each *bus cycle*. A single transaction may be subdivided into two *phases*...

- *Address*

- *Data transfer*

The *address phase* involves transmitting the following messages...

- *Address*

- *Read/Write*

The protocol of the *address* channel is simply made up of *timing* and word length. That of the *read/write* channel is, once again, its timing and just a single bit which indicates the *direction* of data transfer.

Since bus transactions occur iteratively, the operation of the two phases are together referred to as a *bus cycle*.

Synchronous transaction protocol

As mentioned above the *protocol* of each of the three component bus channels relies heavily on timing. This is achieved using the system clock and is best explained by a diagram, Figure 9.4. The duration of the first phase is the time taken to...

- *Setup (render valid) address and R/W*

- *Send physical message*

- *Decode address*

...and is measured in clock-cycles (ticks). In the diagram example each phase takes just two clock-cycles.

An address must be *decoded* in order that the required memory register may be connected to the bus. Phase two comprises...

- *Connect memory register to data bus*

- *Setup (render valid) data*

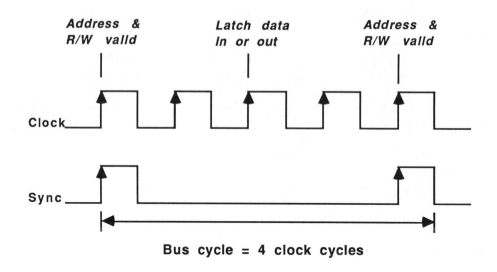

Figure 9.4: Bus cycle showing address and data transfer phases

- *Send physical message (either direction)*

- *Latch data*

Both address and data must remain valid long enough to physically traverse their channel and be successfully latched [4].

Synchronous transaction protocol for slow slaves

The time taken by a memory device to render valid data onto the data bus varies according to the device concerned. Because of this, a transaction protocol specifying a *fixed* interval between valid address and valid data would require that interval to be appropriate to the *slowest* slave device ever likely to be encountered. This would imply an unnecessarily slow system since, as pointed out earlier, bus bandwidth limits overall system performance.

Wait states are states introduced in the bus cycle, between *address valid* and *data valid*, by slow devices to gain the extra time they need (Figure 9.5). Any number of wait states are permitted by most contemporary bus transaction protocols. Note that an extra control signal *(Rdy)* is necessary and that such a protocol implies a slight increase in processor complexity.

---

[4] The physical means of sending and receiving messages is discussed in Chapter 1 and Chapter 5. The timing restrictions of accessing any *physical* memory device are discussed in Chapter 5. In summary these are the *setup time, hold time* and *propagation delay*.

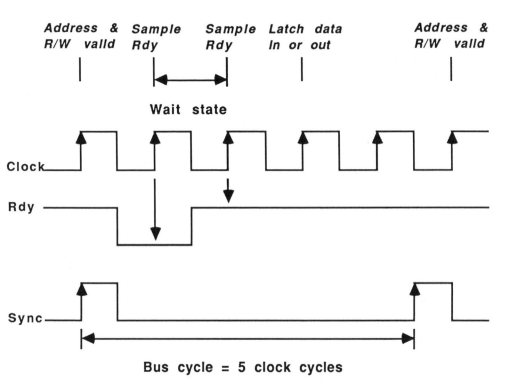

Figure 9.5: Bus cycle with a single wait state inserted

Address/data multiplexing

The fact that the address bus and data bus are active at distinct times may be used to reduce the cost of the physical system at the expense of a slight reduction in system bus bandwidth.

Multiplexing is the technique of unifying two (or more) *virtual* channels in a single physical one. It was introduced and discussed in Chapter 6 where it was shown how to construct a *multiplexer* and *demultiplexer*. *Time-multiplexing* cyclically switches the physical channel between the processes communicating address and data at both ends.

Required bus width is a significant factor in the expense of implementing a system. As has been pointed out previously, when discussing control units[5], *interconnect* can be particularly expensive given a *two-dimensional technology*. Assuming equal data and address bus width, the required interconnect may be *halved*. A single *address/data bus* may be employed, passing the address in the first phase of the bus cycle and transferring data in the second half.

The performance overhead incurred is simply the extra time required to effect the switching at either end. The address must be latched by the slave and then removed from the bus by the master. A delay must be allowed between phases to ensure that two devices do not attempt attempt to transmit on the same physical channel simultaneously.

9.1.4 Asynchronous bus transactions

System events

There is another form of communication which requires a physical channel. The behaviour of the running processes will typically be conditionally dependent upon *events* occurring within the system. Devices must communicate the occurrence of an event to the processor as shown in Figure 9.6.

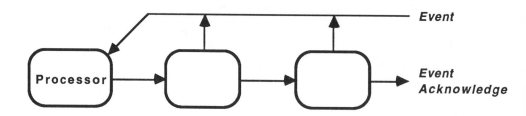

Figure 9.6: Event signal (interrupt request) and daisy chained event acknowledge (interrupt grant)

---

[5]See Chapter 7.

Note that events can occur within the processor as well [6], For example, the control unit should be capable of detecting an attempt to divide by zero. Such a *processor event* is typically dealt with by exactly the same mechanism as for *system events*. The set of system events and that of processor events are collectively known as *exceptions*.

System events are associated with communication, both internal and external. Completion or failure of *asynchronous* communication transactions must be *signalled* to the processor. A signal that an event has occurred is called an *interrupt* since it causes the processor to cease executing the "main" program[7] and transfer to an *interrupt service routine*.

Event protocol

Before a system event can be processed it must first be *identified*. There are two principal methods...

- *Polling*

- *Vectoring*

Event *polling* means testing each and every *event source* in some *predetermined* order (see discussion of *event prioritization* below). Clearly this will occupy the processor with a task which is not directly getting the *system task* done. Care must be taken to test the most active sources first to minimize the *average* time taken to identify an event.

Given a *pure signal*, there exists no choice but polling to identify an event. Commonplace in contemporary system architectures is a more sophisticated protocol which includes transmission of the event identity by the source.

Whether or not a running process on the processor *will* be interrupted or not depends on the event which caused the attempted interrupt. The interrupt signal is thus more properly referred to as an *interrupt request*. In order to decide whether interruption will indeed occur, the event protocol of the system must include some form of *arbitration*. If no event is currently being serviced, the request will be successful and an *interrupt grant* signal be returned.

Thus a complete picture of the required event protocol may now be presented. There are *three* phases...

1. *Event signal (interrupt request)*

2. *Event acknowledge (interrupt grant)*

3. *Event identify (interrupt vector)*

---

[6] ...as discussed in Chapter 7.

[7] The "main" program may be thought of as a routine executed in response to an *interrupt* signalling that a *reset* or *boot* event has occurred.

The symbol used to identify the event may be chosen so as to also serve as a pointer into a table of pointers to the appropriate *interrupt service routines*. This table is called the *interrupt despatch table*. Its location must be known to the processor and hence a base pointer is to be found at either of the following...

- *Reserved memory location*

- *Reserved processor register*

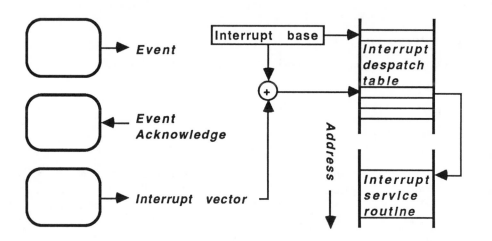

Figure 9.7: Event identification by vector

The event protocol and its efficient means of vectoring a processor to the required interrupt service routine are depicted in Figure 9.7.

Event arbitration

Event protocols must include some means of deciding which event to service given more than one pending. There are three fundamental schemes...

- *FIFO*

- *Round robin*

- *Prioritization*

Prioritized arbitration is the most simple to implement in hardware and is the one depicted in Figure 9.6. *Event acknowledge* channels are arranged in a *daisy chain*. Each device passes on any signal received that it does not require itself. Devices, regarded as *event sources*, must simply be connected in the daisy chain in such a way that higher priority processes are closer to the processor. Software prioritization is also extremely simple. The order of polling is simply arranged such that sources are inspected according to priority. Note that this may well conflict with the efficiency requirement that sources be inspected in order of event *frequency*. *Daisy chain* and *prioritized polling* require only *signal* event protocol.

Prioritization of a *vectored* event protocol, as depicted in Figure 9.7, requires a little more hardware but still uses standard components. A *priority encoder* is used to encode the *interrupt vector/event identity* and thus ensures that the one transmitted is the highest priority provided that event sources are connected appropriately.

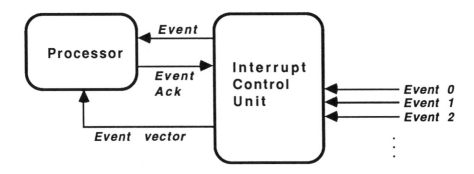

Figure 9.8: Event prioritization and control using an interrupt control unit (ICU)

An *interrupt control unit*, Figure 9.8, is an integrated device which will usually provide *prioritized vectored event protocol* as well as *FIFO* and *round robin*. In addition it may be expected to provide *event masking* as well, Figure 9.9.

Note that, in any prioritized event protocol, if a higher priority event occurs, while a lower priority event is being serviced, interruption of the current interrupt service routine *will* take place. This is equivalent to *preemption* of a running process as in any other *process scheduler*. The event protocol employed effectively determines the scheduling algorithm for the lowest level processes of an *operating system*. This becomes *programmable* to a large extent given a contemporary ICU and thus must be decided by the operating system designer.

Direct memory access (DMA)

As pointed out earlier, the processor is unique among bus masters in requiring continuous, high priority, access to the memory device containing the executable program code. Other bus masters require *direct memory access* and must request it from the *bus arbiter*, which is implemented, together with the processor, in a single device called the *central*

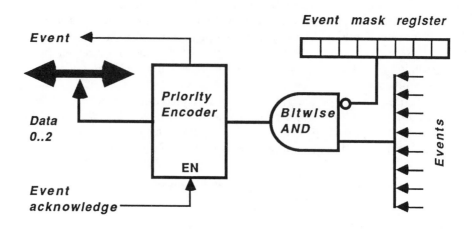

Figure 9.9: Event masking and prioritization using priority encoder

processor unit. These bus masters must report *asynchronous communication events* to the processor.

Typically a bus master will require to read or write a *block* of data to or from memory. The size of the block and location in memory for the transfer will need to be under *program control*, although the actual transfer need not be. To facilitate this a *direct memory access controller (DMAC)* is used which is said to provide a number of *DMA channels* under program control. The DMAC conducts the transfers programmed independently of the processor. A schematic diagram is shown in Figure 9.10.

The protocol employed for communication between the DMAC and the (would-be master) devices may be simple. For example a *busy/ready* protocol might be employed where the device transmits a *ready* signal, announcing that it is ready to transfer data, and the DMAC may assert a *busy* signal continuously until it is free to begin. In addition a *R/W* channel will be required to indicate the direction of transfer.

A simplified picture of the programmable registers is shown in Figure 9.11. One control bit is shown which would determine whether an event is generated upon completion of a transfer. Other control parameters which may be expected are *channel priority* and *transfer mode*. The transfer mode defines the way in which the DMAC shares the system bus with the *CPU*. The three fundamental modes are as follows. . .

- Block transfer mode . . . *completes the whole transfer in one operation and thus deprives the CPU of any access to the bus while it does so*

- Cycle stealing mode . . . *transfers a number of bytes at a time, releasing the bus periodically to allow the CPU access*

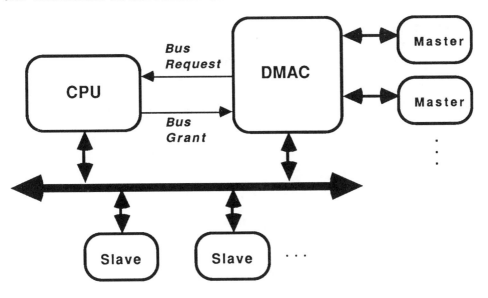

Figure 9.10: Direct memory access controller (DMAC) connected to CPU and system bus

- Transparent mode ... *makes use of bus cycles that would otherwise go unused and so does not delay the CPU but does seriously slow up the speed of data transfer from the device concerned*

There are some devices which require *block transfer mode* because they generate data at a very high rate, once started, and are inefficient to stop and restart. Magnetic disc and tape drives usually require this mode.

Although a degree of efficiency is possible by careful design, the fact remains that the system bus is a *shared resource* and currently sets the limit to overall system performance.

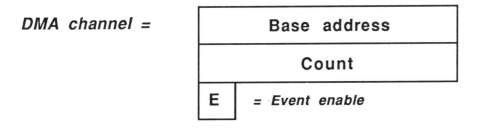

Figure 9.11: DMAC channel registers

9.2   Memory organization

9.2.1   Physical memory organization

Requirements

The memory sub-system of a computer must fulfill some or all of the following requirements, depending on application...

- *Minimum mean access time*

- *Minimum mean cost*

- *Non-volatility*

- *Portability*

- *Archival*

The first three items apply to all systems, regardless of application. The last two
really only apply to *work-stations* (which represent a just a small proportion of working
systems).

Minimum mean access time (per access)   ...of memory partially determines the *bandwidth* of the *system bus* and thus the performance of the entire system (see preceding
section). It is not necessary to have *all* memory possessing the minimum attainable
access time. That would certainly conflict with other requirements, particularly that of
minimum mean cost. The mean access time should be considered over all *accesses*, not
over locations. It is possible to minimize mean access time by ensuring that *the fastest
memory is that most frequently accessed*. *Memory management* must operate effectively
to ensure that the data most frequently referenced is placed in the memory most rapidly
accessed. We shall see how to achieve this later on in this section.

Minimum mean cost (per bit)   ...over all memory devices employed largely determines
the cost of contemporary machines. This is because the majority (~90%) of the fundamental elements (e.g. switches) contained therein are employed in implementing system
memory, rather than the processor or external communication [8]. This is simply true of
the kind of computer we are building now. There is no fundamental reason it should be
this way.

The requirements of *minimum cost per bit* and *minimum access time per access* can
be made consistent by ensuring that *as large a proportion of memory as possible is
implemented in the lowest cost technology available*, while the remainder is implemented
using the fastest.

---

[8] In fact, the greatest cost element in contemporary computer fabrication is that of *interconnect*.
Manufacturers of electronic *connectors* tend to make much bigger profits than those of *integrated devices*.
Of these, those which sell memory do much better than those who sell processors.

Non-volatility ...of memory means that its contents do not "flow away" when the *power supply* is turned off. It is essential that at least some of system memory be *non-volatile* in order that *boot code* be available on *power-up* and that data may be saved for a later work session. Non-volatility is difficult to achieve with *electronic* switches. It is currently only understood how to make switches which "leak" electrons and thus require a constantly applied *potential* to retain their state. As we shall see later, it is possible to minimize the problem by continually "topping up a leaky bucket".

Magnetic technology is able to provide memory devices which are non-volatile *on the timescale of interest*, i.e. up to tens of years. More recently, *optical* and *magneto-optical* non-volatile technologies have matured to the point of commercial competitiveness.

Portability ...of at least a section of system memory is essential for *archival* of data and to allow work to progress on different machines (e.g. should one break down). Magnetic or optical technology offers an advantage here in not requiring physical contact with media, thus greatly reducing wear and the possibility of damage due to repeated insertion and removal.

Archival ...of data means the maintenance of a *long life* copy of important data. This poses similar technological demands to those posed by *minimum mean cost* and *portability*. The only potential difference is *longevity* of memory media, which is sometimes limited by environmental constraints such as temperature variations. Periodic *refreshing* of archival media can be expensive due to sheer volume of data.

Technological constraints

It is *impossible* to fulfill all memory requirements with a single memory device. It probably always will be because *different physical limits* are imposed on optimization against each requirement.

Access time is limited first by the switching necessary to *connect* the required memory register to the data bus and secondly by the time taken for that memory state to be read and latched. The underlying physical limitation, assuming an efficient *physical memory organization*, is the *charging time* required to close a switch. This matter is fully discussed in Chapter 5.

Cost is limited by the production cost, per element, of the device. This may be subdivided into materials and production process. There is no reason why cheap manufacture should coincide with device performance.

Non-volatility and *portability* require *durability* and the avoidance of physical contact with the host. The latter suggests that only a comparatively small physical potential will be available to change the state of a memory element. This is true of magnetic technology but, recently, optical technology has become available, in the form of the *laser*, which demonstrates that this need not be the case.

Archival requires immunity from environmental effects and *long term* non-volatility.

Physical memory devices

A *flip-flop*, Figure 1.3, is referred to as a *static memory* because, if undisturbed, its state will persist for as long as power is provided to hold one or other *normally-open switch* closed. *Dynamic memory* is an alternative which, typically, is easier to implement, cheaper to manufacture and *consumes less power*.

The idea is simply to employ a reservoir (bucket) which represents 1 when charged and 0 otherwise. Implementation in electronic technology requires merely a capacitor. Capacitances are not just cheap to fabricate on an integrated circuit, *they are hard to avoid!* Roughly *four times* the memory may be rendered on the same area of silicon for the same cost.

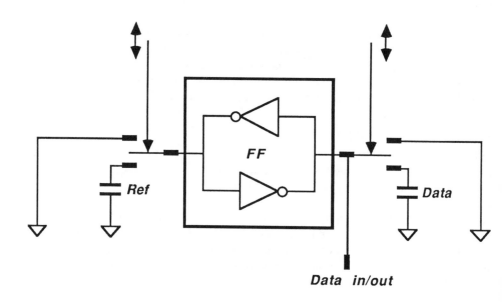

Figure 9.12: Sense amplification to refresh a dynamic memory

Nothing comes for free. The problem is *leakage*. Any real physical capacitor is in fact equivalent to an ideal one in parallel with a resistance, which is large but not infinite. A dynamic memory may be thought of as a "leaky bucket". The charge will slowly leak away. The memory state is said to require periodic *refreshing*. Contemporary electronic dynamic memory elements require a refresh operation approximately every two milliseconds. This is called the *refresh interval*. Note that as bus bandwidth increases, refresh intervals remain *constant* and thus become less of a constraint on system performance.

Refreshing is achieved using a flip-flop as shown in Figure 9.12. First the flip-flop is discharged by moving the switches to connect to zero potential. Secondly the switches are moved so as to connect one end of the flip-flop to the data storage capacitor and the other to a *reference capacitor*, whose potential is arranged to be exactly *half way* between that corresponding to each logic state. The flip-flop will adopt a state which depends solely on the charge in the data capacitor and thus recharge, or discharge, it to the appropriate potential. Flip-flop, reference capacitor and switches are collectively referred to as a *sense amplifier*. Note that memory *refresh* and *read* operations are *identical*.

A cost advantage over *static* memory is only apparent if few flip-flops are needed for sense amplification. By organizing memory in *two dimensions*, as discussed below, the number of sense amplifiers may be reduced to the *square root* of the number of memory elements. Thus as the size of the memory device grows so does the cost advantage of dynamic memory over static memory. For small memory devices, static memory may still remain cost effective. The principal disadvantage of dynamic memory is the *extra complexity* required to ensure *refresh* and the possible system bus *wait states* it may imply.

Note that all forms of electronic memory are volatile. The need for *electrical contacts*, which are easily damaged and quickly worn, generally prohibit portability. Cost per bit is also high since each element requires fabrication. Small access time is the dominant motivation for the use of electronic memory.

That which follows is intended only as an *outline* and not a full description of a real commercial *optical memory device*, which is rather more complicated. However the general operation of *optical memory*, which currently looks set to gain great importance, should become clear. What follows should also serve as an illustration of the exploitation of physical properties of materials for a memory device offering *low cost per bit*.

Figure 9.13 shows how a *laser* is used as a *write head* to write a 0. A laser[9] is a source of intense light (visible electromagnetic radiation) whose beam may be very precisely located on a surface (e.g. of a rotating disc). Once positioned, a pulse of radiation causes the surface to melt and resolidify forming a small crater or *pit*. A second, lower power, laser is pointed at the location to be read. Since the surface there has been damaged, its radiation will be *scattered* and only a very small amount will fall on a *light sensitive detector*, to be interpreted as a 0. Together, the lower power laser and detector form the *read head*. The damage is impossible to undo, hence the data *cannot be erased*.

Reading a 1 follows the same procedure except that the write head delivers no pulse and thus leaves the surface undamaged. Mirror-like *specular reflection* will now be detected by the read head which will thus register a 1, Figure 9.14.

The scheme outlined above should more properly be termed *opto-mechanical* memory

---

[9] Light amplification by stimulated emission of radiation.

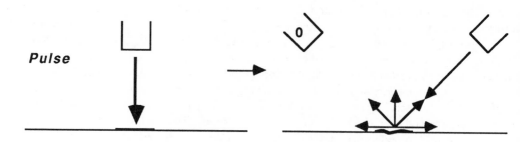

Figure 9.13: Writing and reading a 0 using opto-mechanical technology

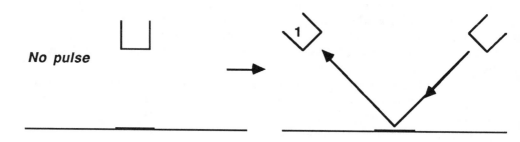

Figure 9.14: Writing and reading a 1 using opto-mechanical technology

since the reference mechanism is *optical* but the memory mechanism is *mechanical*, having two states... *damaged* and *undamaged*. An alternative approach, termed *magneto-optical* memory, uses a laser write head which alters the *magnetic* rather than the physical state of the surface. This in turn affects its optical properties which may be sensed by the read head. In contrast to opto-mechanical memory, magneto-optical memory may be reused again and again since *data may be erased*. It thus offers competition for purely magnetic memory with two distinct advantages...

- *Significantly greater capacity per device*

- *Improved portability*

...in addition to the *non-volatility* and extremely low *cost per bit* which both technologies offer. *Access time* and *transfer rate* are similar, although magnetic devices are currently quicker, largely because of *technological maturity*. The *portability* advantage of the optical device arises out of the absence of any physical contact between medium and read/write heads. Further reading on optical memory is currently scarce, except for rather demanding journal publications. An article in *BYTE* magazine may prove useful [Laub 86].

There is an enormous gulf separating an idea such as that outlined above and making it work. For example, a *durable* material with the necessary physical properties must be found. Also, some means must be found to *physically transport* the heads over the disc while maintaining the *geometry*. A *myriad* of such problems must be solved. Development is both extremely risky and extremely costly.

Physical memory access

Whatever the physical memory element employed, a very large number must be arranged in such a way that any one may be individually referenced as rapidly as possible. The traditional way to arrange memory is as a *one-dimensional array* of *words*. Each word is of a specified length which characterizes the system. A unique *address* forms an index which points to a *current location*. This arrangement presumes access of just *one location at a time*.

The essential physical requirement is for *address decoding* to enable the selected word to be connected, via a *buffer*, to the data bus. Figure 9.15 depicts this arrangement.

If there is no restriction on choice of element referenced, the device may be referred to as *random access*. *Linear* devices, e.g. those which use a medium in the form of a *tape*, impose a severe overhead for random access but are extremely fast for *sequential access*. A *magnetic tape* memory can present the storage location whose address is just one greater than the last one accessed immediately. An address randomly chosen will require winding or rewinding the tape... a very slow operation. Tape winding is an example of *physical transport* (see below).

An alternative arrangement is a *two-dimensional array* of words. Figure 9.16 shows this for a single bit layer. Other bits, making up the word, should be visualized lying on a vertical axis, perpendicular to the page. No further decoding is required for these, only a buffer connecting each bit to the data bus. Each decode signal shown is connected to a vertical slice, along a *row* or *column*, through the memory "cube".

Externally the 2-d memory appears *one-dimensional* since words are accessed by a single address. Internally this address is broken into two, the *row address* and *column address* which are decoded separately. The advantage of *row/column addressing* is that the use of dynamic memory can yield a cost advantage, using current technology, as a result of needing just one sense amplifier for each entire row (or column). This implies that only $\sqrt{n}$ flip-flops are required for n memory elements.

Extra external hardware is required to ensure that every element is refreshed within the specified refresh interval. A *refresh counter* is used to generate the refresh address on each *refresh cycle*. Assuming that a sense amplifier is provided for each *column*, it is possible to refresh an entire *row* simultaneously. Care must be taken to *guarantee* a refresh operation for each row within the given refresh interval.

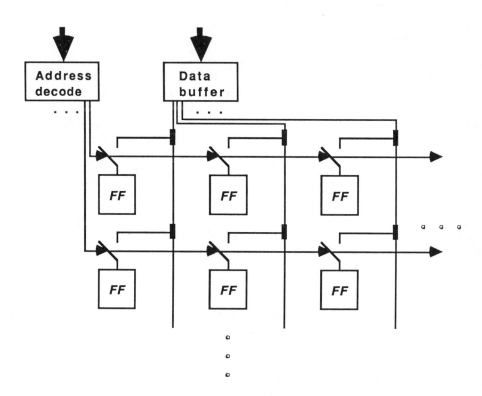

Figure 9.15: One-dimensional organization of memory

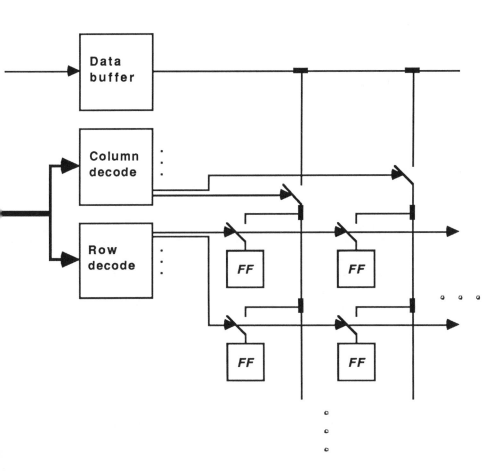

Figure 9.16: Row/column addressing and multiplexing

Note that row address and column address are *multiplexed* onto a local address bus which may thus be *half* the width of that of the system bus. Reduction of *interconnect* reduces cost at the expense of speed and complexity. The following signals must be provided in such a manner as not to interfere unduly in system bus cycles...

- *Row address strobe (RAS)*

- *Column address strobe (CAS)* [10]

These are used to implement a protocol for the communication of row and column addresses, i.e. to *latch* them.

Most contemporary memory devices which offer...

- *Low cost per bit*

- *Non-volatility*

- *Portability*

...require some kind of *physical transport*. For example, devices using *magnetic* technology require transport of both read and write *heads* which impose and sense respectively, the *magnetic field* on the medium [11]. As discussed briefly above, *optical* devices typically require movement of one or more *lasers*, with respect to the medium which act as *read/write heads*.

Two performance parameters of memory devices requiring physical transport are of importance...

- *Access time (random access)*

- *Data transfer rate (sequential access)*

Access time is the time taken to physically transport the read/write heads over the area of medium where the desired location is to be found. This operation is known as a *seek*. The *data transfer rate* is the rate at which data, arranged sequentially, may be transferred to or from the medium. This also requires physical transport, but in one direction only, and without searching.

Figure 9.17 shows the arrangement of the *winchester disc* which possesses a number of solid *plattens*, each of which is read and written by an *independent* head. Each *sector* is referenced as though it belonged to a 1-d memory *via* a *single address* which is decoded into three subsidiary values...

- *Head*

---

[10] *"Strobe"* is a common term meaning simply *"edge signal"*.

[11] Usually a plastic tape or disc coated in a magnetic material.

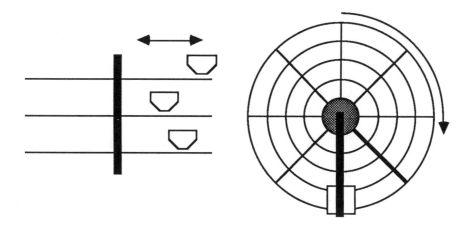

Figure 9.17: Memory access involving physical transport

- *Track*

- *Sector*

Note that the term *sector* is used with two distinct meanings... a sector of the circular disc *and* its intersection with a *track*!

Whatever the arrangement, as far as the *system bus* is concerned, each individual memory element may be visualized simply as a *flip-flop*, internally constructed from a pair of *normally-open switches* or, if one prefers, a pair of *invertor gates*. Only one connection is actually required for both *data in* and *data out* (level) signals. However these must be connected to the data bus in such a way as to...

- *Render impossible simultaneous read and write*

- *Ensure access only when device is selected*

Figure 9.18 shows how this may be achieved. Note that it is the *output buffer* which supplies the power to drive the data bus and not the poor old flip-flop! This avoids any possiblity of the flip-flop *state* being affected by that of the bus when first connected for a read operation.

Modular interleaved memory

Here we discuss a method for enhancing system bus *bandwidth* and which also provides a measure of security against the failure of a single memory device.

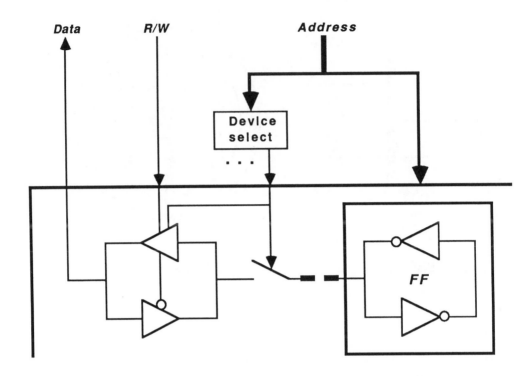

Figure 9.18: Connection of memory device to bus

Memory is divided up into n distinct *modules* each of which decodes a component of the address bus, the remainder of which ($\log_2 n$ bits) is decoded to select the required module. The arrangement is shown in Figure 9.19. Note that the data bus width is four times that for an individual module and hence requires that each *bus master* data buffer be correspondingly wide. This implies extra *interconnect* and hence extra *cost*. The number of modules required is decided by the ratio of *processor cycle* to *bus cycle* (usually the number of clock cycles per bus cycle). Typical for current electronic technology is $n = 4$.

Address interleaving is the assignment of each member of n consecutive addresses to a separate *module*. The most obvious scheme is to assign the module number containing address x to be x *modulo n*. It requires that n be a power of two.

Arguably the greatest advantage of *modular, interleaved memory* is that an *instruction cache* may be filled with fewer memory references as overhead. Given $n = 4$ and single byte, zero-address format, four instructions may be read using just one bus cycle. As discussed in Chapter 8, the efficiency of an instruction cache is dictated by the *condi*

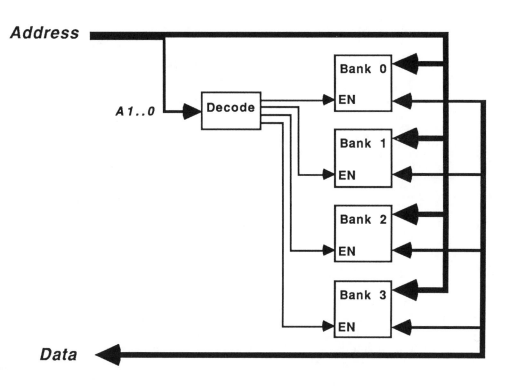

Figure 9.19: Address interleaving over a modular memory

tional branch probability since a branch, following the success of a condition, will render useless the remaining cache contents.

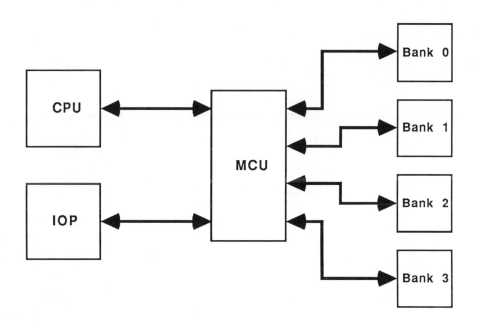

Figure 9.20: Shared access to a modular memory

Simultaneous, independent references to distinct modules are possible. Thus a measure of support for *shared memory multiprocessing* is afforded. Such benefit extends to the model of CPU plus *input/output processor (IOP)* [12], which effects all external communication, including that with *mass storage* memory devices. Each processor may possess its own connection to the modular memory, *sending* an address and *receiving* data. An extra *memory control unit (MCU)*, Figure 9.20, decides whether two simultaneous requests may be serviced *in parallel* and, if so, effects both transactions. If two simultaneous requests require access to the same module then the MCU must take appropriate action, typically inserting wait states into the lower priority processor (IOP) bus cycle.

Associative cache

The *associative cache* (Figure 9.21) is a means of reducing the average *access time* of memory references. It should be thought of as being interposed between processor and

---

[12] ...incorporating *direct access memory controller.*

"main" memory. It operates by intercepting and inspecting each address to see if it possesses a local copy. If so a *hit* is declared internally and *Rdy* asserted, allowing the *bus cycle* to be completed with the cache, instead of main memory, placing data on the data bus. Otherwise, a *miss* is internally declared and the job of finding data and completing the bus cycle left to main memory. The ratio of *hit* to *miss* incidents is called the *hit ratio* and characterizes the efficiency of the cache. Provision is shown for main memory to assert *Rdy* if the cache has failed to do so. The device implementing main memory must be designed with this in mind. Also the processor must be capable of the same brevity of bus cycle as is the cache.

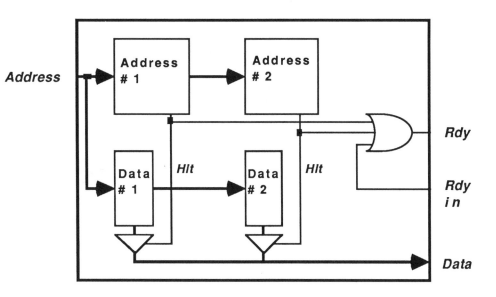

Figure 9.21: Two-way associative cache memory

Crucial to the performance of the cache is the *associativity* between the internally recorded *address tag* and the address on the address bus. *Full association* implies recording the *entire address* as the address tag. An address is compared with each tag stored *simultaneously* (in parallel). Unfortunately this requires a lot of address tag storage, as well as one *comparator* for each, and is thus expensive. There is a better way.

Set association reduces the number of comparators and tag memory required by restricting the number of locations where a match might be found. If that number is n the cache is said to be *n-way set associative*. Although many schemes are possible an obvious and common one is to divide the address into two components and use the least significant word to simultaneously *hash*[13] into each of n banks of tag memory. The most

---
[13] *Hashing* (here) means using the value as an index into an array.

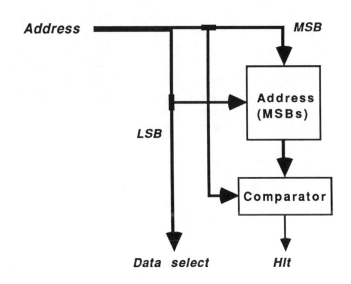

Figure 9.22: One-way (direct mapped) set associative cache

significant word is used as a tag. A hit is declared if any of the n tags found matche
the most significant word of the address. Remember that all n comparators functio
simultaneously. Direct-mapped association, the limiting case where $n = 1$, is shown i
Figure 9.22. *n-way association* may be achieved simply by iterating the structure show

Set associativity requires a *replacement algorithm* to determine which of the n possibl
slots is used to *cache* a data element, intercepted on the data bus from main memor
following a *miss*. Several possibilities include. . .

- *Least recently used (LRU)*

- *Least frequently used (LFU)*

- *First In First Out (FIFO)*

LRU is easily implemented in a *two-way associative* cache by maintaining a single bi
for each entry which is set when referenced and cleared when another member of the se
is referenced. *LFU* requires a *counter* for each member of each set. *FIFO* requires th
maintenance of a *modulo n* counter for each entry, pointing to the next set member t
be updated. *Locality* suggests that *LRU* should give the best performance of the three

Error detection and correction

Where reliability is required to exceed that inherent in the memory devices employed, *error detection*, or even *error detection and correction*, may be employed. Any such scheme implies an extra field added to *every word* of memory.

Parity offers the simplest and cheapest error detection. A single extra *parity bit* is updated on every write transaction. Two alternatives exist...

- *Even parity*

- *Odd parity*

...according to whether the parity bit denotes that an *even* or *odd* number of 1s are present in the word. *Even parity* may be computed in a single *exclusive-or (XOR)* operation according to...

$$p = d_n \oplus d_{n-1} \cdots \oplus d_0$$

Only *single* errors may be detected using a single parity bit. No correction is possible, only an *event* reported to the processor whose response may be programmed as an *interrupt service routine* if an *interrupt* is enabled for such an *event*. Any memory error is as likely to be *systematic* as *random* nowadays. Hence, on small systems, it is now often considered satisfactory simply to report a memory device fault to the poor user or systems manager.

Hamming code offers *single error correction/double error detection (SECDED)*. Although only a single error may be *corrected*, double errors may be *detected* and reported as an *event*. First, consider what is required of an additional *syndrome word* which is capable of indicating whether a word is correct and, if not, which of all possible errors has occurred. Given a data word length of n bits and a syndrome word length of m bits there are $n + m$ possible error states. Including the correct state, there are thus $n + m + 1$ possible states of a memory read result. Thus the *syndrome word* length is defined by...

$$2^m \geq n + m + 1$$

This implies the relationship shown in Table 9.1 between data word length, syndrome word length and percentage increase of physical memory size.

It is obvious from this that such a code is only economic on systems with large data bus width. Further, it would be useful if the syndrome word possessed the following characteristics...

- *Value = zero $\Rightarrow$ No Error $\Rightarrow$ No correction*

- *Value > zero $\Rightarrow$ Error, Value $\rightarrow$ Bit in error (Invert to correct)*

Data bits	Syndrome bits	Percentage increase in memory size
8	4	50
16	5	31
32	6	19
64	7	11

Table 9.1: Relationship between parameters for *Hamming* error detection code

Hamming code achieves all these desirable features by forming subsets of the data word and recording the parity of each. Each bit of the syndrome word in fact just represents the parity of a chosen subset of the data bits. It is possible to choose these sets in such a way that any change in parity, detected by an XOR between recorded and calculated syndrome words, indicates, not just an error, but precisely *which bit* is in error. For example, the *5-bit odd parity* syndrome of a *16-bit* data word is calculated via...

$$p_0 = d_2 \oplus d_5 \oplus d_{10} \oplus d_{11} \oplus d_{12} \oplus d_{13} \oplus d_{14} \oplus d_{15}$$
$$p_1 = d_4 \oplus d_5 \oplus d_6 \oplus d_7 \oplus d_8 \oplus d_9 \oplus d_{10} \oplus d_{15}$$
$$p_2 = d_1 \oplus d_2 \oplus d_3 \oplus d_7 \oplus d_8 \oplus d_9 \oplus d_{14} \oplus d_{15}$$
$$p_3 = d_0 \oplus d_2 \oplus d_3 \oplus d_5 \oplus d_6 \oplus d_9 \oplus d_{12} \oplus d_{13}$$
$$p_4 = d_0 \oplus d_1 \oplus d_3 \oplus d_4 \oplus d_6 \oplus d_8 \oplus d_{11} \oplus d_{13}$$

The *error vector* is calculated via...

$$E = \{(p_0 \oplus p_0'), (p_1 \oplus p_1'), (p_2 \oplus p_2'), (p_3 \oplus p_3'), (p_4 \oplus p_4')\}$$

...where p_i are stored as the syndrome and p_i' are computed after a *read*. $E = 0$ indicates *no error*, $E \neq 0$ indicates one or two errors, each (or each pair) of which will cause E to take a unique value, allowing the erroneous bit(s) to be identified and corrected.

9.2.2 Virtual memory organization

Requirements

Virtual memory simply means the memory as it *appears* to the *compiler* and programmer. The requirements may be summarized...

- *Single linear memory map*

- *Security*

single linear memory map ...hides the complexity and detail of *physical memory* which hould be of no interest whatsoever to the compiler or machine level programmer. Physical memory organization design aims should be considered distinct from those of virtual nemory organization. In other words, as far as the compiler is concerned *all of memory s unified into a single memory map*. This memory map will be typically of a volume approximately equal to that of the low cost (mass storage) device and of access time approximately equal to that of "main" memory. *Memory management* encapsulates the ask of ensuring that this is so. *All* virtual memory should be considered non-volatile.

These requirements pose severe problems for conventional programming techniques where the poor *user*, as well as the programmer, is required to distinguish between memory devices by *portability* (e.g. "floppy" *vs.* "hard" disc) and by *volatility* ("buffer" *vs.* "disc"). It is hardly surprising that computers are only used by a tiny proportion of those who would benefit (e.g. ~7% for business applications). The most promising new paradigm, which might *unify* user and programmer classes, is that of the *object*.

Objects[14] are internal representations of "real world" entities. They are composed of...

- *Methods*

- *State*

State simply means *variables* which are *private* to the object. *Methods* are *operations* which affect state. Objects communicate by *message passing*.

The important point is that neither user nor compiler need give consideration to physical memory organization. Objects are *persistent*, a fact consonant with the *non-volatility* of virtual memory. By rendering communication *explicit* the need for a visible *filing system* is obviated. The intention here is to point out the relationship between *objects* and *virtual memory*[15]. It is not appropriate to give a full introduction to *object oriented systems* here. The reader is referred to an excellent introduction in *BYTE* magazine [Thomas 89] and to the "classic" text [Goldberg & Robson 83].

Security ...of access becomes essential when a processor is a *shared resource* among multiple processes. The simplest approach, which *guarantees* effectiveness *given a suitable compiler*, is for each process to be allocated *private memory*, accessible by no other. The problem is that no such guarantee is necessarily possible *at the architecture level*. A careless or malicious programmer can easily create code (e.g. using an *assembler*) which accesses the private memory of another process *unless the architecture design renders this physically impossible*.

To achieve a secure architecture, memory access must be controlled by the *process scheduler* which is responsible for *memory allocation* to processes when they are created.

---

[14] See Chapter 2.
[15] A full treatment of the subject of *virtual memory* implementation more properly belongs in a text on *operating system*, e.g. [Deitel 84].

Memory device hierarchy

In order to address the problem of meeting the requirements of a *virtual memory*, we begin by adopting a *hierarchical* model of physical memory (Figure 9.23).

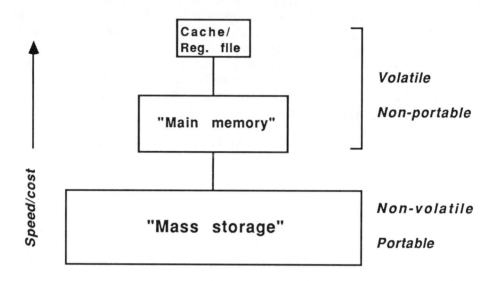

Figure 9.23: Hierarchy of memory devices

The topmost volume exists to render the *fastest possible mean access time per reference*. The bottom volume exists to render the *lowest possible cost per bit*. Memory managment ensures that optimal use is made of each resource.

Given a *cache*, the top two layers are directly accessible on the system bus. The means of unifying them into a single memory map, accessible via a single *physical address*, is discussed above. The task of unifying the result with *mass storage*, via a single *virtual address*, is discussed below.

Virtual to physical address translation

The primary sub-task of memory management is *address translation*. The *virtual memory map* is split up into a sequence of *blocks* which may be either fixed or variable in size, called *pages* or *segments* respectively. As a result the *virtual address* may be split into two fields...

- *Block number*

- *Offset into block*

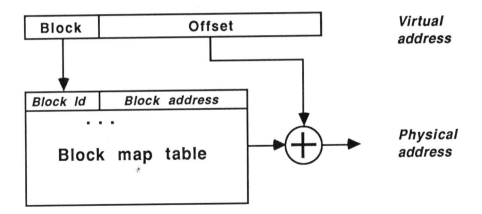

Figure 9.24: Virtual to physical address translation

All device memory maps are divided into *block frames*, each of which holds some or other *block*. Blocks are swapped between frames as required, usually across device boundaries, by the *memory manager* [16]. The *physical* location of every block is maintained in a *block map table*.

Address translation requires two operations...

- *Look up base address*

- *Add base address to offset*

...as shown in Figure 9.24.

Paged memory

For the moment we shall simplify the discussion by assuming a *paged memory*, though what follows also applies to a *segmented memory*. The size of a *page* will affect system performance. *Locality* has been shown to justify a typical choice of 512 bytes.

In fact the block map table must also record the physical memory device where the block is currently located. If it is not directly addressable in *main memory* a *page fault event* is reported to the processor. Whether software or hardware, the memory manager must respond by *swapping in* the required page to main memory. This strategy of swapping in a page when it is first referenced is called *demand paging* and is the most common and successful. *Anticipatory paging* is an alternative strategy which attempts to predict the need for a page *before* it has been referenced.

---

[16]Note that this activity used to require *software* implementation, which would form part of the *operating system*. It is now typically subject to *hardware* implementation.

Security may be afforded by each scheduled process possessing its own distinct *page map table*. This may be used in such a way that no two processes are physically able to reference the same *page frame even if their code is identical*. It is only effective if no process other than the *operating system* is able to initialize or modify *page map tables*. That part of the operating system which does this is the *memory allocation* component of the *process scheduler*. It alone must have the ability to execute *privileged instructions*, e.g. to access a *page map table base address* register. Note that data or code may be *shared* by simply mapping a page frame to pages in more than one page map table.

A *page replacement strategy* is necessary since a decision must be taken as to which page is to be *swapped out* when another is *swapped in*. Exactly the same arguments apply here as for the replacement strategy used for updating the contents of an *associative cache* (see above). As before, the principle of *locality* suggests that the *least recently used (LRU)* strategy will optimize performance given structured code. Unfortunately it is very difficult to approximate efficiently. See [Deitel 84] for a full treatment of this topic.

Lastly, because address translation must occur for every single memory reference, speed is of the highest importance. As pointed out above, a *table look up* and an *addition* is required for each translation. Addition of page frame address to offset merely requires *concatenation* [17]. Hence it is the table look up that limits performance. Because of this it is common to employ a *dedicated associative cache* for page map table entries deemed most likely to be referenced next. This typically forms part of a processor extension called a *memory managment unit (MMU)* which is also usually capable of maintaining the entire page map table *without software intervention* by independently responding to all page fault events.

Segmented memory

Everything said above about paged memory also applies to *segmented memory*, which offers an advantage in the ease of rendering *security* of access at the cost of significantly more difficult memory management due to possible *fragmentation* of the memory maps of *every* physical memory device.

Security is easier to achieve since the *logical entities* which require protection (e.g. the state of a *process* or *object*) will naturally tend to *vary in size*. It is easier to protect one segment than a number of pages.

Fragmentation is the term for the break up of a memory map such that *free memory* is divided into many small areas. An example schematic diagram is shown on Figure 9.25. It arises due to repeated swapping in and out of segments which, by definition, vary in size. The damaging consequence is that, after a period of operation, a time will arrive where no *contiguous* area of memory may be found to frame a segment being swapped in.

---

[17] Only the page frame number is needed, rather than its complete base address, because it is sufficient to completely specify page frame location on account of the fixed size of a page. The physical base address of a page frame is just its number followed by the appropriate number of zeros, e.g. nine zeros for a page size of 512 bytes.

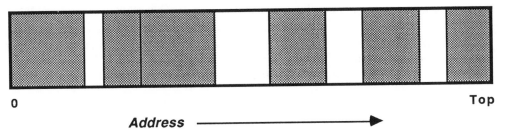

Figure 9.25: Fragmentation of a segmented memory

At the expense of considerable complexity, it is possible to enjoy the best of *both* worlds by employing a *paged segmented memory*. Here the memory may be considered first divided into segments and subsequently into pages whose boundaries *coincide* with those of pages.

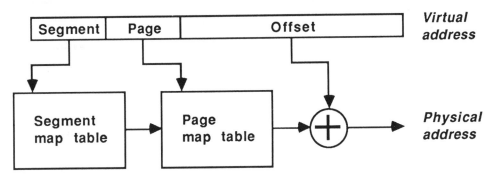

Figure 9.26: Address translation in a paged-segmented memory

Figure 9.26 shows how address translation is now performed. A virtual address is composed of a *triplet*...

- *Segment*
- *Page offset within selected segment*
- *Word offset within selected page*

The segment number selects the page map table to be used. The page number selects the page, offset from the segment base. Finally the word number selects the word, offset from the page base. Note that, although only a single addition is required, *two* table look ups must be performed. That is the potential disadvantage. *Very* fast table look ups must be possible. Benefit from caching both tables is impossible if frequent segment switching occurs, e.g. between code and data.

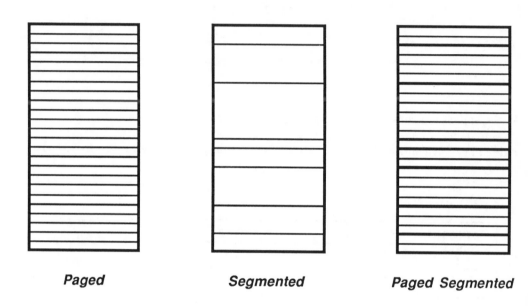

Paged   **Segmented**   **Paged Segmented**

Figure 9.27: Three different kinds of virtual memory organization

Figure 9.27 allows comparison of the appearance of the three different *virtual memory organization* schemes discussed.

9.3   External communication (I/O)

9.3.1   Event driven memory mapped I/O

Ports

A *port*, in the real world, is a place where goods arrive and depart. In a computer the same purpose is fulfilled except that it is *data* which is *received* or *transmitted*. The most efficient way for a processor to access a port is to render it *addressable on the system bus*.

Each port has its own distinct address. A *read* operation then receives data while a *write* transmits it. Because ports thus appear within the main *memory map* this technique is known as *memory mapped I/O*.

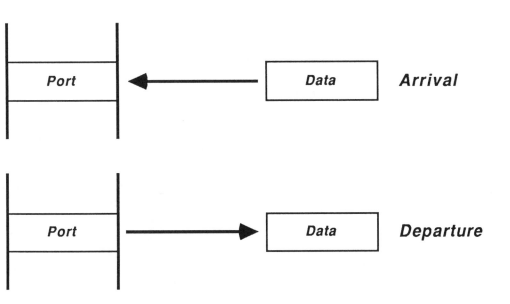

Figure 9.28: Port arrival and departure events

Communication is inherently *asynchronous* since the port acts as a *buffer*. Once data is deposited there, either a processor or external device, depending on direction of data transfer, may read it whenever it is ready. *Synchronous communication* is possible if...

- *Port arrival*

- *Port departure*

...*events* are reported (Figure 9.28).

Ports may be *unidirectional* or *bidirectional*, the direction of data transfer being under *program control*.

Device drivers

The process to which arrival and departure events are reported is called a *device driver*. Any system with more than one port for input or output *must* be *multiprocessing*, at least at the *virtual* level. In the now rare case where no interrupt generation is possible, polling of all ports must be *iteratively* undertaken to determine when events have occurred and select[18] the appropriate device driver to generate a response.

The *software architecture* for a collection of *synchronous communication port drivers* is shown below expressed in *Occam*...

```
PAR i=0 FOR devices
   WHILE running
      c.event[i] ? signal
      port[i] ? data
      process(data)
```

This code assumes the availability of a separate channel for each event. If only a single such channel is available it will be necessary to *wait* for a signal upon it and subsequently poll event sources.

If a compiler is unavailable for a language which supports such *real-time systems* programming, *interrupt service routines* must be individually coded and placed in memory such that the interrupt control mechanism is able to vector correctly. Note that at least two separate routines are required for each device. *Portability* is lost. It is not sufficient that a language supports the encoding of interrupt routines. It must also *properly* support programming of multiple concurrent processes.

In many *real-time* applications the process which *consumes* the data *also* acts as the device driver. This is not usually the case with general purpose computer *work-stations*. Most programs for such machines could not run efficiently conducting their *I/O via* synchronous communication. In the case of input from a keyboard the running program would be idle most of the time awaiting user key presses. The solution is for the keyboard device driver to act as an *intermediary* and communicate synchronously with the keyboard and asynchronously with the program, via a *keyboard buffer*[19].

The function of the event driven device drivers, which form the lowest layer of the *operating system* in a work-station, is to mediate between running programs and external devices. They usually communicate *synchronously* with the devices and *asynchronously* with running processes.

Protocol

External communication channel *protocols* may be divided into two classes...

- *Bit serial*

- *Bit parallel*

---

[18] ...using a *CASE* construct.

[19] Asynchronous communication implies the use of a buffer which must be protected from simultaneous access by both *consumer* and *producer* via *mutual exclusion*.

Parallel protocols support the transfer of all data bits simultaneously. *Bit serial protocols* support the transfer of data bits sequentially, one after the other.

Serial protocols must each include a *synchronization protocol*. The receiver must obviously be able to unambiguously determine exactly when the first data bit is to appear, as well as whether it is to be the most or least significant bit. One method of achieving synchronization is to transmit a continuous *stop code* until data is to be sent, preceded by a *start code* of opposite polarity. The receiver need only detect the transition between codes. However it must still know fairly accurately the duration of a data bit.

Serial interfaces are easily and cheaply implemented, requiring only a *bidirectional shift register*[20] at each end of a *1-bit* data channel.

Both serial and parallel protocols require *transaction protocol*. Perhaps the simplest such is called the *busy/ready protocol*. Each party emits a *level signal* indicating whether it is *busy* or *ready* to proceed. Each transaction commences with the sender asserting *ready*. When the receiver ceases to assert *busy*, data transfer commences and the receiver re-asserts *busy*, so indicating *acknowledgement* to the sender. The entire cycle is termed a *handshake*. Finally when the receiver port has been cleared it must resume a *ready* signal, allowing the next word to be transmitted.

Note that all protocols are *layered*. Layers of interest are...

- *Bit*

- *Word*

- *Packet (Frame)*

- *Message*

Only the first two have been discussed here. The rest are more properly treated in a text on digital communications.

Peripheral interface devices

Here two commercially available *peripheral interface devices* are introduced. What follows is in no way intended to be sufficient to prepare the reader to design working systems. Rather, it is intended to impart something of the nature of current commercially available devices[21].

The *6522 Versatile Interface Adaptor (VIA)* implements a pair of *parallel ports* whose function is subject to *program control* via the provision of a *control register* and *status register*. Further assistance is given the systems programmer in the provision of two programmable *timers and* a programmable *shift register*[22]. Each port, each timer and

---

[20] See Chapter 5.

[21] Their practical exploitation would require *data sheets* which are easily obtainable from electronic component suppliers.

[22] ...which may, with a little difficulty, be used as a *serial port*.

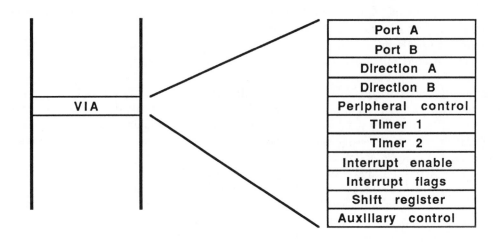

| Port A |
| Port B |
| Direction A |
| Direction B |
| Peripheral   control |
| Timer 1 |
| Timer 2 |
| Interrupt enable |
| Interrupt flags |
| Shift register |
| Auxiliary control |

Figure 9.29: Parallel port registers of the 6522 VIA mapped into memory

the shift register are capable of generating interrupt requests. Figure 9.29 depicts the
device as it appears in the main *memory map.*

Data direction registers are included for each of the two ports, *A* and *B*. Each bit
within determines whether the corresponding bit in the port is an *output* or an *input*
Thus, if required, each port can be subdivided into up to eight subsidiary ports by
grouping bits together.

The *peripheral control register* determines the protocol of each independent port
Automatic input and/or output hansdhaking are provided as options. Other options
include, for example, the polarity of the handshake signals of the external device.

The VIA generates a single interrupt request following each type of event for which
it is so enabled. Interrupt requests are enabled by setting the appropriate bit in the
interrupt enable register. The device driver (interrupt service routine) must respond by
polling the *status* of the VIA by reading the *interrupt flag register* which records the
event which has occurred (Figure 9.30).

The *auxiliary control register* decides whether or not data is *latched* as a result of a
handshake, which would usually be the case. It also controls the shift register and the
timers.

Timer control allows for *free running*, where it repeatedly counts down from a value
stored in it by the processor, or *one shot* mode, whereby it counts down to zero just
once. Timers are just counters which are decremented usually by the system clock. An
extremely useful option is to cause an *event* on each *time-out*, allowing the processor
to conduct operations upon timed intervals. Timers may even be used to generate a
waveform on a port output pin, by loading new values after each time-out, or count *edge*

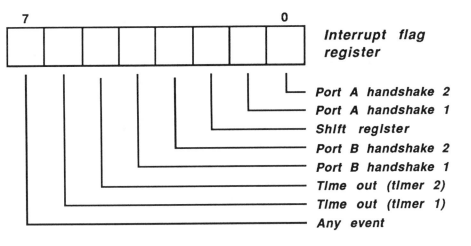

Figure 9.30: Parallel port status register of the 6522 VIA

signals arriving on a port input pin.

Shift register control allows for the shift timing to be controlled by...

- *System clock tick*

- *Timer time-out*

- *External clock tick*

...events. It also determines whether the shift direction is *in* or *out* and allows the shift register to be *disabled*. Note that no provision is made for a *transaction protocol*. This would have to be implemented in *software* using parallel port bits.

Serial communication is much better supported by the *6551 Asynchronous Communications Interface Adaptor (ACIA)*, whose memory mapped registers are shown in Figure 9.31.

Bit level synchronization is established by use of an accurate special clock and predetermining the *baud rate* (the number of bits transferred per second). The *control register* allows program control of this and other parameters, such as the number of bits in the *stop code* (between one and two) and the length of the data word (between five and eight).

Like the VIA/IFR the *status register* encodes which event has occurred and brought about an interrupt request (Figure 9.32). The device driver must poll it to determine its response. Note that *parity error detection* is supported.

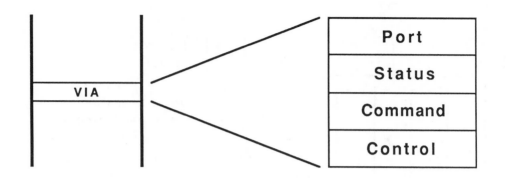

Figure 9.31: Serial port registers of the 6551 ACIA mapped into memory

The *command register* provides control over the general function of the interface device. *Parity* generation and checking may be switched on or off. Automatic *echo* of incoming data, back to its source, is also an option. Other options are the enabling/disabling of interrupt request generation on port arrival/departure events and the altogether enabling/disabling of transactions.

Serial communication has been traditionally used for the communication between a *terminal* and a *modem*, which connects through to a remote computer. For this reason the handshake signals provided on commercial serial interface devices are called...

- *Data terminal ready (sent)*

- *Data set ready (received)*

Terminal communication

Thus far the mechanisms whereby the familiar *terminal* communicates data both in, from the keyboard, and out, to the "screen", remain unexplained in this volume. Here is an overview of how a *keyboard* and a *raster video display* is interfaced to the system bus in a memory mapped fashion.

Every *keyboard* is basically an array of switches, each of which activates one *row signal* and one *column signal*, allowing its identity to be uniquely characterized by the bit pattern so produced. An encoder is then employed to produce a unique binary number for each key *upon a "key press" event*. It is not a difficult matter to arrange the codes produced to match those of the *ASCII* standard.

Figure 9.33 shows the encoder connected to the system by means of a *VIA* port. The *handshaking* is not shown. Here the keyboard *ready* signal equates with *key press event*

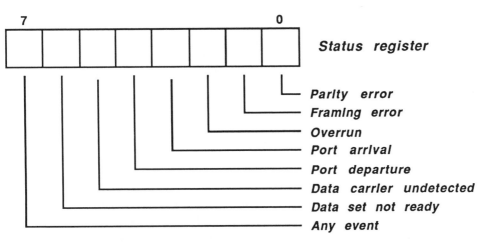

Figure 9.32: Serial port status register of the 6551 ACIA

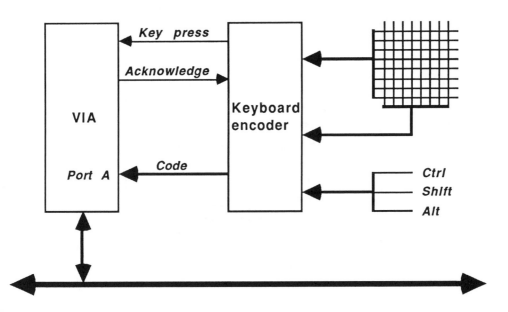

Figure 9.33: Keyboard interface using a VIA port

and should cause the *VIA* to generate an interrupt request and a handshake response (*acknowledge*).

The key matrix need not be large since certain bits in the character code output by the encoder are determined by the three special keys...

- *Control (bits 5,6)*

- *Shift (bits 4,5)*

- *Alt (bit 7)*

A minimum of 64 character keys, plus the four special keys, are usually required Thus a 8 × 8 matrix would be sufficient.

The *raster video display* is much more difficult. Current technology relies on the *cathode ray tube (CRT)* for physical display. It may be briefly summarized as an *electron beam* scanned across a very large array of *phosphor* dots, deposited on the inside of a glass screen, causing them to glow. The beam is scanned *raster* fashion (Figure 9.34), typically with approximately one thousand lines. By varying the *intensity* of the beam with time, in accordance with its position, the screen is made to exhibit a desired brightness pattern, e.g. to display characters. The rapidity with which the intensity may be varied depends upon the quality of the CRT and determines the maximum number of picture elements or *pixels* which may be independently rendered of different brightness.

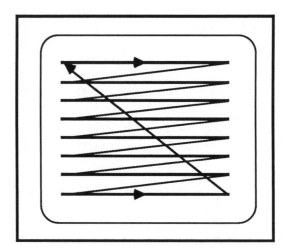

Figure 9.34: Raster scan of a phosphor screen

Base address	Base + 1	Base + 2	Base + 3	Base + 4	Base + 5
Base + width	Base + width + 1	Base + width + 2	Base + width + 3	Base + width + 4	Base + width + 5

Figure 9.35: Byte mapped raster video display

The screen is divided up into a two-dimensional array of pixels. It is arranged that this array be *memory mapped* so that a program may modify the brightness pattern displayed simply by modifying the values stored in the array (Figure 9.35). Typically, given a word width of one byte, a zero value results in the corresponding pixel being black (unilluminated) and FF_{16} results in it being white (fully illuminated). The *digital* values must be converted to an *analogue* of the intensity (usually a voltage) by a *digital-to-analogue converter (DAC)*. Such a system would offer *monochromatic graphics* support. *Colour graphics* support uses one of two possible techniques...

- *Colour look up table (CLUT)*

- *Red, green and blue primary colour planes (RGB)*

In either case a CRT is required which is capable of exciting *three* different phosphors, one for each primary colour. Typically this is done using three separate electron beams whose intensity is determined by the outputs of *three* separate DACs. A *CLUT* is a *memory* whose address input is the *logical colour*, stored in each *pixel* location in the screen map, and whose data output is the *physical colour* consisting of the digitally encoded intensities of each of the three primary colours.

In a *RGB* system a distinct screen map is stored for each primary colour. *Address interleaving* may be employed to give the impression of a single screen map accessible, for example, as a two-dimensional array of 4-byte words. Each pixel location has one byte for each primary colour intensity and one reserved for other kinds of *pixel labelling*.

Extra hardware is required for drawing characters. Returning to the simpler monochromatic graphics system, we shall now look at how characters are displayed.

A *character* is an *instance* of a *class* of *graphic object* of that name. In fact the class "character" may be subdivided into a number of *subclasses* called *fonts*, so that each displayed character is an instance of one or other *font* as well as of *character* and *graphic object*.

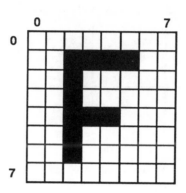

Figure 9.36: Simple example of font character design

Each character (instance of a font) is most simply defined as a two-dimensional array of pixel values. Usually character pixel values may only be black or white[23]. Figure 9.36 shows an example. *Font design* requires good software and much artistic skill. Modern work-stations support user expansion of a *font library*, usually by purchasing commercial designs[24].

The *screen map* must be accessible both from the *system bus* and from a *raster display controller*[25]. A memory accessible from two separate buses is known as a *dual port memory*. *Mutual exclusion* must be enforced to prevent simultaneous access by both controller and system.

The raster display controller generates the addresses of locations for digital-to-analogue conversion synchronized with display beam position. Synchronization with the display is achieved *via...*

- *Horizontal sync*

- *Vertical sync*

---

[23] A very high quality system might define characters using *grey levels* as well.

[24] *Font marketing* is a rather telling example of a new product which is *pure information*. One day a major share of the world economy might be the direct trade of pure information products over public communication networks.

[25] ...more commonly referred to as a *cathode ray tube controller (CRTC)*. An example is the *6545 CRTC* integrated device.

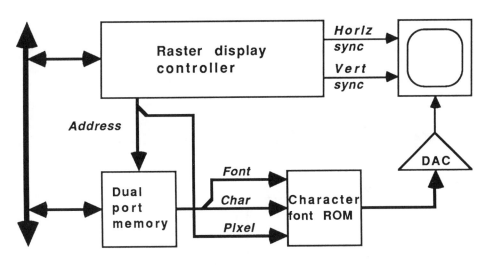

Figure 9.37: Use of raster display controller to interface with a video display

...signals. Upon receipt of *horizontal sync* the beam moves extremely rapidly back to the left-hand side of the screen and begins a new *scan line*. Upon receipt of *vertical sync* it *flies back* to the top left-hand corner to begin scanning a new *frame*. Three parameters alone are enough to characterize a *raster display...*

- *Frame rate*

- *Line rate*

- *Pixel rate*

Figure 9.37 shows how a *raster display controller* is connected to the system bus, the *dual port memory* holding the screen map and the display itself.

In a pure graphics system the *font ROM* would be bypassed and the *whole* address required for the (much larger) screen map memory. Mutual exclusion of the screen memory may be achieved by inserting a wait state into the bus cycle if necessary. The necessary buffering of each memory connection (port) is not shown in the diagram.

In the *character-oriented* system shown, the screen map is made up of a much smaller array of *character values*, each one a code (usually *ASCII*) defining the character required at that position. A typical *character-oriented display* would be twenty-four lines of eighty characters. The code is used as part of the address in a *font ROM*[26] which stores the graphical definition of every character in every available font. The least significant bits

---

[26] It need not in fact be a *ROM* but usually this is the case.

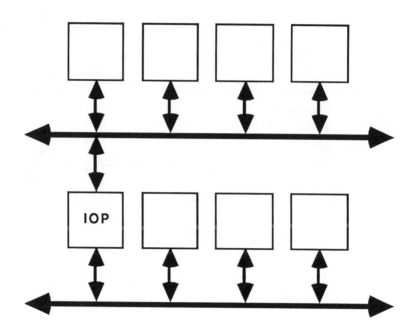

Figure 9.38: Connection of system bus to external communications bus via an IOP

determine the pixel within the character definition and are supplied by the controller. Just as a *colour graphics display* requires multiple *planes*, an extra plane is required here to define the font of each character location. For example, *address interleaving* may be employed to give the appearance of a single two-dimensional array of 2-byte words. The least significant byte holds the character code, the most significant holds the font number, used as the most significant address byte in the font ROM.

Systems which are capable of overlaying, or partitioning, text and graphics on the same display are obviously more complicated but follow the same basic methodology.

9.3.2   External communication (I/O) processors

Small Computer Systems Interface (SCSI)

There are typically many external devices with which a system must communicate. Some of these may be *mass storage* devices offering cheap, non-volatile but slow memory. Others may facilitate communication with other systems, via a network interface, or communication with users, for example via a *laser printer*.

One approach, which has become commonplace, is to connect all external devices ogether onto an *external bus* interfaced to the *system bus* by an *I/O processor (IOP)*. Figure 9.38 shows such an arrangement. An example of such is the *Small Computer Systems Interface (SCSI)*[27] [ANSI 86], which is well defined by a *standards committee* and well supported by the availability of commercially available integrated interface devices (e.g. *NCR 5380*). A detailed account of a hardware *and* software project using this chip may be found in [Ciarcia 86].

Every device must appear to have a single *linear memory map*, each location of which is of fixed size and is referred to as a *sector* or *block*. Each device is assigned a *logical unit number* whose value determines arbitration priority. Up to eight devices are allowed including the *host adaptor* to the system bus. The system then appears on the external bus as just another device, but is usually given the highest priority. A running program may in turn *program* the SCSI to undertake required operations, e.g. the *read* command shown in Figure 9.39.

Each *SCSI* bus transaction is made up of the following phases...

1. *Bus free*

2. *Arbitration*

3. *Selection*

4. *Reselection*

5. *Command*

6. *Data transfer*

7. *Status*

8. *Message*

Arbitration is achieved *without a dedicated arbiter*. Any device requiring the bus asserts a *BSY* signal on the control subsidiary bus and also that data bit channel whose bit number is equal to its logical unit number. If, after a brief delay, no higher priority data bit is set then that device wins mastership of the bus.

Selection of *slave* or *target* is achieved by asserting a *SEL* control signal together with the data bit corresponding to the required *target* and, optionally, that of the *initiator*. The target must respond by asserting *BSY* within a specified interval of time. If the target is conducting a time intensive operation such as a *seek* it may *disconnect* and allow the bus to go free for other transactions. Afterwards it must arbitrate to *reselect* the initiator to complete the transaction.

---

[27] ...pronounced "scuzzy"!

SCSI seeks to make every device appear the same by requiring that each obeys an identical set of commands. The command set is said to be *device independent* and include the following commands...

- *Read*

- *Write*

- *Seek*

Byte	Bit							
	7	6	5	4	3	2	1	0
1	Opcode = 08							
2	Logical unit			Logical address (hi)				
3	Logical address (mid)							
4	Logical address (lo)							
5	Transfer length							
6	Reserved						Flag	Link

Figure 9.39: SCSI Read command

An example of the format of a typical command is shown in Figure 9.39. Note that by setting a *link* flag, commands may be *chained together* to form an *I/O program*. Chained commands avoid the time consuming process of arbitration. Integrated SCSI interfaces, such as the *NCR 5380*, are capable of reading an *I/O program* in the memory of the host automatically via DMA.

Status and *message* phases are used to pass information about the progress and success of operations between initiator and target.

Hard channels (Links)

The severe limitation imposed on using *bus* communication is that *bandwidth* is fixed for the whole system. As more devices are added to an *external bus* a point will be reached beyond which performance will fall. An alternative approach is inspired by the model of external devices as *processors* running *processes* in their own right. *Data flow* between processors is facilitated by providing dedicated *hard channels*. Bandwidth then expands to whatever is required, as long as sufficient hard channels are available.

So far only one architecture offers hard channels. The *Inmos Transputer* is a complete computer with processor, memory and four hard channels *(links)*, integrated into a single

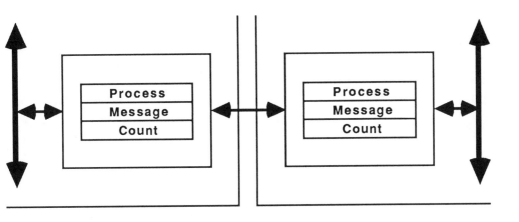

Figure 9.40: Registers and connection of link processors

physical device. Links may be connected *directly* to other Transputers or indirectly, via *link adaptors*, to *"alien"* devices.

Each *link* is controlled by a *link processor* which implements *synchronous communication* by means of *rendezvous*[28] at a *dedicated* memory location. It is programmed by means of dedicated instructions (**in** and **out**) which transfer three values into its own private registers (Figure 9.40). The local *process* is identified by its *workspace pointer* which in turn identifies the PC value. It is stored to enable the process to be *rescheduled*, when the transaction is complete, simply by copying it to the tail of the *ready queue*. The *message* is identified simply by a pointer. A *count* of the bytes to be transferred is decremented each time a byte has been successfully transferred. The transaction is complete when the count reaches zero. Then the locally participating process, be it sender or receiver, is rescheduled and thus allowed to proceed and execute its next instruction as soon as its turn comes to run again.

The *link protocol* consists of byte data transfers, each in a *frame* with two *start bits* and one *stop bit*. An *acknowledge* handshake, confirming reception, is returned by the receiver even *before* the data transfer is complete (Figure 9.41) requiring no delay between transactions.

The advantages of a system composed of a number of Transputers over a purely bus based system may be summarized as follows. . .

- *Communication bandwidth increases linearly with number of Transputers*

- *Arbitration is accounted for in scheduling mechanism*

---
[28] See Chapter 8.

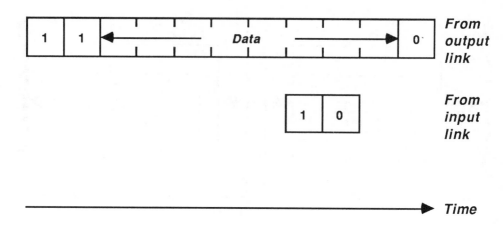

Figure 9.41: Protocol of a hard channel (link)

- *Link adaptors are easier to implement than bus adaptors, requiring no dedicated software overhead*

See Chapter 10 for more about Transputers, which certainly represent a very great step change in paradigm and not just in the area of external communications.

Exercises

Question one

Show by an example why it is that a *two-dimensional memory* is most efficiently rendered *square*.

The *cost per bit* (c_i), *size* (s_i) and *access time* (t_i) of memory device i in a given *memory hierarchy* are such that...

$$
\begin{array}{ccc}
c_{i-1} & > & c_i & > & c_{i+1} \\
s_{i-1} & < & s_i & < & s_{i+1} \\
t_{i-1} & < & t_i & < & t_{i+1}
\end{array}
$$

The *hit ratio*, h_i, of each device is defined as the proportion of references satisfied by device i without recourse to one lower in the hierarchy.

Give expressions for the following...

- *Mean cost per bit*

- *Mean access time*

- *Cost efficiency (expressed as cost per bit of cheapest device over mean cost per bit)*

- *Access efficiency (expressed as access time of fastest device over mean access time)*

What is the overall *cost efficiency* and *access efficiency* for the memory hierarchy described below (typical for a contemporary work-station)...

Cost (pence per bit)	Size (bytes)	Access time (ns)	Hit ratio
10^1	10^3	10^1	0.9
10^0	10^6	10^3	0.9999
10^{-2}	10^8	10^7	1.00

What would the hit ratio of the topmost device have to be to yield an overall access efficiency of 10%?

Question two

Summarize the component signal channels of the *system control bus*. Include channels for *all* signals mentioned in this chapter.

ii Draw a timing diagram for *daisy chain* bus arbitration. Explain how a lower priority device, which requests the bus simultaneously with a higher priority one, eventually acquires *mastership*.

iii Some system bus implementations use *polled arbitration* whereby, when the bus is requested, the arbiter repeatedly decrements a *poll count* which corresponds to a *device number*. As soon as the requesting device recognizes its number, it asserts a *busy signal* and thus becomes *bus master*. It is therefore ensured that, if more than one device issues a requests the bus, the one with the highest number is granted it.

Contrast the advantages and disadvantages of the following three *bus arbitration protocol*

- *Daisy chain*
- *Polled*
- *SCSI bus method*

Question three

i Draw a schematic diagram showing how an *interleaved memory*, three *DACs*, a *raster display controller* and a *RGB video monitor* are connected together to yield a *three plane RGB colour graphics display*.

ii Show how the following components. . .

- *VIA*
- *Modulo 8 counter*
- *3-bit decoder*
- *3-bit encoder*

. . . may be connected in order to read a very simple 64-key unencoded *key matrix* which consists simply of an overlaid row and column of conductors such that the intersection of each row and column pair may be shorted, Figure 9.42. Explain how it is read to produce a 6-bit *key code*, upon a *key press event*.

Question four

The *LRU replacement strategy*, for either an *associative cache* or a *demand paged virtual memory*, is difficult and slow to implement since each entry must be labelled with a *time stamp* and all entries consulted to determine when one is to be replaced.

Devise an alternative implementation which *approximates* LRU yet is efficient both in extra memory for entry labelling and in the rapidity with which the entry to be replaced may be determined. The *minimum* amount of combinational logic must be employed.

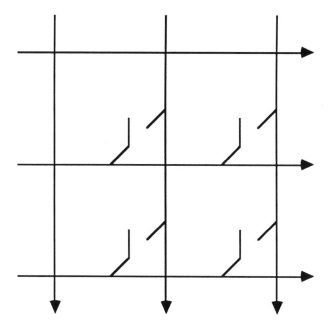

Figure 9.42: 64-key unencoded key matrix

Question five

i Using the *Hamming code* described in this chapter, derive the *syndrome* for the data word $FAC9_{16}$.

ii Show that every possible error, both in data *and* in syndrome, produces a distinct *error vector* when the *Hamming code* described in this chapter is employed.

Chapter 10

Survey of contemporary processor architecture

10.1   Introduction

The objective of this chapter is *not* to provide the reader with sufficient knowledge to author a compiler code generator *or* design a hardware system. Rather it is intended to illustrate ideas conveyed throughout the text as a whole and demonstrate that they really do appear in real commercial devices. However, a clear overview should result of the major features of each example and references are provided.

It is part of the philosophy of this book not to render it dependent on any single commercial design but to concentrate attention on those concepts which are fundamental. The reader should bear this in mind. Lastly, each of the sections below is intended to be self-contained and self-sufficient in order to allow the possibility of consideration of any one system alone. As a result *some* material is necessarily repeated. However, the reader is strongly advised to read all three. Much may be learned from the comparison of the three machines.

Note: The *NS32000* is considered as a *series* of processors whereas only the *M68000* itself is presented, and not its successors... M68010, M68020 etc.. This is justified on two counts. First, *all* NS32000 series processors share the same *programmer's architecture* and machine language. This is not true of the successors to the M68000. Secondly, it seemed desirable to first consider a simpler architecture without "enhancements" and "extensions".

10.2   Motorola 68000

10.2.1   Architecture

Design philosophy

The *Motorola 68000* was a direct development of an earlier 8-bit *microprocessor* (the *6800*) and is fabricated in a self-contained integrated device using *VLSI* electronic technology. It has succeeded in both the *work-station* and *real-time control* markets.

From a software engineering point of view it satisfies the following requirements...

- *Reduction of semantic gap*

- *Structured (procedural) programming support*

- *Security for multi-user operating system*

The M68000 fully qualifies as a *complex instruction set computer (CISC)*. A large instruction set and range of "powerful" addressing modes seek to reduce the *semantic gap* between a statement in a *high level language* and one, of equal meaning, in machine language. Several instructions are included in order to allow compact, fast execution of programming *constructs* and *procedure* invocation, entry and return. Complex addressing modes similarly support the efficient referencing of both *dynamic* and *static* structured or elemental, data. It should be noted that the ease with which this support may be utilized when machine code is automatically generated by a compiler is a separate issue outside the scope of this book[1].

The M68000 also provides support for secure operation of an *operating system*. Two operating modes are possible... *user* and *supervisor*. The current mode is always indicated by a flag in the *processor state register*. Certain instructions are *privileged* to the supervisor to protect first the operating system and secondly users from each other. Privilege violation causes a *trap*[2] which can be dealt with by the operating system. A **trap** instruction allows invocation of operating system procedures. A single operand defines an offset into a table of sixteen vectors to operating system procedures.

There follows a list of the most important features of M68000 architecture...

- *Complex instruction set (CISC)*

- *One or two address instructions*

- *Register file for expression evaluation (no windowing)*

- *Stack for procedure, function and interrupt service subroutine implementation*

---

[1] It is one of the criticisms of the CISC approach that compilers cannot easily optimize code on CISC architecture because of the extent of choice available. See [Patterson & Ditzel 80], [Tabak 87].

[2] A *trap* is a software generated processor *interrupt* or *exception*.

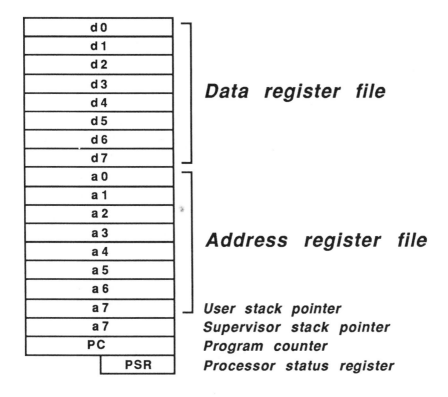

Figure 10.1: M68000 programmer's achitecture

• *Vectored interrupt mechanism*

Instruction opcodes may require one or two operands. Most instructions executed
operate on two operands. Operands may be of one, two or four bytes in length[3]. Vectored
interrupts are prioritized and may be *masked* to inhibit those below a certain priority
specified within the *processor state register (PSR)*.

Programmer's architecture

Figure 10.1 shows the *programmer's architecture* of the M68000. Two register files are
provided, one for addresses and one for data. a7 is in fact two registers each of which
is used as a *stack pointer (SP)*. Two stacks are maintained, one for supervisor mode,
which is used for interrupt service routines, and one for user mode, which is used for

---

[3] In M68000 terminology, "word" refers to two consecutive bytes and "long" refers to four.

Flag	Write access	Meaning when set
T	*Privileged*	Trace in operation causing *TRC* trap after *every* instruction
S	*Privileged*	User stack, not supervisor stack
$I_{0...2}$	*Privileged*	Interrupt priority (lower priority interrupts inhibited)
X	*Any*	Extension beyond word length following arithmetic, logical or shift operation
N	*Any*	Negative result of *twos-complement* arithmetic operation
Z	*Any*	Zero result of arithmetic operation
V	*Any*	Overflow in *twos-complement* arithmetic operation
C	*Any*	Carry after an addition, borrow after a subtraction

Table 10.1: Flags in the M68000 processor state register and their meaning (when set)

subroutines. Any of the remaining address registers may be used as a *frame pointer* from which to reference local variables within procedures, and as a *static base* pointer from which to reference global variables.

On *reset* the processor boots itself using code located at an address found in the *interrupt despatch table* (Figure 10.2). The supervisor stack pointer is initialized with an address found below the *reset vector* at the bottom of the interrupt despatch table and hence at the bottom of memory at address zero.

The *boot code* must initialize the user stack and interrupt despatch table and then load (if necessary) and enter the remainder of the operating system *kernal*. Figure 10. depicts the much simplified form of the *memory map*.

Figure 10.4 shows the PSR. Processor state recorded supports both cardinal and twos-complement signed integer arithmetic operations plus current interupt enable, trace enable and supervisor/user mode. The lower byte is called the *condition code register* (*CCR*), and may be universally accessed. The upper byte however is reserved for privileged access by the supervisor only. Table 10.1 summarizes the condition code flags and their meaning.

Addressing modes

Table 10.2 summarizes the addressing modes available on the M68000 together with their *assembly language* notation and effective address computation. Note that "[...]", i

#0	SSP	Reset supervisor stack ptr.
#1	PC	Reset boot code address
#2	ERR	Bus error trap
#3	ADD	Address error trap
#4	ILL	Illegal operation trap
#5	DVZ	Divide by zero trap
#6	CHK	`chk' instruction trap
#7	TRAPV	`trapv' instruction trap
#8	PRI	Privilege violation trap
#9	TRC	Trace trap
#A		Opcode 1010 emulation trap
#B		Opcode 1111 emulation trap

#18	Spurious Interrupt
#19 ⋮ #1F	Vectored Interrupts
#20 ⋮ #30	`Trap' instruction vectors
#40 ⋮ #FF	User vectors

Figure 10.2: M68000 interrupt despatch table

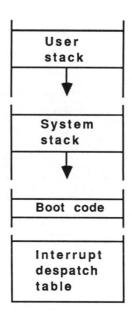

Figure 10.3: M68000 memory map

the *effective address* column, should be read as "contents of...".

An addressing mode is specified within the basic instruction in a 6-bit field. This is divided into two sub-fields... *mode* and *reg*. The latter may be used either to specify a register number or to qualify the mode itself. For example, both *absolute* and *immediate* modes share the same value (111_2) in the *mode* field. The *reg* field dictates how the necessary instruction extension shall be interpreted. In the case of *data register direct* mode (000_2) *reg* contains the number of the data register to be accessed. *Address register indirect* is encoded similarly (mode = 010_2).

Indexing and displacement modifiers are permitted to allow referencing elemental data via an offset from a pointer, and elements within an array using a variable index stored in an address register (for efficient modification).

Predecrement and *postincrement* addressing modes render easier the maintenance and use of stacks and queues. They allow a `move` instruction to implement *push* and *pop* stack operations as opposed to merely copying or inspecting an item on the top of stack.

Byte or word operations affect only the lower order fields within data registers. Hence `move.b d0,d1` will copy the contents of the least significant byte in *d0* into that of *d1*. None of the upper three bytes in *d0* will be affected in any way. It is as though they did not exist and the register was simply one byte long. The same applies to arithmetic and logical operations. In the case where memory is addressed, *word or long word alignment*

Addressing mode	Notation	Encoding	Effective address
Immediate	#<value>	111100_2	*None*
Absolute	<value>	111000_2	*Value* (word)
	<value>	111001_2	*Value* (long)
Data register direct	d<n>	$000 < n >_2$	*None*
Address register direct	a<n>	$001 < n >_2$	*None*
Address register indirect	(a<n>)	$010 < n >_2$	$[reg]$
Address register indirect with postincrement	(a<n>)+	$011 < n >_2$	$[reg]$
Address register indirect with predecrement	-(a<n>)	$100 < n >_2$	$[reg]$
Address register indirect with displacement	<disp>(a<n>)	$101 < n >_2$	$disp + [reg]$
Address register indirect with index and displacement	<disp>(a<n>,d<m>) <disp>(a<n>,a<m>)	$110 < n >_2$	$disp + [reg1] + [reg2]$
Program counter relative with displacement	<disp>(PC)	111010_2	$disp + [PC]$
Program counter relative with index and displacement	<disp>(PC),d<n> <disp>(PC),a<n>	111011_2	$disp + [reg] + [PC]$

Table 10.2: M68000 addressing modes

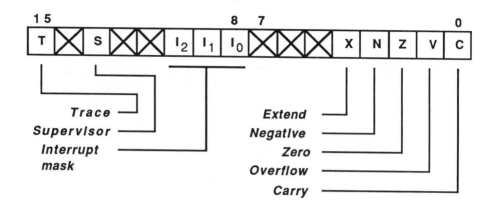

Figure 10.4: M68000 processor state register

is necessary. An attempt to access, say, a word at an odd address will result in failure and a *bus error* trap.

Immediate addressing includes the possibility of a short, *"quick"* operand stored within the instruction. Many constant operands in a typical code segment are small, e.g. loop index increments. A "quick" operand in an arithmetic instruction is just three bits long whereas for a **move** it is eight bits.

Instruction set

Tables 10.3, 10.4 and 10.5 summarize the M68000 instruction set. Where relevant, instruction variants are provided for operation on byte, word and long operands.

Program control is facilitated by a suite of instructions for condition evaluation and conditional branch. A *compare multiple element* (**cmpm**) instruction is included to allow simple, optimized implementation of array and string comparison[4]. Table 10.6 shows all possible conditional branches, with the processor state flag on which they depend, and their meaning.

In the case of two-address instructions the first is referred to as the *source* and the second the *destination*. The result of the operation will be placed in the destination which usually *must* be a register. Where operand *order* is important, for example with subtraction or division, one must take care since ordering is *right to left*. Hence **sub.w (a0),d0** means subtract the contents of the memory location whose address is in *a0* from the contents of *d0* into which register the result is to be placed. Similarly **divu #4,d7** means

---

[4]Among architectures in general, it is not necessarily the case that a **cmpm** instruction will execute faster, or be easier to code-generate, than a sequence of **cmp** instructions. The compiler author should always verify these things.

Group	Mnemonic	Operation
Comparison and	`cmp.<b|w|l>`	Compare
test	`cmpa`	Compare addresses
	`cmpi.<b|w|l>`	Compare immediate
	`cmpm.<b|w|l>`	Compare multiple
	`chk`	Check effective address within bounds
	`btst`	Bit test (result in Z)
	`bset`	Bit test and set
	`bclr`	Bit test and clear
	`bchg`	Bit test and change
Branches and	`b<cond>`	Branch on condition (see table below)
jumps	`bra`	Branch always
	`db<cond>`	Decrement and branch on *negated* condition
	`bsr`	Branch to subroutine
	`jsr`	Jump to subroutine
	`jmp`	Jump always
	`rts`	Return from subroutine
	`rtr`	Return & restore condition codes
	`rte`	Return from exception routine *(privileged)*

Table 10.3: Instruction set of the M68000: Program control

Group	Mnemonic	Operation
Moves	move.<b|w|l>	Move
	movea.<w|l>	Move address
	movem.<w|l>	Move multiple
	movep.<w|l>	Move peripheral
	moveq	Move quick operand
	lea	Load effective address
	pea	Push effective address
	exg	Exchange content of two registers
	swap	Swap upper & lower words of register
	move ccr	Move *to* condition code register
	move sr	Move to/from status register, *privileged*
	move usp	Move user stack pointer
Integer arithmetic	add.<b|w|l>	Add
	adda	Add address
	addq	Add quick operand
	addi.<b|w|l>	Add immediate
	addx.<b|w|l>	Add extended (operands + X)
	sub.<b|w|l>	Subtract
	suba	Subtract address
	subq	Subtract quick operand
	subi.<b|w|l>	Subtract immediate
	subx.<b|w|l>	Subtract extended (operands - X)
	muls	Multiply signed (word to long)
	mulu	Multiply unsigned (word to long)
	divs	Divide signed (word to long)
	divu	Divide unsigned (word to long)
	neg.<b|w|l>	Negate (twos-complement)
	negx.<b|w|l>	Negate extended
	clr.<b|w|l>	Clear
	ext.<w|l>	Sign extend

Table 10.4: Instruction set of the M68000: Expression evaluation (continued in next Table)

Group	Mnemonic	Operation
Logical and Boolean	and.<b|w|l>	And
	andi.<b|w|l>	And immediate
	or.<b|w|l>	Or
	ori.<b|w|l>	Or immediate
	eor.<b|w|l>	Exclusive or
	eori.<b|w|l>	Exclusive or immediate
	not.<b|w|l>	Not (complement)
	noti.<b|w|l>	Not immediate
Shifts	lsl.<b|w|l>	Logical shift left
	lsr.<b|w|l>	Logical shift right
	asl.<b|w|l>	Arithmetic shift left (preserve sign)
	asr.<b|w|l>	Arithmetic shift right
	rol.<b|w|l>	Rotate left
	ror.<b|w|l>	Rotate right
	roxl.<b|w|l>	Rotate left through X
	roxr.<b|w|l>	Rotate right through X

Table 10.5: Instruction set of the M68000: Expression evaluation (continued from last Table)

Mnemonic	Processor state	Condition
bcs	C	Carry set
bcc	$\bar{C}$	Carry clear
beq	Z	Equal
bne	$\bar{Z}$	Not equal
bpl	$\bar{N}$	Plus
bmi	N	Minus
bhi	$\bar{Z}.\bar{C}$	Higher than
bls	$Z + C$	Lower than or same
bgt	$N.V.\bar{Z} + \bar{N}.\bar{V}.\bar{Z}$	Greater than
blt	$N \oplus V$	Lower than
bge	$\overline{N \oplus V}$	Greater than or equal
ble	$Z + (N \oplus V)$	Less than or equal
bvc	$\bar{V}$	Overflow clear
bvs	V	Overflow set

Table 10.6: Conditional branching on the M68000

divide the contents of d7 by four. Note that instructions for short "quick" operands exist for addition and subtraction but *not* for multiplication and division.

A *load/store* programming approach may be taken with the M68000 since...

- *Immediate to register*

- *Memory to register*

- *Register to memory*

...moves are efficiently supported and encouraged. Only move instructions allow *memory to memory* movement. All arithmetic and logical operations place their result in a data register which all but forces a load/store approach.

A problem remaining with the M68000, although it represents a great improvement over earlier machines, is that the instruction set is not wholly *symmetric* with respect to addressing modes. Care must be taken to ensure that use of a selected addressing mode is permitted with a given instruction. This can cause complication for the compiler author.

The *instruction format* typically includes fields for...

- *Opcode*

- *Operand length*

- *Addressing mode for each operand*

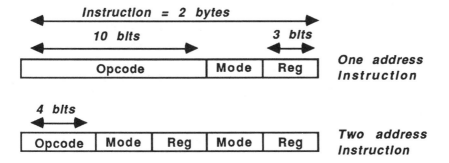

Figure 10.5: M68000 basic instruction formats

Instruction encoding depends strongly on the instruction concerned. The opcode begins at the *most significant bit* in the *operation word* or *basic instruction* (Figure 10.5). In the illustration, the field marked "opcode" includes a 2-bit sub-field which encodes operand length. Shown are two common formats. Several other formats are possible including those for single direct register addressed operand and conditional branch instructions.

The following instruction extensions may be required depending on addressing mode...

- *Index word*

- *Immediate value*

- *Displacement*

- *Absolute address*

Zero, one or two extensions are allowed. Figure 10.6 shows the instruction extension formats.

An excellent concise summary of the M68000 architecture, together with information required for hardware system integration, is to be found in [Kane 81]. A complete exposition which is suitable for a practical course on M68000 system design, integration and programming, is to be found in [Clements 87].

10.2.2   Organization

Processor organization

The organization of the M68000 is a fairly standard contemporary design consisting of a single *ALU* and a fully microcoded control unit. External communication must be fully

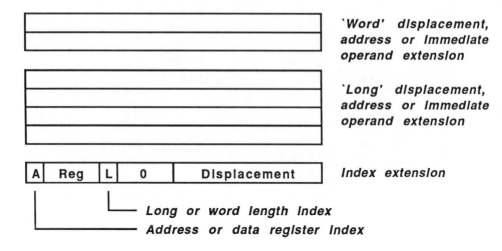

Figure 10.6: M68000 instruction extension format

memory-mapped since no explicit support exists (such as dedicated i/o instructions or control signals). Later derivatives, such as the M68020, possess an instruction cache and *pipelining*.

Physical memory organization

The system bus is non-multiplexed with address bus width of twenty-four bits giving a uniform, linear 16-megabyte memory map. The data bus is of width sixteen bits although byte access is permitted. A drawback of the design is the requirement of *word alignment*. *Words* may only be accessed at even addresses, *long words* at addresses divisible by four.

Bus timing signals (Figure 10.7) include *AS (address strobe)*, which asserts that a valid address is available, and *DTACK (data acknowledge)*, which asserts that valid data has been received or transmitted. If DTACK has not been asserted by the second half of the final clock cycle the start of the subsequent bus cycle will be delayed until it appears. *Wait states* (extra clock cycles) are then inserted into the bus cycle. One extra *level signal* is sent by the bus master for each byte of the data bus to indicate whether each is required or not. That the more significant data bus byte carries data from/to an *even* address, and the less significant byte data for an *odd* address, reflects the fact that data is stored with less significant bytes lower in memory[5].

---

[5] Such an organization is sometimes referred to as *"little-endian"*.

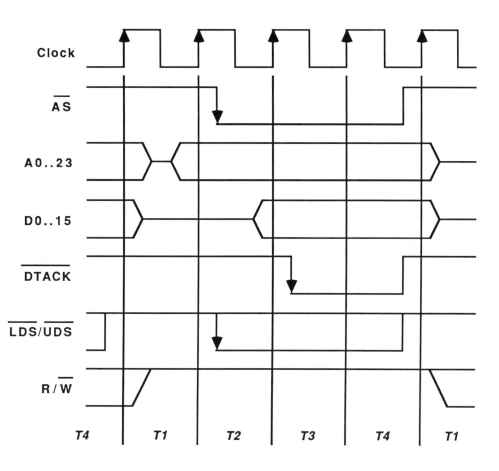

Figure 10.7: M68000 bus timing for a read operation

10.2.3   Programming

Constructs

Some closure of the semantic gap has been obtained by the designers both by careful selection of addressing modes for data referencing and by the inclusion of instructions which go far in implementing directly the commands of a *high level language*. Code generation is intended to produce fewer instructions. However, the instructions themselves are more complex. In other words the problem of efficiently implementing *selection* and *iteration* is to be solved *once and for all* in *microcode* instead of code.

A *"for"* loop always requires *signed addition of constant, compare* and *conditional branch* operations on each iteration. This is a very common construct indeed. The constant is usually small, very frequently unity. The designers of the M68000 included a single instruction to this end (**db<cond>**, with condition set to *false*) optimizing its implementation in microcode once and for all. To take advantage of this instruction, a slight extra burden is thus placed upon the compiler to isolate loops with unity index decrements. There is more to **db<cond>** however. It checks a condition flag *first*, before decrementing the index and comparing it to -1. This may be used to implement loops which are terminated by either the success of a condition or an index decrementing to zero. An example is that of repeatedly reading data elements into a buffer until either the buffer is full *or* an *end of stream* symbol is encountered. Unfortunately it is not always easy for a compiler to detect this kind of loop. There follows a code skeleton for each kind of loop discussed.

```
move.b ntimes,d<n>          move.w #len,d<m>
; loop start                ; loop start
                            move.w input,d<n>
...                         ...
dbf     d<n>,-<start offset>    cmpi.w #eos,d<n>
                            dbeq    d<m>,-<start offset>
```

Below are shown two alternative implementations of a *case* construct, each with its disadvantages. The result of the computation of the *case expression* is first moved into a data register where it may be efficiently manipulated. Comparisons are then performed in order to detect which offset to use with a branch. Each offset thus directs the "thread of control" to a code segment derived from the high level language statement associated with a particular *case label*. *Each selectable code segment must end with a branch to the instruction following the case construct end.* It is usual to place case code segments above the case instruction. The disadvantage of this implementation is that quite a lot of code must be generated and hence executed in order to complete the branch and exit from the code segment selected. Its advantage is that the code produced is relocatable without effort since it is *position independent*.

```
move.w  result,d<n>              move.w  result,d<n>
cmp.w   #value 1,d<n>            asl.w   #2,d<n>
beq.s   <offset 1>               move.l  5(PC,d<n>),a<m>
cmp.w   #value 2,d<n>            jmp     (a<m>)
beq.s   <offset 2>               <address 1>
...                              <address 2>
bra.s   <else offset>            <address 2>
                                 ...
```

The method shown on the left is inefficient if the number of case labels is large (greater than about ten). However, for a small number it is more compact and hence usually preferred. In effect it is simply a translation of *case* into multiple *if... then... else* constructs at the machine level.

In the implementation on the right, known as the *computed address* method, a table of addresses is employed. Address computation is effected, prior to indirection, by use of *PC relative with index and displacement addressing*. The offset into the table must first be computed from the case expression value by shifting left twice (each address is four bytes long). The computed address method requires the compiler to generate the case label bounds together with code to verify that the case expression value falls within them. If it fails to do so an offset should be used which points to a code segment generated from the *"else"* clause in the construct. All table entries not corresponding to case label values should also point to the *else* code. The disadvantage here is that the table generated has to include an entry for every possible *case expression* value between the bounds rather than every stated case label value.

You should be able to see why, *from the point of view of the contemporary machine*, widely scattered case label values cause either poor performance *or* excessive memory consumption depending on the compiler case implementation. In the latter instance the programmer may prefer to use a number of *if... then... else* constructs. However such a decision would mean that the architecture has dictated (and complicated) software design. Where possible, it is better to design an architecture to efficiently support the implementation of source constructs rather than the other way around.

Procedures

Invocation of a procedure is very straightforward since the instruction set offers direct support through dedicated instructions for saving and restoring registers and creating and destroying a *stack frame* for local variables. link should be used at the start of a procedure. It creates a stack frame of the size quoted (in bytes). unlk should appear at the procedure end. It automatically destroys the stack frame by copying the frame pointer into the stack pointer and restoring the frame pointer itself (from a value saved by link on the stack). Any of the address registers may be employed as frame pointer.

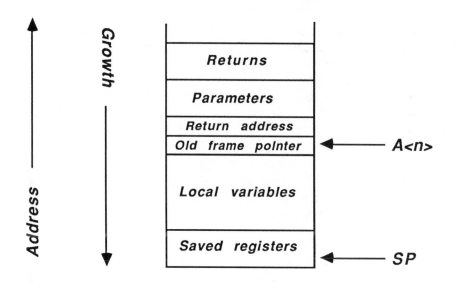

Figure 10.8: M68000 stack following subroutine invocation and entry

In order to save registers on the stack which are to be used within the procedure, movem may be employed as shown in the code segments which follow the next paragraph.

Figure 10.8 depicts the stack contents following execution of movem and link, on entry to a procedure. Finally, the last instructions in a procedure should be movem,lea,rts to restore registers and throw away items on the stack which were passed as parameters thus no longer required, by simply adjusting the value of the stack pointer. A return from the procedure is then effected by copying the return address back into the *program counter (PC)*. In the case of a *function procedure*[6] one must take care to leave the return value on the top of stack.

---

[6] ...using the Modula-2 terminology. Pascal users would normally use the term *"function"*.

```
move.w  0,-(SP)                        movem.l d<n>-d<m>/a<p>-a<q>,-(SP)
move.w  <parameter 1>,-(SP)            link    a<r>,#<frame size>
...                                    ...
move.w  <parameter n>,-(SP)            ...
bsr     <offset>                       ...
move.w  (SP)+,<result>                 unlk    a<r>
                                       movem.l (SP)+,d<n>-d<m>/a<p>-a<q>
                                       lea.l   +<parameter block size>(SP),SP
                                       rts
```

The above code skeletons show how a function procedure call and return may be effected. Prior to the **bsr** *(branch to subroutine)* space is created for the return value by pushing an arbitrary value of the required size (long shown). Parameters are then loaded onto the stack in a *predetermined order*. On procedure entry, any registers to be used within the function procedure are saved, so that they may be restored on exit, and the stack frame then created.

Expression evaluation

The M68000 is a *register machine* for the purposes of *expression evaluation*. For example[7], the following code segment may be used to evaluate $RootSquared := (b^2 - 4.a.c)/2.a\ldots$

```
move.w a, d0
muls   #2, d0
move.w c, d1
muls   a, d1
muls   #4, d1
move.w b, d2
muls   d2,d2
sub.w  d1, d2
divs   d0, d2
move.w d2, RootSquared
```

The processor was *not* designed to perform expression evaluation on the stack. There are two reasons why it would not be sensible to attempt it. Firstly, it would be inefficient. Only very rarely would the compiler require more than eight data registers. Registers are accessed *without* bus access cycles. Secondly, the arithmetic instructions are designed to leave the result in a *data register*. Stack evaluation simply is not supported. The instruction set is designed with the intention that *registers* be used to the maximum

---

[7]See Chapter 8, question four and solution.

effect.

Data referencing is usually performed using *address register indirect with displacement*. The register used is the. . .

- *Frame pointer if the variable is local*

- *Static base pointer if the variable is global*

Two-address registers should be reserved for use in this way.

Accessing elements within an array is achieved by *address register indirect with displacement and index*. The displacement locates the *base* of the array (or string), offset from frame or static base pointer, and the index locates the required element.

M68000 assembly language programming

Programming the M68000 using *assembly language* requires detailed documentation of the *assembler, linker* and *loader* to be employed. The *Motorola* standard mnemonics and symbols are documented, together with an excellent treatment of assembly language programming in general and of the M68000 in particular, in [Kane, Hawkins & Leventhal 81]. However, it does not detail the programming tools required. Many contemporary workstations are built around the M68000 or its derivatives including the *Apple Macintosh* and *Sun 300* series. A very thorough and extremely readable exposition of the *Macintosh 68000 Development System* tools is to be found within [Little 86].

10.3   National Semiconductor 32000

10.3.1   Architecture

Design philosophy

The *National Semiconductor 32000* was designed in the early 1980s to meet the market for very high performance systems in both the *real-time control* and *work-station* markets. Principal characteristics of the design are. . .

- *Reduction of semantic gap*

- *Structured programming support*

- *Software module support*

- *Virtual memory*

- *Security for multi-user operating system*

The three most distinctive characteristics are listed at the top. Both *instruction set* and *addressing modes* are designed to reduce code size and execution time of *high level language* statements. Single instructions replace several required in earlier machines. Most revolutionary, however, is explicit support for *modular* software. Items in *external* modules may be directly referenced, be they procedures or data.

There follows a list of features present...

- *Complex instruction set (CISC)*

- *Two-address instructions*

- *Instruction cache (queue)*

- *Register file for expression evaluation (no windowing)*

- *Stack for procedure, function and interrupt service subroutine implementation*

- *Demand paged virtual memory with self-maintained associative translation cache*

- *Vectored interrupt mechanism with programmable arbitration*

- *Symmetric architecture with respect to...*

    - *Number of operands (two)*
    - *Addressing mode usage (any instruction may use any mode)*
    - *Register usage (general purpose; address, data or array index)*
    - *Processor (8, 16 and 32 bit versions use common machine language)*

Among these the only truly original feature is that of *symmetry*. Almost any instruction may employ any addressing mode. Any register may be used for any purpose, address or data, and each is thus referred to as a *general purpose register (GPR)*. This is intended to make compiler code generation easier.

Interrupt/event arbitration protocols available are...

- *Polling (software control)*

- *Fixed priority*

- *Rotating priority*

Only a higher priority event may cause *pre-emption* of an interrupt service routine.

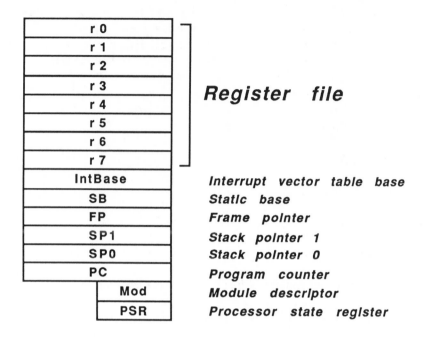

Figure 10.9: NS32000 programmer's architecture

Programmer's architecture

Figure 10.9 shows the *NS32000 programmer's architecture*. Eight *32-bit general purpose registers* are provided which has been shown to be adequate for the vast majority of expression evaluations.

Six *special purpose registers (SPR)* define the *memory map* (Figure 10.10) for any running program. Three SPRs point to areas of (virtual) memory containing data. *static base register (SB)* points to the base of *static* or *global* memory. *frame pointer (FP)* points to *local* memory where variables, local to the currently executing procedure, are *dynamically* stored in a *stack frame*. *program pointer (PC)* points to the next instruction to be executed. Figure 10.11 shows the *processor state register (PSR)* which defines the processor *state*. The state recorded in each flag is summarized in Table 10.7. *Supervisor access only is allowed to the most significant byte* to prevent users from interfering with the operating system in a multi-user environment.

SP0 and *SP1* point to the "tops" of the *supervisor stack* and *user stack* respectively. Both stacks actually grow *downwards* in memory so that the addition of an item actually *decreases* the value of the address stored in the relevant *stack pointer*. *Supervisor stack* access is *privileged* to the *operating system* alone and is used for system subroutines.

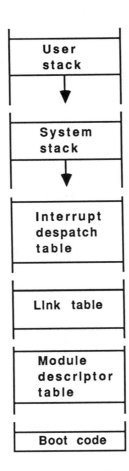

Figure 10.10: NS32000 memory map

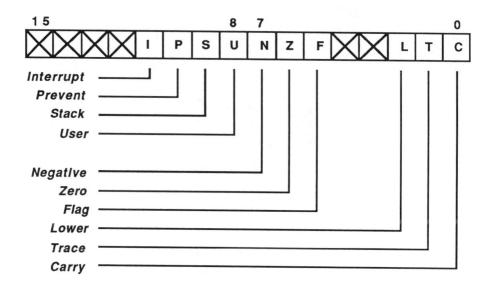

Figure 10.11: NS32000 processor state register

Most or all of these will be invoked via interrupt or trap *exceptions*. The *supervisor call* (svc) trap instruction is used by a program to invoke *operating system* procedures.

IntBase points to the base of the *interrupt despatch table* (Figure 10.12) containing *external procedure descriptors* (see below) for all exception handling subroutines. The first sixteen are of fixed purpose. From there onwards are those for subroutines selected *via* a *vector*, read from the data bus after an interrupt, which serves as an index into the table.

MOD points to the current *module descriptor* (Figure 10.13) which describes the *software module* to which the procedure currently executing belongs. It is only 16 bits in length which implies that *all loaded module descriptors should reside in the bottom 64k of memory*. As far as the machine is concerned a module is described via a pointer to the base of its global variables (SB), a pointer to the base in memory of its executable program code, and a pointer to the base of a *link table* (Figure 10.13).

The program code of a module is simply a concatenation of its component procedures. Each procedure may be referenced, from within another module, by an *external procedure descriptor* (Figure 10.14). This is composed of two fields. The least significant sixteen bits form a pointer to the parent module descriptor. The most significant sixteen bits form an offset from the base of program code, found in the module descriptor, where the *entry point* of the procedure is to be found.

It is these which are used as "vectors" in the *interrupt despatch table*. They also

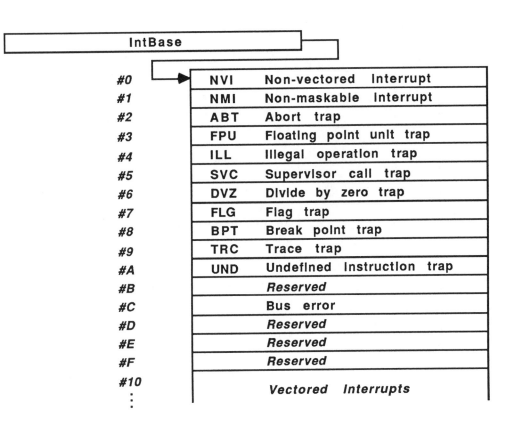

Figure 10.12: NS32000 interrupt despatch table

Flag	Write access	Meaning when set
I	*Privileged*	Inhibit all interrupts except *NMI* (Traps unaffected)
P	*Privileged*	Prevent a trace trap occurring more than once per instruction
S	*Privileged*	User stack, not supervisor stack
U	*Privileged*	User mode hence *privileged* instruction causes *undefined instruction* trap
N	*Any*	Negative result of *twos-complement* arithmetic operation
Z	*Any*	Zero result of arithmetic operation
F	*Any*	Flag used for miscellaneous purposes e.g. arithmetic overflow
L	*Any*	Lower value of *second* operand in comparison operations
T	*Any*	Trace in operation causing *TRC* trap after *every* instruction
C	*Any*	Carry after an addition, borrow after a subtraction

Table 10.7: Flags in the NS32000 processor state register and their meaning (when set)

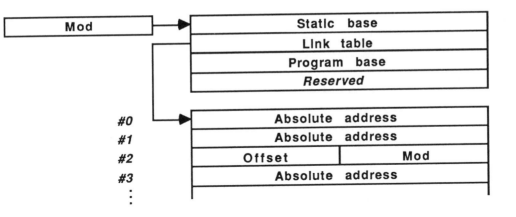

Figure 10.13: NS32000 module descriptor and link table

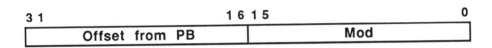

Figure 10.14: NS32000 external procedure descriptor

form one kind of entry in the *module link table* to describe procedures referenced which belong to other modules. The other kind of entry in the link table is simply the *absolute address* of a variable belonging to another module. *Hence whenever an application is loaded, the descriptors and link tables for all its component software modules must be initialized in memory.*

Addressing modes

Table 10.8 offers a summary of NS32000 addressing modes together with their encoding and *effective address* computation. Note that "[...]" in the *effective address* column means "contents of...".

Any principal addressing mode may be extended by addition of a *scaled index*. The scaling indicates whether the array is one of...

- *Bytes*

- *Words*

Addressing mode	Notation	Encoding	Effective address
Immediate	$<value>	10100_2	*None*
Absolute	@<value>	10101_2	*disp*
Register	r<n>	$00 < n >_2$	*None*
Memory space	<disp>(FP)	11000_2	$disp + [FP]$
	<disp>(SP)	11001_2	$disp + [SP]$
	<disp>(SB)	11010_2	$disp + [SB]$
	* + disp	11011_2	$disp + [PC]$
Scaled index	<mode>[r<n>:b]	11100_2	$ea(mode) + ([reg] \times 1)$
	<mode>[r<n>:w]	11100_2	$ea(mode) + ([reg] \times 2)$
	<mode>[r<n>:d]	11100_2	$ea(mode) + ([reg] \times 4)$
	<mode>[r<n>:q]	11100_2	$ea(mode) + ([reg] \times 8)$
Register relative	<disp>(r<n>)	$01 < n >_2$	$disp + [reg]$
Top of stack	tos	10111_2	$[SP]$
Memory relative	<disp1>(<disp2>(FP)	10000_2	$disp1 + [disp2 + [FP]]$
	<disp1>(<disp2>(SP)	10001_2	$disp1 + [disp2 + [SP]]$
	<disp1>(<disp2>(SB)	10001_2	$disp1 + [disp2 + [SB]]$

Table 10.8: NS32000 addressing modes

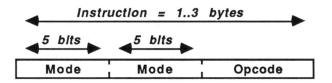

Figure 10.15: NS32000 basic instruction format

- *Double words*

- *Quad words*

. . . where the term *word* is interpreted as meaning *two bytes*.

Instruction set

Tables 10.9 and 10.10 show almost all of the NS32000 instructions together with the operation caused by their execution. The . . . `<i>` notation denotes one of the following operand lengths. . .

- *Byte (i = b)*

- *Word (i = w)*

- *Double word (i = d)*

The instruction set is thus also symmetric with respect to data length. For example **movw** means *"move a word"*.

Table 10.11 lists all the possible *branch conditions* of the processor state and the associated branch instruction mnemonic. The possibility of branching according to the simultaneous state of *two* flags helps close the *semantic gap* with *if. . . then. . . else* selection. Note that semantic gap closure for *selection* and *iteration* is also assisted via the inclusion of *add, compare & branch* and *case* instructions (see below).

The general instruction is composed of a *basic instruction* (Figure 10.15) of length *one, two or three* bytes possibly followed by one or two *instruction extensions* containing one of the following. . .

- *Index byte*

- *Immediate value*

- *Displacement*

Group	Mnemonic	Operation
Comparison and test	cmp\<i>	Compare
	cmpq\<i>	Compare *quick* operand
	cmpm\<i>	Compare multiple bytes (up to 16)
	cmps\<i>	Compare strings
	index\<i>	Recursive index generation (n-d arrays)
	check\<i>	Check array index bounds
	tbit\<i>	Test bit
	sbit\<i>	Test and set bit
	cbit\<i>	Test and clear bit
	ibit\<i>	Test and invert bit
Branches and jumps	br	Unconditional branch
	b\<cond>	Conditional branch
	acb\<i>	Add, compare and branch
	case\<i>	Case (multiway branch)
	bsr	Branch to subroutine
	jump	Jump (copy value to PC)
	jsr	Jump to subroutine
	cxp	Call external procedure (link table)
	cxpd	Call external procedure (descriptor)
	svc	Supervisor (system) call trap
	flag	Flag trap
	bpt	Breakpoint trap
	ret	Return from subroutine
	rxp	Return from external procedure
	rett	Return from trap *(privileged)*
	reti	Return from interrupt *(privileged)*
Register manipulation	save	Save list of registers on stack
	restore	Restore list of registers from stack
	enter	Save registers/allocate stack frame
	exit	Restore registers/de-allocate stack frame
	adjspr\<i>	Adjust stack pointer
Operating system (privileged...)	lpr\<i>	Load private register *(...if PSR or IntBase)*
	spr\<i>	Save private register *(...if PSR or IntBase)*
	bispsr\<i>	Set PSR bits *(...if $i \neq b$)*
	bicpsr\<i>	Clear PSR bits *(...if $i \neq b$)*
	lmr	Load MMU register
	smr	Save MMU register
	rdval	Validate virtual read address
	wrval	Validate virtual write address

Table 10.9: Instruction set of the NS32000: Program control

Group	Mnemonic	Operation
Moves	mov\<i\>	Move
	movq\<i\>	Extend and move *quick* operand
	movm\<i\>	Move multiple bytes (up to 16)
	movs\<i\>	Move string
	movzbw	Move and zero extend byte to word
	movz\<i\>d	Move and zero extend to double word
	movxbw	Move and sign extend byte to word
	movx\<i\>d	Move and sign extend
	addr	Move effective address
	ext\<i\>	Extract bit field
	ins\<i\>	Insert bit field
Integer arithmetic	add\<i\>	Addition
	addq\<i\>	Add *quick* operand
	addc\<i\>	Add with carry
	sub\<i\>	Subtract
	subc\<i\>	Subtract with carry
	neg\<i\>	Negate (twos-complement)
	abs\<i\>	Absolute value
	mul\<i\>	Multiply
	quo\<i\>	Quotient (rounding towards zero)
	rem\<i\>	Remainder from quotient
	div\<i\>	Divide (rounding down)
	mod\<i\>	Modulus (after div\<i\>)
	mei\<i\>	Multiply to extended integer
	dei\<i\>	Divide to extended integer
Logical and Boolean	and\<i\>	Bitwise *and*
	or\<i\>	Bitwise *or*
	xor\<i\>	Bitwise *exclusive or*
	com\<i\>	Bitwise complement
	bic\<i\>	Clear selected bits
	not\<i\>	Boolean negate (complement lsb)
Shifts	lsh\<i\>	Logical shift (left or right)
	ash\<i\>	Arithmetic shift (left or right)
	rot\<i\>	Rotate (left or right)

Table 10.10: Instruction set of the NS32000: Expression evaluation

Mnemonic	Processor state	Condition
beq	Z	Equal
bne	$\bar{Z}$	Not equal
bcs	C	Carry set
bcc	$\bar{C}$	Carry clear
bhi	L	Higher
bls	$\bar{L}$	Lower or same
bgt	N	Greater than
ble	$\bar{N}$	Less or equal
bfs	F	Flag set
bfc	$\bar{F}$	Flag clear
blo	$\bar{Z}.\bar{L}$	Lower
bhs	$Z + L$	Higher or same
blt	$\bar{Z}.\bar{N}$	Less than
bge	$Z + N$	Greater than or equal

Table 10.11: Branch conditions for the NS32000

- *Pair of displacements*

...depending on both the instruction, which may have an *implied* operand, and each of the two addressing modes, one or both of which may require qualification. The basic instruction encodes...

- *Opcode*

- *Operand length*

- *Addressing mode for each operand*

Figure 10.16 shows the format of a *displacement* extension which may be one, two or four bytes in length.

A complete description of the NS32000 instruction set and addressing modes may be found in [National Semiconductor 84].

10.3.2   Organization

Processor organization

Figure 10.17 shows the organization of the *NS32332*. This an evolved member of the NS32000 series. The design is a hybrid stack + register machine, offering the convenience of a *stack* for procedure implementation and the speed and code compactness afforded by *register file* expression evaluation. An *instruction cache* queues instructions fetched

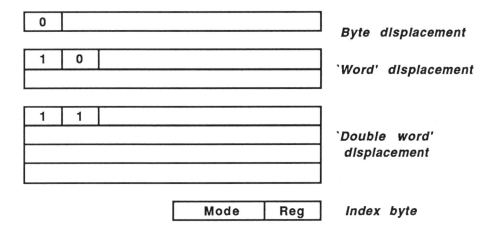

Figure 10.16: NS32000 displacement instruction extension format

when the bus is otherwise idle. A dedicated barrel shifter and adder are provided for rapid *effective address calculation*. Address and data are multiplexed on a common bus. Additional *working registers* are provided. These will be invisible even to the compiler and are used by the microcode in implementing instructions.

Physical memory organization

Physical memory of the NS32000 is organized as a simple, uniform linear array where each address value points to a single byte. Hence it is said to offer *byte-oriented addressing*. However, depending on the data bus width of the processor in use, two or even four bytes may be read simultaneously.

A *modular interleaved memory* is supported as shown in Figure 10.18. Four signals are provided by the processor to *enable* each memory bank to partake in any given bus transaction depending on the address and word length required. This allows byte-oriented addressing *without word alignment access restrictions*. Hence, for example, a two-byte word can be read at an odd address[8]. Table 10.12 shows a table of all possible modes of bus access. Figure 10.19 shows the timing diagram for a bus transaction *without* address translation.

---

[8] NS32000 documentation reserves the term "word" to mean two bytes, "double word" four bytes and "quad word" eight bytes. In the text here the term is used more generally.

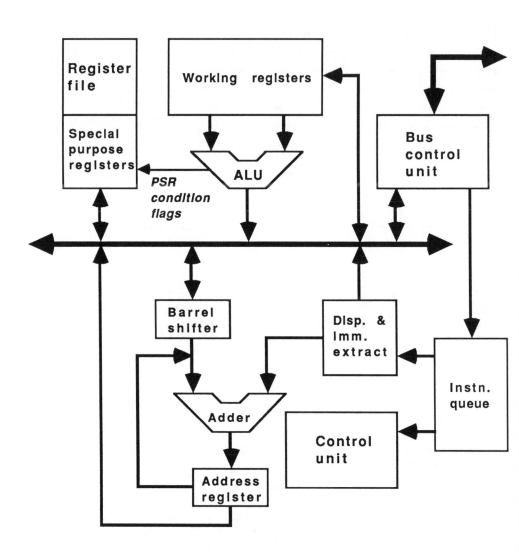

Figure 10.17: NS32332 processor organization

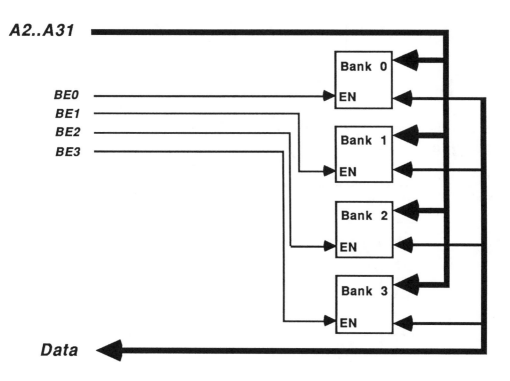

Figure 10.18: NS32000 modular interleaved memory

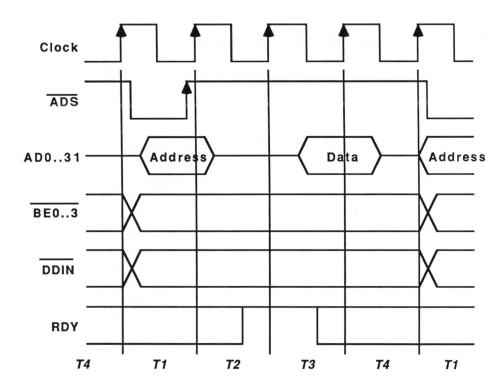

Figure 10.19: NS32000 bus timing

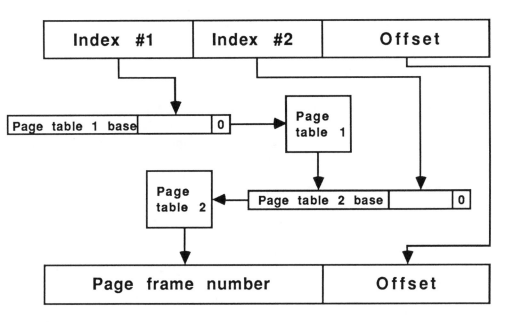

Figure 10.20: NS32000 virtual to physical address translation

Type	Address bits 0,1	Bus enable Active low	Bytes read
1	00	1110	1
2	01	1101	1
3	10	1011	1
4	11	0111	1
5	00	1100	2
6	01	1001	2
7	10	0011	2
8	00	1000	3
9	01	0001	3
10	00	0000	4

Table 10.12: NS32000 bus access types

Virtual memory organization

The NS32000 employs a two level *demand paged* address translation scheme as shown
in Figure 10.20. A page size of 512 bytes is used to optimize the trade-off between page
table size and program locality. Each page present in memory is pointed to by one of
128 entries in a special page called a *pointer table*. Each pointer table is pointed to by
one of 256 entries in a *page table*. The page table itself is located via a pointer register
in the *memory management unit (MMU)*. Only 132k of memory need thus be allocated
to provide *complete* virtual to physical address mapping. However, usually only the page
table and pointer tables *currently in use* are kept in memory. Each process running on
the system may have its own private page and pointer tables. This affords both *security*
and the possibility of *sharing* physical pages.

    An *associative translation cache* is employed to avoid the need for extra bus cycles
being required to look up entries in the page and pointer tables, otherwise address translation would be hopelessly slow. The *cache replacement algorithm* employed is *least
recently used (LRU)* and cache size is just thirty-two entries. Note that *page faults* can
occur because either the desired page *or* the pointer table is absent from memory. When
one occurs the MMU signals the *central processing unit (CPU)* to abort the current instruction and return all registers to their state before it began. The PC, PSR and SP are
saved on the interrupt stack and an *abort* trap occurs, whereupon the *page swap* may
be carried out. The MMU is designed to support a *least frequently used (LFU)* page
replacement algorithm.

    Security is afforded in the following ways...

- *Separate "supervisor" page table*

- *Separate page table per process*

- *"Page protection"* attributes to each page and pointer table entry

- *Supervisor alone may modify page and pointer tables*

Figure 10.21 shows the bus timing modified to allow address translation. Note that only one extra clock cycle per transaction is required provided a *hit* is obtained by the *associative translation cache*, which is 98% efficient!

10.3.3 Programming

Constructs

Closure of the semantic gap has been obtained by the designers both by careful selection of addressing modes for data referencing and by the inclusion of instructions which go as far in implementing directly the commands of a high level language. Code generation is intended to produce fewer instructions. However, the instructions themselves are more complex. In other words the problem of efficiently implementing *selection* and *iteration* is solved *once and for all* in *microcode* instead of code.

A *"for"* loop always requires *signed addition of constant, compare* and *conditional branch* operations on each iteration. Since this is a very common construct indeed, and the constant is usually small, the designers of the NS32000 included a single instruction (acb) to this end, optimizing its implementation in microcode once and for all.

```
mov<i> ntimes,index                case<i> *+4[r<n>:<i>]
; loop start                       <offset1>
...                                <offset2>
acb<i> $-1,index,*-<start offset>  ...
```

Above are code "skeletons" for the implementation of both *for loop* and *case* constructs. case effects a *multi-way branch* where the branch offset is selected according to the value *placed previously* in r<n>. This is used as an index into a table of offsets which may be placed anywhere but which it is sensible to locate directly below the case instruction. The argument to case is the location of an offset to be added to the PC which is addressed using *PC memory space mode*. Each offset thus directs the "thread of control" to a code segment derived from the high level language statement associated with a particular *case label*. Each selectable code segment must end with a branch to the instruction following the case construct end. It is usual to place such code segments above the case instruction.

The compiler must generate code to evaluate the *case expression* which may then simply be placed in the index register. It should also generate the case label *bounds*, an offset table entry for *every value within the bounds* and code to verify that the case expression value falls within them. If it fails to do so an offset should be used which points to a code segment generated from the *else* clause in the case construct. Any offset not corresponding to a case label value should also point to the *else* segment. You should be able to see why *widely scattered case label values indicate an inappropriate use of a*

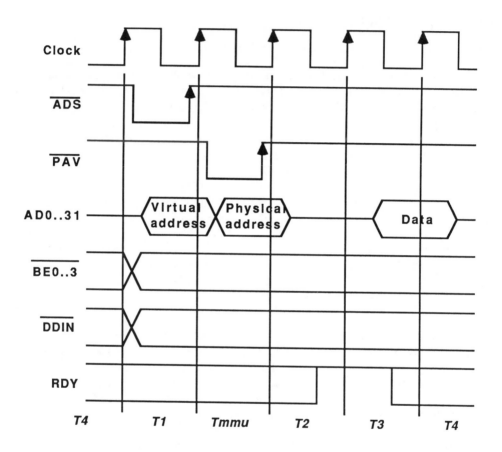

Figure 10.21: NS32000 bus timing with address translation

ase construct. In such circumstances it is better to use a number of *if... then... else* onstructs (perhaps nested).

'rocedures

nvocation of a procedure is very straightforward since the instruction set offers direct upport *via* dedicated instructions for saving and restoring registers and creating and lestroying a *stack frame* for local variables. **enter** should be used as the first instruction of a procedure. It saves a nominated list of registers and creates a stack frame of the size quoted (in bytes). **exit** should be the last but one instruction. It restores a nominated ist of registers and automatically destroys the stack frame by copying the *frame pointer* nto the stack pointer and then restoring the frame pointer itself (from a value saved by **enter** on the stack).

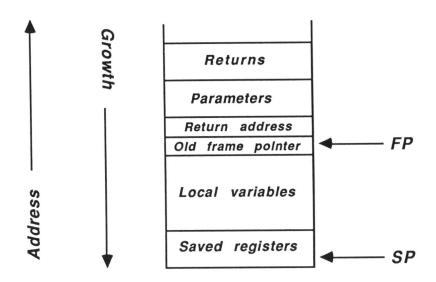

Figure 10.22: NS32000 stack following subroutine invocation and entry

Figure 10.22 depicts the stack contents following execution of **enter** on entry to a procedure. Finally, the last instruction in a procedure should be **ret<i>** which throws away the items on the stack which were passed as parameters, and thus no longer required, by simply adjusting the value of the stack pointer. It then effects a return from the procedure by copying the return address back into the *program counter (PC.* In the case of a *function procedure*[9] one must take care to specify the argument of **ret(i)** so as to

---

[9] ...using the Modula-2 terminology. Pascal users would normally use the term *function*.

leave the return value on the top of stack.

```
movqd 0,tos                          enter [<reg list>],$<frame size>
movd  <parameter 1>,tos              ...
...                                  ...
movd  <parameter n>,tos              ...
bsr   <offset>                       exit [<reg list>]
movd  tos,<result>                   ret  $<parameter block size>
```

The above code skeleton shows how a function procedure call and return may be effected. Prior to the **bsr** *(branch to subroutine)* space is created for the return value by pushing an arbitrary value of the required size onto the stack (double word shown). Parameters are then loaded onto the stack in a *predetermined order*. On procedure entry any registers to be used within the function procedure are saved, so that they may be restored on exit, and the stack frame created.

External procedures, i.e. those which reside in other software modules of the application, may be invoked using either **cxp** *(call external procedure)* or **cxpd** *(call external procedure via descriptor)* instead of **bsr**. The argument to **cxp** is simply an offset (displacement) within the current *module link table*. That of **cxpd** is an *external procedure descriptor* (see above). **rxp** *(return from external procedure)* must be used in place of **ret**.

Expression evaluation

The NS32000 is a *register machine* for the purposes of *expression evaluation*. For example[10], the following code segment may be used to evaluate $RootSquared := (b^2 - 4.a.c)/2.a$ ...

```
movd  a, r0
muld  $2, r0
movd  c, r1
muld  a, r1
muld  $4, r1
movd  b, r2
muld  r2,r2
subd  r2, r1
divd  r1, r0
movd  r0, RootSquared
```

The processor was *not* designed to perform expression evaluation on the stack. There

---

[10] See Chapter 8, question four and solution.

are two reasons why it would not be sensible to attempt it. Firstly, it would be inefficient. Only very rarely would the compiler require more than eight registers. Registers are accessed *without* bus access cycles. Secondly, the stack is only modified if a *tos* operand *access class* is *read* as is the case with the first, *but not the second*, operand in an arithmetic instruction. Hence **add 4(SP),tos** will leave the stack size unaltered. The first operand will remain. The instruction set is designed with the intention that *registers* be used to the maximum effect.

Data referencing is usually performed using *memory space mode*, in particular...

- *Frame memory space mode if the variable is local*

- *Static memory space mode if the variable is global*

Accessing elements within an array is achieved by concatenating a *scaled index* address modifier to a memory space mode.

NS32000 assembly language programming

Programming the NS32000 using *assembly language* requires detailed documentation of the *assembler*, *linker* and *loader* to be employed. The *National Semiconductor* assembler is documented in [National Semiconductor 87]. This runs under the *Unix* operating system and hence allows standard *Unix* tools to be used. [Martin 87] is devoted to the subject and is highly readable.

10.4   Inmos Transputer

10.4.1   Architecture

Design philosophy

The introduction of the *Transputer* represents nothing less than a revolution in computer architecture. Although a *single* Transputer is capable of a higher instruction throughput than almost any other processor integrated into a single device, its real power is extracted when used as a single node in a *homogeneous* network. Parallel processing computers may be constructed extremely easily and with a *cost/performance* ratio that puts super-computing within the purchasing power of the *individual*, or small organization, rather than just huge centralized units. However, its main market is for the many new real-time embedded control applications which it makes possible.

The Transputer is the first device to exploit electronic *VLSI*[11] technology to integrate an *entire* computer in a single device (processor, memory and communication channels) rather than simply to expand the power and complexity of one or other of its components. It is this approach which gives rise to the advent of affordable parallel computation. Also

---

[11]Very Large Scale Integration.

included is an external memory interface which permits easy, cheap "off-chip" memory expansion. This is needed because of the current limit to the scale of integration. As technology improves a decision has to be made about the use of newly available "silicon real estate"... *more memory, more processor or more links?*

Two forms of parallelism are exploited by the Transputer...

- *Division of load*

- *Division of function*

Division of load is achieved simply by connecting a number of devices into a network. *Division of function* is achieved "on-chip" due to the fact that each communication channel is effected by a separate *link* processor. They may function independently of each other and of the *central processor*. Hence an individual Transputer may, for example, execute *input*, *output* and *assignment* in parallel! These three operations are the *primitives* or *atoms*, of the *process-oriented* programming model.

Of equal importance to being the first fully integrated parallel processing element is that the Transputer is the first computer to be developed hand-in-hand with a programming language (*Occam* [Inmos 88#1,Burns 88]). In addition the programming model has a secure *formal* (mathematical) foundation in CSP[12]. This unlocks the possibility of using formal system verification techniques right down to the architecture level. Indeed a system is available for compiling Occam programs directly into silicon [Inmos 88#5 page 45].

Lastly, although the designers never actually proposed it as such, the Transputer may be understood, at least in part, as a *Reduced Instruction Set Computer (RISC)*. Table 10.13 summarizes the "RISCiness" of the Transputer[13]. It fails on only two points. It lacks a register file for storage of local variables and *register windowing* for subroutine linkage. Neither of these are a loss. Fast, "on-chip" memory compensates for the lack of a register file large enough to accommodate local variables. It is three times faster to access than external, "off-chip", memory. Subroutine linkage is effected using the evaluation stack registers. As long as no more than three parameters are to be passed, no memory access is necessary. Even if more are required, they may be placed in workspace in the fast internal memory.

It only *partially* succeeds in the single cycle execution requirement. One of the motivations for keeping small the instruction set is that a *hardwired* control unit becomes economic, both in development timescale and in processor complexity. Current Transputers use *microcoded* control units presumably for their advantage in flexibility, which

---

[12]Communicating Sequential Processes, [Hoare 78,Hoare 85].

[13]A more thorough appraisal of the Transputer as a RISC is to be found in [Tabak 87], although an assertion therein, that $\sim$ 80% of *executed* instructions take just one clock cycle, is mistaken. This is the correct figure for the proportion which are encoded in a single byte, [Inmos 88#5, page 23], but only an unknown proportion of instructions executed do so in a single cycle. About half of the *1-byte* instructions available require only a single cycle.

Criterion (idealized)	Met?	Comments
Small set of compact instructions	Yes	$\sim$ 110 instructions $\sim$ 80% executed are single byte
...optimized for high level language	Yes	Occam 2
Single instruction format	Yes	4-bit opcode + 4-bit operand Prefixing allows instruction set extension
Single cycle instruction execution	Partial	Most common are 1 or 2 cycle
Single addressing mode	Yes	Dedicated instructions for constants and indirection
Load/store register file expression evaluation	Yes	Three register stack Memory to memory move for assignment and communication
Register local variable storage	No	Fast (on-chip) memory compensates
Register window linkage	No	Registers + workspace used instead

Table 10.13: Transputer satisfaction of RISC criteria

is of obvious value when the product is new, and because some of its operations are inherently impossible to perform in a single cycle anyway.

The principal points of Transputer design philosphy may be summarized as. . .

- *Parallel/concurrent processing support*

- *Integration of entire computer in single device*

Transputer design features may be briefly summarized. . .

- *Reduced instruction set (RISC)*

- *Parallel operation of CPU and links*

- *Links (currently four input + four output @ $20Mbits.sec^{-1}$)*

- *Process queue support for each of two priorities*

- *Integrated "on-chip" memory (currently up to 4k)*

- *Integrated support for external "off-chip" memory*

- *One-address extensible instruction set*

- *Code independent of word length*

For full documentation of the Transputer see [Inmos 88#2,Inmos 88#3] and for Occam see [Inmos 88#1,Burns 88]. Very useful ancillary information and documentation of example applications may be found in [Inmos 89].

Programmer's architecture

Figure 10.23 depicts the *programmer's architecture* of the *T414 Transputer*. The *O* (operand) register acts rather like an *accumulator* in that it is the default source of the operand for almost all instructions. *A, B, C* form an *evaluation stack* which is affected both by special *load/store* and by arithmetic instructions. Whenever data is loaded it is in fact *pushed* into *A*, whose content is pushed down into *B*, whose content is in turn pushed down into *C*. The content of *C* is lost, so it is the responsibility of the compiler to save it if necessary. Similarly, a store instruction moves *C* into *B* and *B* into *A*. The new content of *C* is undefined. Only *O, A, B, C* are directly manipulated by instructions. The rest are arranged to be taken care of automatically[14]. One further register, *E*, is *hidden* and used by Transputer *block move* instructions.

I contains a pointer to the next instruction to be executed and hence performs the function of a *program counter*. A departure from traditional *program control* is that

---

[14] . . . except on booting (see later).

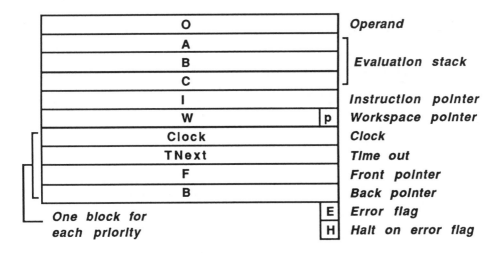

Figure 10.23: Transputer programmer's achitecture

none of the familiar processor state flags are present (e.g. carry, zero). Instead A is used to contain the value of a Boolean expression encoded as 1 for *true* and 0 for *false*. Multi-precision arithmetic is expected to be performed solely using dedicated instructions which use the evaluation stack exclusively without the need for the usual *carry*, *overflow* and *negative* flags.

Flags *are* employed to assist with performance verification and analysis, which is particularly difficult in multi-processor systems. *Error* is set following a processing error, such as arithmetic overflow, divide by zero or array bounds violation. It causes the processor to *halt*[15], i.e. to *STOP*, *if* the *HaltOnError* flag was set. The status of *Error* is reflected on a hardware signal which is *transmitted to all other Transputers* in order to cause them to *STOP* also, depending on the state of their *HaltOnError* flag. Hence a very simple mechanism facilitates an entire network of *Transputers* to *halt* should an error occur *anywhere* therein, allowing software to be verified and if necessary corrected. This is essential since otherwise a problem on a single processor may go undetected until its effects propagate. Facilities are also provided to interrogate and *analyse* the state of each Transputer to determine the cause of an error.

The Transputer is designed to support a *process-oriented* programming model that does not allow variables to be shared by concurrent processes, which instead communicate through *channels*. Variables local to a process, together with information describing process status, are located within a *workspace* pointed to by W which is *word aligned*.

---

[15]Upon a *halt* the transputer will either idle, waiting for link communication, or reboot from ROM depending on the hardware level signal *BootFromROM*.

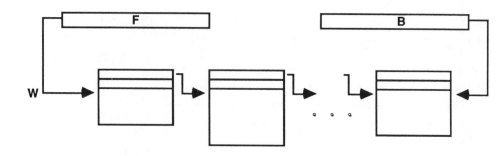

Figure 10.24: Transputer process queue

The least significant bit of W is used to indicate the priority of the current process. A *process descriptor* is made up of...

- *Pointer to process workspace*

- *Process priority*

...which both conveniently fit into a single word.

Further support for concurrent processing comes in the form of *front* and *back* pointer registers which implement a *process ready queue* (Figure 10.24) for each of *two* priorities.

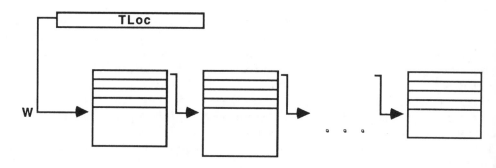

Figure 10.25: Transputer timer list

   Time dependent processing is directly supported also. In the programmer's architecture this becomes visible as two *time* registers. *Clock* contains a measure of time and in fact is two registers, one for each priority. The low priority clock ticks once every $64\mu s$, high priority every $1\mu s$. The full cycle times are respectively $\sim 76hours$ and $\sim 4ms$

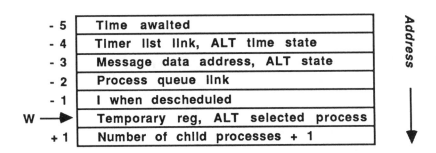

- 5	Time awaited
- 4	Timer list link, ALT time state
- 3	Message data address, ALT state
- 2	Process queue link
- 1	I when descheduled
W →	Temporary reg, ALT selected process
+ 1	Number of child processes + 1

Figure 10.26: Transputer workspace usage for process scheduling

independent of processor clock rate!. The low priority clock gives exactly 15625 ticks per second. *TNext* indicates the time of the *earliest awaited event* and allows the process which awaits it to be "woken up" and rescheduled. The process is located by means of the *timer list* (Figure 10.25), a pointer to the start of which is kept in a reserved memory location (see below).

Figure 10.26 shows the use of reserved workspace locations for process status description. $W - 2$ and $W - 4$ form the links in the dynamic *process ready queue* and *timer list* respectively, should the process be currently on either one. It cannot be on both structures since it will be suspended if awaiting a timer event. $W - 5$ contains the time awaited, if any. When the process is suspended, $W - 1$ houses the value to be loaded into I when eventually rescheduled and run. An Occam *PAR* process spawns a number of subsidiary "child" processes and cannot terminate until they do. The number of offspring which have still to terminate *plus one* is recorded in $W + 1$. Lastly, $W + 0$ is used like an extra register by certain instructions. If these are in use it must be kept free.

In addition to processor registers, a number of reserved memory locations are employed to facilitate communication and process scheduling (Figure 10.27). The bottom eight words are the *rendezvous* locations for eight *hard channels (links)*. This is the *only* way in which links are visible to the compiler. Other than fixed versus definable rendezvous location, there is *no* distinction whatsoever between hard and soft channels at the level of the machine language. One further channel, *EventIn (of pure signal protocol)*, has fixed rendezvous location directly above those of the links.

Scheduling algorithms differ for the two priorities. High priority processes simply run until completion or until they are suspended to await either communication or a time. Low priority processes may be suspended for the same reasons but are allowed to run for no longer than two *timeslices* of $\sim 1ms$[16]. After *two* timeslice "ends" have occurred the process is suspended at the next available *suspension point* (Table 10.14). *A, B, C* are

---

[16] 1024 ticks of *high priority* clock.

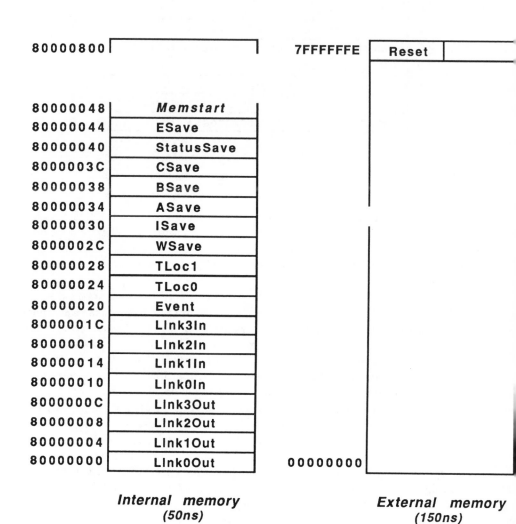

Figure 10.27: Transputer memory map

ot saved when a process is suspended so these instructions should not be executed while
an expression is being evaluated. (*O* is cleared by *every* instruction after its operation is
performed.)

Communication	Alternation/ Timer wait	Termination/ Stop	Branch/ Loop end
in out outbyte outword	altwt talt tin	endp stopp stoperr	j lend

Table 10.14: Instructions where the Transputer may suspend a process

Low priority processes may be *pre-empted* by any high priority process immediately
it becomes ready. The low priority process is said to have been *interrupted* and may
resume *only* if there are no other high priority processes waiting. Interruption can only
happen once at a time. As a result seven more words are reserved as a save area for
processor register contents of the *interrupted* low priority process.

Booting may be achieved either from *ROM* or over a link. On power-up an external
level signal called *BootFromROM* is inspected. If set then the instruction at the top
of (external) memory is executed which must always be a backward jump into a *ROM*.
Processor *reset* state is...

$$
\begin{aligned}
I &= 7FFFFFFE_{16} \\
W &= MemStart \vee 1 \\
A &= I_{old} \\
B &= W_{old} \\
C &\quad is\ undefined
\end{aligned}
$$

If *BootFromROM* is clear then the Transputer listens to the first link to receive a
byte. Sending a reset Transputer a zero byte, followed by an address and then data,
effects a *poke* of that data into a memory location. Similarly a value of one, followed
by an address, effects a *peek* where the contents of that address are returned on the
corresponding output link. Any value greater than one is interpreted as the length of a
string of bytes forming the *boot code* which is loaded into internal memory starting at
MemStart. It then executes that code starting with the following state...

$$
\begin{aligned}
I &= MemStart \\
W &= First\ free\ word \vee 1
\end{aligned}
$$

$$A = I_{old}$$
$$B = W_{old}$$
$$C = Pointer\ to\ boot\ link$$

"First free word" is the first word in internal memory whose address is $\geq MemStart-$ *code length*. The *OR* of W with 1 ensures that the boot code runs as a *low priorit*
process.

Analysing the Transputer state is highly desirable when diagnosing faults on a net
work. By simultaneously asserting the *Analyse* and *Reset* hardware signals the Trans
puter is persuaded to reboot. **testpranal** *(test processor analysing)* may be used a
the start of ROM *boot code* to determine whether to reboot the most senior systen
process or to perform state analysis. If booting from link, *peek* and *poke* messages ma
be employed to examine state (see above).

Following *Analyse/Reset* a Transputer will *halt* program execution as soon as a sus
pension point for the current process priority is reached (Table 10.14). However th
current process is *not* suspended. Subsequently both clocks are stopped, I and W value
are to be found in A and B respectively. State available for analysis includes. . .

- *Error*

- *W and I*

- *Channel status*

- *Ready queue*

- *Timer list*

- *Any low priority process interrupted by one of high priority*

saveh and **savel** save the high and low priority queue registers respectively in a pai
of words pointed to by A. This facilitates inspection of the *ready queue*.

Addressing modes

One of the most RISC-like features of the Transputer is that each instruction defines th
operand addressing mode. In this sense it may be said to have just one mode. However
overall there is more than one way in which the location of an operand is determined
Table 10.15 shows these.

Instructions which specify a constant operand may be said to use *immediate mode*
As far as variable data is concerned, *local mode* is the one used for referencing *scala*
data in compiled Occam. *Non-local mode* is provided (by means of *load/store non-loca*
instructions) for accessing within *vector* data. An offset must be derived in O and $\imath$
pointer in A before loading or storing data.

Addressing mode	Effective address
Immediate	*None*
Local	$disp + [W]$
Non-local	$disp + [A]$

Table 10.15: Transputer addressing modes

All references are *relative* to allow *position independent code* and avoid *relocation editing*. Data is referenced relative to W or A and code relative to I. Although instruction mnemonics j and cj stand for "jump" and "conditional jump", they in fact represent *branch* instructions. Their operands are *added* to the content of I and do not replace it.

Structured immediate mode data may be referenced by means of ldpi *(load pointer to instruction)* whose operand is an offset from the current value of I.

Instruction set

A somewhat cunning approach gives the Transputer instruction set the following qualities...

- *Extensibility with small average instruction size*

- *Operand may be of any length up to word*

- *Operand representation is independent of word length*

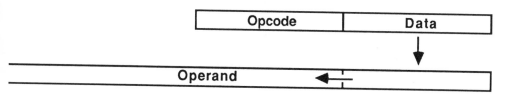

Figure 10.28: Transputer basic instruction format

At the simplest level each instruction is just one byte, consisting of 4-bit opcode and operand fields (Figure 10.28). The *thirteen* most commonly used instructions are encoded in a single nibble. One of the remaining three possible codes (*operate*) *executes its operand as an opcode*, allowing in all twenty-nine effective operations to be encoded within a single byte.

Group	Mnemonic	Operation	nibbles	Cycles
Data access	ldc	Load constant	1	1
	ldl	Load local	1	2
	stl	Store local	1	1
	ldnl	Load non-local	1	2
	stnl	Store non-local	1	2
	rev	Reverse A and B	2	1
	ldlp	Load local pointer	1	1
	ldnlp	Load non-local pointer	1	1
	ldpi	Load pointer to instruction	2	2
	bsub	Byte subscript	2	1
	wsub	Word subscript	2	2
	bcnt	Byte count	2	2
	csub0	Check subscript from 0	4	2
	ccnt1	Check count from 1	4	3
	xword	Extend to word	4	4
	cword	Check word	4	5
	xdble	Extend to double	4	2
	csngl	Check single	4	3
	wcnt	Word count	2	5
	mint	Most negative integer	4	1
	norm	Normalize	4	≤ 36
Integer arithmetic	adc	Add constant	1	1
	add	Add	2	1
	sub	Subtract	2	1
	mul	Multiply	4	38
	div	Divide	4	≤ 39
	rem	Remainder	4	37
	sum	Sum (modulo)	4	1
	diff	Difference (modulo)	2	1
	prod	Product (modulo)	2	$4 \rightarrow 36$
	fmul	Fraction multiply	4	40
	ladd	Long add	4	2
	lsum	Long sum (modulo)	4	2
	lsub	Long subtract	4	2
	lmul	Long multiply	4	5
	ldiv	Long divide	4	8

Table 10.16: Instruction set of the Transputer: Expression evaluation (continued in next Table)

Group	Mnemonic	Operation	nibbles	Cycles
Logical	and	And	4	1
	or	Or	4	1
	xor	Exclusive or	4	1
	not	Not (bitwise)	4	1
Shifts	shl	Shift left (n bits)	4	$n+2$
	shr	Shift right (n bits)	4	$n+2$
	lshl	Long shift left (n bits)	4	$n+3$
	lshr	Long shift right (n bits)	4	$n+3$

Table 10.17: Instruction set of the Transputer: Expression evaluation (continued from last Table)

Two *prefix* instructions allow the extension of the operand, right up to the word length limit, by shifting *its* operand up four bits in O. (All instructions begin by loading their operand into O and, except for prefixes, clear it before terminating.) To generate negative operands, a *negative prefix* instruction *complements* O prior to the left shift. Its operation may be described...

$$(1) \quad O_{LSN} \quad \leftarrow \quad (O \wedge Instruction_{LSN})$$
$$(2) \quad O \quad \leftarrow \quad BITNOT(O)$$
$$(3) \quad O \quad \leftarrow \quad (O \ll 4)$$

In short, the argument to **nfix** appears in the *least significant nibble (LSN)* of O and is complemented (via *BITNOT*) before being shifted left by a nibble. It is not at all obvious how one acquires a desired (twos-complement) value in O *so one doesn't*, one leaves it to a compiler or assembler to work out! For the sake of illustration we will investigate how to acquire an operand value of -256. It requires just **nfix #F**, then the required operator with argument zero. Using the above description, the least significant sixteen bit field of O evolves as follows...

$$0000.0000.0000.0000$$
$$0000.0000.0000.1111$$
$$1111.1111.1111.0000$$
$$1111.1111.0000.0000$$

Note that the result will still be correct *regardless of word width!*

The principal design aim responsible for the operand register mechanism is to minimize the number of bits required to describe a set of operations. As a result the useful work done by the processor is made much less dependent on the bandwidth of the processor-to-memory communication channel. For equivalent "horsepower", less money need be spent on acquiring fast memory.

Tables 10.16, 10.17, 10.18 and 10.19 show the instruction set of the Transputer divide
into expression evaluation, program control and scheduling/communication categorie
Single instructions are provided which implement *input*, *output* and *assignment...* tl
three primitives of Occam. In addition, no (run-time) operating environment is need
to conduct any of the work associated with process scheduling. The onus is on tl
compiler to generate code to take care of that. Without a language capable of expressir
concurrency, this could not be so.

Expression evaluation instructions are provided which assist the implemention of bot
double precision and fractional integer arithmetic. For example **ladd** is used as the la
step in multiple length addition, according to $A \leftarrow A + B + C_{lsb}$. Earlier steps u
lsum which performs the same operation, *without checking for overflow*, and leaves au
carry in B_{lsb}. The need for a *carry* flag is avoided since storing a result and loading
subsequent pair of words onto the evaluation stack will force any carry into C_{lsb}.

Process ready queue management is facilitated by the **startp** and **endp** instructior
which *schedule* and *terminate* processes respectively. **startp** assumes the new proce:
to be of the same priority as the parent. **runp** does the same job but allows the priorit
to be explicitly specified, otherwise **ldpri** and **or** may be used to set the priority of tl
process descriptor in A.

Synchronous communication is made possible by **in** and **out** instructions which su
pend receiving or transmitting process if the other is not ready to communicate. *Re*
dezvous is achieved at a memory location, which effectively implements a *channel*, and
determined on channel declaration. *Hard channels (links)* are programmed using exactl
the same instructions in exactly the same way, except for the reserved locations for lin
rendezvous.

Synchronization with *external* events is made possible by what may be regarded a
a special link whose protocol is simply a *signal* input, *(EventIn)*, followed by a *sign*
output *(EventAcknowledge)*. Again no extra, dedicated instructions are required.

Timer list management is also automatic. *Timers* are an abstraction treated as thoug
they were *channels*. Descheduling and insertion of a process into the list is a result c
tin (timer input). This allows the specification of a time (clock value) prior to whic
the program may not proceed. This is equivalent to the Occam...

```
clock ? AFTER deadline
```

...which allows processes to be endowed with time dependent behaviour. Simpl
loading a timer value (**ldtimer**) and then performing a timer input can *delay* a proces
for a predetermined period, so implementing the Occam...

```
clock ? time
clock ? AFTER time PLUS delay
```

ALT (process selection by guard event) gets explicit support. A number of instruc
tions are provided to this end which are illustrated below. Implementation of *ALT* ma
be summarized...

Group	Mnemonic	Operation	nibbles	Cycles
Comparisons	eqc	Equal constant	1	2
	gt	Greater than	2	2
Branches &	j	Jump (branch)	1	3
linkage	cj	Conditional jump	1	2 or 4
	lend	Loop end	4	10 or 5
	call	Call subroutine	1	7
	gcall	General call	2	4
	ret	Return	2	5
	ajw	Adjust W	1	1
	gajw	General adjust W	2	2
Error handling	stoperr	Stop on error	4	2
	testerr	Test error and clear	4	≤ 3
	seterr	Set error	4	1
	clrhalterr	Clear halt on error	4	1
	sethalterr	Set halt on error	4	1
	testhalterr	Test halt on error	4	2
	testpranal	Test processor analysing	4	2
Instruction	pfix	Prefix	1	1
generation	nfix	Negative prefix	1	1
	opr	Operate	1	n/a

Table 10.18: Instruction set of the Transputer: Program control

Group	Mnemonic	Operation	nibbles	Cycles
Communication	in	Input message (length w words)	2	$2.w + 18$ or 20
	out	Output message (length w words)	2	$2.w + 20$ or 20
	outbyte	Output byte	2	25
	outword	Output word	2	25
	move	Move message (length w words)	4	$2.w + 20$ or 20
	lb	Load byte	2	5
	sb	Store byte	4	4
	enbc	Enable channel	4	≤ 7
	disc	Disable channel	4	8
	resetch	Reset channel	4	3
Timers	tin	Timer input	4	?
	ldtimer	Load timer	4	2
	sttimer	Store timer	4	1
	enbt	Enable timer	4	8
	dist	Disable timer	4	?
Scheduling	startp	Start process	2	12
	endp	End process	2	13
	runp	Run process	4	10
	stopp	Stop process	4	11
	ldpri	Load current priority	4	1
	alt	ALT start	4	2
	altwt	ALT wait	4	?
	altend	ALT end	4	6
	talt	Timer ALT start	4	4
	taltwt	Timer ALT wait	4	?
	enbs	Enable SKIP	4	3
	diss	Disable SKIP	4	4
	sthf	Set *FrontHi*	4	1
	sthb	Set *BackHi*	4	1
	stlf	Set *FrontLo*	4	1
	stlb	Set *BackLo*	4	1
	saveh	Save *FrontHi, BackHi*	4	4
	saveh	Save *FrontHi, BackHi*	4	4

Table 10.19: Instruction set of the Transputer: Process scheduling & communication

1. *Enable all guards*

2. *Suspend if none ready/Reschedule when one becomes ready*

3. *Disable all guards/Determine which became ready*

4. *Run selected process*

Briefly, alt sets the *ALT state* $(W - 3)$ to *Enabling.p* (a predefined value). enbc and/or enbs (enable channel, enable SKIP) instructions may then be employed to check whether any guard is ready to proceed, in which case it modifies *ALT state* to *Ready.p* another predefined value). altwt will suspend the process if no guard was ready. On rescheduling, due to a channel being ready to communicate, diss and/or disc (disable SKIP) are used to determine *which* guard succeeded and to place its process descriptor n workspace $(W + 0)$. altend then causes that process to be *immediately executed*.

A problem occurs if more than one guard is ready during either *enabling* or *disabling*. Both Occam and *CSP* call for *nondeterministic selection* in this circumstance. The Transputer lacks a mechanism for this, so selection is according to the *first ready guard disabled*.

10.4.2 Organization

Processor organization

The Transputer is an an entire computer *integrated into a single device* and consists of a processor, memory and a number of communication links (currently four input and four output) which may be considered as *i/o processors* and use *DMA* (Figure 10.29). These all communicate on a very fast internal bus (currently thirty-two bits wide) which completes a transaction in just one clock cycle (50ns for current 20MHz devices).

A comparatively low frequency clock is required by the Transputer (5MHz). Much higher speed clocks are derived internally from it. This approach has two valuable advantages...

- *All Transputers may use the same clock regardless of their internal speed*

- *The nasty problem of distributing a high speed clock signal is avoided*

An external bus interface allows "off-chip" memory expansion (currently up to 4Gbytes). *All* necessary signals are provided for direct connection to *dynamic ram*, so avoiding much of the usual "glue" logic. External memory is typically *three times slower* than internal, so placement of less frequently referenced items externally pays high dividends in performance.

Each link uses three registers...

- *Process workspace pointer*

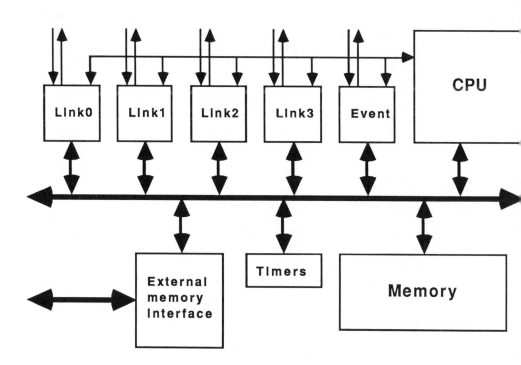

Figure 10.29: Transputer organization

- *Message data/buffer pointer*

- *Message count*

... and needs no user programming. Its operation and protocol is exactly as described ı 9.3.2.

Peripheral interfacing may be achieved conventionally using *memory-mapped periph-* *ral adaptors* such as the *VIA* and *ACIA* discussed elsewhere in this text. However, to ake advantage of the Transputer ability to synchronize processing and communication ; is highly desirable instead to use a *link adaptor* as an interface to the peripheral device hich may then be regarded, for software and system design purposes, simply as an- ther processor externally communicating with the Transputer. It merely then becomes nother in a network of *communicating sequential processes*.

Physical memory organization

Iemory is byte addressed. Word length varies with version and may currently be either wo or four bytes. The Transputer is "little-endian" meaning that the least significant yte in a word always occupies the lowest address.

The memory map (Figure 10.27) is divided into internal and external ("on-chip" nd "off-chip") memory. Internal memory is said to have *negative* address, starting t $MostNeg...80000000_{16}$. External memory runs from the end of internal memory, 80000800_{16} on the *T414 Transputer*) upwards (to $7FFFFFFF_{16}$ on the *T414 Trans-* uter).

Figure 10.30 shows a read cycle of the *T414 Transputer* external memory interface *EMI*). The clock shown is the internal one. There are six states in the cycle, $T1...T6$. During $T1$ the address is presented on the *multiplexed* data/address bus and is latched on he downward edge of *notMemS0*. This is a *nonprogrammable* timing signal convention- lly used as an *address latch enable (ALE)*. Data is then presented on the $MemAD0...31$ nd must be valid on the rising edge of *notMemRd*. Note that the least significant two its of address are not required as an entire four byte word will be presented anyway. 'he required bytes may be selected internally. On a write cycle four output signals, otMemWrB0...3, are provided to select the bytes to be written. Data must be valid nd latched on their rising edge. Early warning of a write cycle is given by the state of *IemnotWrD0* in $T1...T2$, which may be latched using *ALE*.

The signals shown are adequate for *static memory*. Further signals are provided y the *EMI* to refresh and synchronize *dynamic memory*. Memory configuration is *pro-* *rammable*, including many timing parameters, by setting a configuration map located at he top of external memory. A full treatment of interfacing *T414* and *T800 Transputers* o all kinds of memory may be found in [Inmos 89, pages 2–25].

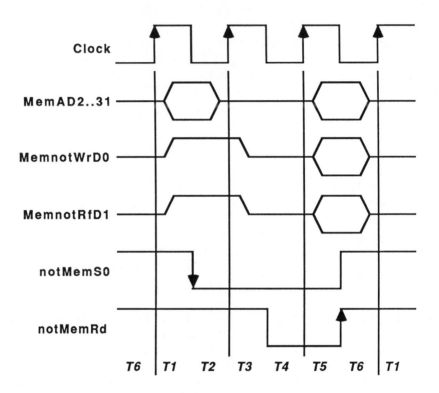

Figure 10.30: Transputer bus timing

0.4.3 Programming

Expression evaluation

The Transputer uses a *stack machine* model for expression evaluation. `ldl` and `stl` *push* and *pop* data between the evaluation stack *(A, B, C)* and workspace. Recall that their operand is an offset into workspace. Constants are loaded using `ldc`.

```
ldl b
ldl b
mul
ldl a
ldl c
mul
ldc 4
mul
sub
ldl a
ldc 2
mul
div
stl RootSquared
```

The above code segment may be used to evaluate[17] $RootSquared := (b^2 - 4.a.c)/2.a$. Order of subexpression evaluation here has not been affected by the fact that the stack is of *depth three only*. However, the compiler must always determine the stack depth required for each subexpression and *evaluate the one needing the greatest depth first*. In this example, at both first and second levels, all subexpressions need an equal stack depth of two.

Because the Transputer stack operators locate their left operand lowest, evaluations are normally performed as they are written, *left to right*. If two evaluations are reversed due to stack depth consideration, *and the operator does not commute* it will be necessary to reverse their values on the stack using `rev` before applying the operator.

If the stack depth required by the second expression exceeds two it will be necessary to evaluate it first and store the result in a temporary variable. *Workspace allocation must allow for this!* The first expression is then evaluated, the result of the second loaded and the operator applied.

`sum`, `diff` and `prod` allow *modulo arithmetic*, that is with *no overflow checking*. `lsum` and `ldiff` permit *multiple precision arithmetic* by treating C_{lsb} as a carry in, and leaving any resulting carry out in B_{lsb}. (Hence zero should be loaded first to clear the first carry in). Storing the result and subsequently loading the next two words leaves the carry

---

[17]See Chapter 8, question four and solution.

correctly positioned for the next operation. The final operator should be one of {lad
lsub} to check for overflow, which when found causes *Error* to be set. Behaviour the
depends on the state of *HaltOnError* (see above).

```
ldc 0                              ldc 0
ldl xlo                            ldl xlo
ldl ylo                            ldl ylo
lsum                               ldiff
stl zlo                            stl zlo
ldl xhi                            ldl xhi
ldl yhi                            ldl yhi
ladd                               lsub
stl zhi                            stl zhi
```

lmul and ldiv support multiple precision multiplication and division. This time
holds the carry *word* of the result and is added to the product of A and B. The leas
significant word of the result is held in A and the most significant (carry) in B. Show
below is the encoding of a *double precision* unsigned multiplication.

```
ldc 0                              . . .
ldl xlo                            ldl xhi
ldl ylo                            ldl yhi
lmul                               lmul
stl z0                             rev
ldl xlo                            stl z3
ldl yhi                            ldc 0
lmul                               rev
rev                               ldl z2
stl z2                             lsum
ldl xhi                            stl z2
ldl ylo                            ldl z3
lmul                               sum
stl z1                             stl z3
. . .
```

Sequential constructs

There is only one processor state flag in the Transputer *(Error)*. There are none of t
familiar arithmetic flags to assist in evaluating conditions. There are two instructio
which evaluate arithmetic conditions, **eqc** and **gt**, which use A to record their resu
using the convention $True = 1$, $False = 0$.

```
ldl <con>      ldl x      ldl x      ldl y
eqc 0          ldl y      ldl y      ldl x
               diff       gt         gt
               eqc 0                 eqc 0
```

Above is shown how these may be employed to encode (left to right) $\neg(cond)$, $x = y$, $x > y$ and $x \geq y$.

Below is shown the encoding of both *for loop* and *case* constructs. Indexed iteration requires two contiguous words in memory. The first is the loop index and the second the number of iterations to be performed. **lend** accesses the index and count via a pointer in B. It decrements the count and, *if further iteration is required*, increments the index and *subtracts* A from I. In other words it causes a branch, whose offset is found in A and is interpreted as negative. This avoids the need for **nfix** instructions.

```
ldc  <start value>            ldl  result
stl  index                    ldc  <case value lo bound>
ldl  ntimes                   diff
stl  index+1                  ldc  3
; loop start                  prod
...                           ldc  5
ldlp index                    ldpi
pfix <start offset hi>        bsub
ldc  <start offset lo>        gcall
lend                          pfix <exit offset hi>
                              pfix <exit offset mi>
                              j    <exit offset lo>
                              ; Jump table start
                              pfix <offset 1 hi>
                              pfix <offset 1 mid>
                              j    <offset 1 lo>
                              pfix <offset 2 hi>
                              pfix <offset 2 mid>
                              j    <offset 2 lo>
                              ...
```

Case implementation may be achieved either by encoding an equivalent series of *if... then... else* constructs or, given more than (say) a dozen case labels, by using a *jump table*. This is composed of a series of jump instructions whose offsets are prefixed all to be the same length, (twelve bits shown above) so that all table entries are the same length (three bytes shown). Hence the address for a **gcall** (general call) instruction may be easily computed. **gcall** expects a destination address in A. In fact all it does is to interchange A and I. The called routine need only first store A in its workspace later to load it back and return by executing another **gcall**!

ldpi loads a pointer into A whose value is I plus an offset found earlier in A. This is interpreted by **bsub** ("byte subscript") as the start address of a structure in memory. It replaces the contents of A with an address B bytes away from the structure start. In this case it is the address of the **gcall** destination. The return **gcall** encounters a jump over the table.

Procedures

Procedure invocation, like expression evaluation, on the Transputer is stack-oriented. This time though W is used as a *stack pointer*. The evaluation stack is used only for passing the first three parameters and for a return. Invocation begins with depositing the first three parameters in A, B, C. W is then adjusted upwards and parameters four onwards are stored in the "bottom" of workspace as shown in Figure 10.31.

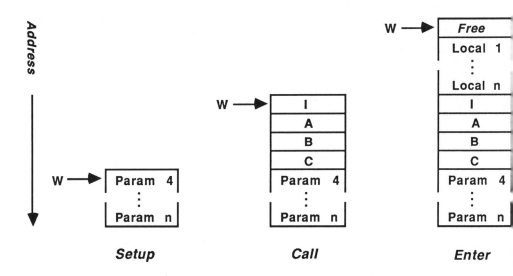

Figure 10.31: Transputer workspace following subroutine invocation and entry

C, B, A, I are then pushed onto the "stack" by **call**. The return address is thus found on top of the stack and is restored to I by **ret**. W must be readjusted to its original state after the return. Code skeletons for both invocation and entry are shown below...

```
ajw   -<n - 3>                          ajw  -<frame size + 1>
ldl   <parameter 4>                     ...
stl   0                                 ajw  +<frame size + 1>
...                                     ret
ldl   <parameter n>
stl   <n - 4>
ldl   <parameter 3>
ldl   <parameter 2>
ldl   <parameter 1>
pfix  <offset hi>
pfix  <offset mi>
call  <offset lo>
ajw   +<n - 3>
stl   <return>
```

Procedure entry requires further stack adjustment to accommodate a *stack frame* for local variables *and temporary variables* for expression evaluation (see above).

Process scheduling

The Occam programming model currently includes only *static* processes. However the Transputer fully supports *dynamic* process start and termination.

Concurrency is expressed in Occam using the PAR construct. Where only a single processor is concerned it may be encoded as shown below...

```
; Initialize PAR process        ; Process 1 code
ldc  <exit offset>              ...
ldpi                            ldlp -<W offset 1>
stl  0                          endp
ldc  n+1                        ...
stl  1                          ; Process n code
; Initialize sub-processes      ...
ldc  <code offset 1>           ldlp -<W offset n>
ldlp <W offset 1>              endp
startp
...
ldc  <code offset n>
ldlp <W offset n>
startp
; If only parent left then exit
ldlp <parent W offset>
endp
```

A count of the total number of processes, *including the parent*, is recorded in $[W+1]$. This will be decremented each time a child process successfully terminates. Following initialization of this, a pointer to code following the PAR is loaded into $[W + 0]$. Each process is then *enqueued* using **startp**, which requires a pointer to the process code in B and its workspace in A. The code pointer will be stored in $[W - 1]$. Priority will be the same as that of the parent. Note that the workspaces of all child processes are located *within* that of the parent.

Processes terminate by executing **endp** with a pointer to the workspace of the parent in A, thus allowing the parent to continue executing at the address held in $[W + 0]$ *if* its process count, $([W + 1])$, equals one. Otherwise the count is simply decremented and the next process is served from the ready queue.

Finally, when the last child process has terminated, the parent may terminate. As with its children, $[W + 0]$ must point to the address of the next code to be executed (the continuation code of *its* parent). This assumes that the whole PAR process was itself a child of another and that it was not a component of a SEQ process. Hence there is no code to be executed directly after its conclusion.

If that were the case, one of the "child" processes could be implemented simply as a continuation of the parent, sharing the same value of workspace pointer value. Only two new processes would then need to be "spawned". *Three* control threads *would exist instead of the four* as in the above implementation. In fact the Occam compiler encodes PAR in this way since it *reduces the scheduling overhead* and makes it easier to compile source code with PAR within SEQ[18].

_____

[18] However such source could never be *configured* over a Transputer network since there is no way for

Communication

Rendezvous to synchronize communication over a channel is implemented by the Transputer instructions **in out**. The evaluation stack is used to describe channel and message in exactly the same manner for both instructions. A contains the message length in bytes, B a pointer to the channel and C a pointer to the message area in memory. Absolutely no difference in usage may be found whether the instructions are used with *hard channels* or *soft channels*, except that hard channels are found at the base of memory.

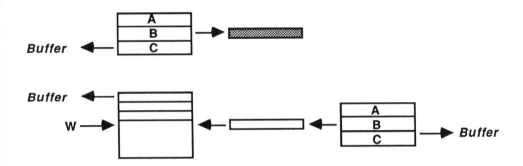

Figure 10.32: Channel communication on the Transputer

Figure 10.32 depicts the first and second process arriving at the rendezvous location. The first finds a reserved value there *(Empty = NotProcess.p)* and deschedules leaving its process "id" (workspace pointer). The second process, on finding a value which is not *NotProcess.p*, is able to complete the transaction, regardless of its direction, since the message area address of the first process is recorded in its workspace (see Figure 10.26).

```
        mint                        mint
        mint                        mint
        stnl #10                    stnl #00
```

The code above shows the initialization of two channels which just happen to be *link0in* (left) and *link0out* (right). Code for sending a message from *link0out* on one Transputer to *link0in* on another is shown below. The two processes will automatically synchronize for the communication transaction.

---

processors executing component processes of the PAR to know when the one executing the parent has reached the point where they themselves may start. It should usually be possible to *transform* the source so that PAR has the broader scope (see [Burns 88, page 141])

```
ldc  <string address>          ldc  <string address>
mint                           mint
adc  #10                       ldc  <message length>
ldc  <message length>          out
in
```

Timers

There is a *clock* register for each priority (Figure 10.23). The high priority clock ticks every $1\mu s$, the low one every $64\mu s$ and give full cycle times of $\sim 4ms$ and $\sim 76hrs$ respectively. There are exactly 15625 low priority ticks per second.

Timers are abstractions of the hardware clocks. *Loading* a timer simply means reading the current priority clock. In Occam timers are declared like channels or variables. They may be *input* from but not *output* to.

```
VAL second IS 15625 :          ldtimer
TIMER clock :                  ldc 15625
INT time :                     sum
...                            tin
clock ? time
clock ? AFTER time PLUS second
```

Above is shown both the Occam and assembly language code to generate a delay of one second in the running of a (low priority) process. The time is first read (loaded) from a timer. One second's worth of ticks are *modulo* added and then a *timer input* performed. `tin` will suspend its parent process unless the value in A is greater than or equal to the value of the current priority clock. The process will then be inserted in the *timer list* (see above) to be automatically added to the *ready queue* when the clock reaches the value awaited. That value is recorded in the process workspace. When it becomes the next time awaited, at the front of the timer list[19], it is copied into *TNext* until the wait is over. Note that the process must wait its turn in the ready queue after the awaited time. Hence when again it runs the clock will read some *later* time. Note also that `tin` does not affect any variables. If the time in A is in the past it has no effect whatsoever, if not its only effect is to suspend and add its process to the timer list.

Alternative construct

The *ALT* construct of Occam is a form of *selection* additional to *IF* and *CASE*. Whereas IF selects according to the values on a list of *Boolean* expressions and CASE according

---

[19] The *timer list* may properly be regarded as a *priority queue* object.

to the value of a single *general* one, ALT selects a process according to the *success of its guard*.

A *guard* in its general sense is any *primitive process*. Here it is assumed to mean an input. Hence the process selected is the one *whose first action may be performed*, where this is an *input*.

In Occam any guard may be qualified by a Boolean expression which allows that input channel to become "deaf", and that process never to be selected, as long as it is false. It is allowable for the guard to always succeed, by use of *SKIP*, so that the entry's selection depends only on a Boolean expression. This also may be chosen to be *TRUE* allowing a default ("else") *TRUE & SKIP* process. Also a guard may be a *timer input*. In summary the following guard types are possible. . .

- *Skip guard*

- *Timer guard*

- *Channel guard*

One great problem exists with implementing the ALT construct. Should more than one process have its guard succeed, and hence become ready, the specification calls for *nondeterministic* selection to ensue. The Transputer, like all other contemporary processors, lacks a mechanism for this. It cannot roll dice. Hence the encoding will dictate an order of priority for process selection.

Encoding of ALT takes the form. . .

1. *Enable guards*

2. *IF no guard is ready THEN suspend*

3. *Start process associated with (first) ready guard*

4. *Disable guards*

Enabling means finding out if any are able to succeed. Prior to enabling the **alt** instruction deposits a reserved value *(Enabling.p)* in $[W-3]$. **enbs** and **enbc** are used to enable skip and channel guards. Should any be ready $[W-3]$ is set to *Ready.p*. Should *any* guard be a timer guard, **talt** must be used which also initializes $[W-4]$ to *TimeNotSet.p*. The first **enbt** instruction will alter this to *TimeSet.p*. The first and subsequent **enbt** instructions will ensure that the earliest time awaited is entered in $[W-5]$.

altwt or **taltwt** will check to see if the *ALT* state is *Ready.p*. If not then it is set to *Waiting.p*, $[W+0]$ is set to *NoneSelected.o* to indicate that no process has been selected, and the process is suspended. *Any* communication or timeout with a waiting *ALT* will set its state to *Ready.p* and adds it to the ready queue.

Disabling means locating the guard which became ready. *It is the disabling order which dictates selection priority given more than one ready guard.* The process descriptor of the process guarded by the first ready guard encountered is placed in $[W + 0]$ by diss, dist or disc instructions.

altend simply branches to the process whose descriptor is stored in $[W + 0]$.

Processes branched to by altend *must* end with a branch to the continuation code after the *ALT*. Those which had a *channel* guard must begin with an input from that channel. Enabling and disabling do not *perform* the input operation. It must be explicitly encoded.

```
ALT                       talt                 . . .
    clock ? AFTER time    ldl time             ldl time
        . . .             ldc 1                ldc 1
    bool & c ? v          enbt                 ldc <offset 1>
        . . .             ldl c                dist
    TRUE & SKIP           ldl bool             ldl c
        . . .             enbc                 ldl bool
                          ldc 1                ldc <offset 2>
                          enbs                 disc
                          taltwt               ldc 1
                          . . .                ldc <offset 3>
                                               diss
                                               altend
```

Above is shown an example of *ALT* implementation. Three guards are shown. Topmost is a *timer guard*, next a *channel guard* and finally a *skip guard* which acts as an "else".

Output to an *ALT* guard *input* uncovers conditional behaviour of the out instruction. enbc in the *ALT* code will have placed a valid process descriptor at the rendezvous even if it arrives first. However, out will check to see if $[W - 3]$ contains a *legal message area address* or the reserved value *Enabling.p*. If the latter it will make no attempt to complete the transaction but instead updates both $[W - 3]$ to *Ready.p* and the rendezvous location to *its own* process descriptor, indicating its own readiness to communicate, and then suspends itself, as though the other party in the communication were not ready.

Workspace locations with offsets $0 \rightarrow 3$ are affected by {alt enbs enbc altwt diss disc altend} instructions. Those with offsets $0 \rightarrow 5$ are affected by the group {talt enbs enbc enbt taltwt diss disc dist altend}.

Booting

As described above, the Transputer will boot either from ROM or the first link to receive a byte value greater than one. If booting from ROM there should be a jump instruction, located at the *ResetCode* address ($7FFFFFFE_{16}$ on the *T414*) branching backwards into memory.

Assuming the Transputer state is not to be analysed, the following actions may be performed by the *boot code*. . .

- *Clear* Error *by executing* `testerr`

- *Initialize* HaltOnError *using* `clrhalterr` *or* `sethalterr`

- *Initialize queue front pointers to* NotProcess.p

- *Initialize link and* EventIn *channels to* NotProcess.p

- *Initialize timer list pointers to* NotProcess.p

- *Start both timers by executing* `sttimer`

The following boot code is suggested, which branches to another routine if the Transputer is being analysed,. . .

```
; Analyse or boot?      . . .                    . . .
testpranal             ; Initialize timer      ; Initialize process
cj  4                  ; queue & link words    ; queue front pointers
pfix <analyse hi>      ldc  0                   mint
pfix <analyse mi>      stl  0                   sthf
ldc  <analyse lo>      ldl  11                  mint
gcall                  stl  1                   stlf
; Initialize Error &   ; loop start            ; Start both timers
; HaltOnError flags    mint                     mint
testerr                mint                     sttimer
sethalterr             ldl 0
. . .                  sum
                       stnl 0
                       ldlp 0
                       ldc 8
                       lend
                       . . .
```

Transputer assembly language programming

Programming the Transputer in assembly language should only be undertaken for the purposes of better understanding its architecture. Very little (if any) extra code optimization is possible over that produced by the Inmos *Occam 2* compiler. This is because the architecture was designed *specifically* for the efficient implementation of Occam. However, the author is of the opinion that structured programming in assembly language is probably the only way to really gain an appreciation of the design of any architecture.

Name	Value	Use
MostNeg	80000000_{16} (32-bit)	Most negative integer
		Base of internal (and all) memory
MostPos	$7FFFFFFF_{16}$ (32-bit)	Most positive integer
		Top of external (and all) memory
NotProcess.p	$MostNeg$	No process (instead of process descriptor)
		"Empty" channel rendezvous
		End of timer list
Enabling.p	$MostNeg$	ALT state: Enabling
Ready.p	$MostNeg + 3$	ALT state: Ready guard while enabling
Waiting.p	$MostNeg + 2$	ALT state: Waiting
Disabling.p	$MostNeg + 3$	ALT state: Disabling
TimeSet.p	$MostNeg + 1$	ALT time state: Timer guard found while enabling
TimeNotSet.p	$MostNeg + 2$	ALT time state: Timer guard not found while enabling
NoneSelected.o	-1	ALT selection: No process yet selected

Table 10.20: Transputer defined and reserved word values (32-bit)

This is as true of the Transputer as of any other machine. Recommended is the *TASM 2* assembler, published by **Mark Ware Associates** of Bristol, UK. The manual is very well produced and full of code illustrations, although the *C* background of its authors discolours it a little. Essential is the *"Compiler writer's guide"*, [Inmos 88#3], whose title is evidence enough of Inmos's distaste for anyone resorting to assembly language to program their progeny.

Reserved values

Process state is recorded in negative offsets from the base of the workspace of each scheduled process. In order to identify the state of each scheduled and suspended process, and that of each communication channel in use, certain word values are *reserved* to have special meaning. These are summarized in Table 10.20.

Exercises

Question one

i When and why is it undesirable for a programmer to employ a *case* construct with many, and widely scattered, *case label* values?

Comment on any implications of this issue for the relationship between the design of *machine architecture* and that of its *programming model*.

ii Either `jump` or `case<i>` NS32000 instructions may be used, in conjunction with *program memory space* addressing mode and *scaled index modifier*, to implement a *case* construct. Explain the differences in implementation and performance. Which is preferable and why?

Question two

i Use the information given in Table 10.21[20] to compare the code size and execution time between the NS32000 and Transputer for a local procedure invocation, entry and exit, where three parameters are passed and no return is made. Assume that *value* parameters are passed as copies of local variables located within sixteen bytes of the *frame*, or *workspace*, pointer and a two byte branch offset. Comment on your result.

ii Use the information given in Table 10.21 to compare the code size and execution time between the NS32000 and Transputer for the implementation of a *case* construct with twelve *case labels*. Assume that the *case expression* has been evaluated and the result stored within sixteen bytes of the *frame*, or *workspace*, pointer and that the case label lower bound takes a value between zero and fifteen. Comment on your result.

Question three

i Using hex notation, give the Transputer machine code (*T-code*) required to load an operand into the *A* register whose *twos-complement* value is -241_{10}.

ii Using pseudocode, give the algorithm for the *T-code* generation of any general signed operand in the *O* register.

---

[20] The information in Table 10.21 is for a *NS32016* 16-bit processor and assumes word alignment of operands and the absence of virtual memory address translation. `enter` and `exit` are asumed to save and restore just *three* registers. In fact the execution times shown may not correspond very well with those actually observed. This is because the instruction queue is cleared by some instructions. Hence execution time will depend on *subsequent instructions*.

Instruction	Bytes	Cycles	Constraints
movew	3	17	Frame to stack
moveb	3	11	Frame to register
subb	3	4	Register to register
bsr	3	23	Word displacement
ret	2	15	Byte stack displacement
enter	3	58	Byte frame displacement Three registers saved
exit	2	60	Three registers restored
caseb	4	17	Byte program offset Index byte

Table 10.21: NS32016 instruction information

iii   Using assembly language notation, give the *T-code* implementation of a *for loop* where the required number of iterations may be *zero*.

Appendix A

ASCII codes

The tables below show the *American Standard Code for Information Interchange* and the function of some of the control codes it specifies...

LSN	Most significant nibble (MSN)							
	0	1	2	3	4	5	6	7
0	nul	dle	sp	0	@	P	`	p
1	soh	dc1	!	1	A	Q	a	q
2	stx	dc2	"	2	B	R	b	r
3	etx	dc3	#	3	C	S	c	s
4	eot	dc4	$	4	D	T	d	t
5	enq	nak	%	5	E	U	e	u
6	ack	syn	&	6	F	V	f	v
7	bel	etb	'	7	G	W	g	w
8	bs	can	(	8	H	X	h	x
9	ht	em	)	9	I	Y	i	y
A	lf	sub	*	:	J	Z	j	z
B	vt	esc	+	;	K	[	k	{
C	ff	fs	,	<	L	\	l		
D	cr	gs	-	=	M	]	m	}
E	so	rs	.	>	N	^	n	~
F	si	us	/	?	O	_	o	DEL

Code	Meaning	Code	Meaning
esc	*Escape*	cr	*Carriage return*
eot	*End of transmission*	lf	*Line feed*
bel	*Cause audible "beep"*	nul	*Null*
del	*Delete*	sp	*Space*
dc1	*Device control 1*	ht	*horizontal tab*
ff	*Form feed*	vt	*Vertical tab*

Control   ... is used to generate control codes. For example, the result of pressing *E* whilst holding down *control*, on a keyboard, is to despatch the *EOT* control character. The code which results should be 40_{16} or 60_{16} less than that obtained by pressing the lower case alphanumeric key alone.

Shift   ... is used to generate upper case characters. The effect of maintaining it down whilst pressing an alphabetic key is to despatch a code with value 20_{16} greater than that obtained by pressing the key alone, and 10_{16} less with a numeric key alone.

Appendix B

Solutions to exercises

From software to hardware

Computation

Question one

Stream protocol is used for the communication between author and reader. Writer and reader processes are *successive*. Communication is *buffered* by the book itself. It is also *layered* into...

- Words: *Streamed character symbols with a space or full stop as EOT*

- Sentences: *Streamed word symbols with a full stop as EOT*

- Paragraphs: *Streamed sentences with a new line and indent as EOT*

i Two examples of communication used in everyday life are the *telephone* and *postal system*. The telephone offers *synchronous comunication* between *concurrent* processes while the postal system offers a*synchronous communication* between *successive* processes. Telephone cables form *channels* and letters *buffers* respectively.

The protocols used are those for spoken and written *natural language* respectively. Spoken language makes use of pauses for EOT of sentences and places heavier reliance on rules of *syntax*. Otherwise the protocol for both is as above.

Question two

i The instruction set is (e.g.)...

- *If (input = {red, red, red} AND state = 'AircraftDetected') Then state := 'Foe'*

389

- If (input = {green, green, red} AND state = 'NoAircraft') Then state := 'Aircraft Detected'

- ...etc.

ii   Example Modula-2 implementation...
```
CONST
  NoAircraft = 0;
  AircraftDetected = 1;
  Friend = 2;
  FailToIdentify = 3;
  Foe = 4;

VAR
  input : CARDINAL;
  state : CARDINAL;

BEGIN
  REPEAT
    CASE input OF
      0C : state := NoAircraft|
      1C : IF state = NoAircraft THEN state := AircraftDetected|
      2C : IF state = AircraftDetected THEN state := Friend|
      3C : IF state = AircraftDetected THEN state := Foe|
    ELSE  IF state = AircraftDetected THEN state := UFO
            ELSE state := NoAircraft
    END
  UNTIL FALSE
END.
```

Question three

A *NAND* gate may be implemented using *normally-open switches* as shown in Figure B.1.

Question four

i   It is easy to think of processes whose subordinates are concurrent. Most systems of interest are thus. Objects of scientific study, e.g. *ecological* and *biological* systems, are composed of concurrent *communicating sequential processes*. Scientists learn a great deal from simulations which it is often too difficult or inefficient to implement sequentially on a single processor computer. The most obvious example, which is benefitting us all dramatically, is weather prediction through simulation of *meteorological* systems.

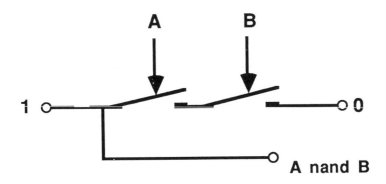

Figure B.1: Nand gate from normally-open switches

It actually proves difficult to think of a natural process, composed only of successive rocesses, which is of any interest. Successive processes are naturally associated with *ueue* structures. The manufacture of a product may be naïvely regarded as sequential...

```
SEQ
    manufacture components
    assemble product
```

The two subordinates would communicate using a buffer such as a box to contain he components. This would not be passed to the assembly worker until full. Either he worker making components or the one assembling the product will be idle while the ther completes his task. Obviously this is very inefficient and bares no resemblance to ny modern production line.

Figure B.2 illustrates the problem and its solution. Communication from A to B and C to D must be *asynchronous* and thus employ *buffers*. Communication from B to D nd C to A must be *synchronous* and thus employ *channels*. The mapping of processes o processors results from the fact that only *channel communication* is possible between listinct processors. In fact there exists a useful *transformation* between two descriptions which are equal in abstract meaning but where only one is physically possible...

```
SEQ                              PAR
    PAR                              SEQ
        A (c.1,v.1)                      A (c.1,v.1)
        C (c.1,v.2)        ≡             B (c.2,v.1)
    PAR                              SEQ
        B (c.2,v.1)                      C (c.1,v.2)
        D (c.2,v.2)                      D (c.2,v.2)
```

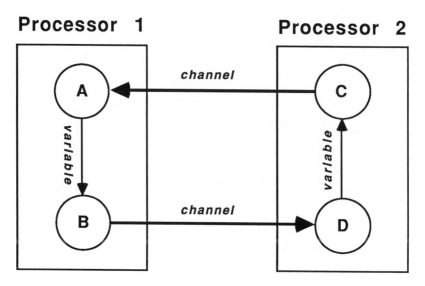

Figure B.2: Mapping of processes to processors

iii   With the information available it must be concluded that deadlock will not occur. However, if the *data dependency* between C and D were reversed then a *dependency cycle* would exist and deadlock could occur. A would be unable to proceed until D had terminated, allowing C to transmit. The system would deadlock.

Software engineering

Question one

Modules are the means of defining and implementing tasks. Each task may be from any level of the top-down diagram. *Definition modules* are written by the design engineer who passes them to a programmer who creates corresponding *implementation modules*. These are then compiled, the resulting *object modules* linked with the necessary *library modules* and then tested to verify that the requirements specification is met.

Top-down diagrams are *decompositions* of tasks into more manageable sub-units. They constitute the first phase of *system design*. No more than three or four levels of decomposition should be expanded before a new analysis is undertaken for each terminal task. The final terminals should be capable of implementation by a single engineer.

Data flow diagrams depict the *communication* inherent in the requirement. Data flows between processes (nodes) via either channels or variables, depending on whether the processes concerned run concurrently or successively. They are useful for *process-oriented design*.

Question two

The phases in the *software life-cycle* are...

1. *Requirements analysis*

2. *Requirements specification*

3. *Design analysis*

4. *Design specification*

5. *Implementation*

6. *Verification*

In addition *documentation* occurs continuously and concurrently with software development. *Implementation documentation* must be embedded with source code to eliminate potential *divergence* between the two. The above will be subject to iteration, when verification fails, as depicted in Figure 2.1.

Definition modules are written as the design specification. *Pseudocode* will usually be employed for procedure algorithm design at the implementation phase.

Question three

i *Library modules* are packages of useful procedures which *reduce the time and effo*
taken to implement applications. As such they greatly reduce the cost of software pr
duction because they reduce the total software which needs to be designed, implemente
and tested for a new application. They also greatly reduce the time taken to deliver
new application to the market.

ii Library modules are *pre-packaged* software. It is wasteful and unreliable to recompil
them each time they are used. Hence the machine language should support the invocatio
of procedures within them. However, the design engineer will encounter them via the
definition modules which are all he/she needs to know! The *implementation enginee*
will simply need to *link* them to his own module for purposes of verification.

Question four

The principal motivation for *machine language* support for software partitions are t
reduce the overhead incurred in crossing an inter-module boundary (e.g. when invokin
an imported procedure or referencing an imported variable).

Machine language

Question one

When a book is translated it is *compilation* since it is completed before anything is read in the destination language.

The *semantic gap* is the difference between a *programming language* and a *machine language*. The main argument for closing it is to gain more rapid execution speed by implementing high level language statements directly in hardware, minimizing the number of actual hardware operations performed. The main argument against closure is that compiler *code generators* rarely use such sophisticated instructions and addressing modes. It is difficult to design one which selects the correct *CISC* instruction and addressing mode from many different alternatives.

Question two

The various operand parameters are tabulated below...

Argument	Access class	Storage class	Addressing mode
r0	RMW	register	register direct
0400	R	memory	absolute direct

Question three

Program to compute **and x, y**...

1. `load x`

2. `nand y`

3. `store x`

4. `nand x`

5. `store x`

Note that **store** must not affect the *processor state* but **load** might without any ill effect. To implement **load** so that it did clear/set the processor state might prove useful in computing other functions.

From switches to processors

Data representation and notation

Question one

i　A 12 bit word maps onto four *octal* and three *hex* digits exactly. (Each octal digi‍ maps exactly onto *three* bits. Each hex digit maps exactly onto *four* bits.)

ii　011001010010000110010 0001 is equivalent to...

- 654321_{16}

- 3124144_{8}

00011111010110001101 0001 is equivalent to...

- $1F58D1_{16}$

- 07654321_{8}

iii　The values represented in binary are...

- 1000.0000.0000.0000.0000.0000.0010.1100

- 111.110.101.100.011.010.001.000

Question two

i　The *twos complement* representation (state) of a value α, given a word width N (modulus $2^N = M$), is...

$$\alpha^{(2)} = M - \alpha$$

The *ones complement* representation (state) of a value α, given a word width N (modulus $2^N = M$), is...

$$\alpha^{(1)} = (M - 1) - \alpha$$

Subtracting both definitions together we may eliminate M...

$$\alpha^{(2)} = \alpha^{(1)} + 1$$

The interpretations possible given the codes shown are...

Representation	Value		
	Sign-magnitude	*xcess-128*	*2s complement*
FF_{16}	-127	+127	-1
$C9_{16}$	-73	+73	-55

Remember that, to work out the 2s complement of a number, you may complement nd add one. Note that the excess-128 and sign-magnitude interpretations are the *sign iverse* of each other!

The sum performed using hex, binary and decimal notations is shown below...

Hex	Binary	Decimal
FF	1111.1111	-1
+C9	1100.1001	-55
1C8	1.1100.1000	-56

Note that the carry is ignored. (Remember the "clock" picture of labelling states!)

Question three

The most important inadequacies of *ASCII* as a terminal protocol are...

- *No cursor control or interrogation*

- *No graphics objects*

- *No WIMP[1] HCI[2]*

- *No file transfer*

- *Only a single character set (font)*

ASCII is a *7-bit* code. If the eighth bit in a byte is not used for *parity* error protection t may be used to switch to an alternative character set.

For extra control, ESC is sent followed by an *escape sequence* of bytes. There exists n *ANSI[3]* standard for an extended terminal protocol which provides some facilities, such s cursor control. *The world awaits new standards!*

---

[1] **Window Icon Mouse Pointer**
[2] **Human Computer Interface**
[3] **American National Standards Institute**

ii   The problem with transmitting raw binary data is that some values will be misinter preted by the receiver as ASCII control codes.

One solution is to pre-encode each nybble of the raw binary as a hex digit, encoded ASCII. On can then transmit an ASCII file and decode it to raw binary at the destination

Question four

i   Two examples of number coding systems which exhibit degeneracy are. . .

- *Sign-magnitude integer*

- *Un-normalized floating-point*

ii $f = mantissa - 1$ where f is the fraction state remaining after removal of the hidden bit. $e = value + 127$ where e is the exponent state.
Normalized 32-bit IEEE floating-point representations are. . .

- $\text{BFB0.0000}_{16}; e = 127_{10}, f = 0110..._{2}$

- $\text{BEC0.0000}_{16}; e = 125_{10}, f = 10..._{2}$

- $\text{BEB0.0000}_{16}; e = 125_{10}, f = 0110..._{2}$

Question five

i   *Floating-point* representation should be chosen, in favour of *fixed-point*, when. . .

- *Dynamic range of abstract quantities is too large for available fixed-point represen tation*

- *Direct reduction of abstract quantities is desired for programming ease if the pro cessing overhead is acceptable or hardware support for floating-point arithmetic affordable*

- *Constant precision, rather than constant resolution, over the range is called for by the abstract nature of the variable*

ii   *The addition of two floating-point values may be considered as composed of three phases.*

Phase 1: The *IEEE single precision* representation of the addition arguments is shown below. . .

Value	Representation	Fraction	Exponent
1.375_{10}	3FB0.0000_{16}	30.0000_{16}	7F_{16}
2.750_{10}	4030.0000_{16}	30.0000_{16}	80_{16}

First we denormalize the representations by matching exponents. We choose to set both exponents to 1 ($7F_{16}$).

Phase 2: Perform the addition...

$$
\begin{array}{ll}
1.375 & 1.0110 \\
2.75 & 10.1100 \\
\hline
4.125 & 100.0010
\end{array}
$$

...remembering to re-instate the *hidden bit*.

Phase 3: Normalize the result by right shifting and incrementing the exponent until the most significant "1" occupies the units (2^0) bit position. This produces...

$$
\begin{aligned}
fraction &= 000.0100.0000.0000.0000.0000_2 \\
&= 04.0000_{16} \\
exponent &= 1000.0001_2 \\
&= 81_{16} \\
result &= 4084.0000_{16}
\end{aligned}
$$

Element level

Question one

A *standard sum of products* may be written...

$$Q_{sop} = A.B + C.D$$

The function derived from a 2-level NAND gate structure is...

$$
\begin{aligned}
Q_{NAND} &= \overline{\overline{A.B}.\overline{C.D}} \\
&= \overline{\overline{A.B} + \overline{C.D}} \\
&= A.B + C.D \\
&= Q_{sop}
\end{aligned}
$$

A *standard sum of products* may be written...

$$Q_{pos} = (A + B).(C + D)$$

The function derived from a 2-level NOR gate structure is...

$$
\begin{aligned}
Q_{NOR} &= \overline{\overline{A + B} + \overline{C + D}} \\
&= \overline{\overline{A + B}}.\overline{\overline{C + D}} \quad (DeMorgan's Laws) \\
&= (A + B).(C + D) \\
&= Q_{pos}
\end{aligned}
$$

Question two

i With *sign-magnitude* representation apply the XOR operator with the *bit mask* 1000.0000, i.e. $msb = 1$.

ii With *twos complement* representation apply the XOR operator with the bit mask 1111.1111, i.e. all 1s, to *complement* the value, then add 1.

Question three

Figure B.3 shows how NAND and NOR gates may be used to implement {AND, OR, NOT}.

	NAND	NOR
NOT		
AND		
OR		

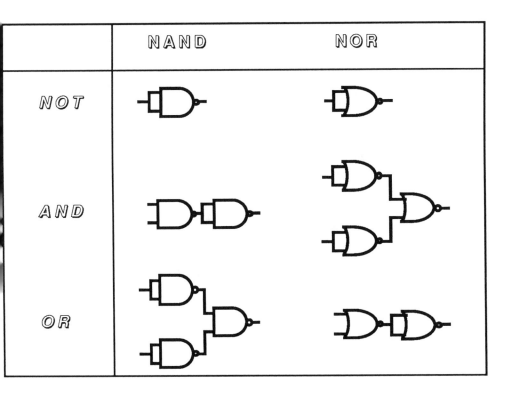

Figure B.3: NAND and NOR implementing {AND, OR, NOT}

Question four

i In each case, *DeMorgan's laws* may be employed to expand the expression as follows. .

$$
\begin{aligned}
Q_{aoi}^{nand} &= \overline{\overline{A.B + C.D}} \\
&= \overline{\overline{\overline{A.B}.\overline{C.D}}} \\
&= \overline{\overline{\overline{A.B}.\overline{C.D}}} \\
&= \overline{(\overline{A.B}.\overline{C.D}).(\overline{A.B}.\overline{C.D})}
\end{aligned}
$$

$$
\begin{aligned}
Q_{aoi}^{nor} &= \overline{\overline{A.B + C.D}} \\
&= \overline{\overline{\overline{A} + \overline{B}} + \overline{\overline{C} + \overline{D}}} \\
&= \overline{(\overline{A} + \overline{A} + \overline{B} + \overline{B}) + (\overline{C} + \overline{C} + \overline{D} + \overline{D})}
\end{aligned}
$$

ii To prove that Q_{aoi} may be employed alone to express any truth function it is enough to show that the {AND, OR, NOT} *sufficiency set* may be implemented. . .

$$
\bar{X} = \overline{X.X + X.X}
$$

$$
\begin{aligned}
X.Y &= \overline{\overline{X.Y + X.Y}} \\
&= \overline{\overline{X.Y} + \overline{X.Y}}
\end{aligned}
$$

$$
\begin{aligned}
X + Y &= \overline{\overline{X.X + Y.Y}} \\
&= \overline{\overline{X.X} + \overline{Y.Y}}
\end{aligned}
$$

A single Q_{aoi} may be used for negation in the implemention of both AND and OR.

Question five

i Figure B.4 shows Figure 5.16 (lower) expanded into *normally-open switches.*

ii An engineer responsible for implementation of the *RS-latch* shown in Figure B.4 would specifications of. . .

- *Fan-out*

- *Setup time*

- *Hold time*

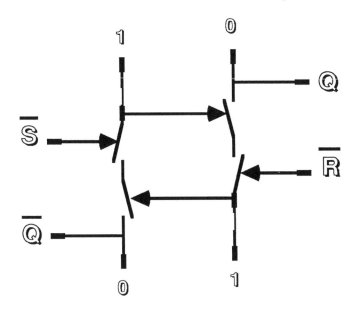

Figure B.4: An RS-latch at switch level

- *Propagation delay*

- *Power consumption*

- *Power dissipation*

See Figure 5.27 for timings.

Fan-out must be traded for operation speed. The implementation technology will set limits on the *product* of these. Power dissipation must also be traded for operation speed. A smaller resistance implies faster operation but higher dissipation. Again the available technology will limit the product of the two.

The technology requirement obviously exists for a switch which is easily closed. *Noise* sets the limit to what is possible. A switch must require more potential to close than might become available through uncontrollable random fluctuations.

Question six

The operation of the clock system shown in Figure 5.28 is easily explained if we consider each side of the capacitor separately. The top gate is referred to below as A, the lower left and right as B and C respectively.

Assume that every point in the system commences at logic 0. All gates will attempt to set their outputs to 1. After $t_{pd} + t_{rc}$ gate C will succeed, causing the system output to become 1[4].

The logic value will now propagate through each gate in turn so that, after $3.t_{pd}$ gate C output, and thus that of the system too, will attempt to become 0. The capacitor must now discharge into the output terminal of gate C. Hence the system output returns to 0 after $3.t_{pd} + t_{rc}$.

The system behaves cyclically in this way.

Question seven

i A *latch* is *enabled* and contains only a single *buffer* whereas a *flip-flop* is *clocked* and contains a *double buffer*. The flip-flop may engage in *synchronous* communication whereas a latch cannot because it is *transparent*, i.e. when enabled the value at the input is visible at the output.

ii The *edge-triggered D-type* flip-flop shown in Figure 5.24 is constructed from three *RS-latches* and an *AND* gate. RS latches have the property of retaining their state when $\bar{R} = \bar{S} = 1$.

$Ck = 0$ implies $\bar{R}_{out} = \bar{S}_{out} = 1$. Hence the output of the final latch, and thus of the whole system, will remain unchanged while the clock input is zero. On a positive clock state transition we must consider the two possible values of D independently.

$D = 0$ implies $\bar{S}_{out} = 1$ while $\bar{R}_{out} = 0$ still, since the upper latch remains in its previous state, having both inputs set. Hence $Q_{out} = 0$.

$D = 1$ implies $\bar{S}_{out} = 0$ while $R_{out} = 1$ since, this time, the lower latch retains its state. The upper latch changes state so that $\bar{S}_{out} = 0$ hence $Q_{out} = 1$.

Use is made of the property of a latch made from NAND gates to maintain a stable state, with $Q = \bar{Q} = 1$ when $\bar{R} = \bar{S} = 0$. This allows $\bar{R}_{out} = \bar{S}_{out} = 1$, regardless of D as long as $Ck = 0$.

Should D change $0 \to 1$ while $Ck = 1$ the lower latch will retain its previous state since $\bar{R} = \bar{S} = 1$, hence so will the whole system. Should D change $1 \to 0$ while $Ck =$ the upper latch will retain its state since the lower one will adopt the "forbidden" state where both inputs are zero and both outputs are one. (The AND gate will effectively disconnect Ck from the $\bar{S}$ input of the lower latch after $\bar{Q}$ of the upper one changes to zero.) See Figure B.5.

---

[4] t_{rc} is the time taken for the capacitor to charge through the resistor.

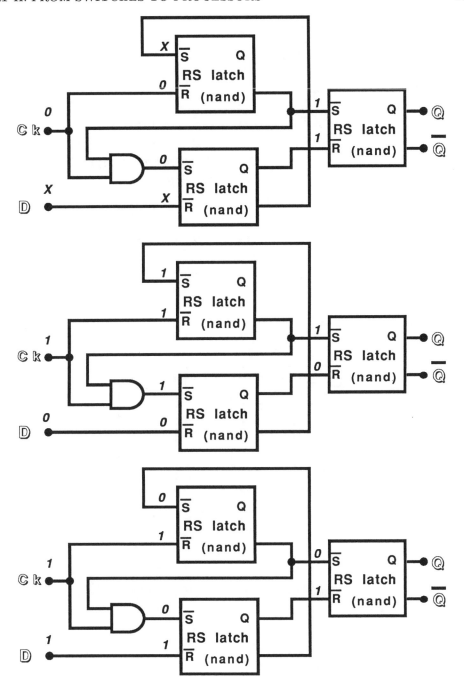

Figure B.5: Edge-triggered D flip-flop operation

Component level

Question one

Boolean recursive absorption...

$$\begin{aligned}
Q_1(A, B, C) &= A.B.C + A.B.\bar{C} + A.\bar{B}.C + \bar{A}.B.C \\
&= A.B.C + A.B.C + A.B.C + A.B.\bar{C} + A.\bar{B}.C + \bar{A}.B.C \\
&= A.B.C + A.B.C + A.B + A.\bar{B}.C + \bar{A}.B.C \\
&= A.B.C + A.B + A.C + \bar{A}.B.C \\
&= A.B + A.C + B.C
\end{aligned}$$

$$\begin{aligned}
Q_2(A, B, C) &= A.B.C + A.B.\bar{C} + \bar{A}.B.C + \bar{A}.\bar{B}.C \\
&= A.B + \bar{A}.B.C + \bar{A}.\bar{B}.C \\
&= A.B + \bar{A}.C
\end{aligned}$$

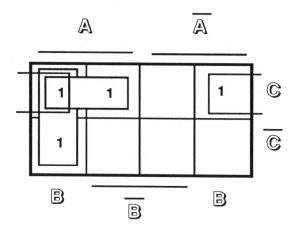

Figure B.6: K-map solutions to question one (i)

Karnaugh map...   Solutions are shown in Figure B.6 and Figure B.7.

Quine-McCluskey...   Solutions are shown in Figure B.8 and Figure B.9.

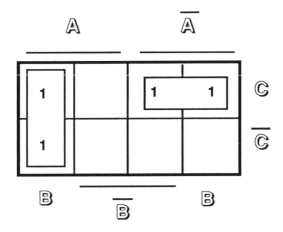

Figure B.7: K-map solutions to question one (ii)

Question two

Truth tables for two half adders and one full adder demonstrate their equivalence (see Table B.1).

A	B	C_{in}	S_1	C_1	C_2	$S_{out} = S_2$	$C_{out} = C_1 + C_2$
0	0	0	0	0	0	0	0
0	0	1	0	0	0	1	0
0	1	0	1	0	0	1	0
0	1	1	1	0	1	0	1
1	0	0	1	0	0	1	0
1	0	1	1	0	1	0	1
1	1	0	0	1	0	0	1
1	1	1	0	1	0	1	1

Table B.1: Truth table for combination of two half-adders

Using Boolean algebra we note...

$$S_{FA} = A.B.C_i + \bar{A}.B.\bar{C_i} + \bar{A}.\bar{B}.C_i + A.\bar{B}.\bar{C_i}$$
$$C_{FA} = A.B + B.C_i + A.C_i$$
$$S_{HA} = A.\bar{B} + \bar{A}.B$$

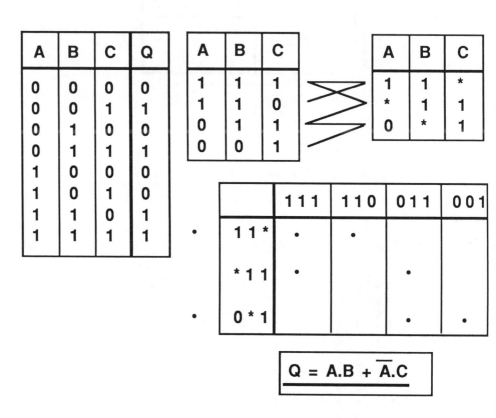

Figure B.8: Q-m solutions to question one (i)

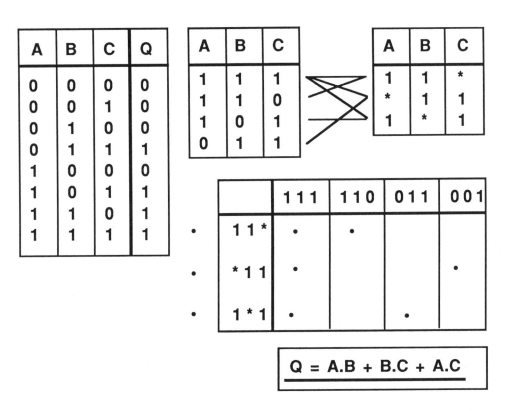

A	B	C	Q
0	0	0	0
0	0	1	0
0	1	0	0
0	1	1	1
1	0	0	0
1	0	1	1
1	1	0	1
1	1	1	1

A	B	C
1	1	1
1	1	0
1	0	1
0	1	1

A	B	C
1	1	*
*	1	1
1	*	1

		1 1 1	1 1 0	0 1 1	0 0 1
•	1 1 *	•	•		
•	* 1 1	•			•
•	1 * 1	•		•	

$$Q = A.B + B.C + A.C$$

Figure B.9: Q-m solutions to question one (ii)

$$C_{HA} \;=\; A.B$$

Substituting for the case of two half adders...

$$
\begin{aligned}
S &= (A.\bar{B} + \bar{A}.B).\bar{C_i} + \overline{(A.\bar{B} + \bar{A}.B)}.C_i \\
&= A.\bar{B}.\bar{C_i} + \bar{A}.B.\bar{C_i} + \overline{A.\bar{B}}.\overline{\bar{B}.A}.C_i \\
&= A.\bar{B}.\bar{C_i} + \bar{A}.B.\bar{C_i} + (\bar{A} + B).(A + \bar{B}).C_i \\
&= A.\bar{B}.\bar{C_i} + \bar{A}.B.\bar{C_i} + \bar{A}.\bar{B}.C_i + A.B.C_i \\
&= S_{FA}
\end{aligned}
$$

$$
\begin{aligned}
C &= A.B + C_i.(A.\bar{B} + \bar{A}.B) \\
&= A.B + A.\bar{B}.C_i + \bar{A}.B.C_i \\
&= A.B.C_i + A.B.\bar{C_i} + A.\bar{B}.C_i + \bar{A}.B.C_i \\
&= B.C_i + A.\bar{B}.C_i + A.B.\bar{C_i} \\
&= C_{FA}
\end{aligned}
$$

ii   The logic for a 4-bit *look-ahead* carry is given by...

$$
\begin{aligned}
C_4 &= A_3.B_3 + (A_3 \oplus B_3).C_3 \\
&= G_3 + P_3.C_3 \\
&= G_3 + P_3.G_2 \\
&\quad + P_3.P_2.C_2 \\
&= G_3 + P_3.G_2 \\
&\quad + P_3.P_2.G_1 \\
&\quad + P_3.P_2.P_1.C_1 \\
&= G_3 + P_3.G_2 \\
&\quad + P_3.P_2.G_1 \\
&\quad + P_3.P_2.P_1.G_0 \\
&\quad + P_3.P_2.P_1.P_0.C_0
\end{aligned}
$$

iii   A *4-bit parallel adder with look-ahead carry* must generate the following outputs...

- $S_i \rightarrow S_{i+3}$

- $P_{i \rightarrow i+3} = P_i.P_{i+1}.P_{i+2}.P_{i+3}$

- $G_{i\to i+3} = G_{i+3} + P_{i+3}.G_{i+2} + P_{i+3}.P_{i+2}.P_{i+1}.G_{i+1} + P_{i+3}.P_{i+2}.P_{i+1}.G_i$

The carry input for the second adder and the carry out are given by...

$$
\begin{aligned}
C_4 &= G_{0\to3} + P_{0\to3}.C_0 \\
C_8 &= G_{4\to7} + P_{4\to7}.G_{0\to3} + P_{4\to7}.P_{0\to3}.C_0
\end{aligned}
$$

Question three

BCD representation uses four bits. Only the first ten binary states are valid. For example 1001_2 represents 9_{10} whereas 1010_2 is invalid and does not represent anything. 45_{10} is
represented, using eight bits, by 0010.0101_2, 938_{10}, using twelve bits, by $1001.0011.1000_2$.

The state table for a *bcd* counter, made from T-type flip-flops, is shown in Table B.2.
Four flip-flops are required since $2^4 > 10 > 2^3$.

Present state				Next state				T excitations			
Q_3	Q_2	Q_1	Q_0	Q_3	Q_2	Q_1	Q_0	T_3	T_2	T_1	T_0
0	0	0	0	0	0	0	1	0	0	0	1
0	0	0	1	0	0	1	0	0	0	1	1
0	0	1	0	0	0	1	1	0	0	0	1
0	0	1	1	0	1	0	0	0	1	1	1
0	1	0	0	0	1	0	1	0	0	0	1
0	1	0	1	0	1	1	0	0	0	1	1
0	1	1	0	0	1	1	1	0	0	0	1
0	1	1	1	1	0	0	0	1	1	1	1
1	0	0	0	1	0	0	1	0	0	0	1
1	0	0	1	0	0	0	0	1	0	0	1

Table B.2: State table for a BCD (modulo-10) counter

The input equations are...

$$
\begin{aligned}
T_0 &= 1 \\
T_1 &= \bar{Q}_3.Q_0 \\
T_2 &= Q_0.Q_1 \\
T_3 &= Q_0.Q_3 + Q_0.Q_1.Q_2
\end{aligned}
$$

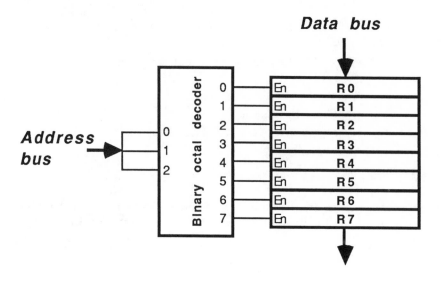

Figure B.10: Use of a binary decoder to enable data registers

Question four

An *octal binary decoder*[5] may be employed to transform three binary *address* digit into eight binary signals which each *enable* a single data register to *read* or *write* data Figure B.10 illustrates the connections required.

Question five

The truth table for a *4-bit priority encoder* is shown in Table B.3. V is a *valid* output signal. Figure B.11 depicts the K-maps. An "X" on the truth table implies two minterms and hence two cells filling on the K-map, one for 0 and one for 1.

We may thus deduce that the logic may be specified via. . .

$$
\begin{aligned}
A_1 &= D_3 + D_2 \\
A_0 &= D_3 + \bar{D}_2.D_1 \\
V &= D_3 + D_2 + D_1 + D_0
\end{aligned}
$$

---

[5] So called because its input may be noted as a single octal digit.

D_3	D_2	D_1	D_0	A_1	A_0	V
0	0	0	0	0	0	0
0	0	0	1	0	0	1
0	0	1	X	0	1	1
0	1	X	X	1	0	1
1	X	X	X	1	1	1

Table B.3: Truth table for 4-bit priority encoder

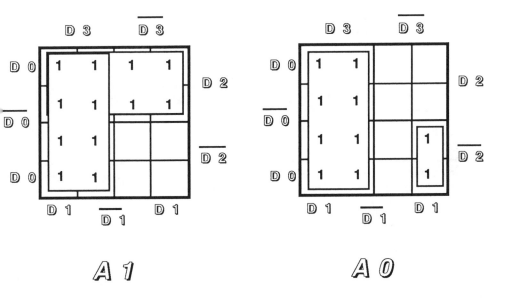

Figure B.11: K-maps for 4-bit priority encoder

Control units

Question one

Control signals making up the *control word* for the processor described are as follows. .

Active registers	$a2r, a2w, a2i, a2d, a2z, a2c, a2sl, a2sr$	(8)
	$a1r, a1w, a1i, a1d, a1z, a1c, a1sl, a1sr$	(8)
	$a0r, a0w, a0i, a0d, a0z, a0c, a0sl, a0sr$	(8)
Program counter	PCr, PCw	(2)
Processor state register	PSr	(1)
Arithmetic unit	$au2r, au1w, au0w, auf1, auf0$	(5)

There are 32 signals making up the whole control word. It is usually advisable to group related signals together. Here, it is appropriate to group signals into two fields. .

- *Active registers*

- *Arithmetic unit*

. . . as shown in Figure B.12. Thus the control word may be represented by eight hex digits, e.g. 0000.0000_{16}.

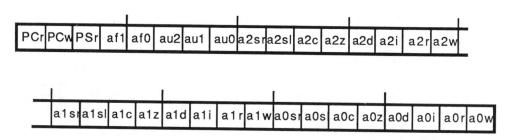

Figure B.12: Control word format for question one

Question two

First we compose the *state assignment table* (Table B.4). Only three states are necessary, hence only two flip-flops are required. Secondly the *state transition table* must be derived, (Table B.5). Lastly, Table B.6 shows the truth table for flip-flop excitation and output generation.

The following are the irreducible expressions which require implementation. . .

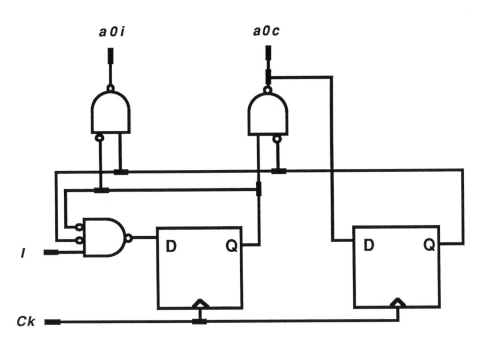

Figure B.13: Control unit satisfying question two

Label	State	Micro-operation
a	00	Inactive
b	01	Complement
c	10	Increment

Table B.4: State assignment table for question two

Input	Present state	Next state	Control word
0	a	a	000.0000_{16}
1	a	b	000.0000_{16}
X	b	c	000.0200_{16}
X	c	a	000.0040_{16}

Table B.5: State transition table for question two

$$
\begin{aligned}
D_0 &= I.\bar{Q}_1.\bar{Q}_0 \\
D_1 &= \bar{Q}_1.Q_0 \\
a0c &= \bar{Q}_1.Q_0 \\
&= D_1 \\
a0i &= Q_1.\bar{Q}_0
\end{aligned}
$$

Figure B.13 shows the control unit which results.

Question three

A simple step to increase performance would be to ensure that `multiplier` takes the smaller of the two values and `multiplicand` the larger. This will minimise the number of loop iterations. This may be achieved by preceding the algorithm with...

I	Q_1	Q_0	D_1	D_0	aoi	aoc
0	0	0	0	0	0	0
1	0	0	0	1	0	0
X	0	1	1	0	0	1
X	1	0	0	0	1	0
X	1	1	0	0	0	0

Table B.6: Truth table for question two

```
IF x > y THEN
  multiplicand := x
  multiplier := y
ELSE
  multiplier := x
  multiplicand := y
END
```

Achieving the comparison will of course imply the overhead of a single subtraction (signed addition) operation. This need not be considered excessive, especially for long word lengths, since the multiplication algorithm typically incurs a number of additions.

Extending the algorithm to cope with signed integers is simple. The above is preceded by...

```
IF x < 0 THEN
  negate x
END
IF y < 0 THEN
  negate y
END
```

Note that the architecture described in question one could easily be extended to allow the conditional negations to be conducted *in parallel*. A further active register control input $(A = Absolute\ value)$ could enable the MSB to signal a control system (the solution to question two) to start. The A control inputs of both registers may be simultaneously activated.

A *microprogram* which implements the unextended given algorithm for the architecture of question one is...

```
zero a2
move a0, au0
add a0
IF zero   THEN
  jump #0000
right a0
IF carry THEN
  move a2, au0
  add a1
  move au2, a2
left a1
jump <start>
```

Question four

The above microprogram contains thirteen *micro-operations*. It is reasonable to assum
that few instructions would prove so complicated to implement. For example, a *regis
ter move* requires only a single micro-operation. Given say twenty instructions for ou
processor, a reasonable assumption for the size of the *MROM* would be 256 location
dictating an address width of 8 bits.

The arithmetic unit and active registers give rise to little *processor state*. A *carr*
and *zero* flag will suffice. In order to force or deny jumping, both logic 1 and logic 0 mus
be selectable. Hence two bits are required in the micro-instruction format.

To summarize, a possible micro-instruction format for a *counter-based* control uni
is...

Jump/Enter	*Bit 42*	*Selection of counter load word*	(1)
Flag select	*Bits 40-41*	*Selection of PSR condition flag*	(2)
Control word	*Bits 8-39*	*(See question one)*	(32)
Jump address	*Bits 0-7*	*(See above)*	(8)

The microcode required to implement the multiplication algorithm of question three
is given in Table B.7. It is assumed that...

- *Jump/Enter = 0 $\Rightarrow$ Jump*

- *Flag select field:*

  - *$0 \Rightarrow 0$*
  - *$1 \Rightarrow 1$*
  - *$2 \Rightarrow Zero$*
  - *$3 \Rightarrow Carry$*

- *Start address = 10_{16}*

Note that, as a result, Jump/Enter and Flag Select fields being clear will cause
jump on condition 0, which always fails, causing the *CAR* to simply increment. Henc
no jump or entry to new *microprogram* occurs if the most significant three bits are clear

Question five

Figure B.14 shows a design of the required control unit, achieved using a simple analysi
of the flow of control. The *END* signal would be used to trigger the *fetch* microprocess
START would be asserted by the instruction decoder on finding the multiplication opcod
at its input.

The control word signals asserted on each timing signal (as enumerated on the figure
are tabulated in Table B.8.

MROM address	Control word	Micro-operations				
10	0.01.10.00.02.00		au0	←	a0,	a2(zero)
11	0.0A.00.00.02.00		au1	←	a0,	au(add)
12	2.00.00.00.00.00	IF Z	CAR	←	0	
13	3.00.00.00.80.15	IF C	CAR	←	15,	a0(right)
14	1.00.00.00.40.10	IF 1	CAR	←	10,	a1(left)
15	0.01.02.00.00.00		au0	←	a2	
16	0.0A.00.02.00.00		au1	←	a1,	au(add)
17	1.04.01.40.00.10		a2	←	au2,	a1(left)
18		IF 1	CAR	←	10	

Table B.7: Microprogram for unsigned integer multiplication instruction

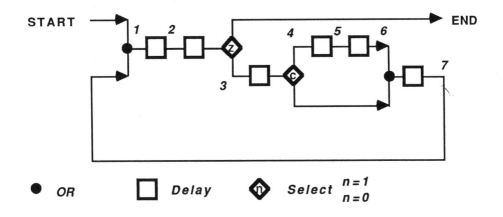

Figure B.14: Shift register control unit for multiplication instruction

Timing signal	Control signals asserted
1	a2z, a0r, au0
2	a0r, au1, af0
3	a0sr
4	a2r, au0
5	a1r, au1, af0
6	au2, a2w
7	a1sl

Table B.8: Control signals asserted vs. timing signal for shift register control unit

From components to systems

Processor Organization

Question one

i *Value parameters* are initialized by the compiler by copying the *value* of the actual parameter into the stack location of its formal parameter counterpart. *Reference parameters* are initialized by copying the *address* of the actual parameter.

ii Figures B.15 depicts the stack structures on invocation of both procedure `HexStringToCard` and function `Real`.

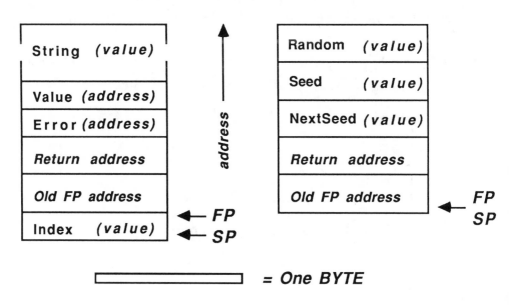

Figure B.15: Stack structure on invocation of procedure `HexStringToCard` and function `Random`

Question two

The *register relative* addressing mode referencing for procedure `HexStringToCard` is..

```
String   +12(fp)
Value     +9(fp)
Error     +6(fp)
Index     -3(fp)
```

and that for function **Random** is...

```
NextSeed    +8(fp)
Seed        +12(fp)
Random      +16(fp)
```

Question three

i It takes longer to perform a *bus operation* than an internal *processor operation* because of the necessarily *sequential* protocol of a bus communication transaction. This is basically composed thus...

- *Send address, read/write signal, data (if write operation)*

- *Delay*

- *Receive data (if read operation)*

The *delay* is necessary for two main reasons...

- *Address decoding*

- *Physical remoteness of memory*

The physical remoteness of memory implies an interval of time to build up potential because the channel itself must be charged, or *'driven"*. In electrical technology this difficulty is measured in the resistance and capacitance *per unit length* of conductor. In a mechanical technology it is represented as the *inertia* of the mechanism.

There is no reason why this should remain a fundamental limitation of computer performance. Address decoding can be rendered as fast as any processor operation. Most important is perhaps the adoption of a technology which minimizes or even *eliminates* the *inertia* of the processor-to-memory communication channel. Three approaches are of importance, though on different timescales,...

- *Processor and memory share physical device*

- *Superconduction (almost zero electrical resistance)*

- *Optical technology (zero inertia medium)*

ii   The number of bus cycles required for each of the two instruction classes, *move* and *arithmetic operator* is tabulated below *versus* architecture...

	Accumulator	Stack	Register file
Move	1	2	1
Arithmetic	1	3	0

iii   The major advantages of a *stack machine* architecture are...

- *Short basic instructions because few are required*
- *Zero or one instruction extension (short since offset only required)*
- *Support for procedure invocation and return*
- *Easy code generation for expression evaluation*

Disadvantages are (in priority order)...

- *Slow due to excessive bus access*
- *Comparatively more instructions required*

Bus access can be dramatically reduced, at the expense of extra processor complexity, by arranging for the topmost three stack items to always appear in three special dedicated registers (see below).

Question four

i   Typical code generated for the *accumulator machine* would be...

```
load a
mul #2
store temp.1
load a
mul c
mul #4
store temp.2
load b
mul b
sub temp.2
div temp.1
store RootSquared
```

Typical code for the *stack machine* and *register machine* would be...

```
            push a                      load  a, r0
            push #2                     mul   #2, r0
            mul                         load  c, r1
            push a                      mul   a, r1
            push c                      mul   #4, r1
            mul                         load  b, r2
            push #4                     mul   r2,r2
            mul                         sub   r2, r1
            push b                      div   r1, r0
            push b                      store r0, RootSquared
            mul
            sub
            div
            pop RootSquared
```

ii The number of instructions, code length and number of bus operations required by the above implementations is tabulated below...

	Accumulator	Stack	Register file	Modified stack
Instructions	12	14	10	14
Code length	54	22	42	22
Bus operations	12	34	4	10

The *register file machine* clearly offers an advantage in execution speed, over the stack machine for expression evaluation *at the expense of code length*. In order to alleviate the problem with code length, which arises not because of the number of instructions but because of the need for *absolute addressing*, and to afford support for procedure invocation and return, it has become common for commercial architectures to include both a register file *and* a stack.

Note just how greatly the execution speed of a *stack machine* is improved by holding the top three stack items in processor registers.

Question five

The following operations must be performed on a stack machine for function *invocation, entry, exit* and *return* (number of bus operations shown in brackets)...

1. (0) *Push space for return value*

2. (6) *Push three parameters*

3. (2) *Branch to subroutine*

4. (1) *Push old frame pointer*

5. (0) *Copy stack pointer to frame pointer*

6. (1) *Increment stack pointer by frame size*

7. (0) *Copy frame pointer to stack pointer*

8. (1) *Pop old frame pointer value to frame pointer register*

9. (1) *Decrement stack pointer by parameter block size*

Note that space for the return value etc. may be accomplished by simply incrementing the stack pointer, without the need for a bus operation. A total of *twelve* bus operations are thus required for any function call where three parameters are passed and the result returned may be accomodated within a single memory word.

ii   A register windowing machine must still perform some similar operations...

1. *Move parameters*

2. *Branch to subroutine*

3. *Increment current window pointer*

4. *Decrement current window pointer*

5. *Move return*

...but the moving of data is all between registers and does not require a single bus operation. The main limitations of *register windowing* are...

- *Number of permitted local variables and parameters (due to window size)*

- *Procedure activation depth (due to number of windows)*

These limitations are known not to greatly affect operational efficiency. Research has shown that...

- *Procedure activation depth exceeds eight on less than 1% of invocations*

- *Number of procedure parameters exceeds six on less than 2% of invocations*

- *Number of local variables exceeds six on less than 8% of invocations*

These results have been reported by more than one research group, [Tanenbaum 78] [Katevenis 85].

Question six

A *procedure* is a *software partition* which has two main motivations...

- *Reduce software development time through repeated use of source code*

- *Reduce code size through repeated use of object code*

By contrast a *process* represents an independent activity whose software may be executed *concurrently* with that of others. Processes do not share variables but instead pass messages to each other. A number of processes may run *concurrently, but not in parallel* on the same processor if a *scheduler* exists to permit sharing of the processor as a resource. Software may be decomposed into a number of sub-processes, each of which may be independently designed and implemented. The interface between processes is stated as a list of *channels* together with their respective *protocols*.

It is possible to utilise either the procedure or the process as an abstraction in *top-down design*. The two alternatives may be termed *procedure oriented design* and *process oriented design*. A procedure abstracts an action[6] whereas a process represents an *activity* which involves *communication*. A procedure requires *parameterization* to serve as a useful object which was worthwhile defining *at edit time*. A process requires *communication channels* and protocols to serve as a useful object *at run time*.

The private state of a process is similar in concept to the local variables of a procedure. However, a procedure shares the scope of the one that called it, and so on out. A process has no access to *any* state but its own.

Perhaps the most significant difference between the two forms of abstraction is that *process abstraction* may be used to model concurrency, at *abstract, virtual* and *physical* levels, whereas *procedure abstraction* cannot. Concurrency implies communication!

---

[6] ...as oppposed to a *function* which abstracts a quantity. The two are sadly frequently confused, particularly when the programming language provides one and not the other (e.g. "C" which provides functions only). The result is identifier names which do not correspond well with abstract (problem level) actions or quantities rendering the program unreadable.

System organization

Question one

i   The cost of a memory is substantially affected by the *address width* required. There
fore a *two-dimensional* memory should be rendered *square* since this minimizes the number of address bits required. For example, given that...

- N = number of memory cells

- A = address width

- x = dimension in x

- y = dimension in y

...we find that...

$$
\begin{aligned}
N &= xy \\
A &= x + y
\end{aligned}
$$

It can be shown that A is a minimum with respect to N if and only if $x = y$ and
provided that N is a *perfect square*. However we shall be content with the example of
$N = 16$ where we observe that...

$$
\begin{aligned}
x &= 8, \; y = 2 \;\Rightarrow\; A = 10 \\
x &= 2, \; y = 8 \;\Rightarrow\; A = 10 \\
x &= 4, \; y = 4 \;\Rightarrow\; A = 8
\end{aligned}
$$

ii   The following are the expressions required for a hierarchy of n devices...

$$
\begin{aligned}
\bar{c}_i &= \frac{\sum_{j \geq i}^{n} c_j . s_j}{\sum_{j \geq i}^{n} s_j} \\[2mm]
\bar{t}_i &= h_i . t_i + (1 - h_i) . \bar{t}_{i+1} \\[2mm]
e_i^c &= c_n / \bar{c}_i \\[2mm]
&= \frac{c_n . \sum_{j \geq i}^{n} s_j}{\sum_{j \geq i}^{n} c_j . s_j} \\[2mm]
e_i^t &= \bar{t}_i / t_i \\[2mm]
&= \frac{1}{r_i + (1 - r_i) . h_i}
\end{aligned}
$$

...where $r_i = \bar{t}_{i+1} / t_i$. For the hierarchy given we obtain...

$$\bar{t}_0 \simeq 10^3 ns$$

$$e_i^c \simeq 50\%$$
$$\bar{t}_1 \simeq 2000$$
$$r_0 \simeq 200$$
$$e_i^t \simeq 5\%$$

An *access efficiency* of 10% with t_0 of 10 requires $\bar{t}_0$ of 1 and hence h_0 of 0.9955. This would be very hard to obtain with current *associative cache* technology.

Question two

i   There follows a summary of *control bus* signal channels...

- *Bus request*

- *Bus grant*

- *Event*

- *Event acknowledge*

- *Clock*

- *Sync*

- *Read/Write*

- *Ready*

- *Address strobe (if multiplexed)*

ii   Figure B.16 depicts the timing for a successful *daisy chain* bus arbitration.

A higher priority device, completing its transaction, will cease to assert *bus request* in order to release the bus for another master *on the subsequent bus cycle* (whose start is marked by *sync*). The *arbiter* will keep asserted *bus grant* if a lower priority device is still maintaining *bus request* asserted. It is up to the higher priority device to *pass on Bus grant* down the chain *immediately* when it ceases to drive *bus request*.

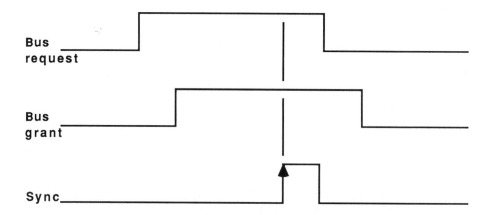

Figure B.16: Daisy chain bus arbitration

iii *Daisy chain* arbitration has the advantage of being very cheap and simple to implement. It is unfortunately rather *unfair* to low priority processes which run the risk of *lock out*. Some *unreliability* is due to a "weakest link" vulnerability. Should any one device fail, e.g. to pass on *bus grant*, all those further down will also suffer. No *software priority control* is possible. The ability to be extended almost infinitely, without overhead in cost, is an advantage.

Polled arbitration offers software control of priority and greater reliability but requires the whole system to be upgraded if extended beyond the limit set by the number of *poll count* signals. The poll count will also take time and possibly reduce bandwidth.

Independent request arbitration usually requires separate *bus request* signals for every device. *SCSI* overcomes this by using *data bus* bits together with the *Busy* signal. With **centralized arbitration**, i.e. with an *arbiter*, software control over priority is possible. The method is reliable and fast.

However *SCSI* illustrates a further distinction in performing **distributed arbitration**. No software priority control is possible but no single device is responsible for arbitration which means the removal of a *common point of failure*. This is extremely important since the majority of *new* applications, particularly in *real time control*, demand very high *reliablity*.

Question three

i Figure B.17 shows the use of an *interleaved memory* in implementing a *3 plane colour graphics display*.

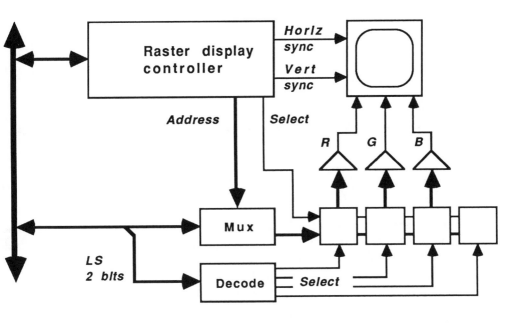

Figure B.17: Interleaved memory in implementing a 3 plane colour graphics display

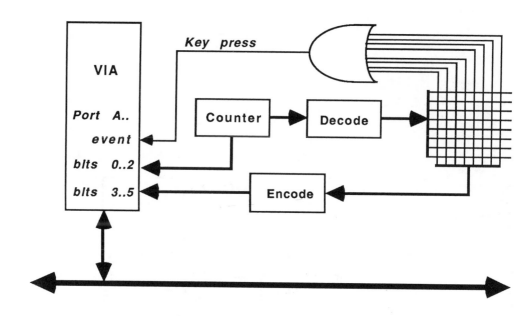

Figure B.18: Connection of unencoded key matrix to system bus

System bus access may select a data word from just one module, asserting just one *select* signal. The *raster display controller* requires all three *RGB* memory modules simultaneously selected. For the sake of simplifying the diagram it is shown using a separate *select* input. On each module the two would be internally *OR*'d together.

ii   Figure B.18 shows how the key matrix is connected to the *system bus*. It is read by the *modulo 8* counter activating each row (or column) in turn via the *decoder*. Any *key press* event will cause the *VIA* to *latch* the (encoded) active column *and* the current row number (counter value) which together form the *key code*.

The counter will need to run quicky enough to catch any key press. A key will remain depressed for a time which is very long compared to the system clock cycle so this will not usually be a problem. However the system must respond to the interrupt and clear the latched *port A* in time for the next key press. A *monostable*[7] should be used on the *event* signal for two purposes...

- *Debouncing of switch*

---

[7]Device with single stable state to which it returns, after a known interval, when disturbed, thus allowing generation of a *pulse* from an *edge*.

- *Pulse generation*

Debouncing means preventing multiple *edge signals* resulting from the switch making contact more than once when depressed (bouncing). A *pulse* is preferred to a continuous level since this would prevent other *event sources* sending event signals.

Question four

The purpose of this exercise was to provoke thought. To have arrived at an efficient, practical implementation would earn praise indeed! However it has been observed that solutions have been found for problems previously thought intractable *when those seeking them have been unaware that they were so deemed.*

A known good approximation to *LRU*, which is efficient and practical to implement, is as follows. Each entry e_i is assigned a single reference bit r_i which is *set* whenever the entry is referenced. Whenever a *miss* occurs, entry e_j is loaded and all entries e_i such that $i \neq j$ are *cleared*. The entry replaced is the first one for whom $r_i = 0$ in a search whose order is predetermined and *fixed*. If all $r_i = 1$ then that entry is replaced which possesses the *smallest* address.

The reader should verify, by thought and experimentation with an imaginary list of addresses, that entries replaced do tend to be those *least recently used.*

Question five

i The following table shows the working which gives an error *syndrome* of 10101_2 for the data word $FAC9_{16} = 1111.1010.1100.1001_2$.

Syndrome bit	Data bits	Data bit values	Odd parity
0	2,5,10..15	00011111	1
1	4..10,15	00110101	0
2	1..3,7..9,14,15	10010111	1
3	0,2,3,5,6,9,12,13	10101111	0
4	0,1,3,4,6,8,11,13	10101011	1

ii The following table shows the *error vector* produced for each possible bit in error. As can clearly be seen each one is distinct and may be decoded (e.g. using a *ROM*) to indicate the bit requiring inversion.

Bit in error	Error vector (Binary)	Error vector (Hex)
d_0	11000	18
d_1	10100	14
d_2	01100	0C
d_3	11100	1C
d_4	10010	12
d_5	01011	0B
d_6	11010	1A
d_7	00110	06
d_8	10110	16
d_9	01110	0E
d_{10}	00011	03
d_{11}	10001	11
d_{12}	01001	09
d_{13}	11001	19
d_{14}	00101	05
d_{15}	00111	07
p_0	00001	01
p_1	00010	02
p_2	00100	04
p_3	01000	08
p_4	10000	10

Note that a *syndrome error* can be distinguished from a *data error* by the *syndrome parity*! The reader should verify that *double errors* produce a non-zero error vector, but unfortunately one which is not unique to each error, and that *triple errors* cannot be detected.

Survey of contemporary processor architecture

Question one

i   Code generation to implement a *case* construct with more than about a dozen case labels will usually employ a *jump table* approach. A table of. . .

- *Offsets*

- *Absolute addresses*

- *Jump or branch instructions*

. . .to the code segment corresponding to each case label is created within the executable file. The size of the table will be decided by the upper and lower case label bounds. An entry is present for *every* value between the bounds. Those not corresponding to case labels point to a code segment which corresponds to the *"else"* clause in the construct.

In practice the result of the *case expression* evaluation will be checked against the table bounds, which must thus also be recorded. If outside the bounds the "else" code must be invoked.

Evidently many, widely scattered case label values may easily result in an unacceptably large table. For example, an integer case expression with more than a dozen case label values scattered from zero to a million will give rise to a table with a million entries! If there are less than a dozen entries a compiler will often substitute a series of *compare* and *branch* instructions. This will result in code length directly proportional to the *number* of case labels instead of their range.

The programmer should only ever need to be aware of the *programming model* and *not* the underlying architecture. This rule breaks down with the use of the *case* construct (unless the programmer can afford not to care about code size). He/she must be aware of the impact on memory consumption, which is an architecture feature, when choosing to use *case*.

The *procedural programming model* is said to be *low level* because it is very close to the classical *architecture model*. *High level* programming models either place greater burden on the compiler or require a more sophisticated architecture model depending on whether the *semantic gap* is to be closed or not. Historically the programming and architecture models have been developed *independently*. Recent machines, such as the *Transputer* and *Recursiv* [Harland 86] signal the arrival of the simultaneous design of both.

ii   Table entries for a `jump` instruction are jumps themselves since the effect of the instruction is only to replace the program counter value with that of an effective address. `case<i>` *adds an operand*, located by the effective address, to the program counter.

Hence table entries need only be offsets. Transfer of control to the selected code only requires the execution of a single branch instead of two jumps and thus to be preferred on performance grounds as well as code size, (smaller table).

Question two

i   The following code *(in order of execution)* is required for procedure invocation, entry and exit by the *NS32000* and *Transputer* respectively...

```
movw  <par1>(fp),tos              ldl   <par1>
movw  <par2>(fp),tos              ldl   <par2>
movw  <par3>(fp),tos              ldl   <par3>
bsr   <proc>                      pfix <proc3>
enter [r5,r6,r7],<frame>          pfix <proc2>
...                               pfix <proc1>
exit  [r5,r6,r7]                  call <proc0>
ret   6                           ajw  -<frame+1>
                                  ...
                                  ajw  +<frame+1>
```

The comparison between the two processors of code size and execution time is shown below...

Processor	Bytes	Cycles
NS32016	19	207
Transputer	12	24

While the code storage requirement differs significantly, but not greatly, the performance overhead in procedure invocation is clearly very much more severe on the *NS32000* than on the Transputer. The principal reason for the enormous difference is the number of memory references required. Only a small proportion of these is due to parameter passing, although the effect of locating parameters in a stack frame is made worse when consideration is given to their reference within the procedure. The real damage is done by the need to *preserve general and special register state* when calling a procedure on the NS32000.

The notion that *a procedure is a named process with private state* in *Occam* means that no mechanism is needed to permit references to variables of non-local scope. Processes cannot be switched whilst the evaluation stack is in use, hence *neither can procedures be invoked*, which guarantees that all registers will be available for parameter passing (and value returning).

ii   The following code (in order of execution) is required for *case* construct implementation by the NS32000 and Transputer respectively...

```
movb <result>(fp),r7           ldl <result>
subb <lo bound>,r7             ldc <lo bound>
caseb *+4[r7:b]                ldpi
<offset table>                 bsub
                               gcall
                               j 24
                               <jump table>
```

The comparison between the two processors of code size and execution time is shown below...

Processor	Bytes	Cycles
NS32016	22	32
Transputer	33	15

This shows that, despite a dedicated NS32000 instruction, the Transputer does not require greater execution time when implementing *case*, although it does require greater code length. The better performance of the Transputer is mainly due to `caseb` taking a long time to calculate its effective address, during which the transputer could have executed `jump` *several times*.

Question three

i   The code required to generate an operand of -241_{10} and load it into the A register is...

```
nfix #F     #6F
ldc  #F     #4F
```

The least significant 16-bit field of O will evolve as follows...

	0000	0000	0000	0000	Cleared by last instruction
nfix#F	0000	0000	0000	1111	$O_{LSN} \leftarrow F_{16}$
	1111	1111	1111	0000	$O \leftarrow BITNOT\ O$
	1111	1111	0000	0000	$O \leftarrow (O \ll 4)$
ldc #F	1111	1111	0000	1111	$O_{LSN} \leftarrow (O \vee F_{16})$
	0000	0000	0000	0000	$A \leftarrow O$

...where *BITNOT* is a *bitwise negation (ones-complement)* operator and *LSN* denotes *least significant nibble*.

ii   The algorithm for deriving a signed operand may be expressed *recursively* and is documented in [Inmos 88#3, page 8] as...

$$prefix(o, v) \quad = \quad IF$$
$$(v < 16) \wedge (v \geq 0)$$
$$o(v)$$
$$(v \geq 16)$$
$$prefix(o, (v \gg 4));$$
$$o(v \wedge F_{16})$$
$$(v < 0)$$
$$prefix(nfix, ((not\ v) \gg 4));$$
$$o(v \wedge F_{16})$$

...where *o* represents an *operation* and *v* represents an *operand*.

iii   The code for a *for loop*, where the loop count may initially be zero, is as follows...

```
ldc   <start value>
stl   index
ldl   ntimes
stl   index+1
ldl   index+1
pfix  <exit offset hi>
cj    <exit offset lo>
; loop start
...
ldlp  index
pfix  <start offset hi>
ldc   <start offset lo>
lend
```

Note that an additional *conditional branch* has to be added at the loop start. No comparison of the loop count with zero is necessary since cj will execute a branch *if the value in A is zero*. Recall that its meaning is *"jump if false"*, where 0 represents the logical value *false*.

Bibliography

[ANSI 86]
American National Standards Institute : 1986, *Small Computer Systems Interface, X3T9.2*
(available from...*X3 Secretariat, Computer and Business Equipment Manufacturers Association, Suite 500, 311 First Street NW, Washington, D.C. 20001, U.S.A.*)

[Arbib 87]
Arbib M. A. : 1987, *Brains, machines, and mathematics*, Springer-Verlag

[Bell & Newell 71]
Bell C. G. & A. Newell : 1971, *Computer structures: Readings and examples*, McGraw-Hill

[Bentham 83]
Bentham, J. Van: 1983 *The logic of time*, Reidel

[Burns 88]
Burns A. : 1988, *Programming in Occam 2*, Addison-Wesley

[Church 36]
Church A. : 1936, "An unsolvable problem in elementary number theory", *American Journal of mathematics*, **58**, *345*

[Ciarcia 86]
Ciarcia S. : 1986, "Adding SCSI to the SB180 computer", *Byte*, **11**, 5, *85* and **11**, 6, *107*

[Clements 87]
Clements A. : 1987, *Microprocessor systems design: 68000 hardware, software & interfacing*, PWS

[Colwell et al. 85]
Colwell R. P., C. Y. Hitchcock, E. D. Jensen, H. M. Brinkley Sprunt & C. P. Koller : 1985, "Computers, complexity & controversy", *IEEE Computer*, **18**, 9, *8*

[Conway 82]
Conway J. H., E. R. Berlekamp, R. K. Guy: 1982, *Winning Ways for your Mathematical Plays*, Academic Press

[Deitel 84]   Deitel H. M. : 1984, *An introduction to operating sys
                                     tems*, Addison-Wesley

[Dowsing et al. 86]   Dowsing R.D, V.J. Rayword-Smith, C. D. Walter
                                     1985, *A first course in formal logic and its application.
                                     in computer science*, Blackwell Scientific Publications

[Goldberg & Robson 83]   Goldberg A., D. Robson: 1983, *Smalltalk-80: The lan
                                     guage and its implementation*, Addison-Wesley

[Halpern et al. 83]   Halpern J., Z. Manna & B. Moszkowski : 1983
                                     "A hardware semantics based on temporal intervals"
                                     *Proc. 19th Int. Colloq. on Automata, languages an
                                     programming*, Springer Lecture Notes in Computer Sci
                                     ence, **54**, *278*

[Harland 86]   Harland, D. M. : 1988, *Recursiv: Object-oriented com
                                     puter architecture*, Ellis Horwood

[Hayes 88]   Hayes J. P. : 1988, *Computer architecture and organi
                                     zation*, 2nd edition, McGraw-Hill

[Hayes 84]   Hayes J. P. : 1984 *Digital system design and micropro
                                     cessors*, McGraw-Hill

[Hoare 78]   Hoare C. A. R. : 1978, "Communicating Sequentia
                                     Processes", *CACM*, **21**, 8, *666*

[Hoare 85]   Hoare C. A. R. : 1986, *Communicating Sequential Pro
                                     cesses*, Prentice-Hall

[IEEE CS 83]   IEEE Computer Society : 1983, *Model program in com
                                     puter science & engineering*, IEEE Computer Societ
                                     Press, (available from *IEEE Computer Society, Pos
                                     Office Box 80452, Worldway Postal Center, Los Ange
                                     les, CA 90080, USA*)

[Inmos 88#1]   Inmos Ltd: 1988, *Occam 2 reference manual*, Prentic
                                     Hall

[Inmos 88#2]   Inmos Ltd: 1988, *Transputer reference manual*, Pren
                                     tice Hall

[Inmos 88#3]   Inmos Ltd: 1988, *Transputer instruction set: A com
                                     piler writer's guide*, Prentice Hall

[Inmos 88#4]   Inmos Ltd: 1988, *Transputer development system*
                                     Prentice Hall

[Inmos 88#5]   Inmos Ltd: 1988, *Communicating process architecture*,
                               Prentice Hall

[Inmos 89]   Inmos Ltd: 1989, *Transputer technical notes*, Prentice
                               Hall

[Kane 81]   Kane G. : 1981, *68000 microprocessor handbook*,
                               Osborne/McGraw-Hill

[Kane, Hawkins & Leventhal 81] Kane G., D. Hawkins & L. Leventhal : 1981, *68000 as-
                               sembly language programming*, Osborne/McGraw-Hill

[Katevenis 85]   Katevenis M. : 1985, *Reduced instruction set computer
                               architectures for VLSI*, MIT Press

[Knepley & Platt 85]   Knepley E., R. Platt: 1985, *Modula-2 programming*,
                               Ruston

[Laub 86]   Laub L. : 1986, "The evolution of mass storage", *Byte*,
                               11, 5, *161*

[Lister 84]   Lister A. M. : 1984, *Fundamentals of operating sys-
                               tems*, Macmillan

[Little 86]   Little G. B. : 1986 *Mac assembly language: A guide
                               for programmers*, Brady/Prentice-Hall

[Mano 88]   Mano M. M. : 1988, *Computer engineering, hardware
                               design*, Prentice-Hall

[Martin 87]   Martin C. : 1987, *Programming the NS3200*, Addison
                               Wesley

[Meyer 88]   B. : 1988, *Object oriented system design*, Prentice-Hall

[Moszkowski 83]   Moszkowski B. : 1983, "A temporal logic for multi-level
                               reasoning about hardware", *Proc. IFIP 6th Int. Symp.
                               on Computer hardware description languages and their
                               applications*, Pittsburgh Pensylvania

[National Semiconductor 84]   National Semiconductor Corp. : 1984, *Series 32000
                               Instruction set reference manual*, National Semicon-
                               ductor Corp., (available, as are NS32000 device data
                               sheets, from... *National Semiconductor Corp., 2900
                               Semiconductor drive, Santa Clara, California 95051,
                               U.S.A.*

[National Semiconductor 87]   National Semiconductor Corp. : 1987, *Series 32000 GNX Release 2.0 assembler reference manual*, National Semiconductor Corp., (available, as are NS32000 device data sheets, from... *National Semiconductor Corp., 2900 Semiconductor drive, Santa Clara, California 95051, U.S.A.*

[von Neumann 46]   Burks A.W., H. H. Goldstine & J. von Neumann : 1946, "Preliminary discussion of the logical design of an electronic computing instrument", in [Bell & Newell 71]

[von Neumann 66]   von Neumann J. : 1966, *Theory of self reproducing automata*, A. W. Burks (ed.), University of Illinois Press

[Patterson & Ditzel 80]   Patterson D. A., D. R. Ditzel: 1980, "The case for the RISC", *Computer architecture news*, **18**, 11, 25

[Pountain & May 87]   Pountain D., D. May: 1987, *A tutorial introduction to Occam programming*, Blackwell Scientific Publications

[Radin 83]   Radin G. : 1983, "The 801 minicomputer", *IBM J. R&D*, **27**, 3, 237

[Rayward-Smith 86]   Rayword-Smith V.J. : 1986, *A first course in computability*, Blackwell Scientific Publications

[Sharp 85]   Sharp J.A. : 1985, *Data flow computing*, Ellis Horwood

[Sommerville 85]   Sommerville I. : 1985, *Software engineering*, Addison-Wesley

[Stallings 87]   Stallings W. : 1987, *Computer organization and architecture, Principles of structure and function*, Macmillan

[Stubbs & Webre 87]   Stubbs D. F., N. W. Webre: 1987, *Data structures with abstract types and Modula-2*, Brooks/Cole

[Siewiorek, Bell & Newell 82]   Siewiorek D. P., C. G. Bell & A. Newell : 1982, *Principles of computer structures*, McGraw Hill

[Tabak 87]   Tabak D. : 1987, *RISC architecture*, Research Studies Press

[Tanenbaum 78]   Tanenbaum A. : 1978, "Implications of structured programming for machine architecture", *CACM*, March

[Taub 82]   Taub H. : 1982, *Digital circuits and microprocessors*, McGraw Hill

[Thomas 89]   Thomas D. :1989, "What's in an object?", *Byte*, **14**, 3, *231*

[Turing 36]   Turing A.M. : 1936, "On computable numbers with an application to the Entscheidungsproblem", *Proceedings of the London Mathematical Society* (Series 2), **42**, *230*

[Turner 84]   Turner R. :1984, *Logics for artificial intelligence*, Ellis Horwood

[Vemuri 88]   Vemuri V. : 1988, *Artificial neural networks: Theoretical concepts*, IEEE Comp. Soc. Press

[Wirth 85]   Wirth N. : 1985, *Programming in Modula-2*, Springer-Verlag

[Yourdon & Constantine 78]   Yourdon E., L. L. Constantine: 1978, *Structured design*, Yourdon Press

Index

Abstract data type, 38
Access class, 63
ACIA, 293
Active register, 187
Addition, modulo, 88
Address
    bus, 256
    translation, 286
    interleaving, 277
    virtual, 286
Addressing mode, 63
    absolute, 64
    immediate, 64
    indexed, 66
    indirect, 66
    M68000, 314
    modifiers, 64
    NS32000, 337
    postincrement, 316
    predecrement, 316
    register, 64
    relative, 64
    stack machine, 231
    Transputer, 362
Address, 57
Alphabet, 18
Alternation, 6, 203, 225, 233
Alternative construct, transputer, 380
AND/OR structures, 113
Application support, 61
    CISC, 78
Arabic numerals, 83
Arbiter, bus, 257
Arbitration
    daisy chain, 264
    interrupt/event, 263
    protocol, 257
Archival, of data, 269
Arithmetic logic unit (ALU), 175, 194
Array, bounds, 99
ASCII, 92
    control code summary, 93

    control codes, 93
    printing code summary, 92
Assembly language programming
    M68000, 330
    NS32000, 353
    Transputer, 383
Assignment, 41, 59
Associative cache, 280, 288, 348
Asynchronous communications interface adaptor (ACIA), 295
Automata, 11

Balanced loading, 33
Bandwidth, 224, 255
Barrel shifter, 342
Base, of number notation, 83
Bi-directional shift register, 182
Binary
    coded decimal (BCD), 191
    decoder, 167
    encoder, 168
    operators, 60
    words, 83
Bistable, 122
Bit, 83
Bitwise logical operations, 114
Block
    page, 287
    segment, 288
Boolean
    algebra, 107
    algebra laws, 108
    expression, 107
    function specification, 149
    operators, 107
    variables, 107
Booting, transputer, 361, 382
Broadcast, 23
Buffer, 23
    double, 134
Bus
    address/data, 262

arbiter, 257
as shared resource, 255
bandwidth, 255
communication, 167
control, 193
cycle, 257, 259
devices, 255
external, 302
grant, 258
master, 257
multiplexing, 262
phases, 259
request, 258
slave, 258
structure, 256
timing, 259
transaction protocol, 259
width, 224
Busy/ready protocol, 293
Byte, 84

Cache
associative, 280, 348
instruction, 323
Case construct implementation, 326
Cathode ray tube (CRT), 298
Causal system, 6
Causality, law of, 6, 116
Cellular automata, 16
Central processing unit (CPU), 257
Channel, 5, 23
DMA, 265
processor to memory, 224
soft vs. hard, 246
virtual, 171
Church thesis, 16
CISC
control unit, 217
description, 77
motivations for complexity, 77
Clock, 129
cycle, 135
phases, 135
two-phase, 205
Code generation, 55
Combinational logic, 108
Communicating Sequential Processes (CSP), 25
Communication
channels, transputer, 379
concurrent processes, 23
physical nature, 115
processor/memory, 196
successive processes, 23

Compilation, 55
Complement, 91
Computability, 16
Concurrency, architecture support, 72
Conditional branch, 57
Connectives, propositional logic, 105
Consistency, 106
Construct processes, 20
Construct programming
M68000, 326
NS32000, 349
Transputer, 374
Context switch, 69
Contradiction, 106
Control bus, 193, 256
Control flow, 57, 60
Control unit
state decoding, 200
state generation, 200

Daisy chain
arbitration, 264
prioritization, 258
Data
archival of, 269
bus, 256
flow graph, 36
register, 178
representation physical, 84
structure, static, 101
structure, dynamic, 101
transfer, 59
type
dynamic range, 93
precision, 93
portability of, 269
Deadlock, 21
Decoder, binary, 167
Degeneracy, 95
Demand paging, 287
Demultiplexer (DEMUX), 171
Design philosophy
M68000, 312
NS32000, 330
Transputer, 353
Deterministic system, 7
Device
bus, 255
driver, 291
independent i/o, 304
prioritization, 258
Dining philosophers, 21
Direct memory access (DMA), 265

channel, 266
transfer mode, 266
discrete digital system, 3
double buffering, 134
dynamic random access memory (DRAM), 270
dynamic range of data type, 93
flip-flop, 134
latch, 133

edge triggered **D flip-flop, 140**
encapsulation, 38
encoder, binary, 168
event, 18
  arbitration, 264
  identification
    by polling, 263
    by vector, 263
  masking, 265
  port arrival/departure, 290
  prioritization, 264
  protocol, 263
  system, 262
Exceptions, 262
excess $M/2$, 96
excess $M/2 - 1$, 97
Execute microprocess, 203
export, 35
Expression evaluation, 59
  M68000, 329
  NS32000, 352
  Transputer, 373
External communication, protocol, 292

Fan-out, 8, 119
Feedback, 118
Fetch instruction microprocess, 201
Fetch operand microprocess, 202
Fetch/execute process, 241
FIFO
  protocol, 264
  scheduling, 245
Fixed-point representation, 93
Flip-flop
  D, 134
  edge-triggered, 140
  JK, 138
  T, 138
Floating-point
  comparison, 96
  degeneracy, 95
  IEEE 754 standard, 97
  operations, 97
  representation, 94

signing, 96
summary, 98
Format, micro-instruction, 219
Formulæ
  propositional logic, 105
  temporal logic, 126
Fractional numbers, 84
Fragmentation, 288
Full-adder, 174

General purpose registers, 59
Graph, 16
Guard, 20

Half-adder, 173
Hamming code, 283
Handshake, 293
Harvard architecture, 57, 224, 244
Hazards, 155
Hex, digit symbols, 85
Hidden bit, 95
Hit ratio, 280
Hoare, Professor, 25
Hold time, 143
Hysteresis, 123

I/O
  device independent, 304
  program, 304
  protocol, 292
IEEE 754 standard, floating-point representation, 97
Import, 35
Indirection, 202
Input, 42
Instruction cache, 241, 323, 342
Instruction pipelining, 241
Instruction set, 11
  M68000, 318
  NS32000, 339
  Transputer, 363
Instructions, 56
  assignment, 59
  control flow, 60
  expression evaluation, 59
  linkage, 61
Interleaved memory, 277
Interpretation, 55
Interrupt, 6, 263
  alternation, 233
  arbitration, 263
  control unit (ICU), 265
  despatch table, 264

identification
    by polling, 263
    by vector, 263
  masking, 265
  microprocess, 203
  prioritization, 264
  request, 203
  routine, 204
  system, vectored, 169
Iteration constructs, 44
  support, 326

JK flip-flop, 138

K-map
  derivation, 152
  limitations, 155
  reduction, 153
  4-variable, 155

Language, requirements, 32
Laser, 271
Latch, 9
  D, 133
  RS, 131
  RS with Set, Clear, Enable, 133
  transparency, 134
Law
  of causality, 6
  first of thermodynamics, 8
  second of thermodynamics, 9
Linear system, 7
Link, protocol, 305
Linkage instructions, 61
Links, 304
List, 39
Load/store
  architecture, 239
  memory access, 75, 321
Locality
  RISC exploitation, 75
  spatial, 75
  temporal, 75
Logic gates, 10, 108
Logic units, processor, 194
Logic, positive & negatve, 115
Look-ahead-carry (LAC) adder, 177
Loop construct, support, 326

M68000
  addressing modes, 314
  assembly language programming, 330
  construct programming, 326

  design philosophy, 312
  expression evaluation, 329
  instruction set, 318
  physical memory organization, 324
  procedure programming, 327
  processor organization, 323
  programmer's architecture, 313
Masking, logical, 114
Maxterms, 112
Mealy machine, 126
  state assignment table, 162
  state transition graph, 164
  state & output excitations, 164
Memory, 9, 122
  management unit (MMU), 288, 348
  memory map, 58
    fragmentation, 288
  1-bit, 131
  device hierarchy, 286
  dynamic random access (DRAM), 270
  error detection and correction, 283
  interleaved modular, 277
  mean access time of, 268
  mean cost of, 268
  non-volatility of, 269
  one-dimensional organization, 273
  opto-mechanical, 271
  physical access, 273
  physical requirements, 268
  physical transport, 273
  physical, 270
  portability of, 269
  program, 62
  random access, 273
  security of access of, 285
  shared by code & data, 57
  technological constraints, 269
  two-dimensional organization, 273
Message passing, 6, 38
Method (of object), 38
Micro-instruction, format, 219
Microcode, 197
Microprocess
  execute, 203
  fetch/execute, 200
  fetch instruction, 201
  fetch operand, 202
  interrupt, 203
Minimization, Quine-McCluskey, 158
Minterms, 112
Modula 2
  applicability, 50
  concurrency, 49

constructs, 49
partitions, 49
primitives, 48
references, 50
Modular interleaved memory, 277, 343
Modules, 29
    interaction, 35
    library, 54
    linkage, 334
    population growth, 33
    software partitions, 47
    support, 334
Modulo addition, 88
Modulus of register, 88
Monitor, 23
Monostable, 122
Moore machine, 127
    state assignment, 159
    state transition graph, 160
    state & output excitations, 160
Multiplex bus, 262
Multiplexer (MUX), 171
Multiplexing, 23
Multiplication algorithm, shift & add, 218

Negation
    arithmetic, 88
    bitwise, 91
    sign/magnitude, 88
    twos complement, 90
Negative logic, 115
Negative number representation, 84
    sign/magnitude, 87
    twos-complement, 88
Nibble, 84
Noise, 123
    immunity, 141
Non-determinacy, 117
Non-volatility, of memory, 269
Normalized form, 95
Normally-open switches, 7
Notation/representation correspondence, 85
NS32000, 78
    addressing modes, 336
    assembly language programming, 353
    construct programming, 349
    design philosophy, 330
    expression evaluation, 352
    instruction set, 339
    physical memory organization, 343
    procedure programming, 351
    processor organization, 342
    programmer's architecture, 332

virtual memory organization, 348

Objects, 38, 285
Occam
    applicability, 52
    constructs, 51
    partitions, 52
    primitives, 50
    references, 53
    replication, 52
Ones-complement, 91
Opcode, 56
Operands
    number of, 62
    quick, 318
Operating system, 69
Operators, binary, 60
Operators, 59
Opto-mechanical memory, 271
Oscillation, 118
Output, 43
Overflow, 91

Page (fixed-size block), 287
    fault, 286
    replacement strategy, 288
Parallel construct, 43
Parallel processing
    building site analogy, 68
    instruction level, 241
Parity, 283
Partitions, software, 29, 38
Peripheral interface devices, 293
Physical memory organization
    M68000, 324
    NS32000, 343
    Transputer, 371
Physical memory, 270
Physical representation of data, 84
Physical transport, 276
Pipelining, 241, 323
    instruction execution, 241
Pixel, 298
Plumbing, processor, 193
Pointer, type, 101
Polarity of logic, 115
Polling, 234, 291
Polymorphism, 38
Portability, 55, 269
Port, 3, 290
    polling, 291
Position independent code, 64, 232, 326
Positive logic, 115

Postincrement addressing mode, 316
Power consumption & dissipation, 118
Precision of data type, 93
Predecrement addressing mode, 316
Predicates, 105
Primitive processes, 20
Prioritization
        bus device, 258
        daisy chain, 258
        event, 264
Procedure, 5
        activation depth, 244
        programming
              M68000, 327
              NS32000, 351
              Transputer, 375
        as software partition, 47
Process, 5
        construct, 20
        economy example, 18
        identifier, 69
        manager, 69
        networks, 245
        primitive, 20
        scheduling, 69
        scheduling, transputer, 356, 377
Processor
        scheduling, 68
        logic units, 194
        networks, 245
        organization
              M68000, 323
              NS32000, 342
              Transputer, 369
        plumbing, 193
        state register (PSR), 56
        central, 257
        internal communication, 193
        /memory communication, 196
Program
        counter, 57
        memory, 62
Programmer's architecture
        M68000, 313
        NS32000, 332
        Transputer, 356
Propagation delay, 116
Propositional logic, 105
Protocol, 5
        arbitration, 257
        bus transaction, 259
        busy/ready, 246, 293
        external communication (i/o), 292

FIFO, 264
link, 305
round robin, 264

Quantization, 3
Queue, 40
        ready, 69
Quick operand, 318
Quine-McCluskey
        reduction, 157
        minimization, 158

Race
        condition, 117
        oscillation, 118
Raster
        scan, 298
        video display, 298
Raw machine, 55
Read-Only-Memory (ROM), 170
Ready queue, 69, 245
Record, 99
Recursion, 20
Reduction
        Boolean expression, 150
        K-map, 153
        Quine-McCluskey, 157
Refresh, dynamic memory, 270
Register
        active, 187
        bi-directional shift, 182
        data, 178
        file, 60, 236
        general purpose, 236
        modulus, 88
        rotation, 182
        transfer language (RTL), 57, 229
        windowing, 237
Rendezvous
        example, 70
        hard channel, 304
        implementation, 246
        Transputer, 379
Representation/notation correspondence, 85
Resume, 69
Ripple-through arithmetic logic unit, 175
RISC
        description, 74
        history, 75
        Transputer as, 353
RS latch, 131

Scheduling

algorithms, 245
    hardware support, 245
    process, 69
    processor, 68
    round robin, 69, 264, 265
    Transputer, 359
Security, 284, 348
    memory access, 285
    pointer object access, 101
    sequential object access, 99
    virtual memory, 287
    virtual memory, 288
Seek, 276
Segment (variable size block), 288
Selection constructs, 44
Semantic gap, 32, 55
    closure by CISC, 78
Separate development, 29
Separate verification, 29
Sequence construct, 43
Setup time, 143
Shared variable, 23
Shift register, bi-directional, 182
Sign/magnitude representation, 87
    pros & cons, 88
Signal protocol, level vs. edge, 258
Small Computer Systems Interface (SCSI), 302
Special registers, 59
Specification of systems, 149
Stack, 40
    frames, 250
    machine, addressing modes, 231
Standard product of sums, 150
Standard sum of products, 150
State, 4, 9
    assignment table
        Mealy machine, 162
        Moore machine, 159
    machines, 13, 127
    transition graph
        Mealy machine, 126, 164
        Moore machine, 160
    transition tables, 128
    & output excitations
        Mealy machine, 164
        Moore machine, 160
    private, 5
    processor, 56
    wait, 260
Statespace, 4
Stochastic system, 7
STOP & SKIP, 19
Storage class, 62

Stream, 5
String, 6
Subroutine, 61, 229
Sufficiency sets (of logical connectives), 106
Suspend, 69
Switch, normally-open, 7
Symmetry, 322
Synchronization, 21, 120
System
    causal, 6
    deterministic, 7
    discrete digital, 3
    events, 262
    linear, 7
    stochastic, 7

Tautology, 106
Temporal logic, 124
    operators, 125
Thermodynamics
    first law of, 8, 118
    second law of, 9, 118
Timers, transputer, 380
Top down task diagram, 32
Traces, 19
Trade off, fan-out vs. propagation delay, 119
Transaction, communication, 21
Translation, 32, 55
Transparency, latch, 134
Transputer (Inmos), 304
    addressing modes, 361
    alternative construct, 380
    assembly language programming, 383
    booting, 361, 382
    communication channels, 379
    design philosophy, 353
    expression evaluation, 373
    instruction set, 363
    physical memory organization, 371
    procedure invocation, 376
    process scheduling, 356, 377
    processor organization, 369
    programmer's architecture, 356
    rendezvous, 379
    reserved values, 384
    sequential constructs, 374
    timers, 380
Traps, 312, 332
Tristate buffering, 178
Truth function, 106
Truth table, 149, 106
Turing, Alan, 13
Turing Machine

origin and purpose, 13
programming, 15
structure, 13
Twos-complement
negation, 90
pros & cons, 91
representation, 88
T flip-flop, 138

Underflow, 91
Unix, 93
Up/down counter, 184

Versatile interace adaptor (VIA), 293
Virtual address, 286
Virtual data type, 88
Virtual memory organization, NS32000, 348
Volatility, 123
Von Neumann J., 16
bottleneck, 224
machine, 57

Wait states, 260
Winchester disc, 276
Word partitions, 84
Words, binary, 83
Word, 4
Workspace, 62

XOR from AND/OR/NOT, 112

Crime
of
Passion

First published in 2016 by
Liberties Press
140 Terenure Road North | Terenure | Dublin 6W
T: +353 (1) 405 5701 | W: libertiespress.com | E: info@libertiespress.com

Trade enquiries to Gill & Macmillan Distribution
Hume Avenue | Park West | Dublin 12
T: +353 (1) 500 9534 | F: +353 (1) 500 9595 | E: sales@gillmacmillan.ie

Distributed in the UK by
Turnaround Publisher Services
Unit 3 | Olympia Trading Estate | Coburg Road | London N22 6TZ T: +44 (0)
20 8829 3000 | E: orders@turnaround-uk.com

Distributed in the United States by
Casemate-IPM | 1950 Lawrence Road | Havertown, PA 19083
T: +1 (610) 853-9131 | E: casemate@casematepublishers.com

ISBN: 978-1910742-56-3

A CIP record for this title is available from the British Library.

Cover image by Anthony Pratt
Additional cover design work by Fergal Condon